Crisis Intervention

Crisis Intervention
A Handbook for Practice and Research

Karl A. Slaikeu

UNIVERSITY OF TEXAS AT AUSTIN

ALLYN AND BACON, INC.

BOSTON   LONDON   SYDNEY   TORONTO

To Diane

Series Editor: Bill Barke

Library of Congress Cataloging in Publication Data

Slaikeu, Karl A., 1944–
    Crisis Intervention.

    Bibliography: p.
    Includes index.
    1. Crisis intervention (Psychiatry)–Handbooks, manuals, etc. I. Title. [DNLM: 1. Crisis intervention–Handbooks. WM 401 S631c]
RC480.6.S54   1983   616.89'025   83–11837
ISBN 0-205-08002-2

Printed in the United States of America

10 9 8 7 6 5 4 3 2   89 88 87 86 85

Contents

Preface

This book is based on the premise that the concept of crisis is an essential building block in any structured understanding of human growth and development. Far too often people think of crises as the unusual, mostly negative, events that should be avoided. The implication is that an ideal world would be one without crises, with things moving along pretty much on an even keel.

Crisis theory, however, takes a very different perspective. Grounded in Erik Erikson's developmental psychology is the idea that crises and major life transitions—similar in their components, varying only in degree and intensity—are the stuff of which life is made. Very few people avoid crises altogether. Adult life, whether neurotic or normal, healthy or ill, optimistic or pessimistic in outlook, is a function of how we have weathered earlier crises, whether these be changing schools, surviving the divorce of parents, dealing with a life-threatening illness, or surviving the loss of a first love.

Crisis is a time when "everything is on the line," so to speak. Previous means of coping and managing problems break down in the face of new threats and challenges. The potential for good or bad outcomes lies in the disorganization and disequilibrium of crisis. A wealth of clinical data suggest that some form of reorganization will begin in a matter of weeks after the onset of crisis. The reorganization may be toward growth and positive development, or toward psychological impairment, or even death, depending upon a host of variables in each case, not the least of which

is the kind of help available during the critical weeks/months of crisis. As its core, crisis theory is provocative since it directs the attention of helpers to episodes in people's lives when tremendous change can occur. The question is whether these helpers will be prepared to make best use of the opportunities given them to assist individuals in working through the crisis experience.

A second premise on which this book is based is that we need to articulate intervention strategies in such a way that they can be systematically studied. The gap between research and practice in the crisis field has been too wide for too long. Though the number of quality studies increased in the 1970s, their results cannot be interpreted in light of any uniform model, either about the natural course of crises, or of helping strategies themselves. Reviews (Auerbach and Kilmann, 1977; Korchin, 1976) have thus been on firm ground in saying that crisis theory is not really a theory, and that crisis intervention is more an *approach* than a set of systematic strategies.

The comprehensive intervention model presented in this volume represents an attempt to change this situation. The model immerged from clinical experience, though it took formal shape through graduate seminars on understanding crises in light of available research data. My goal has been to both summarize and reorganize existing techniques, and to describe an intervention model which can continually serve as a guide for future research. In a very real sense, this model is intended to be not an end point, but a beginning toward refining existing strategies for helping people negotiate life crises.

A third premise ties directly to community psychology: In order to achieve maximum impact on individuals and families, crisis services must be integrated into a wide range of community systems. In Part III of this volume, we apply the crisis model to workers from eight such systems: lawyers, police officers, clergy, health care practitioners, emergency room workers, telephone counselors, school personnel, and supervisors in work settings. In each chapter, the goal is to summarize existing literature, and offer guidelines on how these workers and their colleagues can use the crisis model to assist clients.

My hope is that this book will be useful to both practitioners and researchers. Among the former, are included professionals and paraprofessionals in health, mental health, and social services, as well as employees in each of the settings just mentioned. I anticipate that many experienced professionals will use this volume as a way to reconceptualize and redirect their expertise to achieve maximum gain with crisis clients/patients.

The first part of the intervention model—psychological first aid—is intended for anyone who first has knowledge of, and the opportunity to help, another person in crisis. The second phase—crisis therapy—goes a step further and is designed to capitalize on the potential for radical change inherent in the crisis experience in such a way as to maximize the probability of growth, and minimize the probability of debilitation (mental and physical) as a result of a crisis. As suggested in Chapter 1, my expectation is that the crisis therapy procedures described in this volume will be of special interest to anyone seeking to reduce health care costs through strategic interventions tied to critical life events.

Advanced undergraduate and graduate students in social work, psychology, medicine, etc., should find this book a rather straightforward introduction to crisis theory and

intervention techniques. Consultants and administrators will find the intervention model (particularly the summary tables) useful in planning, implementing, and evaluating training programs for community workers such as those discussed in Part III. Finally, by including research sections in each chapter, I hope to entice behavioral science colleagues to conduct further investigation in this exciting field. To this group, the volume can serve as a source book for research ideas and methodology (see Chapter 18).

ACKNOWLEDGEMENTS

The list of colleagues who contributed to the formation of the ideas in this book is long indeed. I am grateful to pre- and post-doctoral students at the University of South Carolina and the University of Texas, plus the hundreds of mental health and social service workshop participants who test me continually, thereby helping to refine various parts of the intervention model. I am also indebted to Gene Brockopp, David Lester, and former colleagues at the Erie County (Buffalo, New York) Suicide Prevention and Crisis Service (now Crisis Services, Inc.) for first introducing me to crisis work and providing financial support for my research as a graduate student at the State University of New York at Buffalo. Murray Levine and Ira Iscoe were mentors who shaped my thinking as a community psychologist, guiding me toward the knowledge that crisis services will come and go unless they are integrated into the systems within which crises occur.

The reconceptualizations of crisis theory (Chapter 2) and the intervention model (Chapter 5) owe a great deal to Coval MacDonald who first introduced me to General Systems Theory as a framework for behavioral science model building. Steve Tulkin first set me on the crisis research path, and has stayed a helpful colleague through the years, serving as a reality check for fresh ideas and critiquing the entire manuscript prior to publication. Juanita Friddell and Bonnie Dennis were particularly helpful in editing the manuscript. In addition, a team of secretarial colleagues at the University of South Carolina—Lottie Harvin, Virginia Rabin, Sheila Ryan, Janet Snead, Jeanette Strauss, Patricia Stone, and Marina Yartzeff—labored on numerous drafts of this book, earning my gratitude for their preseverence and good work.

I am especially grateful to Nancy Land for outstanding service in guiding the book through the production process, to Jane Stewart for her help with final proofing, and to Ruth Bounous for her assistance in preparing the indices.

Finally, Diane Slaikeu did more than anyone to keep this massive project on track for three years. Without her constructive critique of my ideas, and her emotional support, this book would not have been possible.

Karl A. Slaikeu

PART I

THEORETICAL CONSIDERATIONS

We begin with a common frame of reference for understanding the nature of life crises, which serves as a foundation for the helping process. Chapter 1 gives an historical background of crisis intervention and summarizes theoretical influences, presenting crisis intervention as a special form of secondary prevention (Caplan 1964). Chapter 2 presents the basic principles of crisis theory and casts them into a general systems framework, stressing the importance of family/social group, community and cultural variables in understanding an individual's crisis. Chapter 3 outlines the central components of developmental life crises, including a summary chart of developmental issues through the life span, disruptions in which might precipitate a life crisis. Finally, Chapter 4 summarizes the literature on common situational crises, drawing out implications for the intervention process.

chapter one

Introduction

NEW YORK (AP) *Students had threatened Susan Hudson before, but when the attack came, she did not expect it: A magazine rolled around some heavy object and secured with a rubber band was slammed full force into her neck. It knocked her down, but the middle-aged remedial reading teacher got up and taught her two remaining classes that day in February 1977. Then she went home. She never returned again to her Brooklyn vocational high school classroom.*

She says she hasn't gone back because of her neck injury—the eternal headaches, the dizziness. But also, she says, she's afraid. "I am petrified when I see more than two youngsters together. If I want to go out in the evening, I have to gird my loins all day."

Ms. Hudson, a ten-year teaching veteran who needs only to complete her dissertation to earn a doctoral degree, slides slowly, involuntarily into tears as she describes her injuries and her feelings about the assault. "I know I'm not handling this very well—I cry easily when I'm reminded about this. It's been two years and I'm getting worse. I'm really very bitter." [1]

LIFE CRISIS: HELPING WHEN THE STAKES ARE HIGH The intense personal cost—both physical and psychological—of tragedies such as the one reported above is all too familiar to mental health practitioners. The idea that the poor resolution of life crises (here the attack and its aftermath) can lead to long-range psychic damage has been one of the cornerstones of crisis theory (Caplan 1964).

In some cases, the possibility of any future adjustment is cut short, as these newspaper headlines indicate:

DISTRAUGHT HUSBAND KILLS WIFE AND SELF.

STUDENT DIES IN PLUNGE FROM TOWER.

VIETNAM VETERAN HOLDS FAMILY OF FOUR HOSTAGE.

For many people, insurmountable problems and life stresses build to such a point that something has to give. Physical harm—to self, family/friends, or even strangers—can be the tragic result.

Historically, however, the concept of crisis has been understood in a positive sense as well. The Chinese symbol for crisis indicates both danger and opportunity. Webster defines crisis as a "turning point," suggesting that the turn can be for good or ill, better or worse. This view of crisis became especially apparent in the popular literature of the 1970s that created tremendous public interest in developmental crisis or passages through *expected* life events

---

[1] True story, ficticious name. From "Teacher's Fear Never Wanes After Assault" by J. S. White, in *Lincoln* (Nebraska) *Star*, 1978. Reprinted by permission of Associated Press.

(Sheehy 1976). Male mid-life crisis took its place alongside adolescent identity crisis as a stage which, if properly understood, would help explain seemingly unexplainable behavior, and help families to cope with difficult events.

What makes one crisis result in growth and another result in immediate harm or subsequent psychological problems? An initial consideration is the severity of the event touching off the crisis. Some occurrences, such as death of a loved one or physical attack, seem in and of themselves to have crisis potential. An individual's personal resources make up a second set of key variables. Whether born that way, or seasoned through life experience, some people are better equipped than others to cope with life's stresses.

A third set of variables includes the social resources present at the time of crisis. Who is available to help in the immediate aftermath of the crisis event, and what sort of assistance do these helpers provide? Since crises are characterized by a breakdown in problem-solving capabilities, outside help is critical in determining how individuals will negotiate these turning points.

Consider the case with which this chapter began—a teacher attempting to cope with the consequences of a physical attack. The first question to ask might be: "Who first knew of the crisis event, the assault?" With a few moments reflection, we might construct the following list of people who, within twenty-four hours of the attack, had some knowledge of its occurrence:

1. other students in the classroom;
2. fellow teachers/colleagues in the school;
3. the school nurse;
4. administrative superiors (principal, disciplinarian dean of the school);
5. spouse;
6. best friend(s);
7. family physician, nurse;

8. pastor/rabbi; and
9. attorney, legal assistant.

It is very likely that several of these people heard of the incident, and even talked with Susan after the assault. According to the model presented in this book, each could have provided first-order crisis intervention. Whether these outsiders' chief role was to provide medical attention, emotional support, administrative action, or legal advice, each was in a position to assist in negotiating the very critical first steps in handling the crisis and its eventual impact on Susan's total life. What would these helpers have done? How much time would it have taken? What skills did they need?

There are a number of other questions we might ask about Susan. In the days immediately following the assault, what decisions did she face? For example, would she/could she/should she return to the classroom? If so, when, and under what circumstances? What preparation or coaching might she need to face the class on the first day back? How would she have dealt with her administrative superiors who, the newspaper account later reported, did nothing to discipline the student involved? Later Susan might consider changing careers. How would this decision be made? How about the impact of this crisis on her family? What role would they play in the ultimate resolution of the crisis? All in all, how could she have dealt better with the psychological reaction which, left untreated, affected both her personal life and career?

In the weeks and months following a crisis event, some people need second-order crisis intervention, or crisis therapy. This involves short-term (several weeks to several months) psychotherapy aimed at assisting individuals in working through traumatic or unsettling events so that they emerge equipped to face the future instead of closed to the prospect.

In Susan's case, helpers in several community systems could have helped her deal with her immediate reaction, and assisted her also in making decisions about the ultimate impact of this critical event on her life. The extreme disorganization that accompanies a crisis experience will soon lead to some form of reorganization, whether positive or negative, for the victim and his/her family. A wealth of clinical data suggests that even in a tragedy such as Susan's, there is a possibility for eventual gain. This might take the form of a change in career, an adjustment in how she handles certain aspects of her current job, the development of new coping strategies, better use of social supports, or a change in significant attitudes about life. Many times these seemingly random events provide the occasion for a person in crisis to re-work old conflicts so that psychological health is actually enhanced.

Some people, especially those whose social supports are readily apparent, and those whose ego strengh is great, work through this process without help. Others, like Susan, do not. For these people, the assistance of a trained therapist or counselor can be very important. The list of possible community settings for such services might include:

1. community mental health centers;
2. hospitals;
3. pastoral counseling centers; and
4. private practitioners.

Susan might have been referred to one or more of these by any one of those who first had contact with her. She might eventually have received short-term therapy from a nurse practitioner working as part of a family-oriented health care team, or from a clinical psychologist, psychiatrist, social worker, pastoral counselor, or a paraprofessional trained to offer short-term therapy under supervision.

We can use the case of Susan Hudson to define crisis intervention as:

> A helping process aimed at assisting a person or family to survive an unsettling event so that the probability of debilitating effects (e.g., emotion-

al scars, physical harm) is minimized, and the probability of growth (e.g., new skills, new outlook on life, more options in living) is maximized.

This process can be broken down into two phases: first-order intervention, which is actually *psychological first aid,* and second-order intervention, which is best thought of as *crisis therapy.* Both are important in determining eventual crisis resolution. Psychological first aid needs to be offered immediately, much like physical first aid, by those who have first contact with the victim. These procedures take only a short period of time (minutes or hours), and can be offered by a wide range of community helpers. Crisis therapy, on the other hand, is aimed at facilitating psychological resolution of the crisis. It takes more time (weeks to months), and is offered by therapists and counselors knowledgeable in specific assessment and treatment techniques. As we shall see later in this chapter, crisis intervention is something which takes place *after* an unsettling event has occurred, though *before* its ultimate resolution, whether positive or negative. We shall return to these concepts after looking first at a brief history of crisis intervention and its chief theoretical influences.

HISTORICAL BACKGROUND The origin of modern crisis intervention dates back to the work of Eric Lindemann and his colleagues following the Coconut Grove fire in Boston on November 28, 1942. In what was at that time the largest single building fire in the country's history, 493 people perished when flames swept through the crowded Coconut Grove Nightclub. Lindemann and others from the Massachusetts General Hospital played an active role in helping survivors, those who had lost loved ones in the disaster. His clinical report (Lindemann 1944) on the psychological symptoms of the survivors became the cornerstone for subsequent theorizing on the grief process, a series of stages through which a mourner progresses on the way toward accepting and resolving loss. Lindemann came to believe that clergy and other community caretakers could play a critical role in helping bereaved people through the mourning process, thereby heading off psychological difficulties later in life.This concept was further operationalized with the establishment of the Wellesley Human Relations Service (Boston) in 1948, one of the first community mental health services noted for its focus on short-term therapy in the context of preventive psychiatry.

Building on the start given by Lindemann, Gerald Caplan, also associated with the Massachusetts General Hospital and the Harvard School of Public Health, first formulated the significance of life crises in adult psychopathology. He stated the matter quite succinctly: "An examination of the history of psychiatric patients shows that, during certain of these crisis periods, the individual seems to have dealt with his problems in a maladjusted manner and to have emerged less healthy than he had been before the crisis" (Caplan 1964, p. 35).

If an examination of adult psychiatric patients concluded that poorly handled crises or transitions led to subsequent disorganization and mental illness, then it follows that prevention should look closely at developmental transitions of childhood and early adulthood. Caplan's crisis theory was therefore cast in the framework of Erikson's (1963) developmental psychology in which human beings were understood to grow or develop through a series of eight key transitions. Caplan's interest was on how people negotiated the various transitions from one stage to another. Early on, he identified the importance of both personal and social resources in determining whether developmental crises (and situational or unexpected crises as well) would work out for better or for worse.

Caplan's preventive psychiatry, with its focus on critical life crisis intervention to promote positive growth and minimize the chance of psychological impairment, led to an emphasis on mental health consultation. Since many of these early crises could be identified and even predicted, it became important to alert and train a wide range of community practitioners on how to help children and young adults manage this disorganization. The role of the mental health professional became one of assisting teachers, nurses, clergy, guidance counselors, and others in learning how to detect and deal with life crises in community settings.

In the early sixties, the suicide prevention movement grew rapidly in the United States, resting in part on Caplan's crisis theory. Centers such as Los Angeles Suicide Prevention and Crisis Service, and Erie County (Buffalo) Suicide Prevention and Crisis Service offered 24-hour, 365 day hotlines aimed at preventing suicide. Linked to the social activist mentality of the 1960s, the centers heavily relied upon the efforts of nonprofessional and paraprofessional volunteers in their telephone counseling programs (McGee 1974). While the centers' early identification was with the prevention of suicides, most moved rather quickly toward an intervention approach aimed at providing assistance for a wide range of crises. The idea was to make supportive counseling immediately available by telephone, any time, day or night. This approach was further developed to include an outreach function where workers would, when necessary, travel to homes, bus stations, playgrounds, and the like, to provide onsite intervention (McGee 1974). Techniques uniquely suited to telephone crisis intervention had to be developed (Fowler and McGee 1973; Knickerbocker and McGee 1972; Slaikeu, Lester, and Tulkin 1973; Slaikeu, Tulkin, and Speer 1975). The chief theoretical framework for this work rested with the life crisis orientation of Caplan. Whether crises of suicide, divorce, unemployment, spouse abuse, or adolescent rebellion, the idea was to understand the severe disorganization and upset in terms of the crisis theory.

Running parallel to the growth of the suicide

prevention centers was the formal emergence of the community mental health movement in the United States. As a means of implementing the recommendations of the U.S. Congress' Joint Commission of Mental Illness and Health, 1961, and with the active support of the Kennedy Administration, Congress passed the Community Mental Health Centers Act in 1963. Congruent with the goal of providing mental health services in community settings (that is, not restricting them to hospitals) was an emphasis on early intervention aimed at keeping minor problems from developing into severe pathology. Crisis intervention and emergency services (24 hour) were considered to be an integral part of any comprehensive community mental health system, so much so that federal funding was impossible unless an emergency services component was included in any center's programming. Though implementation of the community mental health concept has not been without its obstacles (Bloom 1977), the immediacy of services component, built in a crisis framework, has endured. The balanced service system of the seventies identified five programming areas: (a) service, (b) administration, (c) citizen participation, (d) research and evaluation, and (e) staff development. The service area was broken into eight subheadings, two of which (crisis stabilization and growth) include activities covered under the Caplanian notion of intervention during life crises (Joint Commission of Accreditation of Hospitals 1979).

As crisis intervention programs were developed in the sixties and seventies, intervention literature began to emerge. Numerous case reports on how to help individuals and families in crisis appeared in the psychiatry, psychology, nursing, and social work journals. Journals were published dealing specifically with crisis topics, such as *Crisis Intervention,* and *Journal of Life Threatening Behavior.* A number of practical instructional books on "how to" do crisis intervention were published (Aguilera, Messick, and Farrel 1974; Crow 1977; Hoff 1978; McMurrain 1975; Puryear 1979), accompanied by edited books of readings, (Lester and Brockopp 1973; Specter and Clairborne 1973).

During this time researchers also turned attention to program evaluation in crisis centers (Fowler and McGee 1973; Heaton, Ashton and Powell 1972; Knickerbocker and McGee 1972; Slaikeu et al. 1975; Slaikeu et al. 1973). By the late 1970s, enough studies had been generated to merit several important reviews (Auerbach and Kilmann 1977; Baldwin 1979; Butcher and Koss 1978; Butcher and Maudal 1976; Smith 1977).

With its reliance on short-term treatment, crisis intervention became even more valued as economic constraints led to an emphasis on diligent use of scarce resources. For example, Cummings and his colleagues at Kaiser Permanante in California demonstrated the cost-effectiveness of short-term psychotherapy (average of 6.2 sessions) in a prepaid health plan (Cummings 1977). Innovative short-term therapy was found to be more effective than long-term psychotherapy, with the cost being offset by the savings from reduced future medical care. Crisis intervention therefore plays an important role in comprehensive health service packages.

Beyond the need to economize, however, the renewed interest in crisis intervention was sparked by the provocativeness of the crisis concept: Emotional pain and suffering is time-limited and holds potential for both positive and negative long-range outcomes. As Viney (1976) points out, the crisis concept

> . . . avoids much of the pessimistic, devaluing, even invalidating approach we . . . often make to patients, by viewing crises as part of normal development, by emphasizing positive coping rather than negative defensive manoeuvres and by proposing crisis resolutions which allow for growth as well as regression (p. 393).

Similarly, Baldwin (1979) suggests that the crisis intervention model, by virtue of its strong interdisciplinary character in both theory and practice, may lend a unifying influence among health professionals. Its ideas are congruent with the increasing emphasis on the interconnectedness of health and mental health care in treating the whole person.

THEORETICAL INFLUENCES

Moos (1976) identifies four theoretical influences on crisis theory. The first is Charles Darwin's theory on the evolution and adaptation of animals to their environment. Darwin's notion of the survival of the fittest examines the struggle for existence of living organisms in relationship to their environments. Darwin's ideas led to the development of human ecology whose distinctive hypothesis is that the human community is an essential adaptive mechanism in man's relation to the environment. (Moos 1976, p. 6).

A second theoretical influence stems from psychological theory regarding human fulfillment and growth. The basic questions concern motivation and drive: What keeps people going and to what end? Freud's idea that motivation is an attempt to reduce tension, that motivation is grounded in sexual and aggressive drive, was challenged in later years by theorists such as Carl Rogers (1961) and Abraham Maslow (1954) who emphasized positive human growth and fulfillment. Both focused on human beings' tendency toward self-actualization, and urge to enrich experience and expand horizons. Maslow's study of outstanding contemporary and historical figures (Abraham Lincoln, Albert Einstein, Jane Adams, and Eleanor Roosevelt) revealed life styles characterized by spontaneity, social interests and altruism, friendships, relative independence of extreme cultural influence, ability to solve problems, and a broad frame of reference or outlook on life. The premise of human self-actualization is also congruent with the emphasis of Buhler (1962) and others that human behavior is intentional, and is constantly oriented toward seeking and restructuring goals. This latter concept is a critical cornerstone to theories which view crises as times when goals become blocked or seem suddenly unreachable.

Erikson's (1963) developmental life cycle focus provided a third chief theoretical influence for crisis theory. Erikson's view of eight stages, each presenting a new challenge, transition, or crisis, provided an alternative to early psychoanalytic theory which suggested that life was essentially based on events in infancy and very early childhood. Erikson's stage theory assumed that, with each transition, subsequent development was "on the line" so to speak. An adolescent who could not resolve the crisis of identity versus role confusion by making choices about career, beliefs, and marriage partner ran the risk of clouding and confusing later adult decisions until the earlier struggle was resolved.

A fourth influence on crisis theory rose from empirical data on how human beings cope with extreme life stress. Studies in this area include coping with the trauma of concentration camps, sudden death of spouses and relatives, major surgery, slow death of a child, and disasters. Broadening this concept to include the impact of a series of smaller events, Holmes and his colleagues demonstrated a relationship between the stress associated with life events and physical health and disease (Holmes and Masuda 1973).

THE UNIQUENESS OF CRISIS INTERVENTION

From its earliest beginnings in the late forties, crisis intervention has had a *preventive* focus. Hotlines trained volunteer workers to prevent callers from committing suicide. Properly working through the grief process was assumed to prevent the possibility of maladjustment later in life. Virtually any intervention aimed at assisting people in managing life crises has been viewed as important since it might prevent psychopathology of some sort later on (Caplan 1964).

In the context of public health, prevention can take three forms (Bloom 1977; Caplan 1964). Primary prevention aims to reduce the incidence of disorders; secondary prevention aims to minimize the harmful effects of events which have already occurred; and tertiary prevention aims to repair damage long after its original onset. In this context, crisis intervention is secondary prevention since it is a process which takes place *after* critical life events have occurred.

Is secondary prevention "second best"? Rather than intervening after crises have already taken place, should we not direct energy toward primary prevention which seeks to keep crises from occurring in the first place? Tyhurst (1958) answers that there will *always* be a critical need for crisis intervention as secondary prevention:

> In such transitions as disaster, migration, or retirement, we have not been impressed by the value of preparation and planning. Unpredictability in disaster, unfamiliarity in migration and denial in retirement have, for example, all interfered with realistic preparation. Instead, as already described, we have been much more impressed by the importance of preventive measures during the period of recoil in disaster, and during analogous periods in migration and retirement. During these phases of turmoil, the individual has tried to act, his assumptions have been in question, and developments at this time will have a crucial bearing upon subsequent psychological events and upon his future health or illness . . .

> To repeat, then, with regard to *the optimum time of intervention*, it is our belief that increasing emphasis will have to be placed upon attempts to intervene during the period of turmoil that is so characteristic of transition states (p. 163).

To state this another way, for many people things have to get worse before they will get better. Growth can only occur after previous patterns have been destroyed and the rebuilding process takes place.

Danish and D'Augelli (1980) contend that the very concept of prevention should be replaced by *enhancement* as we think about life crises. They suggest that prevention language actually implies that we should keep people from experiencing crises in the first place in the hope of reducing the chance of psychological debilitation later on. As an alternative, they offer an enhancement model of human development:

> . . . growth is preceded by a state of imbalance or crisis which serves as the basis for future development. In fact, without crises, development is not possible. Caplan (1964) recognized this quality of crisis in arguing that the way crises are resolved has a major impact on their ultimate role in mental health. In striving to achieve stability during crises, the coping process itself can result in the achievement of a qualitatively different "stability." Thus, contrary to the view that crises are destructive, we contend that they may initiate a restructuring process toward further growth (Danish, 1977). If crises can result in either negative or positive outcomes, the goal of intervention is not to prevent crises, but rather to *enhance* or *enrich* individuals' abilities to deal constructively with these events (p. 61).

As Table 1.1 indicates, crisis intervention can be understood as a strategy bounded on the one side by enhancement strategies (primary prevention) before critical life events occur, and on the other side by treatment strategies (tertiary prevention) administered well after the crisis events and their consequences have taken place. Crisis intervention is the strategy which take place *at the time of the severe disorganization*, resulting from a crisis. As such, according to Tyhurst, it comes at the time when breakdown has occurred, and reorganization will take place, for good or ill. In developmental models it is viewed as the supreme opportunity for growth, since old patterns have been found wanting, and new ones must re-emerge. How people conceptualize the events, that is, interpret them in

TABLE 1.1 CRISIS INTERVENTION IN CONTEXT

	Primary Prevention	Secondary Prevention	Tertiary Prevention
Goal	Reduce incidence of mental disorders; Enhance human growth and development through the life cycle.	Reduce debilitating effects of life crises; Facilitate growth through crisis experience.	Repair damage done by unresolved life crises, that is, treat mental/emotional disorders.
Techniques/strategies	Public education, public policy changes re: environmental stressors; Teaching problem-solving skills to children.	*Crisis Intervention: Psychological First Aid; Crisis Therapy.*	Long-term psychotherapy, retraining, medication, rehabilitation.
Target population	All human beings, with special attention to high risk groups.	Victims of crisis experiences and their families.	Patients, psychiatric casualties.
Timing	Before crisis events occur.	Immeidately after crisis event.	Years after crisis event.
Helpers/community systems	Government (legislative, judicial, executive branches); schools; churches/synagogues; mass media.	Frontline practitioners (attorneys, clergy, teachers, physicians, nurses, police, etc.); Families/social networks; Psychotherapists and counselors.	Health and mental health practitioners in hospitals and outpatient clinics.

light of life's expectancies and long range goals, is critical to future development. As Table 1.1 indicates, crisis intervention is intended to reduce the probability of debilitating effects, and to maximize the probability of growth or mastery for the individual. Target populations are crisis victims and their immediate families and friends. The chief instruments of change are front-line community caretakers, as well as counselors and therapists. This is not to suggest that many crises are not worked out naturally in community settings. Indeed, we know that this is often the case. However, for many the assistance of outside helpers will be critical in determining the ultimate resolution of the crisis. Finally, the strategies of crisis intervention are two-fold: immediate psychological first aid (offered by those closest to the event) and short-term crisis therapy (offered by trained counselors and therapists).

By contrast, primary prevention takes place well before crisis events actually occur. True prevention literally means keeping some events from happening in the first place through public policy changes (e.g., reducing unemployment), and other interventions at social systems levels (e.g., changing laws and parole policies to reduce prison populations). When the external stimulus cannot be affected, enhancement strategies aim at teaching individuals problem-solving and coping skills so that they will be better prepared to weather critical life events. Whether referred to as prevention or enhancement, these strategies take place *before* events occur. They are the mainstay of such fields as community psychology and community psychiatry (Danish and D'Augelli 1980; Rappaport 1977; Reiff 1975).

Treatment or tertiary prevention includes strategies whose aim is to reduce impairment and emotional disorders which result from poor resolution of life crises. Its goal is to repair damage already done to patients who are psychiatric casualties of life stress. It draws on a wide range of psychotherapeutic and pharmaceutical techniques, and is primarily the purview of mental health practitioners, whereas enhancement/prevention falls to planners and educators.

Susan Hudson's case, as noted earlier in this chapter, illustrates the various interactions in Table 1.1. Prevention strategies would have aimed at keeping the assault from taking place in the first place. This would include efforts to reduce class size or to increase educational and staff resources in the school. Although it is possible to say that Susan herself might have taken steps to prevent this occurrence, a true primary prevention focus would have been on the school system itself. Crisis intervention would have aimed at working with Susan in the immediate aftermath of the tragedy. Its concern would have been with what occurred, the impact on Susan and her family, the relative absence or presence of strengths and resources available to her, and with helping her work through the entire episode. Its focus would be to prevent the outcome which actually occurred in her case—bitterness and debilitation two years after the fact. While it might seem naive to talk about growth through such a tragic episode, there were possible new directions in Susan's life after this crisis (such as new career, new approach to teaching, greater assertiveness in dealing with students and administrators). Treatment or rehabilitation would involve helping Susan years after the incident, at which time she was so closed to living (unable to return to school) that she was

not fully functioning. Crisis intervention could have helped Susan to cope more effectively with the situation, and to become more open to future life experiences.

PLAN OF THIS BOOK A review of the main topics covered in this chapter gives a clue to the approach to crisis intervention taken throughout the rest of this volume. The next chapter describes crisis theory, casting it into a general systems framework. The emphasis will be on considering any individual's crisis in the context of family and social group, community systems, and cultural values. This will be followed by chapters devoted to analysis of both developmental and situational types of life crises. Important findings will be reviewed, with particular emphasis given to intervention implications. In Part II, a comprehensive model for crisis intervention will be described, followed by descriptions of both first-order (psychological first aid) and second-order (crisis therapy) interventions, including an analysis of sample cases for each.

Part III includes concrete applications of the crisis model by key practitioners in various community systems, followed by a chapter which offers a model for research on crisis intervention.

Throughout the rest of the book, our primary concern will be with the practice of crisis intervention. Material presented will be offered with a view to its eventual application by practitioners such as those listed in Part III. At the same time, by continual reference to a general systems framework for crisis theory and the intervention process (Chapters 2 and 5), we will attempt to delineate directions for future research. Most chapters will contain a research section intended primarily to summarize trends, expose gaps, and offer suggestions for further work in this area.

chapter two

Crisis Theory: A General Framework

Tom visits the university health center asking for "tranquilizers" to calm his nerves. He hasn't gotten much sleep lately, and last night his wife of three years informed him she is leaving him for another man. The upset precipitated by this news and the fact he is now facing a week of final exams in this last semester of his senior year have made him a "complete wreck." He seems to be holding in a lot of feelings and complains of stomach pains. In discussing his situation with the nurse, he vacillates from energetic nervous talk about getting through all this mess to vague suggestions that perhaps it really isn't worth it after all and he might not make it.

By most definitions of the word, Tom is in "crisis." Visibly upset, he is experiencing a great deal of stress at home and at school, and he seems unable to handle it all. What if the situation were one where Tom was having marital problems but no difficulty at school? Would it still be considered a crisis if Tom were nervous, though not hinting at suicide? Why would we not simply say that Tom is under a great deal of "stress," instead of "in crisis"? Or, is Tom's crisis a sign of neurosis or other form of psychopathology?

All of these questions lead us to the need for a definition of crisis, and an explication of what can be called "crisis theory." From a theoretical point of view, if the crisis state cannot be distinguished from noncrisis states, the whole concept is meaningless. From a practical vantage point, it is important to understand when a person is in crisis in order to provide the appropriate help.

CRISIS THEORY IN A NUTSHELL

A *crisis* is a temporary state of upset and disorganization, characterized chiefly by an individual's inability to cope with a particular situation using customary methods of problem solving, and by the potential for a radically positive or negative outcome.

This brief definition captures the main features of crisis as described by various theorists. Caplan's (1964) emphasis is on the emotional upset and disequilibrium, plus the breakdown in problem solving or coping during the crisis state. Taplin (1971) emphasizes the cognitive component of the crisis state, namely the violation of the person's expectancies about life by some crisis event, or the inability of an individual's "cognitive map" to handle a new and dramatic situation. Others focus on the interaction between the subjective crisis state and some objective environmental situation (Schulberg and Sheldon 1968).

THE SEMANTIC ROOTS OF CRISIS A semantic analysis of the word *crisis* reveals concepts that are rich in psychological meaning. The Chinese term for crisis *(weiji)* is composed of two characters which signify danger and opportunity occurring at the same time (Wilhelm 1967). The English word is based on the Greek *krinein* meaning to decide. Derivations of the Greek word indicate that crisis is a time of decision, judgment, as well as a turning point during which there will be a change for better or worse (Lidell and Scott 1968).

Perhaps the best way to explain our definition of crisis is in terms of crisis theory, as follows:

> All humans can be expected at various times in their lives to experience *crises* characterized by great emotional disorganization, upset, and a breakdown of previously adequate coping strategies. The crisis state is time limited (equilibrium is regained in four to six weeks), is usually touched-off by some precipitating event, can be expected to follow sequential patterns of development through various stages, and has the potential for resolution toward higher or lower levels of functioning. Ultimate crisis resolution depends upon a number of factors, including severity of the precipitating event, the individual's personal resources (ego strength, experience with previous crises), and the individual's social resources (assistance available from "significant others").

The most important principles of crisis theory, each of which will be discussed further, are included in this paragraph. Few writers or researchers in this area argue that crisis theory is a theory in the purest sense of that word, that is, data-based principles able to explain events that have already occurred and predict those that have not yet occurred. Instead, crisis theory is actually a cluster of principles or assumptions upon which seasoned practitioners and researchers generally agree. Indeed, one of the purposes of this chapter is to summarize these principles and to place them in a general systems framework. The aim is to organize current knowledge and, at the same time, pave the way for future research to refine, or possibly redirect, various aspects of the theory. We begin by identifying the major assumptions of our "nutshell" version of crisis theory.

MAJOR ASSUMPTIONS OF CRISIS THEORY

Precipitating Event

Crises have identifiable beginnings. Since clinicians and theorists began reflecting on the nature of life crises in the aftermath of Boston's Coconut Grove Nightclub fire in 1941, the crisis experience has been understood as being precipitated or touched off by some specific event. Viney (1976) summarizes a number of studies that isolate specific life events having the potential for precipitating a life crisis: pregnancy and birth of a child (Caplan 1960; Shereshfsky and Yarrow 1973; Levy and McGee 1975); unmarried motherhood (Floyd and Viney 1974); the transition from home to school (Klein and Ross 1958) and from home to university (Silber et al. 1961); engagement and marriage (Rapoport 1964); surgery and illness (Janis 1958; Titchener and Levine 1960); bereavement (Lindemann 1944; Parkes 1972); relocation/migration (Brown, Burditt, and Liddell 1965; Viney and Bazeley 1977); retirement (Cath 1965); natural disaster (Baker and Chapman 1962); and rapid social and technological change (Toffler 1971).

Some events are so universally devastating that they are almost always capable of precipitating a crisis, for example, the unexpected death of a loved one, or rape. Other events, however, are not in and of themselves of crisis proportion, but must be viewed in the context of the individual's total development. Danish and D'Augelli (1980) refer to these events as developmental markers. For example, to understand how the birth of a child, marriage, the "empty nest," or retirement can precipitate a life crisis, one needs to look both at the external event and what it means to the person in the context of his or her developmental history. Nowak (1978) suggests that the impact of a particular life event depends upon its timing, intensity, duration, sequencing, and the degree of interference with other developmental events. Whether distinguished by its suddenness and severity (a natural disaster), or by its subtlety (one's fortieth birthday), a basic principle of crisis theory is that the onset of crisis is tied to some event in the life of the individual.

Quite often the event is interpreted by the person in crisis as being the last straw, or a seemingly minor happening at the end of a long list of stressful events. Holmes and Rahe (1967) investigated the association between physical health and major life changes as stressful events (e.g., death of a spouse, divorce, pregnancy, change in residence). Life events are given numerical weights (life change units) which are added together to quantify the change a person experiences during a particular time sequence. (See Table 2.1.) According to this model, life crisis is defined as any clustering of life change units amounting to 350 points or more in one year.

Situational and Developmental Types

Situational crises are accidental or unexpected, the most salient feature of which rests with some environmental factor. Individuals experiencing loss of loved ones through natural disaster (fire, flood) and those who are victims of violent crimes (mugging, rape) are examples of situationally induced crises. This category also includes crises centering on events such as moving, divorce, and unemployment.

Developmental crises, on the other hand, are those associated with movement from one developmental stage of life to another, from childhood on through to old age. Each developmental stage is associated with certain developmental tasks, and when there is interference in achieving these tasks, a crisis is possible. From the viewpoint of crisis theory, this means that many such crises are "predictable" since we know ahead of time the developmental issues people face at various times in their lives. The distinction between situational and developmental crises is commonly accepted in articles and books on crisis intervention, and will be followed in this book with a chapter devoted to each (Chapters 3 and 4).

The Cognitive Key

A cognitive perspective on crisis (Taplin 1971) suggests that it is how a person perceives the crisis event, especially how the event fits in with the person's existing frame of reference about life, that makes the situation critical. Taplin's view is that we should consider a person's cognitions and expectancies very much like a computer programmed to receive data, process it, and behave accordingly. Looked at in this way, crisis is a time when the new information received by the computer is either (a) completely dissonant with the existing program, or (b) comes in such great quantities that the computer experiences some form of overload and malfunctions.

An example is the unsuspecting husband who finds his wife has been having an affair for the past year and now wants to leave him for her new lover. The ensuing crisis for the husband results from the conflict between the new information (my wife is having an affair and has been unfaithful to me for the past year), with an existing cognitive framework or set of expectancies about life (my wife loves me only, has been and always will be true to

TABLE 2.1
SOCIAL READJUSTMENT RATING SCALE*

Rank	Life Event	Mean Value
1	Death of spouse	100
2	Divorce	73
3	Marital separation	65
4	Jail term	63
5	Death of close family member	63
6	Personal injury or illness	53
7	Marriage	50
8	Fired at work	47
9	Marital reconciliation	45
10	Retirement	45
11	Change in health of family member	44
12	Pregnancy	40
13	Sex difficulties	39
14	Gain of new family member	39
15	Business readjustment	39
16	Change in financial state	38
17	Death of close friend	37
18	Change to different line of work	36
19	Change in number of arguments with spouse	35
20	Mortgage or loan for major purchase (home, etc.)	31
21	Foreclosure of mortgage or loan	30
22	Change in responsibilities at work	29
23	Son or daughter leaving home	29
24	Trouble with in-laws	29
25	Outstanding personal achievement	28
26	Wife begin or stop work	26
27	Begin or end school	26
28	Change in living conditions	25
29	Revision of personal habits	24
30	Trouble with boss	23
31	Change in work hours or conditions	20
32	Change in residence	20
33	Change in schools	20
34	Change in recreation	19
35	Change in church activities	19
36	Change in social activities	18
37	Mortgage or loan for lesser purchase (car, TV, etc.)	17
38	Change in sleeping habits	16
39	Change in number of family get-togethers	15
40	Change in eating habits	15
41	Vacation	13
42	Christmas	12
43	Minor violations of the law	11

*Reprinted with permission from *Journal of Psychosomatic Research,* 11 (2), 213–218, T. H. Holmes and R. H. Rahe, "The Social Readjustment Rating Scale," 1967, Pergamon Press, Ltd.

me, and it is on this basis that our relationship rests). An understanding of this crisis is based on the latter cognition, that the relationship depends upon mutual fidelity. In a cognitive framework, the external event is threatening since it is incompatible with the husband's understanding of the conditions for survival of a long-term relationship.

An event can also touch off unfinished business or personal issues from the past (Perls et al. 1951), thereby precipitating a crisis. In the example just given, if the husband has a poor self-image (possibly as a result of unpleasant experiences during childhood, or lack of positive identity formation during adolescence), the news that his wife is having an affair with another man takes on great intensity. At the heart of the man's crisis is the fact that the infidelity unleashes painful memories and feelings of inadequacy. As will be discussed next, this perspective is the key to understanding the powerful nature of the crisis experience. It tells us why some events can be so psychologically devastating, and reveals the danger and opportunity dimension of crisis as well. Depending on how the husband works through the experience, the crisis can reaffirm his negative self-image or it can become an opportunity to face squarely and rework the identity and image issues in a new direction, resulting in growth and improved functioning.

Rapoport (1965) suggests that an initial blow can be perceived as (a) a *threat* to either instinctual needs or to the sense of physical and emotional integrity, (b) a *loss* (a person, an ability, or a capability), or (c) a *challenge* that threatens to overtax an individual's capacities. In each case, cognitive processes mediate between the event and the individual's response to it. Clinically, it is most important, after determining the precipitating event, to find out what the event *means* to the person in crisis. It is a cardinal clinical error to assume knowledge of what the crisis event means to the client. As Viney

(1976) suggests, "Just as one man's meat is another man's poison, one man's crisis may be another man's ordinary train of events." It is not simply the nature of the event that is critical to understanding the crisis state. It is necessary to know also how the event is perceived to be a threat, or more specifically, what cognitive map or set of expectancies about life has been violated and what unfinished personal issues have been brought out by the crisis event.

Disorganization and Disequilibrium

One of the most obvious aspects of crisis is the severe emotional upset, or disequilibrium, experienced by the individual. Miller and Iscoe (1963) describe the feelings of tension, ineffectualness, and helplessness of the person in crisis. Crow (1977) teaches crisis counselors to look for crises which come in three colors—yellow (anxiety), red (anger), and black (depression),—reflecting the emotional aspects of the crisis state. It is not uncommon for clinicians to witness not only emotional reactions (crying, anger, remorse), but also somatic complaints (ulcers, stomach cramps), and behavioral disorders (interpersonal conflict, and inability to sleep, perform sexually, or to carry on work activities).

Halpern (1973) attempted to define crisis empirically by comparing the behavior of people not experiencing crises to the behavior of people undergoing crises. Persons in crisis experienced the following symptoms significantly more than those not in crisis:

1. feelings of tiredness and exhaustion,
2. feelings of helplessness,
3. feelings of inadequacy,
4. feelings of confusion,
5. physical symptoms,
6. feelings of anxiety,
7. disorganization of functioning in work relationships,
8. disorganization of functioning in family relationships,
9. disorganization of functioning in social relationships, and
10. disorganization in social activities (p. 345).

The list lends detail to Caplan's notion that the crisis state is characterized by disequilibrium or imbalance. As Halpern's research incates, the disorganization, confusion, and upset of the crisis state can affect several aspects of a person's life at one time: feelings, thoughts, behavior, social relationships, and physical functioning.

Vulnerability and Reduced Defensiveness

A part of the disorganization of the crisis state is the individual's vulnerability and suggestibility (Taplin 1971). This is also referred to as *reduced defensiveness* (Halpern 1973). When an individual is no longer able to cope, and everything held dear seems to have disintegrated, it is almost as if there is nothing left to defend. In Taplin's cognitive framework, the overload from the precipitating event leaves the organism confused and open to suggestions. Clinicians report that at certain times during the crisis state, clients are ready for new conceptualizations to help them explain the data, and to understand what has happened, or is happening. As Tyherst (1958) suggests, this vulnerability, suggestibility, or reduced defensiveness is what produces the opportunity for change characterizing life crises.

Breakdown in Coping

Central to almost any definition of crisis is the idea that coping, or problem solving, has broken down. The assumption is that as we mature each of us develops various methods to deal with life's difficulties. The onset of crisis, whether the result of a major threatening event, or a series of stressful events resulting in a burden too great to bear, calls into play whatever problem-solving devices are available. Maneuvers that might have worked before, such as redefining the situation, ignoring it, talking to a friend, or taking a vacation, are not adequate. The person in crisis may feel strapped, or wholly incapable of dealing with a new unsettling circumstance.

Caplan summarizes seven characteristics of effective coping behavior as follows:

1. actively exploring reality issues and searching for information,
2. freely expressing both positive and negative feelings and tolerating frustration,
3. actively invoking help from others,
4. breaking problems down into manageable bits and working them through one at a time,
5. being aware of fatigue and tendencies toward disorganization, while pacing efforts and maintaining control in as many areas of functioning as possible,
6. mastering feelings where possible (accepting them when necessary), being flexible and willing to change, and
7. trusting in oneself and others and having a basic optimism about the outcome. (Caplan 1964).

This list is congruent with the theoretical model developed by Richard Lazarus (1980) in which *coping* is defined in terms of two main activities. The first activity involves changing the situation—problem solving. This includes from Caplan's list, exploration of reality issues (1), invoking help from others (3), breaking the problem into manageable bits (4), trusting oneself and others (7), and having a confident attitude toward one's ability to solve the problem. The second aspect of coping for Lazarus involves managing the *subjective* components of the problem. This would include managing positive and negative feelings and tolerating frustration (2), dealing with fatigue and tendencies toward disorganization while

pacing efforts, and maintaining control and basic mastery of feelings (5,6).

To understand Lazarus's notion of coping, it is necessary to go back one step. He suggests that when a threatening event occurs, the individual makes a primary and then a secondary appraisal of the situation. The first appraisal answers the question "Is there anything at stake here?" This assumes that events can be either (a) irrelevant as far as his or her well-being is concerned (laying off employees at another factory or in another department), (b) benign or positive (receiving a small increase in wages), or (c) stressful. Stressful events in Lazarus's model can be viewed as one of three types. First of all, the event may represent harm or loss (loss of limb, divorce, untimely death of a loved one). Second, a stressful event may represent a threat to one's present well-being. Third, a stressful event may represent a challenge, an opportunity for growth, mastery, or gain. Before any coping takes place, the primary appraisal is a cognitive process determining whether or not anything is at stake, and if so, what the stakes are.

Secondary appraisal, in the Lazarus model, is also a cognitive strategy, but it is concerned with coping, that is, "what to do." Secondary appraisal aims at changing the situation and at managing the subjective components (feelings, thoughts, physical well-being, behavior) related to the situation.

The crisis state is characterized by the breakdown in these processes. Rational probelm solving is impossible (Caplan's exploration of reality issues, invoking the help of others, breaking the problem into manageable pieces), and the person in crisis has difficulty managing the subjective aspects of the situation (physical complaints, feelings of anxiety, fear, exhaustion). As we shall see in subsequent discussions of the helping process, this analysis provides a framework for decisions on how best to be of assistance during the time of crisis.

Time Limits Most therapists think of the crisis state as being acute (sudden onset, short duration) as opposed to chronic (building over time, lasting months to years). Caplan's notion, reiterated uniformly in the clinical literature, is that the crisis typically will be resolved in four to six weeks. The magical six-weeks figure has led to some confusion. Many writers cite crises which were not resolved in such a short period of time. Lewis, Gottesman, and Gutstein (1979) administered psychological tests and conducted a follow-up with a group of crisis patients undergoing surgery for cancer, as well as a group undergoing surgery for less serious illnesses. They found that the duration of crisis was greater than six weeks but less than seven months, and concluded that though the six-weeks figure is misleading, there are limits to the duration of a crisis. Lazarus (1980) noted that the resolution of a crisis of bereavement may take years.

To clarify the meaning of the six-weeks period, it is important to draw a distinction between restoration of equilibrium and crisis resolution. It is most useful to think of the six-weeks period as a time during which equilibrium is restored, that is, erratic behavior, emotions, and somatic complaints are reduced from the intense state characterizing the early part of the crisis. The assumption is that human beings will not tolerate high levels of disorganization for long periods of time. Most theorists consider the crisis state as a temporary period of instability, bounded on either side by times of greater stability. It is the instability or disorganization which is time-limited (Caplan 1964).

This does not mean, however, that the crisis has been constructively resolved. While equilibrium may have been restored, it may be restored in what will later prove to be a dysfunctional direction for the person and his or her family. The spouse who falls apart on hearing that his wife left him may no longer feel the extreme pain seven or eight weeks later, but the reduction in pain may come about through a commitment "never to trust a woman again." The time limit on the crisis state, with the potential for reorganization in a positive or negative direction (discussed next), is the heart of crisis theory. The time limit is intended to suggest that not only is the potential for gain or loss very high, but the basic track or direction for either is usually set in the weeks immediately following onset of the crisis. As discussed in subsequent chapters, this fact alone has powerful implications for arranging the delivery of crisis services.

Phases and Stages: From Impact to Resolution The state of crisis is considered to progress through a series of relatively well-defined stages. Caplan (1964) describes the onset of crisis as follows:

1. There is an initial rise of tension from the impact of an external event, which in turn initiates habitual "problem-solving responses."
2. The lack of success of these problem-solving responses, plus the continued impact of the stimulus event, further increases tension, feelings of upset, and ineffectuality.
3. As the tension increases, other problem-solving resources are mobilized. At this point, the crisis may be averted by any of the following: reduction in the external threat, success of new coping strategies, redefinition of the problem, or giving up tightly held goals which are unobtainable.
4. If none of these occurs, however, the tension mounts to a breaking point, resulting in severe emotional disorganization.

Horowitz (1976) describes reactions to severe stress (unexpected death of a loved one) to give further detail on the stages of crisis. (See Figure 2.1.) In this model, the first reaction to a threatening event is the outcry, an

FIGURE 2.1   THE STAGES OF CRISIS

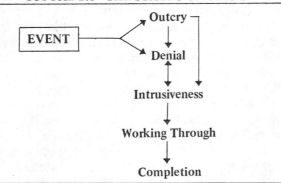

Source: "Diagnosis and treatment of stress response syndroms: General principles" by M.J. Horowitz, in H.J. Parad, H.L.P. Resnik, and L.G. Parad (Eds.), *Emergency and Disaster Management* (Bowie, Maryland: The Charles Press Publishers, Inc., 1976). Reprinted by permission.

almost reflexive emotional reaction such as weeping, panic, screaming, fainting, or moaning. The reaction may be quite obvious to others (a woman sobbing in anguish upon hearing that her husband just died in a work accident), or not so obvious (a person who, hearing the same news, feels a lump in the throat and tears welling up in the eyes). *Outcry* refers to the initial reactions at the impact of the event.

The arrows in Figure 2.1 indicate that outcry leads to either denial or intrusiveness. *Denial* refers to a blocking of the impact. It can be accompanied by emotional numbing, not thinking of what happened, or structuring activity as if the event had not occurred. Horowitz notes that a widow may enter this stage at the time of the funeral, busying herself with activities to meet the needs of relatives, leading them to conclude that she is very strong, or, she is doing very well.

Intrusiveness includes the involuntary flooding of ideas and pangs of feeling about the event, whether a loss or some other tragedy. Recurrent nightmares, or other daily images and preoccupations with what has happened are characteristic of this phase. The widow may experience this after the relatives

have gone, when she lets down, and the full impact of the loss is felt. The flood of thoughts that accompany the intrusive phase may include statements, spoken or unspoken, about the loss and its impact ("I can't go on."). As shown in Figure 2.1, some individuals skip the denial phase and move directly to an intrusive phase. Others vacillate back and forth between these two states.

Working through is the process in which the thoughts, feelings, and images of the crisis experience are expressed, identified, and aired. Some individuals progress and work through these feelings and experiences naturally, whereas others do so only with outside help.

Completion is the final phase of the crisis experience and refers to an integration of the crisis experience into the individual's life. The event has been faced, feelings and thoughts have been identified and expressed, and reorganization has been either accomplished or begun. While mention of loss, for example, may still bring sadness or the thought that "this couldn't have happened," the main disorganization characteristic of the crisis state is passed.

This is similar to Levine's (1976) description of the adaptation process for American expatriots (young draft evaders and military deserters) in dealing with self exile in Canada. A period of disorganization (confusion, ambivalence, loneliness, and general distress) at the beginning was followed by an acting out stage characterized by noninvolvement, superficial relationships, and sometimes aggressive antisocial behavior. A third stage of searching, taking stock, developing closer interpersonal ties, and maturing was followed by a final phase of adaptation and integration, in which the individual became thoroughly involved in a new life style and viewed himself more as a Canadian than as an "American in exile."

The framework offered by Horowitz is congruent with others described in the crisis literature (Baldwin 1979; Caplan 1964; Aguilera, Messick, & Farrell, 1974). For example, Fink, Beak & Taddeo (1971) described a four-stage model for crisis resolution: shock, defensive retreat, acknowledgement, and finally, adaptation and change, each phase characterized by different experiences, perceptions of reality, emotions, and thoughts.

As shown in subsequent discussions of crisis resolution (next and in the intervention chapters in Part II), since each of these phases is characterized by unique activities in terms of thoughts, feelings, and behavior, this model brings us a step closer to understanding which treatments might best facilitate productive crisis resolution.

Outcome of Crisis: For Better or Worse

Theoretically, we can talk of three possible outcomes of crisis: change for better, change for worse, or return to previous level of functioning. However, since crises are so upsetting, the third category has little meaning. Crises are viewed as critical turning points where danger and opportunity co-exist and where the stakes are high. In a very concrete sense, dangerous outcomes may be either physical or psychological. Suicide, homicide, and other less lethal (though frightening) forms of physical violence (spouse battering, child abuse) are examples of one end of the danger continuum. As discussed in Chapter 1, in the United States the suicide prevention movement has historically been linked to the crisis intervention movement, with suicide considered one possible lethal outcome of a life crisis. In the midst of severe disorganization and inability to cope, some individuals decide that there simply is no hope or that the pain is too great, and make the decision to take their own lives (Lester and Brockopp 1973; Faberow and Shneidman 1961). There are also individuals who lash out at others, resulting in physical violence in families and neighborhoods.

In discussion of the intervention process, assessment of lethality, followed by appropriate protections, is a central aspect of the intervention process (Chapters 6 and 7).

In addition to the threat to life, the threat to psychological health is implicit in the crisis concept. Miller and Iscoe (1963), building on the early work of Caplan (1964), discuss it this way:

> After a period of time the crisis will pass or be resolved in some manner. This solution may be healthy or unhealthy, and it is assumed that the type of solution that is reached will have implications for the individual's future functioning. Successful solution of life crises is seen as resulting in a more confident, more highly integrated personality with increased strength to deal with future life stresses. In fact, a person's present state of mental health can be viewed as a product of the manner in which a series of crises have been solved in the past (pp. 196-197).

This raises the question of how to define *crisis resolution*. Viney (1976) suggests that the concept includes, in addition to restoration of equilibrium, cognitive mastery of the situation and the development of new coping strategies, including changes in behavior and the appropriate use of external resources. Building on the idea that crisis resolution somehow involves reorganization and reintegration of functioning, positive crisis resolution can be defined as:

> *Working through* the crisis event so that it becomes *integrated* into the fabric of life, leaving the person *open* instead of closed to the future.

Each of these italicized words represents an important aspect of the process of crisis therapy. *Working through* involves assisting the person in exploring the crisis event, and his/her reaction to it. It assumes that an individual's reaction to a crisis event must be viewed as a complex process, as R. Lazarus (1980) indicates:

> In stressful transactions, psychological events are constantly moving and changing. Depending on what happens in the environment and within the person, anger gives way to anxiety or guilt, or it melts or grows stronger with each successive interchange. A stressful episode is not just a momentary, static stimulus in the environment to which the person gives a single response, say, a thought, act, or somatic reaction, as in the analogy of a single, still photo; rather, it is a continuous flow of events over time, sometimes a short time as in an argument that quickly ends when one party leaves the room, at other times a long, tortuous, complex, sometimes repetitive process of achieving a new equilibrium in a relationship. (p. 39).

As a process, crisis therapy involves facilitating experiences which include: reflecting on the event and its meaning to the person in crisis, expressing feelings, maintaining at least a minimum degree of physical well-being during the crisis, plus making behavioral and interpersonal adjustments appropriate to the situation. We can refer to all of this as *working through* the crisis. Baldwin (1979) summarizes it this way:

1. defining issues, dealing with feelings, making decisions, or learning new problem-solving or coping behaviors;
2. identifying and at least partially resolving underlying conflicts represented in or reactivated by the crisis;
3. defining and mobilizing an individual's internal and external resources toward solving the crisis; and
4. reducing unpleasant or uncomfortable affect associated with the crisis.

To suggest that the goal of crisis therapy includes *integrating* the event into the fabric of life simply means that for the crisis to be resolved, the event and its aftermath must eventually take their places alongside the other life events and markers in the person's life, forming one part of an evolving life experience. The opposite of this functional integration is artificially compartmentalizing it, blocking it out of awareness, pretending it did not happen or somehow denying its existence. While such denial or blocking is often part of *early* reactions to a crisis event (Horowitz 1976), ultimate resolution of the crisis experience must move past this reaction toward integrating the experience with other life experiences. Even for traumatic experiences such as rape, loss of a limb, or loss of a loved one, the eventual resolution hopefully will find the crisis victim able to say or think something similar to the following:

> Yes, that happened to me. I suffered a great deal. I went through emotional pain, felt upset, and even thought at times I could not go on. I talked about it, expressed my feelings, made use of friends, and found that with this, and the passage of time, the event no longer has the same hold on me that it did in the beginning. I even find that some parts of my life which were previously dormant (particular friendships) have been strengthened in positive ways. My outlook on life has changed from being dismal to appreciating what I still have and the new strengths I have found. And now? The emotional scars are healing, though they're still there. Yes, I can remember; I know what I went through. But the whole thing is becoming just one of many experiences that make up my total life. I am ready to go on now. I can, of course, think back and even feel what it was like. At times I can even relive some of the experiences and the hurtful feelings. The bulk of the working through, however, is over. I'm ready to face the future.

Being *open* to facing the future and ready to go about the business of living may also be thought of as being equipped to face the future. Some casualties of psychological crises seem literally to close down many areas of their lives after a crisis—they withdraw from relationships, are unable to work, have difficulty in finding enjoyment in life, or experience concrete behavioral symptoms such as not leaving the house (agoraphobia) or have continued somatic complaints. Openness to the future, on the other hand, refers to a willingness and readiness to continue in the process of living.

Baldwin (1979) calls this an adaptive resolution, characterized by the acquisition of new coping behavior, reduced vulnerability (since underlying conflicts have been resolved and will not be reactivated), and greater maturity. In the present volume, this readiness to face the future is operationalized in terms of specific changes in behavioral, affective, somatic, interpersonal, and cognitive functioning. (See the next section and Chapter 8 concerning BASIC personality framework.) This allows us to think of growth following a crisis as improvement in one or more of these areas.

How an individual responds to a precipitating event and later works through the crisis experience depends on his or her material, personal, and social resources.

Significant *material resources* during a crisis include money (availability as well as amount), food, housing, and transportation. A deficit in any of these areas has the potential of turning a moderately stressful event into a crisis (availability of food stamps during a period of temporary unemployment, inability to pay for medical services). Crisis intervention procedures must therefore assess the extent to which a lack of material resources is exacerbating the situation and the extent to which efforts should be directed toward finding emergency relief (monetary or otherwise) that might facilitate other positive (psychological) coping efforts.

The individual's *personal resources* make up the second major factor in determining both the intensity and the ultimate course of

any crisis. Ego strength, previous history of coping with stressful situations, the existence of any unresolved personality problems, and physical well-being all play a part in determining whether a particular event will lead to a crisis. Miller and Iscoe (1963) describe crisis as a time when an event awakens "problems from the past" or unresolved personality conflicts in such a way that disorganization and emotional upset ensue. An example is a graduate student whose young adult life has been characterized by an unrealistic preoccupation with pleasing parents in both personal life (dating) and career choice. The threat to completion of graduate studies may lead to panic grounded in a fear of not living up to parental expectations. The intensity of the crisis can be understood, not simply in terms of an external event, but in light of the fact that this young adult is still working to meet his parents' expectations rather than to achieve his own goals and objectives. As shown in subsequent chapters, the notion that crisis events touch off unresolved personality issues is one of the encouraging and hopeful aspects of the theory. It provides the opportunity for individuals to complete unfinished business and to rework dysfunctional beliefs and life patterns.

Social resources refer primarily to the people in the individual's immediate environment at the time of crisis, such as family, friends, and work associates. R. Lazarus (1980) discusses the roles of these resources in bereavement.

> What happens at the outset when discovery of the loss occurs—the shock, dazed state, confusion, bustle of activity of family and friends taking care of necessary tasks such as the funeral and giving emotional support—changes greatly as time passes. Ultimately the full realization of the loss must occur, then its acceptance, and finally, after perhaps a period of depression and withdrawal, a reinvestment in living and a search for new commitments. These coping tasks are accomplished in multiple

encounters, with the children, financial accounts, the car, lawyers, friends, family, people at work, new social contacts, many or most of these encounters engendering many forms of stress and calling for varieties of coping processes (p. 39).

Unger and Powell (1980) describe three types of aid that social networks can apply during times of crisis. The first is instrumental support, consisting of material aid such as food, clothing, shelter, or money to alleviate financial burdens. Social networks also provide emotional support, specifically communicating to a person in crisis that he or she is loved, cared for, and valued by family and friends. Finally, social networks provide information and referral to other helping resources. By their words and actions, family members and friends can affect the way a person in crisis will interpret events and which coping strategies will be tried. Similarly, an individual's social network is usually the first (and often most trusted) source of information on where to go for further help, whether for counseling, day care, medical assistance, or something else.

From an intervention vantage point, it is important to know both *who* is available to help and *what sort of help* they will provide. Do family and friends offer comments which lead to a greater understanding of the crisis, mastery of the situation, and increased confidence? Or, do their words and actions make the individual feel less worthy, less capable, more dependent and shaky about the months and years ahead? Effective intervention seeks to assess the nature of the social supports and guide their influence in a positive direction.

More than Stress

Since both stress and crisis involve discomfort, these concepts are often confused. Viney (1976) offers the following distinctions between the two:

1. The coping patterns during crisis are different from those associated with stress. In an empirical study of coping patterns of women during crisis, Bazeley and Viney (1974) concluded that specific crises were dealt with differently from worries or unhappy periods. Coping during crises seemed to be more "personal," using less nuclear family and informal supports.
2. During the crisis state, the individual tends to be less defensive and more open to suggestions, influence, and support (Halpern 1973), though this is not characteristically true of stress.
3. The outcome of crisis can be either debilitation or growth. Stress, on the other hand, is usually associated with pathology and has as its most optimistic outcome adaptation to the wear and tear caused by life's circumstances or return to the status quo (Selye 1976).
4. Crisis is viewed as occurring during a relatively short period of time (about six weeks), whereas stress is not considered to have this self-limiting quality. Stress is more often viewed as a chronic condition building over time, whereas a crisis is associated with a sudden onset.

Not Mental Illness

It is not uncommon for an individual in crisis to be so frightened of the emotional upset and disorganization that he or she comes up with the idea that, "I must be going crazy!" Similarly, some of the "symptoms" of crisis (anxiety, sleeplessness, and interpersonal difficulties) are also characteristic of certain forms of psychopathology. There has even been some confusion among clinicians about when certain symptoms are to be interpreted as a sign of a life crisis and when as a sign of psychopathology.

A chief tenet of crisis theory is that *anyone* can have a crisis. Indeed, the theory suggests that crises happen to everyone at some time or another, though the frequency and intensity of full-blown crises varies. An individual can be quite "normal" for thirty-five years and suddenly be quite disorganized as a result of a crisis event. This disorganization may be considered as a "normal response to an abnormal circumstance." Severe disorganization (somatic complaints, sleeplessness, emotional upset, and the like) is *not*, in the context of this theory, interpreted as a sign of psychopathology. Instead, it is interpreted as an individual's reaction to encountering an insurmountable obstacle blocking a life goal.

This is not to suggest that individuals diagnosed as neurotic or psychotic will not also have life crises. The definition of crisis presented in this chapter applies to these diagnostic categories as well. The key consideration in understanding crisis is seeing it as disorganization or instability bounded on either side (before and after) by periods of greater stability. The prior stability could be "neurotic" or "normal."[1] Crisis, then, does not necessarily indicate either psychopathology or normality. It is characteristically viewed, however, as a positive, growth- and health-oriented concept, instead of one related to sickness or disease.

A GENERAL SYSTEMS FRAMEWORK It may already be apparent to the reader that the formulation of crisis theory used here dwells heavily on *intrapsychic* variables, and that not much has been described concerning the social context within which life crises occur. Practitioners

have long understood that crises do not take place in a vacuum; crises are imbedded in the network of social living (Hill 1958). For example, a parent's crisis can have a profound effect on the children. The upset of an adult head of the household, faced with a crisis precipitated by unemployment, has a great impact on the rest of the family. One family member may even experience a crisis for the family as a whole. Usually this person, called the identified patient, is the one referred to therapists for assistance.

While the emphasis on social supplies and supports in crisis resolution is as old as the theory itself (Caplan 1964, 1976), theoretical models which include both the person and the social context have not been formulated until recently. Moos (1976) examined life crises in a social ecology framework, with an emphasis on the transactions between the person and environment. Stevenson (1977) recently suggested a general systems theory framework for understanding the crises of adult life extending from young adulthood through old age. Notably absent in the clinical reports and research literature, however, is the application of these models to either a theory of how life crises develop or to a format for intervention toward productive crisis resolution. Since the primary focus of this book is on intervention, it is important to cast the various theoretical principles just listed into a framework that allows their application to the helping process. General systems theory (GST), developed by Ludwig von Bertalanffy, has the potential for integrating these theoretical principles in such a way as to provide a backdrop for thinking about the intervention process.

General systems theory suggests that we look at the context within which the person lives, and in particular, at the interactions between the person, various subsystems, and the environment (family and community). It is this dynamic interchange between person and immediate environment that can give

---

[1] This analysis is congruent with recent trends in the study of psychopathology which emphasize vulnerability hypotheses in understanding, for example, schizophrenia. Zubin and Spring (1977) discuss schizophrenia in this way: "It is assumed that exogenous and/or endogenous challengers elicit a crisis in all humans, but depending on the intensity of the elicited stress and the threshold for tolerating it, that is, one's vulnerability, the crisis will either be contained homeostatically or lead to an episode of disorder."

clues to the onset of crisis, as well as to its duration and ultimate outcome. Consequently, it can be of help both to researchers trying to understand the crisis process and to clinicians attempting to intervene with clients going through this process.

A complete description of general systems theory is beyond the scope of this book. Several excellent reviews exist (Berrien 1968; Seiler 1967; von Bertalanffy 1968; Buckley 1968), including one which applies general systems theory to adult life crises (Stevenson 1977). Our purpose will be served by briefly listing the key concepts from general systems theory and by relating them to earlier principles of crisis theory. The principles listed next provide the framework within which each of the preceeding crisis theory assumptions can be organized, providing a backdrop for discussions of the intervention process throughout the rest of this volume.

People as Systems   It is useful to consider the individual person as a system made up of various subsystems. The history of psychology reveals numerous ways of describing human personality in a comprehensive and systematic manner. Recent trends in clinical psychology have emphasized holistic approaches to personality, including assessment along a number of dimensions. A. Lazarus (1976, 1981) for example, considers seven modalities—behavior, affect, sensation, imagery, cognition, interpersonal behavior, and the use of drugs in understanding clinical problems. We have found it useful to adopt Lazarus's approach while collapsing certain categories to form a more consolidated systems approach.[2] We can then consider an individual person as a system whose BASIC functioning includes five subsystems: *B*ehavioral, *A*ffective, *S*omatic, *I*nterpersonal, *C*ognitive. (See Table 2.2 for variables included under each of the five subsystems.) Assessment must be made in each area to determine a person's unique response to a crisis event, whether it be the loss of a loved one, physical injury, losing a job, or some other event. The crisis state will be characterized by disruption in one or more of these five subsystems.

The Context of Crisis   Since nothing takes place in a vacuum, all aspects of a crisis must be examined in light of various contexts. In general systems language, these contexts are "suprasystems." Bronfenbrenner (1979) describes three such suprasystems, each increasing in size and complexity, which are relevant to the coping behavior of an individual. The *microsystem* represents the family and immediate social group. The *exosystem* represents social structures in the community, for example, the world of work, neighborhood social networks, and community governmental structures (including social services). Finally, the *macrosystem* is the largest contextual framework and includes cultural values and belief systems which impinge upon communities, families, and ultimately upon individuals.

---

[2] We have included the behaviors of drinking alcohol, smoking tobacco, and taking other drugs under the behavioral modality, thereby eliminating Lazarus's (1976) drugs category. All aspects of an individual's physical functioning—some of which Lazarus codes under drugs, and others under sensation —we have included under the somatic label. Our somatic modality therefore replaces the sensation category and includes all aspects of physical health, including sensitivity of touch, taste, vision, hearing, and smell. Since imagery and cognition are two aspects of mental functioning, we have coded them under one heading—cognitive functioning. Collapsing the two mental modalities under the cognitive modality is not meant to blur the distinction between right and left hemispheres of the brain, the former mediating verbal cognitions, and the latter mediating visual-spacial processing (Hammond and Stanfield 1977; Woolfolk 1976). Our consolidated system gives considerable attention to both mental pictures/images and mental statements/thoughts as the major subheadings under the cognitive modality (see Chapter 8). Chapter 8).

TABLE 2.2 BASIC PERSONALITY PROFILE*

Modality /System	Variables/Subsystems
Behavioral	Patterns of work, play, leisure, exercise, diet (eating and drinking habits), sexual behavior, sleeping habits, use of drugs and tobacco; presence of any of the following: suicidal, homicidal, or aggressive acts. Customary methods of coping with stress.
Affective	Feelings about any of above behaviors; presence of feelings such as anxiety, anger, joy, depression, etc; appropriateness of affect to life circumstances. Are feelings expressed or hidden?
Somatic	General physical functioning, health. Presence or absence of tics, headaches, stomach difficulties, and any other somatic complaints; general state of relaxation/tension; sensitivity of vision, touch, taste, sight, hearing.
Interpersonal	Nature of relationships with family, friends, neighbors, and co-workers; interpersonal strengths and difficulties; number of friends, frequency of contact with friends and acquaintances; role taken with various intimates (passive, independent, leader, co-equal); conflict resolution style (assertive, aggressive, withdrawn); basic interpersonal style (congenial, suspicious, manipulative, exploitive, submissive, dependent).
Cognitive	Current day and night dream; mental pictures about past or future; self image; life goals and reasons for their validity; religious beliefs; philosophy of life; presence of any of the following: catastrophizing, overgeneralizing, delusions, hallucinations, irrational self-talk, rationalizations, paranoid ideation; general (positive/negative) attitude towards life.

*Data sources for this table include the clinical interview, reports of family members, friends and referral source, questionnaires. (See Table 8.2 and Appendix B.)

As Table 2.3 indicates, each of the four systems, in increasing levels of complexity, is made up of subsystems. The person system is understood in terms of the five modalities which make up BASIC personality.

The family/social group (microsystem) describes he immediate social milieu within which a person lives. Essentially, this refers to Caplan's "social supplies" and is critical to understanding any individual's life crisis. The immediate social group can be a source of support and a source of stress. In some crises, the precipitating event comes from the family/ social context (marital fight). Also, family and social groups are capable of offering psy-chological first aid, or first-order crisis intervention. From the viewpoint of crisis theory, the family/social group is the chief provider of support. Caplan (1976) summarizes the function of support systems in this way: "They tell him [the individual] what is expected of him and guide him in what to do. They watch what he does and judge his performance." He notes further that interpersonal supports provide assistance in managing emotions and in controlling impulses, a parallel to Lazarus's (1980) description of the process of coping.

Rueveni (1979) bases crisis intervention firmly on interventions within the family

TABLE 2.3   CRISIS IN CONTEXT: SYSTEMS VARIABLES

System	Variables
Person	Behavioral, affective, somatic, interpersonal and cognitive (BASIC) aspects of an individual's functioning.
Family/Social Group	Family, friends, and neighbors, and the nature of their relationships with the person in crisis (cohesion, communication patterns, roles and responsibilities, flexibility and openness, values).
Community	The characteristics of an individual's community, including: geography; material and economic resources; the policies of political and governmental structures (executive, judicial, legislative); the individual's place of employment plus other businesses and industries; schools; churches; and neighborhood organizations.
Culture	Predominate values, traditions, norms, customs.

and neighborhood networks. In a family networking approach to crisis intervention, as many as forty or fifty people might be assembled to assist the person and family in dealing with the situation. The goal in such gatherings is to work through the current crisis and to mobilize support to continue the process in the months ahead.

As Table 2.3 indicates, in identifying the role of community systems, particular attention is given to governmental, political, and social service structures which can exacerbate crises as well as assist in their resolution. What support services are available, such as hotlines, hospitals, outpatient clinics, churches? Also, what geographic (burial of chemical wastes) and economic (lay-off at a factory) conditions might contribute to the occurrence of crises in a community?

Cultural variables include both national policy issues (funding for community mental health programs, disaster preparedness plans, and the like), and the traditions, customs, and values which determine how particular individuals will work through crises.

The Whole Is Greater . . . than the sum of its parts. An individual is much more than the sum of behavior, feelings,

physical attributes, interpersonal relations, and thoughts. When these aspects of individual functioning are examined in their totality, they make up a life structure which is a function of the state of these subsystems as well as the interactions between them. The same is true of a family. To understand its unique character, one must look at the personalities of the individual members as well as at their interactions with one another, and the gestalt which emerges when they are seen together as one unit.

Systems Transactions   Systems are continually engaged in transactions with one another. The behavior of an individual person affects his/her family and friends, and vise versa. Similarly, families affect communities and communities affect families, and so on. In systems language, these transactions are viewed as *input, throughput,* and *output.* A mother, for example, experiences certain family pressures (input), has thoughts and feelings about these pressures (throughput), and responds to the original source of stress in what she says and does to her family and friends (output). A sixteen-year-old boy living at home receives ideas and values about life from his family, and is provided with certain physical resources for living (money, use of the family car), as well as a certain degree of social support. He, in turn, gives back to the family his own ideas about living (often at variance with parents), makes contributions to family life through chores around the house, through his relative absence/presence at meals and other family/ social gatherings, and the like. These everyday "transactions" provide the backdrop for our consideration of the ultimate course of an individual's crisis. During the crisis itself, analyses of transactions between the person and immediate social milieu focus on the coping process—problem solving and managing feelings/emotions in the context of family life. (See also Holahan and Spearly, 1980.)

Interdependence of Systems

By virtue of these transactions, subsystems are interdependent upon one another. Since everything is connected with everything else, it is impossible for a major change to occur in one area without having some noticeable impact in other systems which impinge upon it. Consider a family in which the parents have recently separated and are moving toward divorce. One can expect the marital separation to have an impact on the children. The particular impact on each child can be measured in terms of the person-system variables discussed previously (BASIC personality functioning). There might be regressive *behavioral* changes such as thumb-sucking. *Affective* impact might be noticed in depressive moods or crying. Stomachaches, cramps, or other *somatic* complaints are possible. *Interpersonal* changes such as increased aggression in school might be observed. The *cognitive* dimension includes the child's attempts to explain the divorce ("It's my fault that mommy and daddy broke up."), and will have a powerful impact on all other modalities.

Under some circumstances, an entire family will experience pressure (stress related to a move from one city to another), but the "crisis" will be experienced by only one person. In some cases, the coping of the other family members (the father burying himself in work) will add to the strain on the rest of the family (the mother carrying a greater load at home, leading to increased stress for mother and children).

The family analogy also has a counterpart in theories about psychological aspects of physical illness, including cancer (Simonton, Matthews-Simonton and Creighton, 1978). Research in this area grows from the hypothesis that severe external stress (loss of an important emotional relationship) can have an inhibiting effect on the body's immune system, thereby permitting a cancer to develop. In the context of the four systems identified (person, family/social group, community, and culture), the external event (loss of relationship) is understood as affecting the individual's cognitions (I cannot go on without this person), with concomitant impact on physiological functioning.

Another way of talking about this interdependence is to say that every behavior or symptom serves some function (Seiler 1967). The task of the clinician is to determine the function being served by a particular symptom. A nervous breakdown by one family member can serve to draw attention away from destructive relationships in the total family system. Figley and Sprenkle (1978) suggest that it is important, in the diagnostic phase, to examine how a family's current attempts to cope with one member's crisis might actually be maintaining the crisis instead of moving it toward resolution.

The principle of utility or functionality means that behavior, thoughts, feelings, and so on, which may at first seem to be wholly negative or harmful should be examined again to see what purpose they may be serving in the context of the family and social group. This means looking at both gains and losses of any set of symptoms during a state of crisis. General systems theory tells us that any obvious characteristics of a system's state (such as anger, fear, disorganized thoughts, disruptive behavior, inability to cope) should be considered as serving some purpose both for the target system (the person), as well as the suprasystem (the family or social group).

Three Functions of Systems

There are three essential functions of any system: (a) adaptation to the environment, (b) integration of the various subsystems, and (c) decision making. Disruption in any one of the three can lead to crisis (Stevenson 1977). In one sense it would be possible to describe crisis as a major disruption in person-environment fit. Neugarten (1979), for example, refers to the relative match or fit between developmental and biological timetables, on the one hand, and social timetables, on the other. A person who develops either too quickly or too slowly according to social timetables could find him/herself out of synchronization with the environment.

The second systems function—integration—relates directly to our definition of crisis resolution. New awareness of self as a result of a crisis experience (divorce), or the need to readjust one's self-image as a result of physical injury (loss of limb), calls for a reorganization of the person-system so that the various subsystems can again work together smoothly. The person in crisis doubts that he/she can pull this off, resulting in imbalance, disorganization, and disequilibrium. Work toward crisis resolution has as its goal assisting the organism in integrating its various subsystems, a requisite of functioning for all living systems.

Finally, the decision-making function of systems is a prerequisite for the concept of coping in crisis theory: namely, managing the subjective components of the crisis, and problem solving. Crisis can thus be understood as a breakdown in coping, or a severe disruption in the organism's decision-making function.

Steady States

All living systems tend toward returning to a steady state, which is a state of homeostasis or equilibrium. This general systems theory concept suggests that systems, whether they be persons or families, cannot tolerate upset and disorganization for any long period of time. The resources of the system can be expected to make the necessary adjustments to bring about a return to some sort of equilibrium. As Stevenson (1977) describes it:

> Steady state refers to the range of flexibility possible for each of numerous components of the units in all living systems. This range of flexibility means that the system can remain stable despite changes and imbalances occurring within and between the units of the system. This range of flexibility has limits.
>
> When the flexibility of the system is exercised beyond its limits, a stress is produced which constitutes a threat to the system. The system must then use its capacities for adaptation, integration, and decision-making to reduce the stress and stabilize the system. . . . An example would be a family that experienced temporary or permanent unit loss (e.g., run-away child, death of a member, divorce between two members). Such a system would go through a series of processes aimed at returning the family to some level of steady state (p. 47).

The tendency of living systems to return to steady state or to restore equilibrium is a more precise way of stating the clinical observation that the intensity of crises tends to abate in a matter of four to six weeks (Caplan 1964). It is important to note that the return to steady state might be for eventual good or ill as far as the family is concerned. Or, in light of the preceding principles, the return to steady state could be positive for one part of the family and negative for others.

Equifinality

Living systems are characterized by equifinality or the ability of two or more systems to achieve the same final state, though under different *conditions and through different routes* (Berrien 1968; von Bertalanffy 1968). Stevenson (1977) offers the example of how various cultures raise children to adult life using different child-rearing practices. The ultimate goal or endpoint (competent, socialized adults) is the same, though the means of achieving it vary from culture to culture. The same could be said of crisis resolution for individuals. The end result (integration into the fabric of life, etc., and readiness to face the future) can be reached in many ways. In general systems context, the equifinality principle runs counter to the idea of simple "cause-effect" relationships because it suggests multiple causation. The clinical task in crisis intervention, then, is to identify variables conducive to positive crisis resolution—variables occurring naturally in the environment (families, churches, schools, and the like), and variables which will need to be formally introduced during the crisis itself, perhaps by a trained counselor or therapist.

IN SUMMARY

We began this chapter with a summary of crisis theory, offering some detail on its twelve basic principles. We pointed out, however, that in order for this intrapsychic theory to be useful, we will need to cast it in a general theoretical framework which gives full consideration to the *context* of life crises.

Crisis theory in a general systems framework can be summarized as follows:

> Prior to a crisis event, the individual (person system) is in a stable, steady state, functioning adequately as a member of a family/social group, which is in turn nested within a community setting, which is a part of the broader social culture. The precipitating event (loss of a loved one, unemployment) impinges on the person from either the family, community, or cultural system. The event interacts with the individual's personality, a process measured in terms of five BASIC subsystems (behavioral, affective, somatic, interpersonal, and cognitive). The individual's reaction in turn affects the other suprasystems (family, community, etc.). In the most immediate sense, spouse, children, and close friends become intimately involved in the crisis. Just as likely, however, neighbors, work associates, and the entire community are affected. In the first few days following the onset of crisis, opportunities for psychological first aid (first-order crisis intervention) from family and community exist. In subsequent weeks, steps will be taken to re-establish coping and to ultimately resolve the crisis. Whether through formal crisis therapy (offered by trained workers through various community systems) or through natural helping resources (family, neighbors, media), equilibrium will eventually occur, whether for good or ill. The resolution of all individual crises will have a considerable effect on the over-all health of neighborhoods, communities, and society at large.

Attention to context during the intervention process is important because all crises involve some sort of interaction between a human being and other people, even when this interaction is "symbolic," as in the case of grief for a lost partner, or loneliness (Baldwin 1979). General systems theory allows us to think of both the person in crisis, and also the family, community, and cultural systems as a backdrop for each particular situation. This basic premise will be elaborated in subsequent chapters. No crisis can be fully understood without understanding the person's family/social milieu, community resources (including both attitudes and services), and cultural backdrop. Our operating premise will be that insofar as any one of these various systems is ignored, the intervention process will bog down; similarly, insofar as attention is given to the impact of each of these various systems on the individual, and the resources from each of these systems are brought to bear on the individual's crisis, positive crisis resolution will be enhanced.

RESEARCH ISSUES The bulk of this chapter has been geared toward explicating crisis theory, stating its key assumptions, and organizing these in a general systems theoretical framework. We have sought to provide working definitions and a general framework within which to discuss situational and developmental crises, and the intervention process itself. As the title of this text suggests, however, there are also important research questions to be addressed. Presently crisis theory is, at best, a well recognized set of assumptions about particular states which occur under particular circumstances. The unfortunate reality is that little has been done to tighten crisis theory as a "theory" so that its usefulness in explanation and prediction (the main criterion of any good theory) is increased. The goal in this section is to highlight major research issues and to point directions for future investigations.

As suggested earlier, crisis theory makes powerful claims about human growth and development, not the least of which is the idea that it is only during the crisis state that many people are vulnerable enough, suggestible enough, open enough, to consider new avenues of development. The idea that "things often have to get worse before they get better" is well accepted by practitioners, though it has not yet been subjected to rigorous research. For what kinds of people is this supposition most true? What variables are conducive to reorganization toward growth as opposed to those conducive to reorganization toward debilitation?

One of the most impressive bodies of research on crisis theory has been that developed by Viney (1976) and her colleagues at the Macquarie University in North South Wales. Going beyond the study of psychologically extreme cases, these researchers have investigated crises in active, healthy, "normal," individuals such as preschool children (Viney and Clarke 1974, 1976), university students (Viney 1973), housewives (Bazeley and Viney 1974), and child-bearing women (Westbrook 1975) successfully coping with crisis. Most encouraging from a research point of view has been these investigators' ability to test the limits of the crisis concept in laboratory analogs. For example, Viney and Clarke (1974) applied the extinction period of an instrumental learning paradigm to kindergarten children (working on a free-choice discrimination task) to test the effects of crisis conditions on subsequent behavior. They found that crises involving loss of reward from social as opposed to nonsocial sources led to greater disorganization and more fixed, rigid responses from children. Crises resulting in nonsocial responses led to trying new responses and less frustration in boys and less giving up in girls; girls whose previous experience included more reliable social sources of supplies withdrew less after a crisis than those with less reliable sources.

Methodologically, studies such as these offer encouragement to those wishing to test crisis theory hypotheses in laboratory settings. In addition, several specific issues deserve the attention of researchers.

(a) Research is needed to specify the relative importance of biological, psychological, and social/environmental variables in determining both the intensity of crisis, and its ultimate resolution. Thomas, Chess, and Birch (1969) document inborn temperamental differences that are stable throughout life, making some individuals slow to adapt to change and/or upset by abrupt changes. Lieberman (1974) suggests that poor cognitive functioning may limit a person's ability to assess strengths and opportunities for adaptation. This is congruent with R. Lazarus's (1980) writings on a cognitive understanding of the coping process. Further, Lieberman suggests that the intensity of the stress associated with crisis is dependent upon the amount of change causing the crisis. It would seem that this latter variable—amount of change—could be quantified at biological, psychological, and social levels.

In a similar vein, Wandersman, Wandersman, and Kahn (1980), investigated different kinds of social support for new parents (birth of a first child), concluding that social support comes in many different forms (instrumental, promotional, and the like) with differing effects. Further, they found that the social support variables accounted for only a small percentage of the variance in post-partum adjustment five or six months later. Future research needs to examine both the complexity of the construct, and its relative importance alongside person variables (parents' resources and coping skills, and their previous adaptations).

(b) The Holmes and Rahe (1967) approach to quantifying life events and their crisis potential could be broadened by investigating the events in the context of developmental transitions/stages (Danish and D'Augelli 1980, and Nowak 1978).

(c) Within the general systems model just presented, the role of cognitive factors in crisis needs to be studied. Taplin (1971) has opened the door in crisis work for looking at cognition and perception as the mechanisms involved in the onset of crisis, though this perspective has generated little research. Also, the crisis literature is silent regarding the potential tie between cognitive modification (Beck 1976; Mahoney 1974; Meichenbaum 1977) and crisis resolution. If, as Taplin suggests, the crisis states occur when expectancies about life are violated or when cognitive maps are found inadequate, then it would seem the intervention process could make use of cognitive modification techniques. (This will be discussed more fully in the intervention section of this book, Part II.)

A number of theorists have suggested that crises progress through various stages (Caplan 1964; Horowitz 1976; Levine 1976; Tyhurst 1958). The crisis experience can be viewed as progressing through three such stages: dis-

organization at onset, working through, and integration. The variables involved in each of these stages need to be specified. For example, at what point might denial (Horowitz 1976) turn toward openness or suggestibility, or reduced defensiveness (Halpern 1973)? Clearly the intervention and helping process must vary according to the state of the crisis along these dimensions. Also, it will be important to collect data on how various people work through crises without outside help. What are the resources in the natural environment which facilitate the working-through process? Crisis therapy may profit by an examination of the natural processes which are found to be facilitative.

Crisis resolution was defined in this chapter as a process aimed at integrating the crisis experience into the fabric of life so that the person emerges open or ready to face the future. This is actually a summary of numerous clinical findings. These constructs need to be operationalized and explored further. For example, what are the behavioral, affective, somatic, interpersonal, and cognitive components of readiness to go on living, or face the future, after a crisis?

The general systems framework presented in this chapter is intended to allow for a study of the relationship between variables during crisis episodes. Belsky (1980) makes the same point in arguing for a systems framework in studying child abuse.

> In addition to providing a scheme for systematically ordering the large body of data on child abuse, this ecological framework can serve as a guide for future empirical inquiry. Specifically, by drawing attention to the nested relationships that exist between causative agents, this framework should stimulate investigators to move beyond the mere identification of individual variables that are correlated with child abuse and neglect to the study of relationships between variables. Although the strategy of identifying individual correlates has proven fruitful in the past . . . , it is clear that the

predictive value of such research is exceedingly limited (p. 321).

The same applies to the study of life crises. The relationships between variables must be investigated so that we can make intelligent, predictive statements about onset, intensity, and resolution.

chapter three

Developmental Life Crises

Perhaps the most striking feature of crisis theory is the idea that crisis can lead to personal growth. This perspective lifts crisis from a tone of despair, negativism, danger, and disorganization (common feelings during crises) to a more positive plane: Suffering can also stimulate personal growth and maturation.

The common theme in developmental crises is that their precipitating events are imbedded in maturational processes. This approach looks beyond the particular crisis event and focuses on the individual in light of his/her developmental history. The question asked is: could this time of upset, danger, and disorganization represent this person's attempt to grapple with a major transition from one life stage to another?

Erikson (1963) first formalized the idea that personality *continues* to develop through the life span. Whereas Freud suggested that personality was largely structured during the early years of childhood, Erikson viewed personality as developing throughout the entire life cycle, indeed, changing radically as a function of how an individual deals with each stage of development. He suggested tracking psychosocial development through eight stages, each of which possesses crisis potential. Depending upon how specific developmental issues are resolved at each level, a person's growth might be arrested at one stage, or might progress to the next higher level.

A review of developmental psychology research indicates that emphasis was originally placed on the extreme ends of the developmental continuum—childhood and old age—and only more recently on adulthood and middle age (Neugarten 1979). This coincides with Erikson's (1978) suggestion that we may now be entering the century of the adult. Even a cursory examination of popular books, undergraduate texts, and research titles suggests that the study of adulthood is taking preeminence in the literature.

Adults searching for clues to marital disruption, radical changes in career, values, and goals turned in the seventies to such books as *Passages* (Sheehy 1976), *Transformations* (Gould 1978), and *Male Mid-Life Crisis* (Mayer 1978). Research studies such as Levinson's *Seasons of a Man's Life* (1978), and Vaillant's *Adaptation to Life* (1977), as well as Lowenthal, Thurnher, and Chiriboga's *The Four Stages of Life* (1975) have provided inspiration for new theorizing and new data collection among developmental scholars.

How do these trends relate to crisis intervention? Unfortunately, research studies in these two fields—crisis intervention and developmental psychology—have not yet been meaningfully integrated. A few books (such as Stevenson 1977) have summarized developmental trends with a view to their practical application, although developmental issues have not yet been tied directly to the intervention process.

In this chapter, our aim is to take steps toward bridging the gap by first discussing assumptions of the developmental approach to life crises, and then reviewing developmental issues at various stages through the life cycle. Intervention implications will be summarized from a developmental perspective, and directions for future research will be suggested. Research in this area is still a long way from identifying, with any degree of certainty, principles upon which the practitioner can depend. Speaking about her colleagues in developmental psychology, Neugarten (1979) said, ". . . . we are not likely soon to have a Dr. Spock of adulthood, for the course of adult change is too complex and the individual differences are too great for any how-to-do-it book" (p. 888). Our goal then will be to summarize assumptions and, in particular, preoccupations through the various stages of development, with a view to highlighting implications of available data for the intervention process.

DEVELOPMENTAL ASSUMPTIONS

The major assumptions behind a developmental approach to life crises include the following:

1. Life, from birth until death, is characterized by continuous growth and change. The change which characterizes the crisis state is unique because it is so extreme, not because of the change per se.

2. Development can be considered as a series of transitions (some say stages) each characterized by certain tasks (Erikson 1963, Havighurst 1952) or preoccupations (Neugarten 1979; Rapoport and Rapoport 1980). Stage theorists contend that the individual must negotiate the tasks of one stage in order to function fully at the next. For example, an adolescent would need to develop a sense of identity to discover who he/she really

is before being able to engage meaningfully in the intimate relationships of young adulthood.

3. Developmental transitions of adulthood are qualitatively different from transitions of childhood and adolescence. While a forty-year-old executive mid-life crisis may look like a second childhood, or take on features of an adolescent identity crisis, it is an over simplification to view it solely in terms of constructs from these earlier stages since the adult crisis is uniquely identified by the adult stage preoccupations or tasks.

4. Although each stage is unique, themes from younger days are usually revisited or reworked throughout the life cycle (Neugarten 1979).

> . . . they do not in truth emerge at only given moments in life, each to be resolved and then put behind as if they were beads on a chain. Identity is made and remade; issues of intimacy and freedom and commitment to significant others, the pressures of time, the reformulation of life goals, stock-taking and reconciliation and acceptance of one's successes and failures—all of these preoccupy the young as well as the old. It is a truism, even though it sometimes goes unmentioned, that the psychological preoccupations of adults are recurrent. They appear and reappear in new forms over long periods of time (p. 891).

Rapoport and Rapoport (1980), for example, discuss development through the life span as being concerned with work, family, and play (a triple helix). All of life's stages are viewed as focusing on some interaction of these three aspects of life. Career, for example, may be something to find at the age of eighteen and something to change at the age of forty-five, though career as a life theme remains constant.

5. Events which precipitate developmental crises must be understood in the context of an individual's personal history. A fight between a seventeen-year-old boy and his father

about friends, curfew, and use of alcohol should be considered in the context of identity formation in later adolescence. Similarly, a forty-year-old executive's dissatisfaction with his job and infatuation with his secretary may be events imbedded in a transition of mid-life.

6. A crisis is an extreme version of a transition. Transitions are turning points or boundary regions between two periods of greater stability (Levinson et al. 1976). These developmental transitions may go smoothly, or may involve considerable turmoil. Developmental crises are disruptions that *precede* growth and, in fact, make growth possible (Danish and D'Augelli 1980; Riegel 1975).

TRANSITION OR CRISIS　There are a number of hypotheses to suggest when a transition might become a crisis. These include:

(a) Crisis can occur when the accomplishment of tasks associated with a particular developmental stage is disrupted or made difficult. Danish and D'Augelli (1980) suggest that transition from one developmental stage to another can be thwarted by a lack of skill, knowledge, or an inability to take risks.

As we shall see in Chapter 8 (Crisis Therapy), deficits in the first two areas—information, skills—are usually easier for the clinician to deal with than when the difficulty involves the more complex matter of risk-taking, which directly engages four of the personality subsystems: behavioral, affective, cognitive, and interpersonal. In addition to these person variables, physical resources (for example, money), and social resources (friends, outside support) can be critical factors determining whether or not, for example, an eighteen-year-old girl moving from small town to the big city will negotiate the transition to adulthood smoothly or with considerable stress. The suggestion is that a deficit in any

of these five variables—skills, knowledge, willingness to risk, physical resources, social supports—can keep a person from achieving developmental tasks or turn a predictable transition into a crisis. Similarly, the birth of a first child requires certain minimum skills, knowledge, etc. for parents as they rearrange their life styles. An absence of skills, knowledge, social supports, money, or willingness to risk new ways of behaving, (Wandersman et al. 1980) can lead to a developmental crisis of parenthood.[1]

(b) Another way of understanding how a transition might become a crisis is to think in terms of demand overload. Brim (1977) states:

> A "male mid-life crisis" will occur for some men if there are multiple, simultaneous demands for personality change; if, for instance, during the same month or year the man throws off his last illusions about great success; accepts his children for what they are; buries his father and his mother and yields to the truth of his mortality; recognizes that his sexual vigor and, indeed, interest, are declining, and even finds relief in the fact (p. 16).

This concept fits with Holmes and Rahe's (1967) definition of life crisis as the accumulation of life events (350 or more Life Change Units in a year). Here, however, each of the events falls into the category of expected pains addressed at mid-life.

(c) A transition could become a crisis if an individual does not accept or is not prepared for the marker events (Danish & D'Augelli

---

[1] The skill dimension from Danish and D'Augelli is not unlike an operational definition of the Peter Principle (Peter and Hull 1969) wherein an individual is viewed as being promoted in an organization until he/she reaches his/her own level of incompetence. Incompetence here refers to the fact that the skills important for success at a lower level in the organization, indeed those which led to promotion in the first place, are *not* functional at the next higher level. Negotiating the move upward in an organization, that is, avoiding living out the Peter Principle, may mean casting off previous ways of working and developing new skills.

1980). Neugarten (1976) discusses both menopause and widowhood as life events for which the woman's expectations are critical in predicting outcome. She suggests that most women go through a subliminal process anticipating widowhood, realizing from statistical chances that they will probably outlive their husbands. Similarly, women in their forties and fifties expect menopause and therefore see it as a natural event. While they may have heard stories which generate some anxiety, they also know that all women survive it. Most women take menopause in stride regarding it merely as "a temporary pause that depresses" (page 19). Many welcome it as a relief from menstruation and fear of unwanted pregnancies. Conversely, individuals who have not been so prepared for developmental marker events are in greater danger of experiencing them as crises. A middle-age man unprepared for the fact that his wife might want to develop a business career outside the home as the children grow older might be jolted by this event, partly because he didn't expect it, and partly because he is unprepared for a new role himself (broader household responsibilities).

(d) Finally, an individual might experience one of life's developmental transitions as a crisis if that individual perceives him/herself as being out of phase with society's expectations for a particular age group. Neugarten (1979) believes that all of us carry around "mental clocks" telling us whether we are on or off time with our peers.

> People talk easily about these clocks. They readily tell an interviewer what they regard as the best age to marry, to have a child, to become a grandmother, when a man should be settled in his career, when he should have reached the top, when he should retire, and even what personality characteristics ought to be salient in successive age periods (for instance, it is appropriate to be impulsive in adolescence, but not in middle age). People will also readily report whether they themselves are on time, and if not, why not (p. 888).

This perspective suggests that leaving home, choosing a partner, bearing children, and the like are indeed normal turning points in life, each calling for changes in self-concept and identity, each having crisis potential if their "timing" is off.

Neugarten continues:

> For instance, for the majority of middle-aged women the departure of children is not a crisis. It is, instead, when children do *not* leave home on time that a crisis is created for both parent and child. For an increasingly large proportion of men retirement is a normal, expectable event. Even death is a normal and expectable event for the old. Death is tragic only when it occurs at too young an age. Even the death of one's spouse, if it occurs on time, does not create a psychiatric crisis for most men or women (p. 889).

To fully appreciate the role of expectations and time for any particular individual, it is important to understand further that timing has social, biological, and psychological aspects, and that each aspect has undergone significant change in progressive generations. Puberty, for example, comes earlier than before for both sexes, and the life expectancy of all people has progressed from the sixties and seventies to a figure nearing the eighties. Similarly, social timing has also undergone change. For example, men enter the labor market (due to the lengthening in the education process) at a later age than two or three decades ago. Changes have also occurred in marriage (earlier) and parenthood (earlier, except for women who have postponed family for career, and fewer children). Since the mean age for widowhood has increased, couples now experience fifteen years or so together after the children leave the household in a period which has been referred to as the "empty nest."

An emphasis on changing biological, psychological and social time tables is congruent with the general systems framework for crisis theory presented in Chapter 2. It is not enough to examine a particular event, nor even a particular individual's developmental stage, without understanding also the individual's perception of the "fit" between him/herself and what society expects.

PREOCCUPATIONS THROUGH THE LIFE SPAN

Table 3.1 offers an overview of developmental stages and the transition issues, tasks, and possible crisis events associated with each. The words *task/preoccupations* are meant to reflect an argument in the developmental literature as to the exact nature and importance of these stages. Some contend that specific boundaries to stages (by age) are important (Levinson et al. 1976), while most suggest that for the reasons cited earlier in this chapter (recurrence of themes through life span), it is a distortion to talk too narrowly of rigid boundaries (Neugarten 1979; Brim 1977). Writers seem more content to associate tasks with childhood than with adulthood, preferring to discuss themes of the latter as preoccupations. Our main goal is to have these themes as a backdrop for considering any individual life crisis. At no point will we conceptually "force" an individual into a stage, or impose a rigid developmental framework on an individual's experience. Rather, we will use this information as a guide for asking questions and testing hypotheses on the way toward specifying an intervention strategy. Just as the age boundaries are somewhat arbitrary (or at least subject to interpretation, depending upon social factors), there may be variations from person to person on the importance of the specific preoccupations associated with each stage.

Perhaps the most important aspect of Table 3.1 for practitioners is the link between precipitating events and developmental tasks/ preoccupations. Here the focus is on how the particular event might either grow from a developmental struggle, or touch off earlier unresolved developmental issues. The practi-

tioner's question in this framework needs continually to be: Might this seemingly insignificant event—marital argument, fight with parent, trouble at school or at the office—be imbedded in this person's attempt to negotiate the transition from one developmental stage to another?

As Table 3.1 indicates, the possible crisis events of *childhood* weigh heavily in the areas of socialization, relationship with parents, friendships, and success/failure in school. Relative success in each of these areas is viewed as necessary for progressing successfully to the next higher level of development. Parents and teachers (see Chapter 16) play a particularly important role in how children cope with disruptions in the learning process during the early years of life. For example, will a nine-year-old girl having difficulty mastering the "three Rs" come to view herself as "stupid," "behind," "different," or as an acceptable human being with both strengths and weaknesses (the latter capable of some change with work and outside help)?

Adolescence provides the occasion for negotiation of identity themes which have career, value, and intimacy components. As any high school teacher or parent of a teenager can attest, the turmoil of adolescence involves a struggle to assert oneself in such a way that an identity is established. Painful though it may seem, the chief values of family and other social institutions must often be rejected so that they may be reclaimed later in life as one's own.

Young adulthood is a stage involving preoccupations with intimacy, parenthood, and getting started in an occupation or career. Tasks can be thought of as carrying a new identity from adolescence into adult relationships with partner, children, friends, and co-workers. Young adulthood has been referred to as a time of settling down and establishing roots, and at the same time moving forward, particularly in career. These developmental preoccupations can, in combination with critical life events, provide the occasion for

TABLE 3.1 DEVELOPMENT THROUGH THE LIFE SPAN: AN OVERVIEW[a]

Stage	Transition Theme	Tasks/Preoccupations	Possible Crisis Events[b]
Infancy (0-1)	Trust versus mistrust	Feeding	Disruption in feeding
		Developing sensory discrimination and motor skills	Physical illness, injury
		Gaining emotional stability	Rejection by primary caretaker
Toddlerhood (1-2)	Autonomy versus shame and doubt	Walking, talking	Physical injury
		Developing sense of independence	Conflict with primary caretaker over increased assertiveness, toilet training, etc.
		Adjusting to socialization demands	
Early childhood (2-6)	Initiative versus guilt	Learning skills and muscle control	Physical injury
		Developing body concepts, and learning about sex differences	Conflict with teachers/parents re: early sex play
		Learning cultural values, and sense of "right and wrong"	Conflict with teachers, peers
		Developing concepts of social and physical reality	Entering school (preschool or kindergarten)
		Developing interpersonal skills (family, peers)	Loss of friends through moving/migration
Middle childhood (6-12)	Industry versus inferiority	Mastering school subjects (three Rs, science, humanities)	Learning difficulties in school
		Developing learning and problem solving skills	Peer conflicts
		Relating to peers, teachers, and unfamilar adults	Conflict with teachers

[a]Stages, themes, and tasks represent summaries from J. E. Brophy, *Child development and socialization*. Chicago: Science Research Associates, 1977; C. E. Kennedy, *Human development: The adult years and aging*. New York: Macmillan, 1978; R. J. Havighurst, *Developmental tasks and education*. New York: Longmans, Green & Company, 1952; J.S. Stevenson, *Issues and crises during middlescence*. New York: Appleton-Century-Crofts, 1977; E. H. Erikson, *Childhood and society*. New York: W. W. Norton, 1963; J. Conger, *Adolescense: Generation under pressure*. New York: Harper & Row, 1979; M. Fiske, *Middle age: The*

TABLE 3.1 (Continued)

Stage	Transition Theme	Tasks/Preoccupations	Possible Crisis Events[b]
		Developing sense of in-dependence within family context	Conflict with parents
		Developing self control and frustration tolerance	Change in schools
Adolescence (12-18)	Identity versus role confusion	Adjusting to bodily changes and new emotions	Menstruation
			Sexual intercourse
			Unwanted pregnancy
		Achieving gradual inde-pendence from parents/caretakers	Graduation from high school
			Going to college
		Questioning values/devel-oping life philosophy	Conflict with parents over personal habits and life style
		Exploring intimate personal relationships	Breakup with girlfriend/boyfriend; broken engagement
		Exploring vocational options	Career indecision
			Difficulty on first job
			Success/failure in: academics, athletics
Young adulthood (18-34)	Intimacy versus isolation	Selecting and learning to live with a mate/partner	Rejection by potential part-ner; extramarital affairs; separation, divorce
		Starting a family (or, not . . .)	Unwanted pregnancy; in-ability to bear children; birth of a child
		Developing parenting skills	Discipline problems with children; illness of son

prime of life? New York: Harper & Row, 1979; R. Kastenbaum, *Growing old: Years of fulfillment.* New York: Harper & Row, 1979.

[b]Whether or not these events present "crises" or not depends upon a number of variables, including timing of the event, as well as financial, personal, and social resources.

TABLE 3.1   (Continued)

Stage	Transition Theme	Tasks/Preoccupations	Possible Crisis Events[b]
			or daughter; inability to manage the various demands of parental role
		Deciding about military service	Entering military service; being drafted; avoiding service
		Getting started in an occupation	Academic difficulties; failure to graduate from high school/college; inability to find satisfactory career; poor performance in chosen career
		Overall development of personal life style in social context	Purchase of home; financial difficulties; conflict between career and family goals; age 30 transition
Middle adulthood (35–50)	Generativity versus stagnation	Adjusting to physiological changes of middle age	Awareness of physical decline
			Chronic illness (self or spouse)
			Climateric
		Adjusting to changes in children (e.g., to young adults)	Rejection by rebellious adolescent children
			Divorce of child
		Dealing with new responsibilities regarding aging parents	Decision about care of aging parents
			Death or prolonged illness of parents
		Increasing productivity and developing socioeconomic consolidation	Setback in career; conflict at work
			Financial concerns
			Moving associated with career advancement

TABLE 3.1 (Continued)

Stage	Transition Theme	Tasks/Preoccupations	Possible Crisis Events[b]
			Unemployment
		Re-examination of earlier life choices (mate, career, children) and reworking of earlier themes (identity, intimacy)	Awareness of discrepancy between life goals and achievements
			Regret over earlier decisions to not marry, not to have children, or vice versa
			Dissatisfaction with goals achieved
		Shift in life structure in light of changes in family and work responsibilities	Promotion
			Break/conflict with mentor
			Marital problems/extra-marital affairs
			Return to work (female), post childrearing
			Death of friend(s)
Maturity (50–65)	Generativity versus stagnation	Adjusting to physiological aging (e.g., changes in health, decreased strength)	Health problems
		Preparing for retirement	Decisions re: retirement (leisure time, new career)
			Change in physical living arrangements (farmhouse to city apartment)
		Developing mutually rewarding relationships with grown children	Conflict with grown children
		Re-evaluating, consolidating relationship with spouse/ significant other, or adjusting to his/her loss (death, divorce)	"Empty nest" (last child leaves home)
			Death of spouse, divorce

TABLE 3.1 (Continued)

Stage	Transition Theme	Tasks/Preoccupations	Possible Crisis Events[b]
		Assisting aging parents	Conflict with parents
		Making productive use of increased leisure time	Resistance to retirement (separation or letting go of work roles/responsibilities)
Old age (65–death)	Ego integrity versus despair	Pursuing second/third career, and/or leisure interest	Financial difficulties
		Sharing wisdom from life's experience with others	Interpersonal conflict with children
			Interpersonal conflict with peers (e.g., in new living quarters)
			Neglect by adult children
		Evaluating past and achieving sense of satisfaction with one's life	Death of friends
			Awareness of loneliness
		Enjoying reasonable amount of physical and emotional comfort	Illness or disability
		Maintaining sufficient mobility for variety in environment	Difficulty in adjustment to retirement

life crises. Possible crises would include, for example, a young woman's conflict about balancing the priorities between career and family. Her choices are not made in isolation, but depend very much on attitudes and behavior of spouse, family, and friends. Similarly, decisions on whether or not to bear children, and if so, how many and when, are addressed by young couples during young adulthood.

Middle adulthood is a time to both rework previous developmental themes, and at the same time confront entirely new issues and challenges. After a number of years devoted to career and raising children, there is a time of taking stock of what has been accomplished in relationships with spouse, children, and the world of work. Books of the seventies (*Passages, Transformations, Male Mid-Life Crisis,* and the like) let everyone know that marital disruption, dissatisfaction with career, and new beginnings might all be expected at mid-life.

It is particularly interesting to note cross cultural studies (Gutmann 1975) which indicate a shift in the priorities of men and women at mid-life. Many men, who have been active and aggressive in pursuing career and economic gain, shift toward a more mellow, affiliative, nurturing stance in their forties and fifties. Many women, on the other hand, take a more active and assertive role as children require less attention. With an increase in the number of women working outside the home, and with an increase in greater sharing of parenting responsibilities, this pattern might become less prominent. The trend does serve, however, to underline how commitments made in young adulthood can satisfy one part of an individual's total self, leaving other needs unmet (Levinson et al. 1976). Appropriate assessment of mid-life crisis, then, involves understanding these commitments and distributions of energy in relation to an individual's total personality.

The new themes of mid-life include parent caring (Lieberman 1974), adjustments to life with adolescent or young adult children (some of whom might be experiencing considerable turmoil themselves, e.g., divorce), and moving toward a changed time perspective (thinking of time left to live instead of time since birth). What arrangements will be made for aging parents? A nursing home, or moving in with children? What impact will this have on existing patterns of family life? Depending on the resources available, preparation, and other variables listed earlier, these issues have the potential for precipitating a crisis.

Later life can be divided into *maturity*—fifties and early sixties until retirement, and *old age*—retirement until death (Kennedy 1978). The increase in life expectancy, and with it, later retirement have lengthened late adulthood. The preoccupations of maturity involve coping with the new freedoms for parents when the children are grown, adjusting to death of a spouse, preparation for retirement (which might include a second or third career), and changes in physical living conditions (moving from a house into an apartment, for example). Erikson's notion of "generativ-

ity" that is characteristic of this stage suggests a preoccupation not only with caring for and guiding one's own offspring but also with the next generation more broadly defined. Neugarten describes the fifties and sixties as a time of increased interiority, which means a shift from an outer orientation to an inner one, away from boldness and risk taking, toward an accommodation of the self to the constraints of the outside world (Neugarten et al. 1964; Neugarten 1979). It is a time for both consolidation of experience and resources, and a reorientation of one's life toward later years.

Erikson's view of old age as a balance between ego integrity and despair is accompanied by several preoccupations. Neugarten (1979) talks about the "triumphs of survivorships," or a recognition that one has savored a wide range of life experiences, knows about life, and has endured both physical and psychological pain in a way that no young person can quite know.

> In old age some old and some new issues arise. Some are related to renunciation; adapting to losses of work, friends, and spouse; the yielding of a position of authority and the questioning of one's former competences; the reconciliations with significant others and with one's achievements and failures; the resolution of grief over the death of others and of the approaching death of self; the maintenance of a sense of integrity in terms of what one has been, rather than what one is; and the concern over legacy and how to leave traces of oneself (p. 890).

This stage is characterized also by attitudes which are quite adaptive in old age, though would be less so in earlier life. Neugarten and her colleagues have studied elderly persons and found a certain adaptive paranoia in which combativeness is a survival asset (Neugarten 1979), suggesting that coping in later life may be a very different process than in earlier years (Lieberman 1978).

MALE MID-LIFE CRISIS: REALIGNING THE LIFE STRUCTURE
One of the more provocative studies of adult development is that by Levinson and his associates (1976) conducted at Yale University in the early seventies. In an attempt to understand an area that had been left relatively untouched by researchers, the Yale team interviewed forty adult males (age 35-40) including ten from each of four occupational groups (business executives, blue and white collar industry workers, academic biologists, and novelists). With an attempt to better understand what they conceptualized as "mid-life transition," Levinson and his associates interviewed subjects for a number of hours and organized the data into an adult developmental framework. While the framework from this study is based on a very limited sample (see research section below), the concepts it generated are powerful and have far-reaching implications for crisis intervention, thus meriting our detailed attention in this chapter. From this study, Levinson hypothesized that a crisis at mid-life came about when his subjects questioned or challenged their life structure. To further understand this idea, and its intervention implications, let us briefly summarize the transition within which it is imbedded.

Levinson's conceptual framework is congruent with the general systems framework for life crises outlined earlier. The life stages are not simply an unfolding of biological process, nor simply a sequence of psychological transitions, for they are also determined by familial, educational, and cultural systems. Levinson talks about "an embracing sociopsychological conception of male adult development periods, within which a variety of biological, psychodynamic, cultural, social-structural, and other timetables operate in only partial synchronization" (p. 21). This is congruent with Neugarten's (1979) idea in which the timing of particular life events is critical in determining whether an individual will experience a crisis or not.

Levinson hypothesized four stages of development on the way toward the mid-life transition. Leaving of the family (LF) is a stage starting around sixteen/eighteen and ending at twenty/twenty-four, encompassing a transition between adolescent life (centered with the family) and entering into the adult world. Associated with Erikson's conflict of identity versus role diffusion, this transition has its external aspects such as moving out of the family home, becoming less financially dependent upon family, and entering new roles and living relationships. It also has internal aspects since there is an increase in differentiation between parent and self, and more psychological distance from the family. LF ordinarily begins around the end of high school. Those who enter college or military life enter a new institutional situation which, in a sense, is an intermediary between family life and adult life. Those who move directly from high school to the labor force, however, have no such institutional matrix to shape the transition. Many young men in this situation continue to live at home for a time in a semi-border status in which they live their own lives yet remain subject to some parental authority.

The LF period ends when there is a shift in the balance from relative connectedness to the family to relative separation from the family, at which time the young man has begun to make a place for himself in the adult world.

The period in the early twenties, extending roughly through the age of twenty-seven to twenty-nine, Levinson et al. (1976) label "Getting Into the Adult World" (GIAW). Associated with Erikson's ego state of intimacy versus aloneness, the overall task is to arrive at an initial definition of oneself as an adult, and to fashion an initial life structure that will provide a link between the self and the broader adult world. As Levinson et al. see it, the life structure has external aspects which refer to patterns of roles, memberships, interests, style of living, goals, and the like, in which an individual relates to and takes a role in society. There are, however, internal aspects as well that refer to the personal meanings that each of these external aspects has for the individual. The internal side of the life structure refers to values, fantasies, and the like. The life structure in this sense provides a *boundary* between the self/individual and the society. It is a means by which to order priorities and to make various life decisions.

Central to the GIAW period is the concept of the dream. Men in Levinson's sample entered adulthood with a dream or vision of what their future would be. Often described in an occupational context—becoming a great novelist, winning the Nobel Prize, making some contribution to human welfare—the dream came to be central in understanding the various transitions in adult life, and in particular, transitions which became crises. Crises at age thirty, forty, or later often turned out to be transitions where men found the dream to be unrealistic, unfulfilled, or somehow damaged by the realities of life events.

Centered around the concepts of life structure and dream, some men in the sample chose a career and then redirected after a year or two, while others remained unsettled through their twenties, leading to a rather desperate attempt to find some direction at approximately age thirty. This age thirty transition can be accompanied by considerable turmoil and confusion, or might involve a more quiet reassessment and intensification of effort.

Settling Down (SD) ordinarily begins in the early thirties, extending to the late thirties or early forties. This period is characterized by the paradoxical combination of order, stability, security, and control, on the one hand, and a desire to "pull out all the stops" and "make it" in one's career on the other. The executive has to get into the corporate structure by age forty or has to be earning at least fifty thousand dollars by that time; the assistant professor has to get tenure by forty,

and so on. Kennedy (1978) describes the late thirties with the phrase, "let's stop dallying and get on with it," which has a sense of urgency about achieving the goals set out in the twenties, making the dream come true.

The next phase, Becoming One's Own Man (BOOM), occurs in the late thirties (typically thirty-five to thirty-nine in the Levinson sample) and represents a high point of early adulthood. It begins with a frustrating awareness that no matter what the man has accomplished to date, he is not sufficiently his own man. The writer feels dependent and constrained by his publisher/editor; the executive feels too controlled by the company; the untenured faculty member wonders when he will be free of the restraints and demands of acquiescing to the university and its desires.

Central to the concept of becoming one's own man is the idea of separation from one's *mentor*. According to Levinson, a mentor is one who is typically eight to fifteen years older, and serves as advisor, teacher, protector of the younger man. He initiates the younger man into the occupational world by showing him around, imparting wisdom, giving critical feedback, and providing a blessing for the dream. The BOOM phase is characterized by separation from the mentor, a termination which is often brought about by increased conflict between mentor and mentee, resulting many times in intense feelings of bitterness, rancor, grief, abandonment, and so on. It is a process of separation from the one who has been responsible for teaching/coaching in the early years, a separation which is necessary for the young man to feel truly "on his own." (Levinson's notion is that it is likely impossible for one to become a mentor, unless one has been a mentee.) Further, it is the mentor's qualities of caring for and helping along younger people that provides the core for, as Levinson sees it, Erikson's ego stage of generativity versus stagnation in adulthood.

During BOOM, the men in the sample showed themselves to desperately want to be affirmed by society in the roles that they valued most. They are trying to achieve that crucial goal that is a sign of progress toward the dream. It may be promotion to a certain level in the company, writing a best seller, or achieving national recognition as a scientist. "Since the course and outcome of this key event take several (perhaps three to six) years to unfold, many men at around 40 seem to be living, as one of our subjects put it, in a state of suspended animation. During the course of waiting, the next period gets under way" (p. 24).

The mid-life transition (MLT) suggests a boundary between the achievement orientation (steady state of high activity) of the thirties and a redirected life in the forties. It is at this point that the concepts of life structure, dream, and self converge to suggest how a mid-life transition might become crisis. At forty, most men have enough experience to be able to look critically at both dream and life structure. The central issue here is not whether he has succeeded or failed in achieving his goals, but in the experience of disparity between what he has gained through his dream, life structure, and behavior, on the one hand, and what he truly wants for himself, on the other. Levinson describes this disparity as being between "what I've reached at this point" and "what I really want." This in turn leads to a soul searching for "what it is that I really want."

Another way to understand this disparity is to talk about a poor fit between the life structure and the self (Levinson et al. 1976):

> A man may do extremely well in achieving his goals and yet find his success hollow or bitter-sweet. If, after failing in an important respect, he comes primarily to castigate himself for not being able to "make it," then he is having a rough time but he is not having a mid-life crisis. He just regrets failure. He is having a crisis to the extent that he questions his life structure and feels the stirrings of powerful forces within himself that lead him to modify or drastically to change the structure (p. 24).

Levinson notes other concomitants of the mid-life crisis. (a) There is a sense of bodily decline and awareness of one's own mortality at about this time. (b) There is a sense of aging, with a feeling of being old rather than young, and thinking in terms of time left to live more than time lived. (c) There is an awareness of denied aspects of self, called the "feminine aspects" by Levinson et al. During earlier years, when masculinity was predominant, and making it in the adult world the chief goal, the tender, nurturing, aspects of self had been denied.

> During the mid-life period there is often a flowering of fantasies about various kinds of women, especially the maternal (nurturing and/or destructive) figures and the younger, erotic figures. These fantasies do not represent simply a belated adolescence, a final surge of lasciviousness, or self-indulgence or dependence (though they may have these qualities in part). The changing relationships to women may also involve the beginnings of a developmental effort. The aim of this effort is to free oneself more completely from the hold of the boy-mother relationship and to utilize one's internal relationships with the erotic transformative feminine as a means of healing old psychic wounds and of learning to love formerly devalued aspects of the self. It is the changing relation to the self that is the crucial issue at mid-life (p. 25).

Crisis at this point involves awareness of a life structure which leaves parts of the self unfulfilled. As the preceding paragraph indicates, relationships at mid-life often correlate with this discovery of heretofore denied aspects of the self, e.g., the executive who falls in love with his secretary who brings out parts of him (feelings, thoughts, awarenesses) not present in the relationship with his wife. The redirection at this point involves re-examination of the life structure (its amendment, or change to better actualize the self).

The Levinson notion of mid-life crisis

(questioning of the life structure) offers a paradigm for assessment and treatment of developmental crises more broadly defined. In its internal aspect (dream, sense of self) it suggests that we examine an individual's goals, aspirations, hopes, and expectations on the way toward understanding what a particular event means to the individual in crisis (Taplin 1971). In its external aspects it allows examination of an individual's roles and responsibilities, family relationships, friendships, work choices and leisure pursuits. In Chapter 2, we stressed the importance of understanding any individual's crisis in the context of family, community, and social variables. The concept of life structure provides a useful bridge between the person (internal aspect of life structure), and the outside world (external aspect). As we shall see in our discussion of crisis therapy procedures and through case examples, the Levinson framework demands assessment of the full range of relevant variables, and suggests steps to be taken in crisis resolution: e.g., modification of imagery (new dream?), changed cognitions, new behavior (roles), and interpersonal style (relationships with spouse, friends, and the like) (Figure 3.1).

INTERVENTION IMPLICATIONS

Close attention to the developmental perspective outlined in this chapter yields a number of practical implications for the process of crisis intervention. Though the gap between research and practice is still quite large, it is nonetheless possible to offer practitioners suggestions which are faithful to existing knowledge.

First, there are assessment guidelines:

1. Consider the possibility that the precipitating event for any crisis might be imbedded in a client's attempt to grapple with developmental tasks. For example, a twenty-year-old college student who falls apart on learning that all his applications for medical school have been rejected faces more than the possible loss of an immediate goal. The disruption and upset becomes all the more potent in the context of developmental tasks of late adolescence which include finding a career direction. As a check on the seeming randomness of crisis events, they should be examined in the light of the preoccupations through the life span from Table 3.1.

2. To be more specific, since crisis can occur through some difficulty with achieving tasks of a particular stage, look for deficits which might be contributing to the difficulty: skills, knowledge, willingness to take risks, physical resources, social resources, and supports.

3. Find out how the individual perceives this particular precipitating event. Does the person feel out of phase or "off time" with societal expectations (having children, career success, and the like)? What are the person's perceptions of social and psychological clocks (Neugarten 1979)?

4. What impact will an individual's developmental struggle have on family and friends? A woman who chooses to go back to school or to go into business might precipitate adjustments for her husband and teenage children at home. Are *they* prepared for these changes?

5. How will this same mother's outward move to the world of business fit with her husband's self-image and life structure, which may also be undergoing change, though in the opposite direction?

6. What is the role of varying community expectations in the course of an individual's crisis? Becoming publicly identified as a homosexual might be a *crisis* for a twenty-year-old in a small rural community, though only a *transition* were he to live in a large urban center.

7. How does the individual's past expectations and anticipations relate to the crisis? What did a sixty-five-year-old retiree believe about retirement before it happened

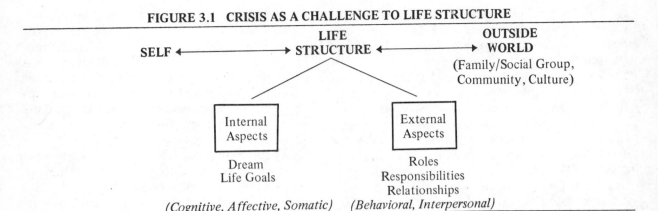

FIGURE 3.1　CRISIS AS A CHALLENGE TO LIFE STRUCTURE

to him? What, if anything, had he done by way of preparation?

Explore the possibility of life structure as a concept to help organize crisis data. It is possible, for example, to gather data under five basic personality modalities (behavioral, affective, somatic, interpersonal, and cognitive) as they relate to Levinson's concept of life structure. A young man's dream and life goals will be reflected in the cognitive modality. Similarly, relationships to mentors and other external role characteristics of life structure yield information about the behavioral and interpersonal modalities. Treatment might take the form of assisting a person in first recognizing current challenges to a life structure and in fashioning new, more appropriate "boundaries" between self and outside world. Some clients might need to be taught new life skills in the service of making a new life structure work (increased assertiveness, or management of time in a career advancement). Others will need support and coaching as they take risks in making developmental leaps. For others, the primary need will be for understanding therapeutic relationships within which they can talk out and explore intense feelings associated with the reality that a current life structure has for some time left a great deal of the self unfulfilled.

During counseling sessions, it might be fruit- *ful to state that a particular crisis could be a reflection of the client's wrestling with developmental issues.* Timing and manner of presentation are very important here. At certain times, individuals simply do not want to hear that they might be going through a phase. On the other hand, if it becomes clear that an individual is preoccupied with fears that the current disruption is a sign of his/her being "crazy" or sick, then the introduction of new labels could signal a breakthrough in an individual's cognitive mastery of the crisis. The idea that the severe upset and emotional pain is actually part of a *normal* transition from one stage to another might be very comforting. A fight with the boss, for example, might be understood as an event which psychologically has to do with separation from a mentor. What feels like the end of the world might be then understood as a new beginning by virtue of the language and conceptual framework introduced.

Other considerations for introducing developmental language in counseling/therapy sessions include the following:

(a)　The concept of phase or stage is not to be considered an "excuse" for various feelings or for certain behavior. Individuals are still responsible for what they think, feel, and do. The developmental

(b) To think of disruption and crisis in a developmental context is to emphasize the potentially constructive outcome of a crisis experience. One popular book on the topic of male mid-life crisis has the subtitle "Fresh Starts After Forty" (Mayer 1978), implying that positive new beginnings can grow from a time of turmoil and upset.

(c) Several other metaphors can be used to describe the process. It is not unlike the idea of rebirth, or of a butterfly coming out of a cocoon. Some describe it as discarding worn clothing, and buying a new suit of clothes to face new possibilities. Or, like getting rid of skis that are too small, and buying a set more appropriate for new challenges. Others find it useful to compare adult transitional crises to the disruption that small children experience during teething, or the pain that accompanies the developmental leaps in infancy (Caplan 1973).

In offering any of these analogies, the goal is simply to provide another image or cognition to explain the current situation, an appropriate alternative to medical or disease-oriented constructs which clients often use to interpret their own crises.

Caution the crisis client against making sudden long-term commitments during the turmoil of a developmental crisis. The executive who falls in love with his secretary at mid-life may, according to Levinson's data, be "in love" as much for how the relationship cultivates heretofore denied aspects of the self as for the desire for a new long-term relationship. To leave wife and family, or to initiate divorce proceedings too quickly, might well be regretted later. As new aspects of the self are discovered, he may find that the new relationship is temporary, and that after discussions/confrontations, opportunities for redirecting old relationships exist where at first they seemed not to. Binding, long-term decisions (divorce) are to be avoided until considerable exploration has taken place, and until a reasonable amount of time has passed to test feelings, tensions, and possible new directions.

Finally, all analyses and suggested connections between precipitating events and developmental preoccupations must be tentative, offered to clients for their consideration, to see how well the client believes they might fit with a particular situation. Boxing a client in, or forcing his/her experience into a framework, can only lead to alienation in the therapeutic relationship and resistance. The attitude of the helper needs to be one of hypothesis testing, or generating and volunteering possible ways of conceptualizing the situation, matching it against the data of an individual's experience, and then acting on the results.

In this same vein, there is a very real danger for the counselor who is knowledgeable of developmental stages and preoccupations to unknowingly support only traditional or normative approaches to life, leaving little room for individual differences and variations. Fiske (1979) suggests that for many people it is not the common preoccupations (Table 3.1) that lead to crisis, but rather their own private developmental markers (falling in love, or achieving a particular private goal). As just mentioned, the crisis counselor needs to help the client understand him/herself, quite often in the light of social and biological norms, though not with a view to being bound by them.

In summary, a developmental perspective on life crises brings with it a number of specific clinical implications which we have noted above. We will find that attention to these issues enriches the assessment and treatment aspects of the comprehensive crisis intervention model presented in Chapters 5-9.

RESEARCH ISSUES   Kennedy (1978) offers an overview of major trends in the study of adult development. He notes that until recently, the formulation of human development theory has been associated primarily with the study of child development. The life span perspective, grounded in the early work of Erikson and Havighurst, has only recently received the attention of researchers. The main contributions in this area have come from work by the Committee on Human Development at the University of Chicago (Neugarten 1968), Lowenthal's research at the University of California at Berkeley (Lowenthal et al. 1975), the work of Maas and Kuypers (1974) at the same institution, longitudinal studies at the Duke Medical Center (Palmore 1974), and the work by Levinson and the Yale group on adult development in men (Levinson et al. 1976). Researchers interested in critical reviews of work to date can consult these sources, plus Datan and Ginsberg (1975), and reviews by Danish and D'Augelli (1980), and Danish, Smyer, and Nowak (1980). An overview of the developmental literature as applied to crisis intervention suggests that research is especially needed in a number of areas:

1. The provocative descriptive analysis by Levinson et al. of men in the twenty-five to forty-five age bracket needs to be replicated with larger samples. The use of questionnaires as the next step beyond the interview format could reduce interviewer bias in results. The Levinson group has provided a great service by introducing constructs such as life structure, although further empirical work is clearly needed.

2. Similar descriptive analyses, with replicable methodologies, are needed for the years outside the twenty-five to forty-five age range in both men, women, and ethnic minorities. Gilligan (1979) and Bell (1977) have suggested that the developmental constructs for women and ethnic minorities are very different than for white males.

Gilligan suggests that when notions of separation (from family, first jobs, etc.) are used to define developmental processes for women, as they now are for men, women continually appear as less developed but that when constructs related to connection, concern for others, and attachment are used, the reverse is the case. Bell suggests that, given the lot of ethnic minorities in the United States, that is, subject to personal and institutional racism, the developmental processes for black and white males are very different. In a variation on Erikson's first stage of trust versus mistrust, Bell suggests that in white America it is very important for young black males to develop a healthy sense of mistrust in the outside world in order to survive. Each of these theorists builds intriging cases for differences not only in developmental processes, but also in the constructs used to describe them, for men, women, and ethnic minorities. Further research is needed to test these hypotheses and outline their practical implications.

3. Neugarten (1976) suggests that transitions from one stage to another are not necessarily crises, presenting data on menopause and the empty nest syndrome in women to support this contention. The question then arises as to whether or not we can be more specific on the ingredients of transitions which become crises and transitions which do not. What variables lead some individuals to grab hold of transition opportunities and turn them into growth experiences, and others to retreat (wait it out) with little gain, or a series of losses?

4. At this point the gap between recent developments in life span developmental psychology (reported in this chapter), and work on the intervention process during crises is quite wide. There is considerable room for studies which examine various intervention strategies applied to specific developmental groups, e.g., late adolescence, young adulthood, and so on.

chapter four

Situational Life Crises

Not all life crises are directly tied to the natural process of maturation; many are completely unpredictable. The loss of one's entire family in an automobile accident, leukemia in an eight-year-old boy, rape, being held hostage under the threat of death—events such as these are called *situational* crises. The most salient characteristic of these crises is that the precipitating event (flood, physical attack, death of a loved one) has little or no association with the individual's age or developmental stage in life. Situational crises can strike virtually anyone at any time.

The chief characteristics of situational crises are:

1. *Sudden onset.* While a struggle with developmental issues usually builds over a number of years, situational crises seem to strike from nowhere, all at once.
2. *Unexpectedness.* While individuals and families might anticipate some life transitions, and thereby prevent a crisis, few prepare for or believe that situational crises will happen to them. In the majority of cases, people tend to believe that "it will happen to someone else."
3. *Emergency quality.* Since many situational crises threaten physical as well as psychological well-being, they often begin as emergencies requiring immediate action. Crisis intervention strategies must therefore allow for priorities to be quickly assessed, followed by the implementation of appropriate action steps.
4. *Potential impact on entire communities.* Some situational crises affect large numbers of people simultaneously, requiring intervention with large groups in a relatively short period of time. A fire such as the one at the MGM hotel in Las Vegas—can leave hundreds of survivors, relatives, and friends all struggling to cope with loss in the weeks and months following.
5. *Danger and opportunity.* While danger may be the chief watchword of situational crises, we must remember that from the disorganization that ensues, some sort of reorganization must eventually begin. This reorganization has potential for moving the person and his/her family to higher as well as lower levels of functioning. At first glance, growth resulting from something as traumatic as physical assault, rape, or loss of a loved one may seem rather farfetched. However, since these events call for new methods of coping and provide the occasion for examining and reworking unresolved personal issues from the past, it is possible for an individual to emerge from the crisis better equipped than before to face the future.

Following the lead of Eric Lindemann (1944), a number of practitioners have reported on the reactions of individuals and families to situational crises. Table 4.1 summarizes representative literature, listing major categories, events associated with each, as well as key resources. We will review significant trends under these important headings, and follow with a list of intervention implications.

PHYSICAL ILLNESS AND INJURY Medical practitioners readily attest to the fact that physical and psychological well-being are intimately connected. Among the most interesting developments in this area has been research investigating the relationship between life events and

stress (Dohrenwend and Dohrenwend 1974; Holmes and Rahe 1967). Further, Cousins (1979) and others have devoted considerable energy toward sensitizing medical professionals to the effects of attitudes on the course of illness. A provocative line of cancer research and treatment developed by Simonton and his colleagues is built on the assumption that certain cancers develop because life events interact with psychological attitudes and thus interfere with the body's immune system (Simonton, Matthews-Simonton, and Creighton 1978). While this particular area of research may not be widely accepted in the medical community, few physicians would not accept

TABLE 4.1 SITUATIONAL CRISES

General Category	Situational Events	Key Resources	References
Physical illness and injury	Surgery, loss of limb, life threatening illness, physical disability.	Health care professionals, clergy, family members, employers, teachers.	Surgery (Auerbach and Kilmann 1977; Kimbrell and Slaikeu 1981); psychotherapy (Capone et al. 1979; Winder 1978; Kopel and Mock 1978; Vachon 1979); life threatening illness (Sourkes 1977; Faust and Caldwell 1979); environmental supports (Bryant 1978); disability (Lane 1976; Levinson 1976; Spink 1976; Bahr 1980).
Unexpected/ untimely death	Fatal accident, fatal disease, homicide, suicide.	Health care professionals, clergy, family members, emergency service personnel, funeral directors, police.	The grief process (Parkes 1970; Lindemann, 1944; Vachon 1979; Sheskin and Wallace 1976); support networks (Caplan 1976; Walker et al. 1977); grief therapy (Carey 1977; Weisman 1976; Lindemann 1944).
Crime: victims and offenders	Assault (mugging, rape); domestic violence (child and spouse battering/abuse); incarceration/release of offenders.	Police, health care professionals, neighbors, family members, clergy, attorneys, parole/ probation officers, social service workers.	Rape (Burgess and Holmstrum 1976; McCombie 1980; Sutherland and Scherl 1976); victims of crime (Symonds 1975); child abuse Belsky 1980; Borgman et al. 1979; Brown 1979; Helfer and Kempe 1976; Parke 1977); spouse abuse (Follingstad 1977; Gelles 1972; 1976; Straus 1973; 1976; Steinmetz and Straus 1974; Walker 1978); offenders (Kantor 1978; Speer 1974; Slaikeu 1977; Stratton 1974).

the critical role of life stress in exacerbating various medical conditions.

From the point of view of crisis theory, physical illnesses and injuries are events which challenge the individual's/family's ability to cope and adjust. As indicated in our list of crisis principles in Chapter 2, events such as the diagnosis of life-threatening illness, surgery, loss of limb, or physical disability retain the potential for being viewed as a loss, threat, or challenge since illness or injury may make life goals unreachable or may even threaten life itself. How the event is interpreted, especially in relation to self-image and future plans, and how behavioral adjustments are made, will be critical in determinating the ultimate course of crisis resolution.

Betty Rollin's (1976) personal account of living through the diagnosis of breast cancer, surgery, and recovery is an excellent chronicle of the various stages through which an individual can be expected to pass. (The book is appropriately titled *First You Cry*.) Important research has been developed concerning surgery patients, attempting to determine whether or not preparation (information about what will happen, and its impact) facilitates subsequent physical and psychological healing (Andrew 1970; Cohen and Lazarus 1973; DeLong 1971). These studies show that

TABLE 4.1 (Continued)

General Category	Situational Events	Key Resources	References
Natural and man-made disasters	Fire, flood, tornado, hurricane, nuclear accident, airline crash.	Emergency service workers, mental health outreach teams, media.	Natural disasters (Birnbaum *et al.* 1976); man-made disasters (Lifton and Olson 1976; Schaar 1980; Titchener et al. 1976; Gleser, Green, and Winget 1981); community planning (Butcher 1980; Cohen and Ahearn 1980; Harshbarger 1976); research (Dynes and Quarantelli 1976).
War and related acts	Invasion or other military action, taking of hostages prisoners of war.	Medical personnel, chaplains, families, psychotherapists.	Combat casualties (Levav et al. 1979; Figley & Sprenkle 1978; Horowitz and Solomon 1975; Ishikawa and Swain 1981; Williams 1980); concentration camps (Davidson 1980; Epstein 1980); hostages (Sank 1979).
Situational crises of modern life	Psychedelic drug experiences, economic setbacks (inflation, unemployment), migration/relocation, separation/divorce.	Friends, health care professionals, personnel workers, employers, attorneys, clergy, counselors, friends.	Psychedelic drugs (Twemlow and Bowen 1979; Brown and Stickgold 1976; Cohen 1977); unemployment (Fagin 1979); migration (Fried 1976; Levine, M. 1976; Levine, S.V. 1976); divorce (Kraus 1979; Cantor 1977; Weingarten and Kulka 1979; Wallerstein and Kelly 1980; Weiss 1975; Coogler 1978; Kessler 1978).

whether or not information will be helpful depends upon the individual's typical mode of dealing with stress. People who tend to deny or avoid stressful situations do not benefit from information about surgery and its impact. On the other hand, those with a history of attacking or facing problems head on profit from information about the impending ordeal. The research underlines the need for crisis intervention strategies which take into account these individual differences in coping styles.

Kimbrell and Slaikeu (1981) have reviewed literature on chronic illness, with a particular emphasis on interventions which reinforce ultimate wellness rather than the development of a sick role. Chronic illness syndrome is one possible result of a crisis followed by serious illness. Crisis intervention aims at assisting these patients and their families in (a) the effective use of denial (management of overwhelming anxiety early in the illness), (b) the development of effective coping strategies for the aftereffects of illness (pursuit of a life that is modified, but not dominated by illness) based on a wide range of interventions including support, cognitive restructuring, and family consultation. This approach encourages medical practitioners to steer away from exclusive attention to the illness and its negative outcomes, and more toward illness in the *context* of broader life experience (Hamera and Shontz 1978; Kling 1980; Miles 1979; Susman et al. 1980).

Work with children who have cancer provides a graphic example of this shift in emphasis. Rather than submitting to preoccupation with impending death, emphasis is placed on how the family copes during the illness, and how the child deals with the illness, so as to maximize the adaptation of the child and family (Eiser 1979). A number of articles suggest specific treatment approaches for families of cancer patients (Kopel and Mock 1978; Winder 1978). Interventions are based on the premise that a change in one part of the family system—cancer in a child or parent—must be felt in the other aspects of the family system as well. Bahnson (1975) describes the situation:

> Whenever an individual is terminally ill and slides out of close relationships with the rest of the family system, the system always attempts to reestablish balance by redistributing hostile and affective charges among the remaining family members. Both loving and angry feelings as well as controlling or dependent attitudes, often become "homeless" when a family member becomes terminally ill and is no longer available in the usual fashion to the family. The family members who gave or took affection and love from the terminal family member now must look for other family members toward whom to discharge, or from whom to receive, these affects and emotions (p. 306).

The role of the outside helper becomes one of assisting the family in dealing with these changes constructively.

Bryant (1978) emphasizes the importance of key figures in a child's external environment and how they can facilitate rehabilitation. Addressing school teachers, Bryant (1978) states:

> Remember that as a teacher you have a special place. You represent the child's normal world; you are an oasis for him. The doctors and the nurses bring shots and machines; the parents hover with tears and anguish. You, however, know that child's work-a-day world. You are a part of his business and social community. You, more than many, can maintain a semblance of his former world by your visits, news of the classroom, and occasional work assignments (p. 239-240).

The diagnosis of emotional or physical disability in a child provides the occasion for another sort of crisis in the lives of parents and siblings. Schild (1977) outlines five psychological tasks facing a family at this time: (1) reaffirming the self-worth of the child; (2) understanding the limitations of the diagnosis and accepting the concommitant loss;

(3) reordering self-concepts for both parents and child; (4) dealing with various aspects of deviance, including the social stigma associated with the diagnosis; and, (5) achieving parent/child roles and relationships which enhance continued growth and personality development.

In a review of literature on the diagnosis of emotional and/or physical disability in a child, Bahr (1980) outlines the various stages of parental reaction in the following manner: (1) impact (news of diagnosis interacts with life goals, self-image, etc.); (2) denial (an adaptative stage allowing for acceptance of reality in increments); (3) grief (expression of feelings, stark reality of contradiction between desired child and real child); (4) focusing outward (working through, developing new cognitions, and coping behavior); and, (5) closure (acceptance, looking toward the future). Crisis workers need to be aware of all these processes in order to help a family through this experience.

In summary, physical illness and injury are events which interact with an individual's coping resources, life structure, self-image, and perceived future. These events may be interpreted as being a challenge, threat, or loss. In systems language, they have an impact on all other aspects of the person systems (feelings, thoughts, etc.), and have a noticeable impact on the next higher suprasystem (family social network). Therapy aims at assisting the individual and his/her family in understanding and coping with the physical illness in the context of these other systems.

UNEXPECTED DEATH

Earlier we discussed the facing of one's own death as a developmental transition of adulthood. Theoretically, awareness of mortality actually begins in childhood with the first thought, "Since someone/something else died, I might also." Anticipation is a critical variable in dealing with impending death, either one's own or

that of a loved one. Developmentally, this becomes especially prominent in middle age with the recognition that life is now to be charted according to time left as opposed to time since birth. Numerous life experiences, such as grieving for a loved one, viewing a motion picture or play on death, or even drawing up a will, are capable of forcing individuals to confront their own mortality.

According to the definition of crisis given in this volume, not all bereavements are crises. In so far as death is anticipated (as in old age), bereavement involves experiencing and working through a loss, though not necessarily with severe disorganization and inability to cope. When comparing the different bereavements associated with suicide, natural, and accidental death, Sheskin and Wallace (1976) found that bereavement was most severe when death was unanticipated or unexpected. Suicide, for example, leaves the surviving spouse wondering what role he/she might have played in causing the death. Sheskin and Wallace (1976) also note that although widows need to share experiences and feelings with others, they fear other people's reactions upon disclosure that death was by suicide.

Easy interaction between the surviving spouse and friends cannot be taken for granted when the problem of disclosure poses such difficult questions. Thus, encouraging these clients to seek social support must be preceded by the clinicians knowledge that support will actually be available from friends and relatives.

The literature suggests that the emotional reactions accompanying unexpected death go through several phases (Lindermann 1944; Parkes 1970; Moos 1976). The first is the response of numbness, or denial of feelings and emotional detachment from the reality of death. This is viewed as a natural self-protective reaction, admitting only as much reality as one can bear. In the second phase, escape from the stark reality of the death can no longer be avoided, and feelings associated with the loss begin to surface. This is a time of preoccupation with the deceased person, and an intense yearning for the lost one. This phase is characterized by emotional upset and disorganization (depression, anger at deceased), disruption of regular routines (work, sleep), and a general inability to function. The third phase is characterized by a gradual acceptance of the reality of the loss, and the breaking of ties with the deceased. This final stage involves movement toward a functioning life without the loved one, and the development of new relationships to replace the lost individual.

The focus is on other aspects of the survivor's life, broadening the view toward the rest of life to be lived.

Weisman's (1976) description of the end of bereavement fits with our earlier definition of crisis resolution:

> Just as most wounds heal and bone fractures reunite, leaving scars but permitting restoration of function, so, too, most people get over bereavements. We may not, of course, wholly forget that a death happened, nor can the loss be totally obliterated. But the process of bereavement is complete when the afflicted survivor becomes operational once again (p. 268).

The mourning process is affected by prevailing community and cultural expectations, and must be understood in terms of many individual variations. Some people express feelings openly to family and friends; others take a more private stance, working through grief on their own. For some, the course of bereavement will include times of humor and frivolity, while for others these will be absent.

In the context of these two principles—the goal of becoming operational, and individual variations in the process—Weisman suggests that a distinction between timely and untimely death provides guidance on ways to facilitate a natural bereavement process.

Timely deaths are those in which observed survival equals expected survival. A person who lives about as long as actuarial tables suggest he/she should, or as long as a particular physical condition (cancer) allows is considered in this framework to experience a "timely" death. Weisman refers to these deaths as being appropriate, that is, life has run its expected course, leading to a sense of an appropriate time to die. Untimely deaths, on the other hand, violate individual expectations for survival. They can come about through premature death (of a child), unexpected death (a middle-aged adult killed in an automobile accident), or calamitous death (unpredicted, violent, and demeaning).

In Weisman's view, other things being equal, timely or appropriate deaths are conducive to a natural bereavement process. On the other hand, bereavement has the potential for taking on crisis proportions when the death is untimely by its prematurity, unexpectedness, or calamitousness.

The intervention process seeks first of all to facilitate a process of bereavement that is *paced* to allow for individual variation, and fits with psycho-social customs and expectations. The ultimate goal is to complete the grief process with a sense of relief, restored equilibrium, and an openness to facing the future. In a very practical sense, Weisman's framework suggests that initial intervention after an untimely death should aim at cognitively transforming the most difficult untimely deaths into more acceptable forms: "More specifically, our task is to change calamitous deaths into unexpected deaths, unexpected deaths into premature deaths, and premature deaths into appropriate deaths" (p. 270).

Weisman offers the example of "breaking the news" to a family member after the death of a loved one, which is a task faced by emergency room personnel, police officers, and clergy, to name a few.

There is no scenario enabling us to break bad news painlessly. Key survivors will be injured, but will survive. Informants should expect disbelief, shock, or bitter antagonism, because, after all, they are the bearers of sad tidings, even the psychological perpetrators of an injustice. Sometimes initial responses are rage, confusion, or aimless, wordless bustling about the room. This may be followed by accusations, self-directed or at the authority whom the family has trusted until that point. In contrast, early numbness and incredulity may give a false impression of calmness and control. Therefore, during these very early moments, following simple but mitigated communication of basic facts, the professional should be prepared to stand by, absorbing various responses, without flinching, without hastening to ameliorate through intellectual explanations, without being defensive, guilty, or hurried, without arbitrary acts of personal contrition.

. . . a woman was crudely told about her husband's death in an automobile accident. She answered the telephone. An unidentified man's voice said, "Mrs. A, this is the police. About an hour ago your husband was killed by a truck. Can you come down to headquarters and identify the body?"

Her reaction was bewildered disbelief, followed quickly by panic and then denial. "Are you serious?", she exclaimed. "Is this a crank call?" An interchange followed, and she was finally persuaded that the call was legitimate. She then waited alone for the police to arrive and take her to the mortuary.

Obviously, this was a calamitous death. But her response could have been somewhat different had the call be less impersonal, cruel, and itself calamitous. Perhaps a professional, even a policeman, might have come to her house, introduced himself, and done something more to mitigate the impact and to prepare her for the unexpected death. Conceivably, he might have said something along these lines: "I am here because there was an accident, a bad accident. Some cars collided—your husband was in his car and was injured very badly. We took him to the hospital right away—but the doctors found that he was hurt too seriously—and I must now tell you that he didn't survive."

This is, of course, a rather brutal example of "hard tell." Long after the woman recovered from her bereavement, she dwelt upon the calamitous way in which the news broke up her life. Not only did she repeat that moment over and over in her mind, but she hated the nameless voice that first called her.

Tact can be taught, not just to make bitter news sound hypocritically sweet, but to change the context in which the information is given. Note that in the version of how she might have been told, the violence of the fatal calamity was changed into an unexpected accident. Her husband's injuries in such a bad accident were depicted as *necessarily* severe. He was not left to die alone, anonymously, but was given appropriate *care*, with an implication of personal concern. Telling the woman that her husband was hurt too seriously to survive, especially after medical examination, shows that suffering was at a minimum, that experts were involved, and that the arbitrary chaos and violence had been diminished. Even the indirect statement, "He didn't survive," muffles without hiding the fact of death (p. 270-271).

This narrative presents key ideas on how an outsider might, with compassion, assist a person in facing the hard realities of the crisis of unexpected death. It should be emphasized that the goal here is not to deny what happened or merely soften the blow, but instead to arrange the realities so the individual can begin to assimilate them, that is, take the first steps toward working through the grief.

CRIME: VICTIMS AND OFFENDERS A number of events associated with criminal activity have been discussed in terms of crisis theory (Slaikeu 1977; Speer 1974; Symonds 1975). Various forms of physical assault such as rape and mugging can be understood as events whose psychological manifestations of upset and disorganization lead to full-blown life crises for the victims (McCombie 1980). A number of investigations of women who have been victims of rape suggest patterns which are congruent with Caplan's stages of life crisis (Caplan 1964). Sutherland and Scherl (1976) describe a first acute phase which is characterized by shock, dismay, and anxiety, lasting anywhere from a few days to a few weeks. The second phase, outward adjustment, includes returning to a normal routine, and temporarily suppressing feelings about the rape in an attempt to reduce anxiety and manage the intense feelings. The final stage of integration and resolution might begin with the surfacing of feelings and the need to talk. In this critical phase, it is important for the victim to work through her feelings, develop and accept a view of herself which includes the rape experience, and resolve her feelings about the assailant.

The rape victim can receive outside help in managing each phase of the crisis. In the acute phase, practical problems must be resolved such as whether to press charges, how to inform family and close friends, and how to get testing for venereal disease and pregnancy. The victim also needs information on expected emotional reactions and help in dealing with feelings of anger, humiliation, and fear. Intervention must address the question of how the woman will discuss the experience with her immediate family. Family sessions might include helping family members to understand the rape, and to see how their attitudes can play in the ultimate psychological resolution of the crisis. According to Sutherland and Scherl, the need for outside help might be denied at this point, though outside helpers need to be available nonetheless. It is in the third phase, characterized frequently by depression and a need to talk, that counseling can be helpful in dealing with obsessive memories, in working through feelings, and in developing cognitive mastery aimed at integrating the crisis event with the rest of the victim's life experience.

Those who have first contact with rape victims (police, emergency workers, hospital personnel) should be aware of expected reactions and be equipped to offer psychological first aid. Those who will be in contact over the next several weeks to months (clergy, physicians, social service workers, and the like) also need to know what to expect during the course of the crisis, and what sort of outside help would be most beneficial. Burgess and Holmstrum (1974b), for example, have developed training programs for front-line workers in the Boston area, offering a model for crisis intervention following rape. Similarly, Bard (1970) and others have developed crisis intervention training programs for police (see Chapter 12 of this volume).

Domestic violence—child and spouse abuse—is another area which has been increasingly understood in terms of crisis theory, particularly in planning interventions to prevent violence (Belsky 1980; Brown 1979; Parke 1977; Warner 1981). Abuse by a parent or spouse can create a crisis for the victim. Beyond the physical danger, there are psychological dangers which spring from the interpretation of events by the abused person, particularly self-attributions of guilt and blame. In addition, the act of abusing a child or a spouse can be understood as a sign of the abuser's inability to cope appropriately. Interventions need to be tailored for both abusers and victims to provide coping mechanisms to diminish the possibility of re-abuse. Borgman, Edmunds, and MacDicken (1979) have outlined how crisis intervention strategies can be used by child protective workers in helping families in which child abuse has occurred or is imminent. (See also Helfer and Kempe (1976) regarding child abuse in family and community systems.) Spouse abuse has also received the increased attention of researchers (Gelles 1972, 1976; Steinmetz and Straus 1974; Straus 1973, 1976). Walker (1978) has offered a cycle theory of battering incidents (tension building, explosion, or acute battering incident, and then a calm, loving reprieve) which highlights the context (antecedent condition) of the battering incident itself. The problems in this area are all the more momentous in light of the fact that one-half to three-quarters of all police calls involve domestic violence of some sort and further, that police are themselves in danger of physical harm when responding to such calls (*Crime in the United States,* 1979).

Attention has also been given to understanding criminal activity in light of crisis theory (Stratton 1974; Kantor and Caron 1978; Speer 1974). The experience of many attorneys and jail personnel is that arrest and incarceration may precipitate crises. (See statement by criminal lawyer Richard "Race Horse" Haynes in Chapter 11 on the difficulty a lawyer faces in interviewing "psychological basket cases.") Regarding incarceration, crisis theory suggests that a number of factors such as public exposure, shame, self-blame, loss of social supports, and restriction of coping possibilities, plus the reality of a noxious jail environment, can combine to create life crises for newly incarcerated offenders. Although jail suicides are not uncommon, adequate training for jail guards

is still the exception rather than the rule (Beigel and Russell 1972; Farberow 1980).

At the other end of the corrections system, it is possible to conceptualize release from an institution as being a transition which might precipitate a crisis for parolees or offenders who have finished serving their time in prison. It has been hypothesized that rapid change in environment, lack of social resources (compounded in most cases by lack of job and physical resources as well), and poor preparation to cope with the challenges of life back in society may combine to make release from prison a crisis, one that can lead to further criminal behavior as a means of restoring equilibrium. In this framework, crisis intervention programs for ex-offenders are viewed as having the potential for preventing new offenses, thereby reducing community crime. This broad hypothesis has received some tentative support. For example, Stratton (1974) found that crisis intervention offered to pre-delinquent and misdemeanor juvenile offenders in San Fernando, California, was associated with reduced number of re-arrests, need for probation services, and number of

---

PEOPLE'S TEMPERS RISING WITH TEMPERATURES*

Tempers are rising with the temperatures, some officials are saying, and the three-week heat wave that has killed 689 people in the South and Midwest may be to blame for a rash of child abuse in Dallas.

The heat prompted Alabama Gov. Fob James to declare a state of emergency yesterday. A state of emergency was put in effect Monday in Missouri.

President Carter directed federal officials to make $6.73 million available in six states to provide relief for poor people put in dangerous situations because of the heat wave. The money will be used to pay utility bills, buy fans and air conditioners, and fund transportation to relief centers.

Carole Bowdry, Director of the Child Abuse Program in the Dallas County Child Welfare Department said that incidents of child abuse have increased steadily since June 23, when the heat wave began in Dallas.

"If you're hot, you're going to get angry faster," Ms. Bowdry said yesterday.

"That applies to parents and especially to children," she said. "Historically our worst cases of child abuse have happened in extremely inclement weather of one type or another," Ms. Bowdry said.

Source: People's Tempers Rising with Temperatures" in *The State* (Columbia, S.C.), July 16, 1980, United Press International. Reprinted by permission.

days spent in detention, resulting in a reduction in cost to the county.

Kantor and Caron (1978) suggest that whether release from prison is a crisis or a relatively smooth transition depends upon the strength of the parolee's social network in prison, and his/her previous parole experience. Speer (1974) suggests that in order to be fruitful, crisis services must be developed in conjunction with job placement and training programs. This view is widely shared by criminal justice professionals. Speer's program featured an innovative attempt to use the county's local crisis hotline as an adjunct to the group counseling sessions in a comprehensive approach to work with ex-offenders.

NATURAL AND MAN-MADE DISASTERS

One of the most striking features of disasters is that they affect many people at the same time. Hundreds may die, leaving many more to cope with the loss. The immediate aftermath of disasters (such as fires, floods, tornados, airplane crashes) is actually a state of emergency; immediate action must be taken to save lives and treat the wounded. The potential for psychological crises comes in the days and weeks immediately following, as individuals attempt to cope with loss. From the vantage point of individuals and their families, natural disasters are for the most part unexpected. They have a potential, then, of

---

TRAGEDY OF A BROKEN HEART*

Aug. 10, 1976, was a warm day in Belfast. That afternoon Anne Maguire, a 31-year-old mechanic's wife, was crushed against a school railing with her four children by a swerving getaway car used by terrorists of the Provisional I.R.A. The car's driver had been shot dead by pursuing British soldiers. Mrs. Maguire was hospitalized in a semiconscious state; it was several weeks before she fully comprehended that three of her children had been killed.

In one sense, Anne Maguire's tragedy was not in vain. Betty Williams, who had witnessed the accident, and Anne's sister, Mairead Corrigan, began a door-to-door campaign, seeking signatures for a petition condemning the continued violence between Ulster's Roman Catholics and Protestants. The movement, known as the Peace People, won the 1976 Nobel Peace Prize for rallying public outrage against the senseless sectarian killings.

But for Mrs. Maguire herself there was no consolation. She emigrated to New Zealand with her husband Jack in 1977 and there gave birth to a second daughter. She suffered a nervous breakdown, and the homesick family returned to Belfast in less than a year. Perpetual grief led to even more breakdowns, even deeper mental depression. Last week Anne Maguire finally gave up. She took her own life, slashing her wrists and throat with an electric carving knife.

The funeral took place in a church only 100 yards from the site of the 1976 accident and was attended by 1,500 mourners, including both Catholics and Protestants. The majority of them were women. In his homily at the Requiem Mass, Father James Kelly told the congregation: "A broken heart was the cause of Anne's death. In truth she died four years ago." An even more tragic truth is that Mrs. Maguire's suffering was not at all exceptional. "There are hundreds of Mrs. Maguires in Northern Ireland whom you never hear about," said one mourner. "They are all widows and mothers."

precipitating a crisis as we have defined it: a state of disorganization characterized by inability to cope, with potential for long lasting damage.

The tragedy in 1972 when a dam constructed by the Buffalo Creek Mining Company broke was a classic example of a disaster which precipitated crises in the lives of survivors. (Gleser, Green, and Winget 1981). When the dam broke, it unleashed more than a million gallons of water into the Buffalo Creek Valley, destroying everything in its path in a period of three hours. One-hundred and twenty-five persons were killed, and four thousand left homeless. A team of social scientists and mental health professionals were subsequently retained by attorneys of the survivors to bring legal action against the mining company, building their case on the psychic impairment (social, vocational, and personal disability) which resulted from the tragedy. In analyzing the symptoms presented, Titchener, Kapp, and Winget (1976) grouped disaster reactions into (1) acute effects of the impact, (2) symptoms which persisted for months and years later, and (3) more pervasive character and life-style disorders. The acute effects included such symptoms as memory disturbances, nightmares, insomnia, irritability, and panic. Symptoms persisting past the acute phase were continued anxiety, phobias, depression, increased use of stimulants and depressants (tobacco and alcohol), and loss of interest in sexual relationships, recreational pursuits, and socializing in general. Children's symptoms included continued sleep disturbances, lack of interest in school, and fear of future disasters (Frederick 1977b). Among the more enduring character and life-style effects were a sense of guilt and shame about surviving, unresolved grief over the loss of loved ones and life style, sense of hopelessness and meaningless about life, and diminished trust. The complex of both transitory and persistent effects came to be called "survivor syndrome."

Lifton and Olson (1976) described the Buffalo Creek survivor syndrome in terms of five categories. The first category was death imprint and death anxiety — indelible images and memories about the disaster, including terrifying dreams such as the following (Lifton and Olson 1976):

> I dream I'm in a car on a pier surrounded by muddy water—or else in a pool of muddy water. I feel like I've got to hold onto the side of the pool. If I do, I'm all right. I know that I can't get out. I have to stay in it (p. 296).

The second category is that of death guilt— the survivors' painful self-condemnation for having lived while others died. This can also be reflected in the description of dreams such as (Lifton and Olson 1976):

> I dreamed we knew the dam was going to break. In the dream Mrs. T. had a white dress on. She asked me to follow her out in the yard. She just kept going back into a hole that looked like a mine. I don't know why she wanted me to come with her—she held her hand out, but I was afraid (p. 298).

Psychic numbing, characterized by diminished feeling and a desensitization to the experience (apathy, withdrawal, depression), is the third category. The fourth and fifth categories of survivor syndrome manifest themselves as: impairment in human relationships, particularly between husbands and wives, and employers and employees, and an internal struggle to find some cognitive formulation for the meaning of the disaster, often in terms of religious convictions.

White and Haas (1975) point out that, with a few exceptions, (Quarantelli and Dynes 1977), research on disasters has been limited to the investigation of local problems, with little theory development or testing of assumptions and hypotheses. There is still some confusion, for example, on the extent of post-disaster psychological harm. Dynes and Quarantelli (1976) contend that:

> . . . as a result of disaster, individual disorganization is somewhat minimal because the poten-

tial effects are mediated through various social structures within which individuals play roles. We are particularly concerned with the family and the larger community as mediating structures. The consequences of such structual mediation are that, in most disaster situations, individuals are able to exhibit situationally adaptive behavior. Rather than being characterized by widespread maladaptive behavior, disaster situations are, in many ways, characterized by a greater proportion of adaptive, goal-oriented behavior than may be true in so-called normal situations (p. 232).

Similarly, Frederick (1977b) points out that research has dispelled the myth of panic reactions in the immediate aftermath of disasters.

> People seldom get so panic stricken that they run amuck during a disaster, unless they are pinned into an enclosed area which is on fire. Although a number of behavioral disturbances are associated with disasters, including some which are dramatic, going berserk is not one of them (p. 45).

For those who do experience severe reactions, the symptoms can be expected to cover the entire spectrum of emotional and behavioral upset, as in the aftermath of the Buffalo Creek tragedy (see Gleser, Green and Winget 1981). Frederick points out that available data suggest that it is not uncommon for hostility to emerge between friends and family, resentment to be shown toward neighbors who have been spared personal loss, or for anger and suspicions to be directed toward helping personnel. The open resentment usually occurs after the initial shock.

The nature of the disaster can also be expected to play a role in individual reactions. Lifton and Olson (1976) reported that the impact of the suddenness and terrifying quality of the Buffalo Creek flood was exacerbated by the fact that it was seen as a man-made disaster—the dam broke because of human negligence. Further, residents were still economically dependent upon those responsible for the disaster after it was over.

Crises following disasters involving toxic chemicals (Love Canal, Niagara Falls, 1978) and nuclear accidents (Three Mile Island, 1979) offer other examples of how the unique character of the precipitating event affects the course of the crisis as well as the resolution process. Reports are now beginning to surface on the mental health effects of these disasters, with interesting implications for the crisis intervention process (A. Levine 1982; Schaar 1980). The immediate effects of noxious odors and chemicals were first noticed in the Love Canal area through reports of unexplained physical and medical problems: abnormal numbers of miscarriages, chronic illnesses, and birth defects (Schaar 1980). The psychological concomitants of these difficulties also became apparent. Stress was related not only to the emergence of physical problems, but also to the uncertainty about long-term effects. In addition, residents were embroiled in a political battle with the government over who was responsible for cleaning up the chemical waste, and for making reimbursements for damage, including relocations to new homes.

Similarly, in the aftermath of the Three Mile Island nuclear accident, attention was drawn to psychological stresses on area residents. As with chemical waste disasters, much concern was centered around the unknown dangers and the controversy over their severity, the full impact of which would not be noticed until 20 or more years down the line. The President's Commission on the Accident at Three Mile Island concluded that psychological stress and mental health problems were among the chief consequences associated with the accident (Kemeny 1979). A review of studies conducted immediately after the accident found that symptoms such as depression and anxiety in area residents continued as much as one year after the accident (Baum et al. 1982).

While the communities involved were not prepared with adequate disaster plans to help deal with these crises, a number of efforts were begun, with some rather interesting results. A report by Richard Valinsky, Coordinator of the Division of Consultation and Education of the Niagara Falls Community Mental Health Center serving the Love Canal area, suggested that the center's early outreach efforts (a pamphlet sent to residents discussing stress and its effects) backfired. The pamphlet was not well received, with residents expressing anger over any suggestion that they were having problems adjusting to the situation. They contended that their main need was for the government to buy their homes so they could move out of the area. Further, "many had a real fear of any so-called mental health help because they were afraid it would be used to say that their relocation or health worries 'were all in their head'" (Schaar 1980, p. 14).

After this initial false start, the center redirected its efforts, keeping a much lower profile and steering clear of any identification of its approach as a mental health effort. A full-time crisis outreach team began to make phone calls and take walks through the neighborhood to make contact with residents, listening to their problems, and assisting them in negotiating with social services. Sociologist Adeline Levine and her associates conducted exploratory research on the impact of the Love Canal incident on residents. She observed that the Love Canal Home Owners Association, which had already been in operation for two years, actually served a considerable mental health function without originally intending to do so. Based on the premise that "nobody can help us unless they have lived through it," the organization represented a significant effort at self-help and support for residents. Though data are not available on the course of crisis for these residents, one might hypothesize that crisis mastery began as much through political action as through information on the expectedness or naturalness of stress reactions which followed the incident. (See Chapter 2 and Chapter 8 for discussion of intervention through several modalities—cognitive, behavioral, etc.—in crisis resolution.)

A number of writers have offered guidelines for planning intervention strategy to be used following disasters (Butcher 1980; Cohen and Ahearn 1980; Frederick 1977a; McGee 1976; Zusman 1976). For example, Frederick suggests that:

(a) Crisis intervention is superior to no intervention at the time of disaster;
(b) The intervention must go beyond standard psychotherapy procedures and emphasize mediative, innovative strategies suitable to the needs of the community, and the nature of the particular crisis;
(c) Outreach programs are more effective than those placed in one particular location;
(d) Mental health language and concepts should be avoided since "people in disasters, who are in need of crisis intervention, do not see themselves as mentally ill and, in point of fact, usually are not."
(e) Health records should be kept to allow for continued research to improve our understanding of the nature of reactions, and the effectiveness of various strategies (p. 49).

McGee[1] has further underlined the importance of nonprofessional volunteers in the delivery of crisis services after a disaster. He suggests that disaster planners make use of existing, already trained volunteers (from hotlines, rape crisis centers, mental health centers, etc.) modeled after the National Guard, i.e., calling workers into action, according to a pre-existing plan, whenever needed.

Finally, Harshbarger (1976) suggests an ecological model for assessing individual and

---

[1] Address given by Richard McGee at conference on "Preventing the Youthful Suicide," Southern Methodist University, Dallas, Texas: November 10, 1976.

group needs, and delivering crisis and social services to large numbers of people. His model identifies both survivors and interveners/helpers as "clients" needing attention in the aftermath of disaster (Figure 4.1). Both formal and informal systems in a community are used in the intervention process to help clients to manage stress and identify resources (e.g., legal aid, welfare or monetary assistance, social supports), and thereby facilitate coping.

WAR AND RELATED ACTS

War and its variations provide another set of events which can lead to crisis. The loss of life and property, and threat to national identity and chosen way of life have far-reaching psychological implications for survivors. As Table 4.1 indicates, important literature has developed in this area, particularly around combat casualties, prisoners of war, and the unusual stress associated with survival in concentration camps.

That such crises can have long-lasting negative impacts has been brought most graphically to the world's attention in recent investigations of second generation survivors of the Nazi Holocaust (Davidson 1980; Epstein 1980). Based on experience in treating concentration camp survivors in Israel for a number of years, Davidson (1980) found increasing numbers of second generation family members "suffering from a wide spectrum of emotional disorders, personality disturbances, borderline and psychotic states which are clearly related to the long-term effects of massive traumatization in the survivor parents" (p. 11).

A number of disruptions in parent/child interactions emerged: (1) over-anxiety, overprotectiveness by mothers; (2) intense emotional investment and idealization of the child by survivor parents; (3) identification of children with siblings and parents lost in the concentration camp; (4) transmission of parental feelings of guilt, shame, and low self-esteem to children who identified with their parents. Many children drew from their parents a sense of danger and distrust, coupled with the burden of trying to live a life in compensation for those whose lives were cut short. Davidson suggests that intensive family therapy is the treatment of choice. He found that when a trusting relationship between therapist and parents (particularly mothers) was established, " . . . parents became able to tell the child in an appropriate way of their traumatic experiences and losses. When no working through was possible because of the parents' disturbances and, if anxiety and depression were overt, they were offered symptomatic and supportive therapy" (p. 19).

Two other areas that have received the attention of therapists in a crisis framework have been treatment of post-traumatic stress disorder in Vietnam veterans (Figley and Sprenkle 1978; Williams 1980) and work with newly released hostages (Sank 1979). It is not uncommon for the trauma of combat experiences to be repressed, and then reactivated by some other life crisis (divorce, unemployment). Figley and Sprenkle (1978) have applied Horowitz and Solomon's (1975) paradigm on the psychological reactions of trauma to their treatment of Vietnam veterans. Veterans who at first resisted attempts to talk through stressful experiences sometimes needed the assistance of an outside therapist for this important task (Figley and Sprenkle 1978):

> When I finally got in the mood to talk about the "blood and guts," I discovered no one really wanted to hear it. The only one halfway willing to listen was my dad, but only about the parts that would make him proud of me—the John Wayne shit. I couldn't really tell him how I was scared shitless or how I risked my ass for nothing or how the guys I loved were wasted for nothing (p. 57).

Treatment also focuses on the veteran's immediate family and social group, often coaching them on how to deal with specific reactions. Spouses, for example, are taught to

FIGURE 4.1*

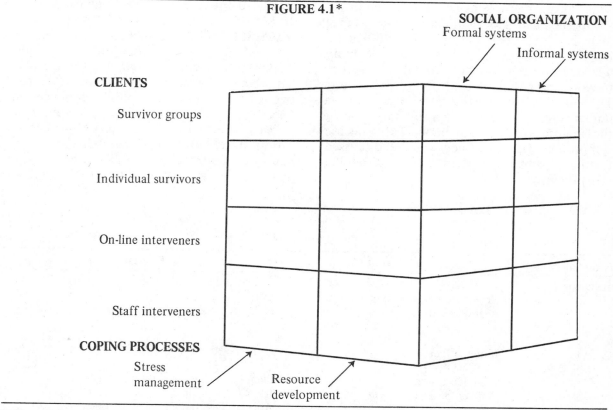

Source: "An ecologic perspective on disaster intervention" by D. Harshbarger, in H.J. Parad, and H.L.P. Resnik, and L.G. Parad (eds.), *Emergency and disaster management: A mental health sourcebook.* Bowie, Maryland: The Charles Press Publishers, Inc., 1976.

resist counterattacking which might lead to further aggression instead of catharsis of violent impulses. Therapists need to model an objective and realistic stance which allows feelings to be expressed without permitting physical and mental abuse. For example:

> . . . it is O.K. for you to feel anger, and I will try to understand what is going on inside you. But I will not let you abuse me or the children (p. 57).

In the political and social turmoil of the sixties and early seventies, a number of groups in the United States chose physical and often violent strategies towards social change, including the taking of hostages. Psychologists and others began attempting to understand psychological aspects of the hostage experience (identification by hostages with captors), as well as processes which were helpful in dealing with the aftermath. Sank (1979) reports on an innovative intervention by therapists from a Washington, D.C., health maintenance organization with 154 men and women who had been held hostage for three days by the Hanfi Muslims at the B'Nai B'Rith National Headquarters in 1977. Immediately after the hostages were set free, they offered group sessions at the site of the takeover (twice weekly for four weeks), with follow-up sessions at three months and one year later. As Table 4.2 indicates, the therapists observed a wide range of problems in survivors, and used group sessions to offer therapeutic assistance in working through the experience in such a way that damaging effects would be minimized, and survivors of the ordeal could return to work and go on about the business of living. The unique feature of this intervention was its immediacy, and its use of a full spectrum of therapeutic treatments aimed at specific symptoms. This approach will be discussed further in subsequent chapters on multimodal crisis therapy.

SITUATIONAL CRISES OF MODERN LIFE

The final category of crises listed in Table 4.1 includes a number of situations that do not belong in previous categories, though they have been of increasing concern in the past two decades. For example, experiences induced by psychedelic drugs offer many of the classic characteristics of life crises (disorganization, disequilibrium, vulnerability, need for new coping strategies) and yield, according to many theorists, opportunities for growth as

TABLE 4.2[a]

Modality	Problem	Treatment
Behavior	Avoidance, Crying, verbally snapping at others, Fear of isolation	In vivo and systematic desensitization DMR,[b] assertiveness Planned program of writing and sharing experience with others
Affect	Muted affect	Encouraged group sharing of experience or writing feelings
	Mild depression	Planning rewarding activities, reassurance
	Anxiety attacks	DMR,[b] coping imagery, assertiveness training
	Anger	Assertiveness training
Sensation	Sleep disturbance	DMR,[b] scheduling usual relaxing activities, exercise, coping imagery
	Headaches	DMR with concentration on muscles of the face, neck, and shoulders
	Stomach and bowel disturbance, palpitations, muscle tightness, back pains	DMR with concentration on trunk muscles
	Fatigue	Permission to sleep more and engage in less rigorous activity
Imagery	Reliving of takeover and Holocaust fantasies	Substituting calming imagery, focus on release
	Being vulnerable in all life situations	Assertion imagery
	Unable to testify in court	Behavior rehearsal, organized review of events

[a]Source: Sank, L.I. "Community disasters: Primary prevention and treatment in a health maintenance organization." *American Psychologist.* 34: 334–338 (1979). Copyright 1979 by the American Psychological Association. Reprinted by permission of the author.

[b]DMR = deep muscle relaxation; RET = rational-emotive therapy.

well as harm (Brown and Stickgold 1976; Cohen 1977; Twemlow and Bowen 1979). Migration and relocation—peaking in the sixties as upward mobility led to promotion and job changes, and leveling off in harder economic times—is characterized by complete environmental change and the accompanying sense of loss, challenge of new beginnings, and the like. The social supplies of individual family members are taken away, necessitating adjustment and new beginnings (Fried 1976; M. Levine 1976; S. Levine 1976). Further,

changing economic conditions—inflation, unemployment—bring social upheaval that clearly has effects on individual, psychological, and family functioning. A study by the United States Government in 1976 attempted to estimate the social costs of national economic policy (*Estimating the Social Costs of National Economic Policy* 1976). The most striking finding was that even a 1 percent increase in unemployment was associated with the following events over a six-year period:

TABLE 4.2a (Continued)

Modality	Problem	Treatment
Cognitions	Obsessive rumination	Thought stopping
	"Awfulizing"	Encourage feedback from group members on
	"This wouldn't have happened if only...."	behavior during takeover
	"I should have...."	
	"You should have...."	
	"I wasn't a hero and I should have been."	
	"Catastrophizing"	RET[b]
	"I'll never get over this."	
	"The Hanafis know my name and address and will come to kill me later."	
	"No place is safe anymore"	
	Isolation	Group sharing, therpists providing limited information about the wide variety of human reactions to stress
	"I'm the only one who had these reactions."	
Interpersonal	Increased dependency and desire for human contact	Coping imagery, assertion training, permission to need the comfort of others
	Suspicious of strangers	Take more realistic precautions (lock car and home, etc.), in vivo desensitization
	Marital and family conflict	Assertion training, referral to family and conjoint therapists
Drugs	Increased use of tranquilizers, medications, alcohol	Substitution of DMR, exercise, RET, coping imagery, limited use of drugs when appropriate
	Somatic disturbances	Medical check after release and before rejoining families, medical follow-ups of new complaints or old ones exacerbated by stress

- 36,887 total deaths, including 20,240 cardiovascular deaths,
- 920 suicides,
- 648 homicides,
- 495 deaths from cirrhosis of the liver,
- 4,227 state mental hospital admissions, and
- 3,340 state prison admissions (pp. 5–6).

The environmental changes represented in economic lows and migration have clear implications for primary prevention, and for crisis intervention as well. Just as child abuse can be expected to increase during inclement weather, the occurrence of life crises can be expected to increase during hard economic times. Calls to suicide centers and hotlines, for example, increase during inflationary times. Recognizing this, some employers have taken steps to soften the blow of migration on family life, and to offer assistance in coping with the disruption which can be expected in families after a move takes place (see Chapter 17 in this volume on life crises in work settings).

The divorce rate rose to almost one in two marriages in 1975 (Kraus 1979). While these statistics have led to considerable alarm, indicating to some that divorce is a sign of pathology in individuals if not in society, others have come to conceptualize divorce as a life crisis whose outcome may just as well lead to growth as to harm. In early research on the impact of divorce, Goode (1956) found that women reported divorce as being most traumatic when they saw it as one sided, i.e., desired by their husbands but not themselves. Much less trauma resulted when the decision was a mutual one.

In a review of divorce literature, Kraus (1979) presents a composite of the various stages through which a crisis of divorce might flow. The first is characterized by denial, acting as if the relationship is still working well. This is followed by anger and guilt in the face of marital discord, with blame for the dissolution of the marriage put either upon oneself or one's spouse. Anger can then mix and alternate with regret and with last ditch attempts to save the marriage, followed by depression in the realization that the old structure has broken down and that further emotional investment will not pay off. Finally, a stage develops which focuses on the individual's own current functioning, with movement toward a reorientation of activities and acceptance of a new lifestyle. Kraus points out that the stages that are represented in the divorce literature do not, however, grow from research data, but from clinical reports, lending some caution as to their universality.

In an attempt to summarize variables considered relevant in understanding the nature of divorce crises, and to pave the way for future research, Kraus (1979) offers an organizational model (Figure 4.2). Special attention needs to be given to the individual's belief system or cognitive interpretation of his or her new status:

> . . . emotional pain is related both to the commitment one had to one's marriage, but also to the belief in marriage itself as the best form of adult life. In the framework of rational emotive therapy . . . , if one holds the irrational belief that a divorce is a catastrophe one can easily make oneself miserable. An individual whose value system says that a divorced person is a failure, and a person without a mate is worthless, will most certainly experience a great deal of distress, if he finds himself in that position. Research examining the relationship between one's belief system and adjustment variables is needed (p. 115).

One of the most encouraging trends in the past decade has been the emergence of divorce mediation centers whose goal is to assist divorcing couples in dissolving marital contracts efficiently and fairly by procedures which seek to manage the intense feelings of bitterness and hostility associated with separation and divorce (Coogler 1978; Kessler 1978; Pearson 1979).

The mediation concept rests on the premise that stress and long-range psychological harm

FIGURE 4.2   IMPACT OF DIVORCE: THE CRISIS MODEL

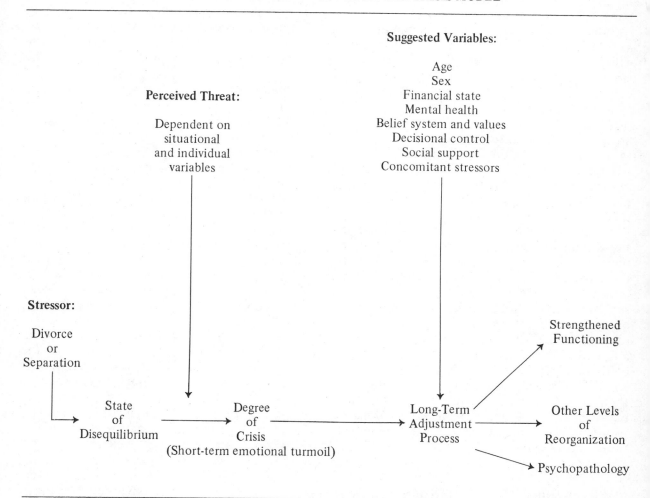

Suggested Variables:

Age
Sex
Financial state
Mental health
Belief system and values
Decisional control
Social support
Concomitant stressors

Perceived Threat:

Dependent on
situational
and individual
variables

Stressor:

Divorce
or
Separation

State
of
Disequilibrium

Degree
of
Crisis
(Short-term emotional turmoil)

Long-Term
Adjustment
Process

Strengthened
Functioning

Other Levels
of
Reorganization

Psychopathology

to children of divorce grow not from one-parent homes *per se,* but from the turmoil involved in continued parental conflicts (Leupnitz 1978, 1979; Wallerstein and Kelly 1980).

Based on social psychological principles of conflict resolution (Deutsch 1973), mediation centers offer third party assistance (a mediator) for a couple as they attempt to manage feelings of anger, hurt, and guilt, and at the same time work toward equitable decisions on the division of property, custody of children, and visitation. In a typical mediation arrangement, a couple meets with a mediator for anywhere from four to ten sessions, each with a particular focus on some aspect of dissolving the marital agreement *and* arranging for post-marital contacts as appropriate (visitation of children). At the end of the mediation period, an agreement is signed by both parties, the mediator, and an attorney (drawn from a panel of consulting attorneys). The agreement can then be taken to a court of law and offered as the divorce settlement. The mediators assists couples in cooperating in the dissolution of their marital contracts, instead of becoming adversaries against one another, the typical stance taken in traditional divorce proceedings. While the right of each party to secure his/her own attorney and "fight it out" in court is always present, a right which is a hallmark of our legal system, mediation is an attempt to circumvent the more negative aspects of the adversary system as applied to domestic disputes.

Mediation centers have sprung up around the country as private operations and as a part of the court system (American Association of Conciliation Courts). Early success of pilot programs has led investigators to examine specific process variables which might predict positive outcome (Pearson 1982). The intent of mediation is, of course, to provide a rational alternative for couples coping with the crisis of divorce. Though research still needs to be conducted in this area, it is entirely possible that crisis intervention techniques on the management of intense feelings could contribute substantially to the success of mediation, especially in its early stages.

INTERVENTION IMPLICATIONS

A review of the findings outlined in this chapter yields several intervention implications which are directly related to the unique nature of situational crises. We can summarize these ideas as a preview of the more general structure of the crisis intervention process presented in Chapter 5:

1. The sense of immediacy associated with situational crises underlines the importance or providing interventions that help clients deal with what is going on *now,* while at the same time diagnosing needs which will require attention later. Situational crises demand a "first things first" approach to the intervention process, e.g., saving lives, finding a place to stay for the night, mediating a domestic quarrel. The severe impact of these events requires that those in crisis receive both symptomatic relief as well as linkage to resources for continued assistance in the weeks and months ahead.

2. Each specific category of situational crisis listed in this chapter accentuates one or more critical aspects of crisis theory itself. The impact of disability or loss of a limb, for example, points to the importance of making behavioral adjustments later on, possibly changing careers and future plans. Expectations (cognitions) are emphasized in understanding how people cope with untimely death. The need for developing strategies for treating large numbers of people at the same time becomes apparent when considering natural and man-made disasters. Similarly, the emergency quality of many situational crises accentuates the importance of training those who are first on the scene (e.g., police for crimes of violence).

3. In each of the situational crises presented, we suggest attending to all four systems levels—person, family/social group, community, and society—in planning interventions. To treat a rape victim without considering the impact of the experience on her relationship with her husband, and including him in the treatment, is just one example of how a limited focus can impede ultimate resolution of the crisis. Similarly, state and federal governmental response can have an effect on the resolution of crises induced by exposure to toxic chemical wastes.

4. By affecting many people at one time, situational crises call for broad-based community planning in order for intervention to take place quickly and appropriately.

McGee (1976) suggests that the chief characteristics of community programs include (a) use of volunteer workers, (b) locating the services so they are conveniently accessible to users, and (c) adopting an outreach attitude.

5. Experience with misguided, though well-meaning, interventions suggests that it is important to pay attention to what victims say they want and need, in addition to what crisis theorists suggest they might want and need. Without client acceptance, intervention efforts are fruitless.

RESEARCH ISSUES   As is characteristic of crisis research in general, the literature on situational crises includes primarily case and program reports, complemented by a few empirical studies. The reports and theoretical articles which have appeared for the past two or more decades, plus the pioneering efforts of researchers cited earlier in this chapter (Janis 1958 regarding surgery; Quarantelli and Dynes 1977 on natural disasters), make the field fertile for more systematic investigation. Interested researchers should give close attention to the following areas:

1. Auerbach and Kilmann (1977) have summarized the research on crises precipitated by surgery. They point out that, with the specific stimulus of impending surgery, and the controlled hospital environment, systematic investigation is perhaps more realistic in this area than in many others in the crisis field.

2. Speer's (1974) program using a 24-hour hotline as an adjunct to crisis intervention with ex-offenders needs to be replicated. The original study suffered because of management difficulties, and thus was not an adequate test of a comprehensive approach to work with ex-offenders.

3. Frederick (1977b) and Quarantelli and Dynes (1977) offer program directions and evaluation guidelines for disaster research. Harshbarger's (1976) ecological model has potential for comprehensive conceptualization of disasters, helpers, and victims in a community context. The precision of future evaluation efforts can be enhanced by use of such a model.

4. In the diaster area it is important for research teams to be ready to quickly implement research designs, well before disasters occur. Following the nuclear accident of Three Mile Island, and toxic chemical crisis at Love Canal, federal money was made available to those who were prepared with a sound research design (Schaar 1980).

5. One productive approach to further refining knowledge and techniques regarding situational crises might be to re-analyze old data using broad based multimodal approaches (Striegel-Moore and Slaikeu 1982). The clinical reports are remarkably consistent on the occurrence of crisis symptoms which involve not only feelings, but also cognitions, behavior, interpersonal relationships, and the like. Much can be done to consolidate directions for the intervention process by using the multimodal perspective offered in this volume (see Chapters 2 and 8).

PART II

INTERVENTION STRATEGIES

Having reviewed literature on the nature of life crises, we now turn to the helping process. Several questions emerge: Who is in the best position to help people in crisis? How should the help be offered? What sort of training is needed? What are appropriate goals, and how can we tell when the goals have been reached? How does crisis intervention by a police officer differ from that done by a telephone hotline volunteer, or a social worker at a mental health center? How does crisis intervention differ from psychotherapy?

Part II of this book addresses these questions directly. Chapter 5 reviews the chief characteristics of crisis intervention as gleaned from a wide range of research and clinical reports, and presents a comprehensive crisis intervention model which distinguishes between First- and Second-Order Crisis Intervention (Psychological First Aid versus Crisis Therapy). Building on this framework, Chapters 6 through 9 provide detailed descriptions of the five components of psychological first aid and a multimodal approach to crisis therapy, including case examples. As we shall see, our success in dealing with the questions raised above depends in large measure upon our ability to clarify the distinctions between these two phases of the intervention process.

chapter five

A Comprehensive Model for Crisis Intervention

Written descriptions of how to do crisis intervention advocate a wide range of therapeutic techniques. However, most published articles are actually clinical reports dealing with small numbers of cases, as opposed to systematic studies on the effectiveness of specific procedures across a large sample (Auerbach and Kilmann 1977; Butcher and Koss 1978; Butcher and Maudal 1976; Slaikeu, Tulkin, and Speer 1975). We are not at a point where we can summarize tried and true principles or strategies of crisis intervention. One of the difficulties has been that few studies examine both process (what therapists say and do) and outcome (what happens to clients as a result). In their review of crisis intervention literature, Butcher and Koss point out that, "The actual processes by which various crisis interventions bring about desired individual changes have not received enough attention to enable evaluation of them . . . In general, with the exception of a few studies, very little research effort has been directed toward examining the theoretical model underlying crisis intervention strategies" (p. 746).

Chapter 18 of this volume discusses research in this area and suggests next steps in consolidating our knowledge. For now, we must admit that we do not know all we would like to about what works and what does not. At the same time, a review of clinical and research reports yields a remarkable consistency across articles with regard to several distinguishing characteristics of crisis intervention. These consistencies provide a starting point for a model on how to help a person through a crisis. Though few of the principles listed here have been the subject of rigorous research, their reappearance in the clinical literature attests to their staying power and provides a challenge to investigators to take note of them as possible variables for future research. For our purposes, they are the important data or raw materials from which a comprehensive crisis intervention model will emerge. What follows, is a look at what practitioners—people who daily help others manage crises—tell us about the distinguishing characteristics of crisis intervention.

CLINICAL PRINCIPLES

Timing

Short-term, time-limited therapy is the treatment of choice in crisis situations. The literature suggests that the helping process should take about as long as the time it takes for most people to regain equilibrium after a crisis event, or about six weeks according to Caplan (1964). Most writers describe crisis intervention as taking anywhere from one to six weeks (Aguilera et al. 1974, Burgess and Baldwin 1981), as distinguished from interventions that go on for months or for years in long-term psychotherapy. More important, short-term therapy is not seen as a second best approach. Having fewer sessions poses clear economic advantages and offering therapy during the immediacy of the crisis has additional therapeutic advantages as well. We maximize the client's chances of growing through a crisis by offering assistance to help him/her gain mastery over the situation, and move toward reorganization of a disorganized life.

An extension of this idea is *Hansel's Law*: The effectiveness of a crisis intervention service increases directly as a function of its proximity in both time and place to the crisis event (McGee 1976). Since the crisis experience is a time of high stakes for both client and family, help needs to be available immediately and in an easily accessible location. Accordingly, twenty-four hour telephone services operating 365 days a year, as well as walk-in counseling services, have been used extensively since the late 1950s (see Chapter 15). In addition, many centers have outreach services allowing counselors to visit people wherever crises occur. The assumption is that if a client has to wait hours, days, or weeks to receive help, the danger factor in the crisis might increase, resulting in loss of life (suicide or homicide). Another danger is that dysfunctional habits and patterns of thinking might become so strongly ingrained in the client's life that they become extremely difficult to change later on. In summary, the emphasis on timing is calculated to both reduce danger and, at the same time, to capitalize on the client's motivation to find some new approach (whether attitudinal or behavioral) to cope with life's circumstances.

Goals

A common theme in the crisis intervention literature is that the chief goal is to help the person regain the level of functioning that existed immediately prior to the crisis event. Some define this as restoration of equilibrium, while others focus on the reattainment of the individual's ability to cope with the situation. As one clinician put it, "My goal is to help people get off the ropes and back into the center of the ring." Notice the difference between this strategy and the goals of long-term psychotherapy—symptom reduction, personality reorganization, or behavior change.

Most therapists recognize, however, that a client never "goes back" to the previous level of functioning. By successfully working through and resolving a life crisis, the person learns new ways of coping. The client may end up conceptualizing life differently than before the crisis occurred (often times more realistically), and may be able to chart entirely new directions for the future. Many clinicians view these outcomes as secondary benefits of crisis intervention. Unfortunately, this view leaves aside the uniqueness of the crisis experience, namely, an opportunity to rework unfinished personal issues, to reorganize one's life after everything has fallen apart. The solution adopted in the present volume rests on the distinction between first-and second-order intervention (discussed later in this chapter). The goal of the former—re-establishing coping—is much more limited, while the goal of the latter—crisis resolution—focuses directly on assisting the client in learning from the crisis, resulting potentially in a higher level of functioning than before the crisis.

Assessment

It is important that assessment involves both strengths and weaknesses of each of the systems involved in the crisis. This intervention principle grows from the general systems perspective on life crises outlined in Chapter 2. Data on what is going wrong in a person's life (crumbling marital relationship) is complemented with data on what is still functional (a supportive network of friends). Social strengths and resources can be used to help a person cope with the distress of crisis. Based on the fact that each person's crisis occurs within the context of family, work, neighborhood, and community systems, the clinician's task is to determine which environmental variables precipitated the crisis, which are maintaining the disorganization and suffering, and which can be mobilized to facilitate constructive change in the situation. Employing this analysis leads to a variety of strategies for change, ranging from such measures as assistance in securing food stamps or legal counsel to a referral for one-to-one counseling or vocational guidance.

Helper Behavior[1]

One of the most salient aspects of crisis work is that therapists are more active, directive, and goal-oriented than in noncrisis situations. Since time is short, therapists become active participants in accessing the difficulty, pinpointing immediate needs, and mobilizing helping resources. In some situations, crisis counselors give advice and initiate referrals to help a person "make it through the night." The challenge of crisis intervention lies not only in working efficiently and effectively with the client, but also in being flexible enough to mobilize a full range of suprasystem resources (family and community) in working toward crisis resolution for the client.

While therapists are relatively more goal-oriented and directive in crisis work, a basic intervention principle holds that clients should be encouraged to do as much as they can for themselves. The crisis counselor takes the more directive action steps (calling a

parent, driving a person home, initiating emergency hospitalization) only when the extreme disorganization and upset preclude the client from acting on his or her own behalf. Implicit in this stepwise approach is an attempt to reinforce clients' strengths as they work toward mastery of the situation. Since clients are expected to be on their own in a matter of weeks anyway, counselor behavior is geared as much as possible towards facilitating/encouraging that subsequent independence.

The intervention literature describes various approaches to helping a person or family survive a crisis. We will summarize several of these approaches as a backdrop for the comprehensive model described in this volume. (See also Aguilera et al. 1974; Burgess and Baldwin 1981; Butcher and Maudal 1976; Crow 1977; Getz et al. 1974; Hoff 1978; Puryear 1979).

McGee and his colleagues identify two areas of counselor performance: clinical and technical effectiveness (Fowler and McGee 1973; Knickerbocker and McGee 1972; McGee 1974). The former refers to the counselor's ability to show empathy, genuineness, and warmth to the client. Technical effectiveness refers to the counselor's ability to assess lethality in suicide cases, explore resources, make an appropriate referral, and the like. Walfish and his colleagues have further developed the latter by designing a crisis contracting scale which looks at the extent to which counselors assess the present crisis, explore resources, and move toward action steps on a contractual basis (Walfish et al. 1976). In this same vein, Berg has outlined five aspects of counselor performance in working with a telephone caller in crisis. Counselors are expected to communicate empathy, demonstrate an understanding of the problem to the caller, summarize the problem, survey resources available to the caller, and assist the caller in developing an action plan (Berg 1970).

Some articles focus both on what counsel-

---

[1] Since crisis intervention is considered to include strategies used by a wide range of professional and paraprofessional workers, throughout this chapter the terms "helper," "therapist," "counselor," and "worker" will be used interchangeably to refer to the person in the help or care-giving role.

ors do *and* on the training required to do it in defining different crisis interventions. For example, Jacobson, Strickler, and Morley (1968) differentiate between four levels of crisis intervention: environmental manipulation (linking a person to a helping resource such as minister, friend, or agency), general support (empathic listening done by neighbors, or bartenders, and the like), the generic approach (short-term work by persons trained in crisis intervention), and individually tailored crisis intervention by persons with extensive training in abnormal psychology, personality theory, crisis theory, and related areas.

Many theorists draw heavily on the early work of Lindemann (1944) regarding the grief process in defining what therapists should do to help crisis clients. In Lindemann's framework, the therapist helps the person accept the pain of bereavement, review the relationship with the deceased, express the sorrow and sense of loss fully, find an acceptable formulation of future relationships with the deceased, verbalize feelings of guilt, and also find persons around whom new patterns for conduct can be established.

In line with this tradition, Pasewark and Albers (1972) talk about crisis intervention as involving three general areas: (1) establishing or facilitating communication (between persons in crisis, significant others, agencies, etc.), (2) assisting the individual or family in perceiving the situation correctly (with a focus on concrete events, their meaning, and possible outcomes) and finally (3) assisting the individual or family in managing feelings and emotions in an open manner.

Similarly, Viney (1976) describes practitioners and researchers as helping clients to: regain the homeostasis lost by the crisis; achieve cognitive mastery over the crisis; and make behavioral changes. The first area relies on techniques facilitating catharsis or working through feelings. In the second area, the therapist assists the person in gaining an understanding of the cognitive maps and ex-

pectancies which have been violated by the crisis event, with a goal of developing new conceptualizations of self and others. In the final area (behavioral), new ways of responding or coping are discussed, rehearsed, and then implemented.

Another set of variables determining helper activity relates to the responsibility of the counselor to take action regarding a specific crisis. McMurrain (1975), for example, distinguishes between four levels of crisis intervention (empathy, assertion, facilitation, control) depending upon the level of crisis involved (catastrophic, critical, or developmental). In cases without threats to life and limb, therapists take a supportive or facilitative stance in working with the person in crisis (listening, suggesting possible solutions). In more lethal situations (child abuse), therapists might take a more assertive (negotiation of a referral) or controlling (reporting child abuse to the authorities, initiating emergency hospitalization) approach.

Along the same lines, Blanton (1976) offers a flow chart for police in dealing with crisis situations. After receiving the call, the officer's responsibilities are to observe the scene, defuse the situation, and then determine the facts. This fact finding may lead to a criminal or noncriminal judgment, the former resulting in arrest or other legal disposition, and the latter leading to: (a) referral, (b) separation of the parties, or (c) mediation. As with McMurrain's approach, the choice between (a), (b), or (c) depends upon the nature of the particular crisis.

FIRST- AND SECOND-ORDER CRISIS INTERVENTION

The themes of the intervention literature regarding timing, goals, assessment, and strategies leave a number of questions unanswered. For example, if interventions range from one to six sessions, how is a "one shot" helping session different from an intervention with more extended contact (several weeks)? How do the interventions differ in terms of goals and procedures? Which community helpers should be involved in each? Do we not expect a different sort of intervention from a busy attorney talking to a distraught divorcee than from a trained pastoral counselor or social worker talking with the same person the next day?

Most intervention articles do not adequately answer these questions. Some writers present crisis intervention as a primarily behavioral enterprise (setting up a referral, finding a place for a client to spend the night), while others clearly indicate that the helping tasks are more psychological in nature. The range of goals for crisis intervention includes everything from a narrow linkage to helping resources at one extreme to broader crisis resolution at the other. Short-term and long-term goals are seldom clearly differentiated and specified in most articles.

A comprehensive crisis intervention model must make a number of important distinctions regarding: techniques, length of treatment, specific services delivered, goals, and training. The model must take into account what we already know about life crises, namely, that crises involve disequilibrium, high stakes, sense of urgency, and immediacy. The model needs to consider the individual as an active participant in many different community systems (family, work, church, neighborhood), a participant who daily engages in interactions/transactions with the environment.

Table 5.1 presents an intervention model designed to address these issues directly. Building on the consistencies represented in existing clinical and research reports, the comprehensive model procedes further by making a distinction between first-and second-order crisis intervention.

We can begin by describing *psychological first aid*, or, first-order crisis intervention which involves immediate assistance and usually takes only one session. Psychological first aid is primarily intended to provide support, reduce lethality, and link the person

TABLE 5.1   CRISIS INTERVENTION: A COMPREHENSIVE MODEL

	First-Order Intervention: Psychological First Aid	Second-Order Intervention: Crisis Therapy
How long?	Minutes to Hours	Weeks to Months
By whom?	Front Line Caregivers (parents, police, clergy, attorneys, physicians, nurses, social workers, teachers, supervisors, etc.)	Psychotherapists and Counselors (psychologists, psychiatrists, social workers, pastoral counselors, school counselors, psychiatric nurses, etc.)
Where?	Community Settings: home, school, work, hotlines, etc.	Therapy/Counseling Settings: clinics, mental health centers, walk-in centers, churches, etc.
Goals?	Re-Establish Immediate Coping: give support; reduce lethality; link to helping resources.	Resolve Crisis: work through crisis event; integrate event into fabric of life; establish openness/readiness to face future.
Procedure?	Five Components of Psychological First Aid (Chapter 6)	Multimodal Crisis Therapy (Chapter 8)

in crisis to other helping resources. Furthermore, it can and should be given by persons who first see the need, at the time and place it arises. Parents can be taught to give psychological first aid to their children just as they are now taught to give physical first aid in emergency situations. (Indeed, some of the early "parenting" literature seemed to have this aim, [Ginott 1965; Gordon 1970]). Police give psychological first aid when they intervene in domestic quarrels, as attorneys do when they take time to counsel an emotional client and then refer him or her for counseling or psychotherapy later on.

As Table 5.1 indicates, psychological first aid is a brief intervention taking anywhere from several minutes to several hours, depending upon the severity of the disorganization or emotional upset of the person in crisis and on the skill on the helper. Following the clinical tradition in crisis work, its goals are limited. Immediate coping is the main focus (getting through the day/night; planning the best next step). In practice, this is broken down into the three subgoals: *providing support, reducing lethality* (in child abuse, spouse battering, suicide, and homicide cases), and *linking to helping resources* (referral for counseling). The entire first aid contact is aimed at these areas, and no more; no effort is made to finalize psychological resolution of the crisis.

A special set of problem-solving procedures, tailored to account for the intensity of crisis situations, provides a guide for counselor/helper behavior. Identified in Table 5.1 as the five components of psychological first aid, these procedures cover the necessary and sufficient steps for the very first critical contact with a person in crisis. Each component entails skills and behaviors which can be taught and measured. A complete explanation of each follows in Chapter 6.

Second-order crisis intervention, or *crisis therapy*, on the other hand, refers to a short-term therapeutic process that goes beyond restoration of immediate coping, and aims

instead at crisis resolution. As Table 5.1 indicates, crisis resolution means assisting the person in working through the crisis experience (expressing feelings, gaining cognitive mastery of the situation, etc.) so that the event becomes integrated into the fabric of life. The desired outcome is for the individual to emerge ready and better equipped to face the future. Put another way, crisis therapy seeks to minimize the chance that the person will become a psychological casuality of the crisis event, whether the crisis is developmental (mid-life transition) or situational (unexpected death of loved one) in nature. As a therapeutic process, crisis therapy is best understood as a short term venture (several weeks to several months). Ideally, it will accompany the six-week plus period during which equilibrium following a crisis is restored.

Not only does crisis therapy require more time than psychological first aid, it also requires more skill and training on the part of the helper than psychological first aid does. "Psychotherapist" is perhaps the best general category under which to include psychiatrists, psychologists, social workers, pastorial counselors, psychiatric nurses, school counselors, and others who have had formal training in short-term therapy.

Similarly, psychological first aid and crisis therapy differ from one another by the location of the service. While psychological first aid can be offered almost anywhere (over the telephone, in a bus station, home, hallway, or office), crisis therapy has the same physical space requirements as any other form of counseling or psychotherapy (private room in which a counselor and client or family can talk/work for an hour or more per session).

Finally, crisis therapy is distinguished by its procedures. Building on the work of Lazarus (1976, 1981), *multimodal* crisis therapy examines behavioral, affective, somatic, interpersonal, and cognitive aspects of any client's crisis. The entire therapeutic endeavor is structured around four tasks of crisis resolution (each of which engages one or more of the person subsystems): physical survival, expression of feelings, cognitive mastery, and behavioral/interpersonal adjustments.

The distinction between first- and second-order crisis intervention provides answers to many of the questions raised earlier in this chapter, such as, the difference between crisis intervention by an attorney (psychological first aid) and a counselor at a mental health clinic (both psychological first aid and crisis therapy). Where the model does not yield immediate clarity, it lays the ground-work for research which can do so. We remember, for example, from reviews of crisis intervention research (Auerbach and Kilmann 1977), that few studies offer clear ties between the process of crisis intervention and client outcome. The psychological first aid and multimodal crisis therapy training procedures can be coded for use in process and outcome research. Initial work in this direction is presented in Chapter 18.

IN SUMMARY   The distinction between psychological first aid and crisis therapy as presented in Table 5.1 is both faithful to the recent clinical history of crisis work, and, at the same time, conductive to the growth of much needed research programs in the field. The remainder of Part II will discuss each set of interventions in detail. We will look closely at how to give psychological first aid using the five components approach, and how to conduct crisis therapy using Lazarus's multimodal format. Each approach is also applied to illustrative cases of situational and developmental crises.

chapter six

First-Order Intervention: Psychological First Aid

A woman asks the crisis hotline volunteer if she should try to break down the door at her boyfriend's apartment. She is afraid he might have taken pills in an attempt to commit suicide.

A twelve-year-old boy calls his minister from a phone booth: "Dad beat me up again. I'm afraid to go home."

A bank teller confesses to his supervisor that "marital problems" are the cause of his recent poor performance at work. Five days ago his wife left him. He has been drinking heavily ever since.

A social worker is asked to talk with two young parents in the emergency room of a general hospital. They've just learned that their four-year-old son died after being struck by a car.

Each of the helpers represented in these cases—hot line worker, minister, bank supervisor, and case worker—is faced with the challenge of giving psychological first aid to a person or family in crisis. We recall from the previous chapter that these first-order interventions are short (usually one session), can be provided by a wide range of community helpers, and are most effective early in the crisis.

GOALS

The chief goal of psychological first aid is to re-establish immediate coping. According to Caplan (1964) and other theorists, life crises are characterized by a breakdown of previously adequate problem-solving or coping abilities.

For the person in crisis, the crux of the matter is that he/she simply feels unable to deal with the overwhelming circumstances confronted at that time. The helper's primary aim, then, is to assist the person in taking concrete steps toward coping with the crisis, which includes managing the feelings or subjective components of the situation, and beginning the problem-solving process (R.S. Lazarus 1980).

There are three subgoals of psychological first aid that give direction to helper activity. *Providing support* is the first and rests on the premise that it is better for people not to be alone as they bear extraordinary burdens. By helping people shoulder part of the load, support becomes one of the more humane aspects of crisis intervention. Concretely, it means allowing people to talk to us, extending warmth and concern, and providing an atmosphere in which fear and anger can be expressed. It also means reinforcing strengths for people who are conscious only of their own weakness during the crisis. Providing support is certainly not a new concept. On the contrary, it is one that runs through the history of such fields as medicine, ministry, and other human/social services.

Reducing lethality, the second subgoal of psychological first aid, aims at saving lives and preventing physical injury during crises. It is not uncommon, especially in a society where violence is so much a part of daily life, for some crises to lead to physical harm (child, spouse battering) or even death (suicide, homicide). Policemen and women, for example, are injured more often through attempts to mediate in domestic crises than in any other aspect of their work. A critical subgoal of psychological first aid, then, is to take measures to minimize destructive possibilities and to defuse the situation. This may involve removing weapons, arranging for the sustained contact of a trusted friend for several hours, talking a person through a stressful situation, or in some cases, initiating emergency hospitalization.

Finally, *providing linkage to helping resources*, the third subgoal, ties directly to our definition of life crisis as a time when personal supplies and resources have been exhausted (Miller and Iscoe 1963). Rather than trying to solve the whole problem immediately, the helper pinpoints critical needs and then makes an appropriate referral to some other helping person or agency. Often this referral will be for individual counseling of the short-term (crisis therapy) variety. Other times it will be for legal assistance or help from a social service agency. In any case, the bottom line in psychological first aid is to provide an appropriate linkage so that the person can begin to take concrete steps toward working through the crisis. Referral provides both guidance and relief for the worker. It directs the helping process, and

also puts limits on what is expected of any one person, whether a parent, hotline worker, neighbor, attorney, or employer.

FIVE COMPONENTS OF PSYCHOLOGICAL FIRST AID

We can conceptualize the process of psychological first aid by building on key elements of representative crisis intervention training models (Berg 1970; Knickerbocker and McGee 1972; Lester and Brockopp 1973; Lister 1976). The common element in each of these, though often not fully articulated, is a basic problem-solving model, amended in light of the intense emotions of crisis situations. What emerges is a five-step approach that includes:

making psychological contact,
examining dimensions of the problem,
exploring possible solutions,
assisting in taking concrete action, and
following up to check progress.

Table 6.1 lists the components as well as the helper behavior and objectives involved in each step of the model.

Making Psychological Contact

Some people describe this component as empathy or "tuning in" to a person's feelings during a crisis. Identified most strongly with Carl Roger's (1951) client-centered therapy, empathic listening is a precondition for any helping activity. In the present context, it means listening for both facts and feelings (what happened, as well as how the person feels about it), and using reflective statements so the person knows we have really heard what has been said. In the disorganization and upset of a crisis, often the newness or strangeness of the experience is the most frightening part. The

TABLE 6.1 FIVE COMPONENTS OF PSYCHOLOGICAL FIRST AID

Component	Helper Behavior	Objective
1. Make psychological contact	Invite client to talk; Listen for facts and feelings; Summarize/reflect facts and feelings; Make empathic statements; Communicate concern; Physically touch/hold; Bring "calm control" to an intense situation.	Client to feel heard, understood, accepted, supported. Intensity of emotional distress reduced. Problem-solving capabilities reactivated.

2. Explore dimensions of the problem	Inquire about:
	  Immediate past;
	    Precipitating event;
	    Pre-crisis BASIC functioning (strengths and weaknesses);
	  Present;
	    BASIC functioning now (strengths and weaknesses);
	    Personal (inner) resources;
	    Social (outer) resources;
	    Lethality.
	  Immediate future;
	    Impending decisions—tonight, weekend, next several days/weeks.
		Rank order:
		  (a) Immediate needs; and
		  (b) Later needs.

3. Examine possible solutions	Ask what client has attempted thus far; Explore what client can/could do now; Propose other alternatives: new client behavior; redefinition of the problem; outside (3rd party) assistance; environmental change.	Identify one or more solutions to immediate needs and later needs.
4. Assist in taking concrete action	See below.	Implement immediate solutions intended to meet immediate needs.

Concrete Action: Helper Behavior

If: (a) Lethality is low, and (b) person is capable of acting on own behalf, then	If: (a) Lethality is high *or* (b) person is not capable of acting on own behalf, then

Facilitative Stance
  "We talk";
  "You act"; and
  Contract for action is between helper and client.
	Directive Stance
	  "We talk";
	  "I may act on your behalf"; and
	  Contract for action might include family and other community resources.

Ranges from active listening to giving advice.	Ranges from actively mobilizing resources to controlling the situation.

TABLE 6.1   FIVE COMPONENTS OF PSYCHOLOGICAL FIRST AID *(CONTINUED)*

Component	Helper Behavior	Objective
5. Follow-up	Secure identifying information; Explore possible follow-up procedures; Set up contract for recontract.	Secure feedback of 3 subgoals of psychological first aid: Support received; Lethality reduced; Linkage to resources accomplished. Set next phase in motion: Later solutions; If (a) immediate needs were met by immediate solutions and concrete action taken, *and* if (b) linkage for later needs is made, then *STOP*. If not, go back to Step 2 (Dimensions of Problem) and *CONTINUE*.

helper's first task, then, is to listen for how the client views the situation, and communicate whatever understanding emerges.

Table 6.1 lists the central helper behaviors involved in making psychological contact, for example, inviting the person to talk, listening both for what happened (facts) and the person's reaction to the event (feelings), making reflective statements, and so on. When feelings are obviously present (nonverbal cues), though not yet put into words and thereby legitimized, helpers gently comment on this, "I can sense by the way you talk how *upset* you are about what has happened," or, "It seems that you also are very *angry* about what has happened, and rightly so."

Crow (1977) talks about the feeling or affective concomitants of crisis as usually being anxiety, anger, or depression ("yellow, red, and black" crises, respectively). He describes the helper's task as not only to recognize these feelings but also to respond in a calm and controlled manner, resisting the tendency to become caught up (becoming anxious, angry, or depressed) in the intensity of the client's feelings.

Psychological contact is not always made solely through verbal communications. Some-

times nonverbal physical contact is most effective, for example, touching or holding a person who is very upset. Clinicians and clients report that a gentle touch or an arm around the shoulder can often have an important calming effect in addition to signifying human concern.

There are several objectives for making psychological contact. The first is for the person in crisis to *feel* heard, accepted, understood, and supported, which in turn leads to a reduction of the intensity of the emotions. Psychological contact serves to reduce the pain of being alone during a crisis, but it actually aims for more than this. By recognizing and legitimizing feelings of anger, hurt, fear, etc., and thus reducing emotional intensity, energy may then be redirected toward doing something about the situation. We shall see later how pivotal the contact part of psychological first aid becomes.

Exploring Dimensions of the Problem   The second component of psychological first aid involves assessing the dimensions or parameters of the problem. Inquiry focuses on three areas: immediate past, present, and immediate future. Immediate past refers to events leading up to the crisis state, especially the specific event which triggered or precipitated the crisis (the death of a loved one, unemployment, injury, separation from spouse).

It is also important to determine the person's BASIC functioning prior to the crisis. Without engaging in a systematic inquiry, the helper can listen for the most salient characteristics of the person's behavioral, affective, somatic, interpersonal, and cognitive life prior to the crisis. What were the most apparent strengths, for example, a steady job (behavioral modality)? What were the person's chief weaknesses or deficits, for example, poor self image (cognitive), few friends (interpersonal), and so on. Why did problem solving break down at this particular time? Has anything like this ever happened before? The inquiry here is guided by the premise from crisis theory that for most people the crisis state has a precipitating event (what is it?), and an inability to cope leads to crisis (why can't he/she cope now?).

Inquiry about the present situation involves the "who, what, where, when, how" questions of an investigative reporter. We need to find out who is involved, what happened, when it happened, and so on. This is most often accomplished by simply having the person tell the story. In addition, it is important to listen for the most salient characteristics of the person's BASIC crisis functioning. How does the person feel right now (affective)? What is the impact of the crisis on family life and friendships (interpersonal) and physical health (somatic)? How has his/her daily routine been affected (behavioral)? What is the nature of the person's mental ruminations, including thoughts and fantasies as well as day and night dreams during the crisis (cognitive)? (See Chapter 2 for other relevant variables under each of the five modalities.)

Attention is given to both strengths and weaknesses during the time of crisis. For example, which aspects of the person's life have not been affected by the crisis? What activities or routines (such as physical exercise) are part of the person's lifestyle and might be called into play in working through the difficult situation? Which family members or friends might be available to help? If there is any indication of physical harm (to the client or to someone else), an assessment of lethality is made. Particular attention is given to previous attempts, the nature of the suicide/homicide plan, and willingness to maintain contact with "significant others," each of which is discussed in detail later in this chapter.

Finally, what are the likely future difficulties for the person and his or her family? A runaway teenager needs a place to stay for the night (week) as decisions are made about what to do next. A woman recently separated from her husband might need counsel on how to manage loneliness and on how to talk to her children about the recent events. Depending upon the circumstances, she might also need short-term counseling later on to help her sort through and learn from the breakup. Whatever the case, in this component of psychological first aid, these needs are noted as *dimensions of the problem.*

The main objective of this second aspect of psychological first aid is to work toward a rank ordering of the person's needs within two categories: (1) issues which need to be addressed immediately, and (2) issues which can be postponed until later. In the confusion and disorganization of the crisis state, people often attempt to deal with everything all at once. Many times there is little awareness of what must be dealt with right away and what can wait a few days, weeks, or even months. An important role for the helper, then, is to assist in this sorting-out process. Examples of issues that might need immediate attention would be: finding a place to spend the night, talking a person out of killing himself tonight, or "buying time" in a family dispute so everyone can talk again in a less heated moment. Later needs cover anything that does not need to be taken care of in the next several hours or days, and might include such things as a need for legal assistance, marital counseling, individual crisis therapy, vocational rehabilitation, and the like. Any of these alternatives might be instrumental in the subsequent psychological resolution of the crisis experience.

Many times, of course, there is little time to explore all aspects of the difficulty, and many of these questions are postponed. Also, more often than not, clients volunteer much of the information so that helpers seldom need conduct a rigorous step-by-step inquiry. Whether he/she is a policeman intervening in a domestic quarrel, a hotline worker talking to a suicidal caller, or a minister visiting a grief-stricken parent at a hospital, the effective intervenor has the preceding framework in mind as she/he talks with the person in crisis. Though the helper may not ask directly about each of the categories mentioned above, he/she listens with these categories in mind. As we shall elaborate, the categories provide a cognitive map to help direct the assessment of crisis situations.

Finally, as with the reflective statements of psychological contact, it is noteworthy that simply telling the story in very concrete terms to someone who cares often yields both emotional release and understanding (by the client) of what needs to be done to get through the crisis. The information-gathering aspect of first aid, then, can have an immediate therapeutic benefit for the client, and also assist both helper and client in planning next steps.

Examining Possible Solutions The third component of psychological first aid involves identifying a range of alternative solutions to both the immediate needs and the later needs identified previously. As Table 6.1 indicates, the helper takes a step-by-step approach, asking first about what has been tried already, then getting the person in crisis to generate alternatives, followed by the helper's adding other possibilities. Pluses and minuses (or gains and losses) of each solution are explored. These are then summarized and categorized as appropriate to the immediate and later needs identified earlier.

Following from a basic principle of crisis intervention (see Chapter 5), we get people to do as much as they can for themselves, even if only in generating alternatives about what to do in this particular situation. The premise is that helplessness can be checked by encouraging the client to generate ideas about what to do next, that is, helping the client operate from a position of strength rather than weakness. This can evolve from asking questions about how the client has dealt with previous problems. Only after exploring client suggestions does the counselor join in a brainstorming process to generate other solutions to the problem.

Two other process issues deserve to be mentioned here. The first is the importance of coaching some clients to even consider the idea that possible solutions exist. The counselor may have to structure the discussion with comments like: "Let's just consider what if you were to . . . (talk to her, go home tonight, call child welfare, call your parents, etc.). What might happen?" In such cases, the counselor makes room in the first-aid process for untried, prematurely rejected options, and guides the crisis client in fully considering them. Similarly the client can be asked, "What kind of solutions might someone else try? Think of someone who might know what to do—what would that person's ideas be?" A second issue is the importance of examining obstacles to implementation of a particular plan, for example, nonassertive manner as an obstacle to face-to-face confrontation of spouse, or lack of car as hindrance to keeping an appointment for individual counseling.

Counselors cannot leave such issues to chance. Instead, they think ahead to possible obstacles and make it their responsibility to see that these are addressed *before* an action plan is set in motion.

Table 6.1 states the objective of this component of psychological first aid as identifying one or more solutions to meet both the immediate and the later needs. This is especially true of the former. Some feasible steps must be identified for addressing the most pressing needs. Psychological first aid is not complete until these steps have been identified. Further, in most cases (barring a client so confused as to be unable to participate in the process), there should be agreement between client and counselor on the acceptability of the solutions chosen. If this has not been accomplished, then some "obstacle" has likely gone unexplored, indicating a need to talk further about the parameters of the problem, solutions, and/or a match between the two.

Taking Concrete Action Relating directly to the action and goal orientation of crisis intervention, the fourth component of psychological first aid involves helping the person to take some concrete action to deal with the crisis. The objective is actually very limited, no more than taking the best next step given the situation. According to Table 6.1 this means implementing the agreed upon immediate solution(s) aimed at dealing with the immediate need(s). The action step may be as simple as an agreement to meet again the next day, or as complicated as initiating emergency hospitalization.

It is important to remember that we want the client to do as much as he/she is capable of doing. Only when circumstances severely impair a client's ability to act does a counselor take an active role, and even then this is done in a stepwise fashion.

Depending upon two major factors (lethality and capability of the person in crisis to act on his or her own behalf), the helper takes either a facilitative or directive stance in helping the client deal with the crisis. If the situation is high in lethality (danger to the client, himself, or to someone else), or if the person is not capable of taking care of him/herself (is drunk, or so emotionally distraught as to be incapacitated), then the helper's stance is directive. When there is no danger to self or others, and when a person, though emotionally distraught and disorganized, is still capable of doing such things as driving home, calling a spouse, enduring a long weekend, then the helper's role is more facilitative than directive.

To further clarify these distinctions (Table 6.1) we can think of the facilitative stance as one in which (1) helper and client talk about the situation, but (2) client takes major responsibility for any action. Further, any (3) contract regarding action is a matter involving only the helper and the client. For example, the client and counselor may talk and then agree that it would be good for the client to talk to her husband on the phone before making any major decisions about leaving home or returning home this weekend. She alone, however, would make the phone call, and later report to the counselor how it turned out. The contract involves just the two, counselor and client.

Under a directive stance, however, the approach is somewhat different. Though the (1) talk is again between client and helper, the (2) action part may include helper as well as client. Similarly, the (3) contract for action might involve others, for example, spouse who is not present during the initial session, or another agency (child welfare, police, hospital personnel).

There are other differences between facilitative and directive action stances. As Table 6.1 indicates, facilitative approaches may range from active listening to advice. The former means primarily listening and reflecting back the content of the message through various phases of the discussion. In other cases, the facilitative stance includes advice or the helper advocating a particular course of action, for example, "I am worried about what might happen to you. I really believe you should. . . ."

Many times the advice has as much to do with thoughts as with behavior, as when the helper provides new labels or ways to define the problem. For most people the extreme disorganization and upset characteristic of crisis are both frightening and new. Lacking ways to conceptualize and understand the experience, many crisis clients talk about being afraid of "going crazy," "cracking up," "losing control," as if their feelings are a sign of mental illness.

The therapist then has the opportunity/responsibility to supply labels that are both accurate and facilitative of crisis resolution. In such situations it is not uncommon for an effective therapist to make statements such as: "You might feel like you're going crazy or becoming mentally ill, but I don't believe you are," or, "Given all that has happened, I would be surprised if you didn't feel disorganized, confused, helpless. It seems to me like you are having a rather normal response to abnormal events. You know, I would be worried about you if you weren't reacting so strongly to all of this." The language of the therapist is critical since the way crisis clients conceptualize their pain plays an important role in subsequent adjustment. People who label themselves as mentally ill often impose limits on their later recovery. On the other hand, people who view their upset and disorganization as something temporary and expected of normal people when life's circumstances are severe can unleash creative energy toward getting over the crisis, thereby developing a hopeful view of their own future.

Directive action ranges from actively mobilizing community resources to taking very controlling action (e.g., emergency hospitalization of a suicidal person). In so far as the client is incapable of taking the steps needed to defuse the situation, to buy time, or to accomplish linkage to helping/supportive resources (whether family or agency), the counselor needs to either get someone else involved or do it him/herself, thereby controlling the shortrun outcome. In the latter case, the counselor acts to ensure that the needed next step is taken. An example of this would be removing an abused child from a home or providing for immediate, constant contact for a homicidal/suicidal person when all other avenues have failed. Congruent with our stepwise approach, such action would occur only when all other less restrictive possibilities have been considered or attempted, and when the high stakes indicate that the situation cannot be left as it is. We will give a more detailed explanation of how to assess lethality, as well as guidelines for initiating directive actions later in this chapter. For now, it is important to note that, in crisis stiuations, certain directive/controlling actions are a legitimate set of activities on the continuum of helper behavior.

Needless to say, the directive stance in crisis work raises a number of important ethical and legal issues. Building on our criteria for directive counselor action (high lethality, incapacitation of client), there are several important guidelines:

1. Any counselor action must be done within existing law. It is incumbent upon crisis workers to be aware of the laws in their community that relate directly to their work. For example, in most states, the law requires human service workers (if not ordinary citizens) to report any knowledge of child abuse to the authorities. Similarly, most communities have laws protecting the rights of citizens concerning involuntary emergency hospitalization. The criterion of "danger to self or others" is common to most jurisdictions as grounds for directive/controlling intervention in crisis cases.

2. As suggested earlier, controlling interven-

tions occur only after everything else has been found wanting.

3. In case of emergency hospitalization, every effort should be made to assist both client and family in combating its negative implications, for example, labeling client as mentally ill for having been hospitalized. Whenever possible, language born of adult life crises/transitions should be used. As discussed earlier, the goal is to supply labels which accurately describe what is happening and, at the same time, facilitate subsequent adjustment and growth.

4. Following both legal precedent and common sense, confidentiality in a therapy context needs to be amended to square with other community realities (Bersoff 1976, re: Tarasoff v. Regents of the University of California.). A physical threat to human life (self or other) takes precedence over supreme allegiance to confidentiality in a helping contract.

5. Finally, by conceptualizing all action plans as part of a contract (whether written or not) between the parties involved (client, counselor, family, agency), counselors can lend both clarity and protection to the process. Contracting in a psychological first aid model refers to agreements reached between helper, person in crisis, and any other relevant parties. In extreme cases, the contract for action involves a legal component, for example, when a judge signs an order for emergency hospitalization of a psychotic or dangerously suicidal person. Usually, however, the contract is not a written legal document, but is, instead, verbal and reflects the agreement between the parties involved about what will take place. Minimally, it involves an oral restatement between helper and the person in crisis of who will take what next steps, and for what reason.

Before any directive action is taken, counselors should think through who will do what, toward what end, for how long, with what

risks, and with what safeguards. Every effort should be made for an "above board" quality to characterize these actions; for example, "If you won't let child welfare visit your home, then I feel I must call them myself. This is why . . . ."

Table 6.1 indicates that the "contract for action" in a facilitative stance involves only two people (helper and person in crisis), but that under a directive stance, it may involve third parties. By giving psychological first aid a contractual quality, our intention is for at least one person in the process to assure that appropriate protections are present, and that a framework conductive to feedback and follow up exists.

Following Up The last component of psychological first aid involves eliciting information and setting up a procedure to allow for following-up to check progress. As Table 6.1 indicates, the main helper activity here is to specify a procedure for client and helper to be in contact at a later time. Follow up can occur through a face-to-face meeting, or by telephone. It is important to specify who will call whom, or who will visit whom, as well as the time and place of contact. All of this fits into what might be called a "contract for recontact." Psychological first aid is not complete until such procedures have been agreed upon.

The objective of following up is first and foremost to complete the feedback loop, or to determine whether or not the goals of psychological first aid have been achieved: support provided, lethality reduced, and linkage to resources accomplished. In addition, following up facilitates other steps toward crisis resolution. It allows the helper to operationalize the later solutions described previously (such as referral for subsequent crisis therapy).

In each case, there is a check on whether or not the particular immediate solution was appropriate for the immediate need. If the immediate needs have been met by one of the agreed upon immediate solutions, followed by the concrete action steps, *and* if linkage for the later needs has been accomplished, then the process is complete and the counselor/helper responsibility terminates. If, on the other hand, these conditions have not been met (for example, the agreed upon action did not help the way it was intended) then the helper goes back to Step 2 (exploring dimensions of the problem) and re-examines the situation as it presently stands. The process then continues through possible solutions, concrete action, and follow-up.

RESPONDING TO THREATS OF SUICIDE OR HOMICIDE: ASSESSMENT OF LETHALITY
As the first helping contact with the person in crisis, psychological first aid includes an assessment of whether or not the person is so upset, desperate, or disorganized that suicide or homicide might be the eventual outcome of the crisis. Every year there are over 20,000 people who commit suicide, and at least that many who commit homicide, in the United States (Crime in the United States 1979; Frederick 1977a). Death by firearms constitutes the greatest number of both suicides and homicides. In 1979, for example, 63 percent of all homicides were by firearms, 52 percent of all the victims were acquainted with their assailants, and 43 percent of all murders involved arguments between acquaintances (*Crime in the United States* 1979).

Prediction of whether or not someone will engage in a lethal act has been the subject of considerable investigation, with results that are far less conclusive than most practitioners would desire (Beck, Resnik, and Lettieri 1974; Farberow and Litman 1975; Lester 1974; Shneidman and Farberow 1957; Wekstein 1979). There is concensus in the literature, however, on the following:

1. There are many possible reasons for the occurence of suicidal behavior: cry for help, attempt to manipulate others, result of psychotic episode (delusions, hallucinations), political statement, hopelessness and helplessness in the face of insurmountable life problems, or a reasoned end to emotional or physical suffering.

2. The desire to end one's life is usually imbedded in a network of *ambivalent* feelings. This may take the form of contradictory messages (e.g., taking a lethal dose of sleeping pills, but allowing oneself to be discovered in time to prevent death) or a simple awareness that a person both wants to live and wants to die. The clinical task is to draw out the client's feelings and other life circumstances on both sides as groundwork for contracting to hold off on the decision to kill oneself.

3. Most people are intensely suicidal for only a short period of time, usually a matter of days, and often change their minds about killing themselves; crisis intervention aims at getting people to postpone irreversible decisions until other help can be brought to bear on the situation.

4. Most people who kill themselves or someone else offer some warning or clue to their intentions well before completing the act (Farberow and Litman 1975). •

5. Danger to human life is highest when someone in crisis has both a lethal plan and the means to carry it out.

6. The goal of saving human life supersedes total allegiance to confidentiality. In extreme cases, relatives or local authorities may need to be informed of the client's potentially suicidal behavior in order to prevent the person from killing him/herself.

7. Since life-saving measures involve either an individual's voluntarily agreeing not to commit a lethal act, or an outside person stopping him/her from doing so, maintaining some form of contact with a potentially dangerous person can be a critical ingredient in preventing suicide or homicide.

TABLE 6.2 FACTORS ASSOCIATED WITH SUICIDAL RISK

1. **Age:** The rate for successful suicide increases with age though recent data indicate a marked increase in the suicide rate for young people (teens and early twenties). From 1965 to 1975, the number of suicides in the twenty to twenty-four age range more than doubled from 1400 to 3000 (Frederick 1977a).

2. **Sex:** Though women attempt suicide more often than men, men are more likely to be successful in their attempts, due in part to the use of more lethal means (Farberow and Litman 1975). After age 60, the gap for commiting suicide between men and women narrows.

3. **Race:** The overall rate for whites is three times that among blacks, though among urban blacks (20-35 age range) the rate is twice that for whites of the same age (Hoff 1978). The rate for American Indians increased a marked 36 percent between 1970-1975. The rate for Indians in 1975 was 21.6 per 100,000 population, which is 70 percent higher than for all races, 64 percent higher than whites and 254 percent higher than blacks (Frederick 1977b).

4. **Suicide Plan:** The more specific and concrete the plan for taking one's life, the greater the risk. An individual who has taken steps in preparation for death (changing a will, giving up cherished possessions, writing notes), has chosen a highly lethal method (guns, lethal dosage of pills, etc.), and has the means to carry out the plan (gun in possession, or pills in the medicine cabinet) is a much higher suicidal risk than an individual for whom suicide is still primarily a thought or fantasy (Farberow and Litman 1975).

5. **History of Previous Attempts:** The number of suicide attempts far outweigh the number of completed suicides in the United States, about 10 to 1 in adults, and 50 to 1 in adolescents (Hoff 1978). Suicidal risk increases as the number of attempts increases since individuals often choose more lethal means with subsequent attempts (guns, as opposed to taking pills or breathing gas with the chance of subsequent discovery). Increased risk is also associated with the increased possibility of dying by accident during a suicidal attempt.

6. **Social Supports and Resources:** Suicidal risk increases as social isolation increases—living alone or withdrawing from social contacts.

7. **Recent Loss:** Common precipitating events—losses—for suicide include death of a loved one; divorce or separation; loss of health through illness, accident or surgery; loss of job; or loss of self-esteem through threat of criminal prosecution (Farberow and Litman 1975).

8. **Emotional Symptoms:** The most common suicidal symptoms are related to depression (apathy and despondency, loss of appetite, weight loss, inability to sleep at night, loss of interest in social activities, and general physical and emotional exhaustion) (Farberow and Litman 1975). Suicidal behavior may also be the result of psychotic states, for example, a patient acting on delusions, hallucinations, or other disorientation in time and place.

9. **Medical Problems:** The diagnosis of debilitating illness can affect both life style and self-image (breast cancer, loss of limb, heart disease), thereby heightening the risk of suicide. Physicians and other health care practitioners also see patients who present relatively minor physical complaints which actually mask depression or other psychological distress. If they do not inquire about life circumstances surrounding the physical complaint, health care practitioners may miss clues to possible suicidal ideation.

10. **Alcohol and Other Drugs:** Drinking increases suicidal risks since it increases impulsive behavior and reduces the number of pills necessary to make a dose lethal (Hoff 1978).

SIX-YEAR-OLD BOY SLAIN AT HOSPITAL*

SPRINGFIELD, Mass (AP)—Rose Lombardi tried desperately to rescue her 6-year-old son when she saw a man swing a thin-bladed boning knife at him. But when it was over, little Anthony Lombardi was dead and Mrs. Lombardi and four other people were wounded in a bloody hospital stabbing spree.

William B. Robinson, a former ice cream factory employee, was charged with murder and eight counts of assault with a dangerous weapon and was hospitalized under police guard after the Monday accident.

His sister said the rampage came one day after Robinson, 42, visited the same hospital, seeking admission and warning he might kill.

"If they had put him in the hospital, this never would have happened." said Edna Hooks. "These people wouldn't have been hurt. He was threatening to kill everybody that got in his way."

According to security guards at the Springfield Hospital Unit of Bay State Medical Center, the man walked into the emergency room about 10 a.m., grabbed a woman and began stabbing her. Guard Harold Ferrier, 62, radioed for help before he was stabbed in the back.

Bishop [sic] heard the call "Somebody's been stabbing everybody over here!" and came running. He said he found the man outside on the ambulance dock, crouched over, with young Lombardi in his arms.

When Bishop told him to drop the knife, the man put down the child and lunged forward. "I'm the King, I'm the King!" he shouted. "I did it. What are you going to do now?"

Mrs. Lombardi, 30, of Agawam, was hospitalized in stable condition with stab wounds received when she tried to save her child. Police said she and her son had gone to the hospital to pick up a patient.

Besides Ferrier and Mrs. Lombardi, three women patients were treated for knife wounds.

Police said the violence began an hour earlier at Robinson's house.

Lt. John Coville said Robinson burst into a bathroom and threw a caustic drain cleaning chemical at his wife, Norma, burning her and his 5-year-old granddaughter, Shanndolyn Reynolds. He then stabbed his wife, police said, and headed toward the hospital.

Mrs. Robinson was in fair condition and Miss Reynolds in good condition at Baystate's Wesson unit.

Robinson, who received first and second-degree burns on his arms and chest from the chemical, was in fair condition at the same hospital.

Source: "Six-year-old boy slain at hospital" in *The Columbia Record*, June 24, 1980, United Press International. Reprinted by permission.

---

8. With stakes as high as life and death, it is especially important that helpers be: (a) aware of their own feelings and attitudes about death and the act of suicide; (b) ready to consult with colleagues or supervisors about the appropriateness of any directive steps taken; (c) prepared to deal with "failure," that is, the completed suicide of a client. Regarding the latter, opportunities for guilt following the completed suicide of a friend, relative, co-worker, or client are much greater than with the "failure" of other attempts to provide help. It is very important that workers develop a network of supportive colleagues for shared decision making during crisis intervention, and for working through the intense feelings generated by suicide intervention work.

Assessment of lethality in psychological first aid involves first listening for clues to

---

MOTHER APPARENTLY "CHICKENED OUT"*

Mount Clemens, Mich. (UPI) A Detroit-area divorcee held in the slaying of her three children left behind a will and apparently planned to kill herself, too, but "chickened out," detectives said Saturday.

Patricia Dueweke faced three counts of first-degree murder in the shootings of her daughter, Cynthia, 16, and sons Mark, 15, and Karl, who would have been 13 Friday. She was held without bond in the Macomb County Jail.

Police speculated that Mrs. Dueweke waited for the children to return home from school Thursday, shooting them one-by-one with a six-shot, .357-magnum pistol she had purchased about a week after her August 23 divorce.

It appeared that the woman sat up all night with the bodies, then telephoned her husband, Ralph, Friday morning to tell him of the shootings. Dueweke was at the home when police arrived.

"She had planned on killing herself but she chickened out," said Lt. Lloyd Rivard, chief of detectives at the Macomb County Sheriff's Department. "She couldn't do it."

Police arriving at the home found the woman "wrote a will leaving everything to her husband. She specified her choice of a funeral home," Detective Sgt. Gail Caudle said.

Police said they found 24 spent bullet casings in the home, some of them in the basement, where Mrs. Dueweke apparently had set up a target to practice with the pistol.

One friend said Mrs. Dueweke, 42, had been despondent over her divorce and the prospect of raising the children alone.

"She was unsure about her future because she had no job training," said Roger Gill, a next-door neighbor and long-time friend of the woman and her ex-husband, a school social worker.

Neighbors said the Duewekes were active in school affairs and led a quiet life prior to the divorce. They enjoyed camping and often were seen canoeing on the Clinton River, which ran near their home.

"She was just a super good neighbor," Caudle said. "She was a timid individual who kept everything to herself and never created any problems for anybody."

Source: "Mother Apparently 'Chickened Out'" in *The Columbia Record*, September 23, 1979, United Press International. Reprinted by permission.

---

physical danger, and then conducting a structured inquiry to gather information as a basis for implementing an appropriate action plan. Clues to either suicide or homicide can take several forms:

Verbal

"I sometimes feel like I can't go on/could kill her/want to end it all/wish I were dead/would like to hurt people/will do something rash, etc."

"If it happens again, I'll kill him," or a victim's recalling that "he was so mad he tried to kill me." (Any statement that in- dicates directly or obliquely that someone could be physically hurt as a part of this crisis.)

Also, any reference to previous attempts at suicide/homicide: "I tried that once before," or reference to previous fights between individuals, or, reports that with more precision, previous injuries might have resulted in death.

Nonverbal

For suicide, increased listlessness, arrangement of affairs and preparation for death (e.g., giving away cherished possessions), abnormal sleep patterns (too much or too little), depressed mood, sudden lifting of depression (as if decision has been made). For homicide, the occurrence of a fight in the bedroom or kitchen, or baiting of the aggressor by the victim with belittling remarks.

Concern of Other People

Report of sudden changes in behavior, or even a gut feeling that a person might hurt him/herself. Regarding homicide, the reputation of the aggressor for his/her impulsiveness or bad temper.

On noting such threatening signs, the helper should look for an opportunity to make a straightforward inquiry to clarify their meaning (Farberow and Litman 1975). The idea that practitioners should be careful lest they give clients ideas that had not been thought of is a common myth of workers new to crisis work. It is far more likely that the person in crisis will experience a sense of relief that someone has heard the distress and cares enough to ask about the situation.

A useful tactic to begin the inquiry is to phrase questions using the individual's own words. For example, "You said that you feel like you can't go on anymore. Tell me what you mean by that." If the forthcoming answers remain vague, the helper should be direct: "Are you thinking of hurting yourself or committing suicide?" The aim of the question is to find out the person's intent and what he/she wants to happen by the fantasy or gesture. Again, this is best determined by direct questions such as: "What do you want to happen?" or, "What would you hope to accomplish by that?" These are not questions offered with a critical or judgmental attitude or with a view to condemn the act or feeling. They are, instead, simple requests for information. Possible answers might be: "To stop the pain, to show him/her how badly I feel; to pay her back for what she did; to die,"

and so on. The information generated by this line of inquiry can be useful later in negotiating for possible alternative means to achieve the same ends. Our assumption here is that suicide or homicide has been chosen as one possible solution to a particular problem. Inquiry in the early stages aims at recognizing the suicidal/homicidal threat or gesture and finding out the problem it was/is intended to solve.

Assessment of dangerousness, whether on a telephone hotline, in a physician's examining room, or in a guidance counselor's office, must include three key variables: plan, history of previous attempts, and willingness to make use of outside helpers should suicide or homicide seem imminent.

1. Plan

How far has the person proceeded in thinking about commiting suicide or hurting someone? If a man is depressed over losing his job and has thought of suicide, but does not know how he will do it, he is less of a risk than if he has indeed gone so far as to plan his death. Further, if he has the means to carry out the plan, he is a greater risk. An individual who has not thought of a plan, or who has thought of a plan to take pills but does not have any on hand at the time, is at less risk. A person who thinks he might shoot himself, and has a gun and ammunition with him at all times, is at high risk.

2. Previous Attempts

A person who has never attempted to commit suicide is a lower risk than one who has attempted to do so previously. The probability of success increases with each attempt. Even though an attempt may be a cry for help or a manipulation, there is the possibility that an individual will die by accident (e.g., taking a higher dose of pills than intended). For each previous attempt, it is important to inquire about what the person's intention was in taking pills, breathing gas, or whatever, *and* what the outcome of the attempt was. The helper should be alert for the difference between taking a dose of pills that the person knew would not be lethal, and being discovered by a spouse returning from work at the *usual* time, as opposed to a truly accidental discovery when the dosage was known by the person in crisis to be lethal. Ask what the person wanted to happen when the previous attempt was made. For homicide threats, the inquiry focuses on previous fantasies and their outcomes, and on previous aggressive behavior and its result. As with suicide attempts, it is important to inquire about what precipitated the action.

3. Willingness To Make Use of Outside Resources

Individuals who live alone and have no family or friends are greater risks than those who have others to whom they can turn. It is particularly important to differentiate between the availability of others and the individual's willingness to reach out to them in a time of real need. To an outsider, the person may appear to have many friends to whom he/she can turn. Indeed, friends may tell the person to "call on me if you need me." It is important, however, to ask the person in crisis if he/she *will* call on these others in time of need. Some people are too depressed to ask for help. Others can give no assurance that they will be able to control their behavior. They need to be treated differently than those who promise to call when the going gets very rough, or if circumstances change in some way. Individuals afraid of their homicidal fantasies may admit that they will not be able to call for help in time, or that they would rather kill than be stopped.

Inquiry in these three areas captures the most critical variables in determining how dangerous a person is and how directive the

helper should be. Lethality is judged to be low if the answers to plan, previous attempts, and isolation are negative. For example, the risk of suicide is low if an individual has been depressed and contemplating suicide, although there is neither a plan nor means to implement one, and there have been no previous attempts. The lethality is lessened further if the individual will maintain contact with outside resources should things take a turn for the worse. According to our psychological first aid model, the helper takes a *facilitative* stance in these cases. On the other hand, dangerousness increases with an affirmative answer to one or more of the three main categories of plan, previous attempt, and isolation. In these cases, the helper takes a *directive* stance with respect to the person and his/her crisis.

Action Steps

If lethality is judged to be low as a result of the previous inquiry, then the helper's approach is to assist by talking through the problem, offering emotional support, and suggesting further outside help, such as referral for counseling. The approach is to draw out the ambivalent feelings of the person in crisis and to explore alternatives for both immediate and later needs. It is especially important to set up an agreement specifying that the person will recontact the helper should there be a change in the situation, such as increased depression and hopelessness leading to further, more concrete suicidal thoughts. The helper should make him/herself available by telephone, or negotiate an agreement that if needed the individual will make use of close friends, family, or other resources in the next several days.

When lethality is high, the helper takes a more directive stance. In each case, a stepwise approach is followed, beginning with the least directive and intrusive avenue possible. An attempt can be made to contract for the following: for the client to not commit suicide in the next several days, to get rid of the lethal means for the time being (guns, pills), to not stay alone over the weekend, and/or to promise to call the helper if things become worse. The aim is to buy time, to postpone irreversible and final decisions, and to take whatever steps are necessary to separate distraught crisis clients from lethal means to take human life. Agreement to such a contract can be facilitated by drawing on the ambivalent feelings which may have emerged in the discussion, such as "I want to die, but I love my children and don't want to hurt them." In such a case a contract for postponing the decision of suicide for the next several days might rest squarely on love for the children and not wanting to hurt them. Whatever tactic is chosen, the objective is to secure cooperation in not commiting suicide for an agreed upon period of time.

If the person cannot or will not make these assurances, then other people (possibly family members, roommate, or, in the case of homicide, potential victim and police) may need to be informed of the dangerousness of the situation. Though the approach depends on the particular obstacle (unwillingness to give up weapon, or inability to promise to call if needed), the assumption is that, when the individual cannot promise to take precautions against suicide or homicide, others in the immediate social milieu must be involved.

In most cases, this can be done with the individual's permission: for example, "I am concerned enough about you right now, Jane, that I think you shouldn't be alone tonight. I think your husband needs to know how bad things are. You could call him or, if you prefer, I will." If such contact or protective observation in the natural environment is not possible, either because no one is available or the individual refuses to include anyone else at that time, then voluntary hospitalization might be needed. Many suicidal people

are quite amenable to a "time away from all of this" to rest, recuperate, and not have to deal with everything. Others will resist the idea because of the negative implications associated with hospitalization. Whatever the situation, the approach (as outlined previously under the five components of psychological first aid) is to deal openly and directly with each of these potential obstacles.

In extreme cases, when lethality is very high (lethal plan, previous attempts, isolation), and cooperation in the service of self-protection is not forthcoming (due to the individual's resistance, psychotic state, or debilitation due to drugs or alcohol), involuntary hospitalization is necessary. When this occurs, it is important that hospitalization takes place according to local law and that family members are helped to deal with the negative implications associated with hospitalization to occur (Armstrong 1980); this can be assessed by following the procedures outlined previously. Following the case of Tarasoff v. Regents of the University of California (Bersoff 1976), helpers also have the responsibility of informing potential homicide victims of imminent danger (See Blocked Insert.)

Extremely dangerous situations are still the exception rather than the rule in crisis work, though they present themselves often enough that practitioners need to be prepared to deal with them. While the research literature does not provide us with hard and fast guidelines to predict all suicides or homicides, we do know the steps that need to be taken to reduce the probability of a lethal outcome. Lethality is reduced if lethal means to complete a violent act are removed; an individual makes a commitment to postpone a lethal act; and/or the dangerous individual is under constant observation. The foregoing procedures are aimed at taking steps to meet at least one of these conditions.

TARASOFF v. REGENTS OF THE UNIVERSITY OF CALIFORNIA
During the course of voluntary outpatient psychotherapy conducted at a university hospital clinic, a client informed his therapist that he was going to murder a young woman when she returned from a summer vacation (Cohen 1978). The woman went unnamed but was readily identifiable by the therapist when the client concluded his visit. The therapist conferred with two other clinicians who decided that the client should be commited to a mental hospital for observation. The psychologist telephoned the campus police (followed by a formal letter) requesting their help in committing the young man. Subsequently, three officers took the client into custody, but, satisfied that he was rational, released him on his promise to stay away from the woman. With the knowledge of the campus policemen's action, the psychologist's superior had the police return the therapist's letter and directed that all copies of it and the therapy notes be destroyed. He ordered no further action with regard to commitment. Two months later, the ex-client carried out his threat and killed the woman.

Parents of the victim filed suit in California State Court against the school's governing body, the therapist, his supervisors, and the campus police. Though the complaint was at first dismissed by the trial judge, the action was later reversed by the Supreme Court of California. The Court ruled that when a psychotherapist determines that threats made by a patient during therapy are neither idle nor remote, public policy dictates that the value of the disclosure of the threat to a third party outweighs the benefits of preserving the confidentiality of the communication. The Tarasoff case set a precedent which has been followed by other Courts, prompting discussions by therapists and lawyers on the practical implications for clinical work (Bersoff 1976). L. Wilson (1981), writing as general counsel to the New Jersey Psychological Association, offers the following general guidelines for practitioners in light of the Tarasoff ruling:

1. Your principal duty is to your patient, not to the relationship between you and not to your ability to help him.

2. Resistance to action, if born of a desire to protect the therapeutic relationship, or of a fear of being wrong, is misplaced. Consider the object of your patient's threats as if he were closely related to you, your child or your spouse.

3. Seek the opinion of colleagues (an appropriate course in any difficult case) and preserve the substance of your conversation in private notes. . . .

4. Don't hesitate to attempt to dissuade a patient from his threatened violence but don't try to play hero. Security personnel are well-trained—and well paid to take personal risk to protect people and property.

5. Don't hesitate to warn a victim or his family solely for fear of legal reprisal by your patient. If you have seen enough to conclude a genuine threat to that person's life or property exists, and you have the means to prevent it, the law says you have a duty regardless of your obligation of confidentiality.

6. It would be well, in every case, to discuss the nature and extent of confidentiality with your patient. While such an agreement is a subject for another occasion, in this context it is appropriate to assure your patient you must act in his best interest, even to the point of preventing him from committing a crime. . . .

7. If you feel justified in repeating a patient's threat to protect a victim, tell the patient what you are doing and why. And then do it. And, unless there are unusual circumstances present, be prepared to move to hospitalize the patient or otherwise have him restrained. (Wilson 1981, p. 37)

PRACTICAL   Several considerations
CONSIDERATIONS   are important in apply-
                      ing the five compo-
nents of psychological first aid to crisis
situations.

1. It is helpful to use the five components as
    a conceptual framework or "cognitive
    map" for guiding helper behavior (state-
    ments, questions, actions). The steps need
    not, however, take place one after the other
    in sequential fashion. This would be artifi-
    cial since many times the process *begins*
    with talk of solutions, then later moves to
    definition of the problem, then back to
    solutions, and so forth. Also, one helper
    statement can actually serve goals under
    more than one component. For example,
    an empathic (contact) statement may also
    serve to further explore parameters of the
    problem. Also, a line of inquiry on dimen-
    sions of the problem may quite readily
    generate possible solutions.

    Instead of sequential steps, then, the
    components are best used as a cognitive
    map or guide for helper statements.
    Helpers should ask themselves through-
    out: What sort of contact have I achieved
    with this person? How well have I explored
    the dimensions of the problem? Are pos-
    sible solutions matched to rank-ordered
    needs? What concrete action needs to be
    taken? Who will take it? Am I clear about
    following up?

    Such an inquiry reminds helpers that they
    have responsibilities under each heading.
    Our assumption is that, in so far as one
    component of psychological first aid is
    neglected, the intervention is incomplete.
    It is not enough, for example, to simply
    offer empathic understanding to an emo-
    tionally distraught client. However, by
    thinking of the five components as a cog-
    nitive map or guidebook, the worker can
    monitor his/her activities at any moment
    during the intervention process. On termi-

nation of the contact, he/she can go through
a mental check to see if any part has been
left out and now needs attention.

2. Another use of the five components is to
    assist helpers when the intervention seems
    to be going poorly. Just as this framework
    can help a worker decide what to do next,
    it is also useful in diagnosing difficulties in
    the helping process. For example, a client
    may resist any discussion of concrete ac-
    tions to address the crisis. The client may
    either give a number of "yes, but's" or
    talk about how nothing suggested will
    work. This is often an indication that
    either the worker needs to spend more
    time exploring dimensions of the problem
    or to simply give more attention to making
    good contact with the client. Many times
    when clients feel that they are not being
    heard or understood in the midst of an
    emotionally distressing situation, they will
    resist overtures to solve the problem. When
    things are not going well in the helping
    process, workers may need to backtrack.
    The first aid framework gives clues on
    areas within which to take temporary re-
    treat until the process becomes unstuck.

3. Although each of the components has been
    discussed in considerable detail, the goals
    of psychological first aid are limited. The
    entire process is only a *first step* toward
    crisis resolution. In evaluating their per-
    formance, workers should have the sub-
    goals in mind: providing support, reducing
    lethality, linking to further resources. Also,
    as a brief (several minutes to several hours)
    first step, helpers might move very quickly
    through various components, spending
    more time on one or the other depending
    upon the circumstances. One sentence (or
    a glance) might serve to establish psycho-
    logical contact between people who al-
    ready know one another, with most of the
    time being devoted to generating viable

DO'S AND DON'TS OF PSYCHOLOGICAL FIRST AID

	Do	Don't
1. Contact	Listen carefully. Reflect feelings and facts. Communicate acceptance.	Tell your "own story" yet. Ignore either facts or feelings. Judge or take sides.
2. Dimensions of problem	Ask open ended questions. Ask person to be concrete. Assess lethality.	Rely on yes/no questions. Allow continued abstractions. Ignore "danger" signs.
3. Possible solutions	Encourage brainstorming. Deal directly with blocks. Set priorities.	Allow tunnel vision. Leave obstacles unexplored. Tolerate a jumble of needs.
4. Concrete action	Take one step at a time. Set specific short-term goals. Confront when necessary. Be directive, if and only if you must.	Attempt to solve it all now. Make binding long-term decisions. Be timid. Retreat from taking responsibility when necessary.
5. Follow-up	Make a contract for re-contact. Evaluate actions steps.	Leave details up in the air, or assume that client will follow through on plan on his/her own. Leave evaluation to someone else.

solutions. In other cases, just the opposite may be true—considerable energy may be devoted toward reaching someone who has cut off contact with friends and potential allies. In sum, helpers work within all five components, while the time and energy spent on any one component will vary with the circumstances; moreover, all this takes place with a view to the limited and important goal of reestablishing coping.

4. The first aid format of this chapter can be used as a guide for the supervision process in human service agencies. It provides a framework within which to critique a worker's/student's performance. For example, "How well did you make contact with this person? Were you able to identify both immediate and later solutions appropriate to the identified immediate and later needs? At the end of the conversation, were both of you clear on what the best next step would be? Was lethality assessed? Were follow-up procedures specified?" A supervisor using the five components to examine a student's work both monitors performance with the immediate case, and at the same time teaches a model which the student can use later for self-critique.

5. Finally, the psychological first aid model can be used in research to code the process of first order crisis intervention in process/outcome studies. In Chapter 5, we noted a major criticism of existing research on crisis intervention, namely, that too often

the process variables are poorly specified (either too vague and broad) or, even when specific, are incomplete. Chapter 18 indicates directions for use of this system in outcome research.

IN SUMMARY   In this chapter, we have identified strategies or components of psychological first aid, and specified the helper behavior and objectives involved in each. For the process to more fully come alive we need to see it in action,

to witness application of the five components in case examples. Chapter 7 serves this function by examining applications of psychological first aid in representative situational and developmental crises, and further pinpointing the critical helper choice points in each. Chapters 8 and 9 will complete our comprehensive crisis intervention model by examining what happens after psychological first aid has been applied: the use of multimodal crisis therapy (second-order crisis intervention) to take the next important steps toward facilitating crisis resolution.

chapter seven

Psychological First Aid: Case Examples

In this chapter, two cases are presented which illustrate the use of the five components of psychological first aid. These early interventions are aimed at helping the person in crisis to take the first important steps necessary to re-establish coping. The marginal headings and the comments section at the end of each case relate the case material to the model presented in Chapter 6.

PSYCHOLOGICAL FIRST AID DURING A MARITAL CRISIS

Bob wondered about the knock at the door. Who would be out at this time—11:30 P.M.—on a cold December night? Having just finished a busy day in his law practice (interviews with clients, four hours in court, three hours in meetings with staff and other attorneys), he was ready to turn in for the night.

He opened the door to find one of his law clerks, Tom, asking if he could come in to talk. As they walked toward the living room, Tom began: "I'm sorry to barge in on you like this, but I've got trouble. It looks like Sue and I are going to **PRECIPITATING** get a divorce." Choking back tears, he spoke rapidly about what had happened **EVENT** earlier that evening. Tom's wife, Sue, had said she "wanted to tell him something." After a little coaxing she confessed that for the last four months she had been having an affair with a man who was a good friend of Tom's. Not believing his ears, Tom reacted at first with a shocked/dazed look, and then with a series of questions, some of which Sue couldn't or wouldn't answer. Struggling to keep feelings of hurt from becoming too apparent, Tom finally broke off the conversation and said he was leaving. He then grabbed his jacket, walked quickly out of the apartment, and drove away. After driving around for about 30 minutes, Tom turned up on Bob's door step.

Tom's first words came out in a torrent, and to hear him tell it, everything, including his marriage, was over. Barely stopping to sip the tea Bob had offered him, he told of loving his wife, not wanting to lose her, but feeling that it was inevitable that he would. After all, she was supposedly "in love" with this other man.

Tom and Sue had been married just over three years. They had moved to this community two years ago so Tom could attend law school. Sue had been the primary bread winner with her job as a high school math teacher. They had dated each other for about four years in college prior to being married at graduation. They grew up in the same small rural southern community, and attended the state university for their undergraduate degrees. Though each had dated other people in high school, neither had any "serious" romantic involvements prior to marriage. Both came from devout Roman Catholic backgrounds, though neither had attended church regularly for the past year or so. For the most part, the marriage had undergone few stresses and strains up to this point. Since they knew each other quite well before marriage, they had many things in common, e.g., interest in music, jogging, etc., and felt comfortable with one another. The main concern over the past year for Tom had been Sue's unexpected flirtatiousness with other men at parties. At first it didn't bother him, though as it became more obvious, it led to frequent quarrels after social events. At no point, however, had he any concern that Sue might go any further than talk.

PSYCHOLOGICAL CONTACT

Bob's reaction to all of this was to listen sympathetically, interrupting every now and then to paraphrase, or play back what he was hearing.

"I can see how upsetting all of this is for you."

"So you're feeling that Sue has really betrayed you by this."

"You also seem to feel that now that she had this affair, you will never be able to stay together."

Bob listened to what Tom was saying and used Tom's own words whenever possible in reflecting back *what had happened* and *how Tom felt* about it. In this particular crisis, Tom felt tremendous emotional pain which he experienced as hurt, almost as if he was wounded. He felt Sue had betrayed him. He was very upset over the fact that she had "lied to him." He also seemed to be turning much of this crisis back on himself, suggesting that he was "no good" since he had been rejected for another man. He saw the whole matter as a reflection on his manhood.

Bob encouraged Tom to talk concretely about how things had been going prior to this "news." Tom reported that he thought their relationship had been a good one. To be sure, Sue's flirtations had bothered him some. Moreover the two had sometimes thought that they might have married too young, allowing for little experience with other people before getting married. Nevertheless the affair was a complete surprise to Tom.

Tom made few distinctions between what happened in the past, his current situation (that very evening), and the future (beginning with tomorrow, and extending into the next several months and years). As a matter of fact, he was collapsing all of these categories together, and talking painfully of how his whole world was coming down on him right now. In this case, his "whole world" referred to his marriage, his self-image, his career ("I'll never be able to study for the exam I have in two days, and I might fail it"), and the rest of his life (talking surely as if he could never trust another woman again). His self-statements were critical:

"What's wrong with me? Why wasn't I good enough for her?"

"It's all my fault!"

Bob continued to listen, offering empathic and understanding responses, all in an attempt to offer support and hopefully thereby ease some of the emotional stress of that evening.

IMMEDIATE   After about 30 minutes of this kind of talk, Bob directed the conversation
PROBLEMS toward the difficulties which confronted Tom immediately:
Where to spend the night—to go home or not;
What to say to Sue the next time he saw her—if not tonight, then tomorrow;
What to do about the exam he needed to take on Friday—two days away— how
to prepare for it when he was so emotionally upset.

ISSUES TO   Other matters would certainly need to be dealt with at some time, but were out
ADDRESS of reach that night. Tom would need to talk to Sue to find out about what the
LATER affair actually meant to her. What were the implications for their relationship?
Was divorce really the only option? Might they not work through this crisis, learn
from it, make adjustments in their marriage because of it, and stay together after
all?

EMPHASIS ON   Bob's approach was to say straight out to Tom: "Let's see what you need to
IMMEDIATE deal with right now, tonight, and what can wait until morning."
CONCERNS   Bob then confronted Tom with the idea that although divorce was certainly a
possibility, it was not something he needed to decide on that night. Bob then
asked Tom what he would like to do about the most immediate needs that had
been identified, i.e., where to stay, how to deal with Sue, and the pending exam.

POSSIBLE Bob's aim was to get Tom to generate as many acceptable solutions as possible,
SOLUTIONS and, if these were found wanting, for Bob to offer some of his own. In his distraught state, Tom had not separated the issues in this way. He also had no solutions to any of these difficulties. He thought he might simply "drive around"
and then sleep in the car. He was afraid to confront Sue, not knowing what to say
to her, and afraid that he would break down and cry in her presence, giving her
yet another reflection against his manhood. The exam increased his panic further.
It was a major exam in constitutional law, given on one day only, with very little
chance of make-up. Besides, if he were to ask for a make-up he would have to admit to his marital difficulties to a very stern professor.

FOCUS   Bob continued to work toward boiling the problems down into smaller pieces,
examining possible avenues for each. He said to Tom that the whole problem
could not be solved right then, so they would need to take the pieces that needed
the most attention and deal with them first. The issue of where to spend the night
was the easiest to deal with. Bob assertively told Tom that driving around would
not be a good idea and that he should stay there that night, sleeping on the couch.
After a little resistance, Tom accepted this idea.
Dealing with Sue presented a different problem. Since Tom's chief concern
seemed to be that he would not know what to say to her, and that he might break
ADVICE down, Bob took it upon himself to offer a few ideas of his own at this point. He
said, first of all, that breaking down was a rather human reaction to this crisis, and
that Tom should be careful about passing judgment on his manhood based on
something like this. In a friendly joking manner, he criticized Tom for assuming
he had to take a "John Wayne" approach to this, i.e., show no emotion for fear it
would be a sign of weakness. Bob suggested that both Tom and Sue see a marriage
counselor soon, even tomorrow, and talk in the presence of a third party.

CONFRONTING   As they discussed options such as the student counseling center on campus, the
OBSTACLES mere mention of a counselor raised other problems for Tom. Would it be confidential? Would seeing a "shrink" be on his record, possibly something he might

have to mention in his application for the state bar? The application had recently come in the mail. Tom had noted that there was a question something like: "Have you ever been treated for a nervous or mental disorder"? Tom certainly felt that at the time he was having a nervous and mental disorder, like he was "cracking up." He didn't want to have to tell anybody about it, surely not the state bar. Bob and Tom talked this one over for several minutes, moving toward an agreement that: this would be marriage counseling, and not something that he would need to list on his bar application. No one was having his/her head "shrunk" by a psychiatrist or anyone else. This would be short-term counseling for working through a crisis. Bob was sure that the records at the student counseling center were confidential. In any case, a decision did not need to be made right then; it would wait until morning. Tom could call the counseling center and ask these questions before setting up an appointment.

They talked over the upcoming exam as well. Tom's chief concern was that he couldn't concentrate enough to study. Again, Bob reminded him that he surely would not be able to concentrate tonight, and that he shouldn't try to study. If he needed to ask for an extension, he should do that. He would not have to tell the professor all of the circumstances. Again, he could see how he felt in the morning. Though he surely didn't feel like studying, he might well be able to put in a couple of hours tomorrow in the afternoon.

The conversation proceeded with Bob helping Tom work toward acceptable solutions to each of the immediate concerns. At times, Tom would try to inject issues about what happened in the past, or about the future (e.g., "I wonder how many times she slept with him," "How long does it take to get a divorce?"). When this happened, Bob recognized that this was a concern (e.g., "I know you must wonder about that"), but reminded Tom that he had time to find out about these things. Surely nothing could or needed to be decided on right now. The strategy was to articulate that these were concerns but that they didn't need to be dealt with now. When they talked again, they would see when, how, and whether these concerns would be addressed.

CONTRACT FOR ACTION After an hour-and-a-half talk, Bob convinced Tom that it was time to get some rest. They had agreed that Tom would sleep there that evening and call Sue in the morning to ask if she would consent to their talking with a marriage counselor that afternoon. Next they had agreed that Tom would call the student counseling center to ask for an appointment, and at the same time ask questions about confidentiality. Finally, Tom would put the whole exam question on a shelf until later in the afternoon, after classes, at which time he would try to put in one or two hours of studying. He would call Bob later that afternoon to let him know how things worked out.

FOLLOW UP

Almost as an afterthought for both of them, they realized that Sue might wonder where Tom was, and whether he would be coming home. Though Tom was reluctant to talk to her right then, he agreed to call and tell her, at least, that he had come over to Bob's for a talk, that he would stay there that evening, and would call her in the morning. Tom made the brief call, and Bob gave him a blanket and pillow for sleeping on the couch. The two then retired for the evening.

Comment

This case demonstrates how a helper can take a facilitative stance (Chapter 6) during the early stages of crisis. We can highlight the more salient features of the help given by discussing them according to the five components of psychological first aid.

Psychological Contact

Bob's main tactic was to listen, and to reflect back what he was hearing about Tom's crisis: facts (what happened) and feelings (how Tom was reacting to it all). Bob avoided the cardinal error of taking sides in the marital dispute: he was careful not to volunteer his own judgment of Sue. Any judgments he had to offer were about how Tom might cope with his most pressing concerns that very night.

Dimensions of the Problem

Tom presented Bob with classic crisis behavior: disorganization, confusion, and worrying over everything all at once. Tom's crisis can be understood from a cognitive viewpoint (Taplin 1971): the affair violated Tom's expectations about marriage and conditions for its survival, that is, fidelity. His panic grew, in part, from his "catastrophizing" ("this one affair means all we had in the past and might have had together in the future is lost") and over interpreting ("her sleeping with this man must be a reflection on me and my inadequacies"). How this crisis event interacts with Tom's values, expectancies, self-image, and the like will need to be addressed in some way or another as Tom works through the crisis. Should he begin short-term crisis therapy, this interaction will be at the heart of the working through process (see Chapter 8).

The meaning of the affair to each spouse will need to be explored. It may be possible to examine this as a developmental issue in Tom and Sue's marriage, discussion of which might lead to a re-examination of a whole range of issues. As a result, everything from sex life to the way they talk to one another, express affection, or divide household chores may be addressed. During psychological first aid, however, these factors are given scant attention. Skilled therapists who offer psychological first aid might pick up on these cues for use in subsequent sessions. As a friend offering help, Bob likely had little understanding of the cognitive processes or mechanisms involved in Tom's specific crisis reaction.

What Bob did do, using the principles of psychological first aid, was to help Tom sort through what needed attention right now and what could wait until the next day; he helped in taking the first steps toward problem solving. Since there was no talk of Tom physically hurting himself or anyone else, Bob did not have to take steps to reduce lethality. (However, he did reduce the chance of an automobile accident by keeping Tom from aimlessly driving around in the early hours of the morning.)

Possible Solutions

It is interesting to note the way Tom began the conversation: "It looks like we will be getting a divorce." It is not uncommon for clients to begin by identifying one solution or a seemingly inevitable outcome to their crises. It needs to be acknowledged that this is one possible solution to a client's problem, one which should be recognized, but not be allowed to bind either the person in crisis or the helper. The tactic is to recognize the solution, state it in words as a possibility, something which may in fact happen (such as divorce), but to generate other alternatives as well. The aim is to keep clients from moving toward singular solutions for complex problems. Bob did this by encouraging Tom to put this issue on a back burner and deal with the most pressing concerns first.

In this case, Bob also had to deal with a

number of obstacles to the solutions generated, for example, what seeing a "shrink" might mean to Tom's law career. Throughout, Bob's tactic was to work toward generating viable alternatives, a process which required rechecking the alternatives with Tom to see how acceptable they really were and whether he would be able to carry them out.

Concrete Action

Since lethality was low, and since Tom, though distraught, was capable of taking care of himself and acting on the best next steps, Bob's stance was facilitative according to the action continuum of psychological first aid (Chapter 6). He became actively involved in the decision-making process, however, since Bob found himself giving Tom advice on certain aspects of the crisis (not driving around that night, not assuming that divorce was inevitable, not assuming that his own manhood was necessarily in question simply because Sue had an affair).

It is important to note that, in each case, the advice given to Tom was limited; its aim was to calm things down, to buy time so issues could be examined more calmly, and to keep options open.

Tom will need to make his own decisions on other aspects of this crisis (e.g., will he stay in the relationship with Sue or not). For now, given the fact that Tom's own state of upset seemed to be standing in the way of several immediate decisions, Bob allowed himself to give *advice* on what to do. Following the "do's and don'ts" of psychological first aid (Chapter 6), Bob attempted to dissuade Tom from making any decisions about the future right then, or drawing any major conclusions about his own self-worth. Instead, Tom was encouraged to wait until he had a chance for marital counseling. All of the advice given by Bob, then, was aimed at specific objectives, namely, managing the immediate situation, and taking initial steps toward problem solving (talking to a marriage counselor).

Follow-up

The agreement to talk to one another over the phone the next afternoon (after Tom's talk with Sue, his law professor, and the student counseling center) satisfied the condition of followup in psychological first aid. The followup agreement added focus to what Tom would do the next day. It signaled Bob's continued interest in Tom's problem, and it built in a feedback loop to see if something else might be needed the next day, such as another counseling resource besides the student counseling center.

At the end of this late night conversation, the three objectives of psychological first aid had been achieved.

(a) Bob had provided support for Tom, through listening and talking, and further offering physical assistance in the form of a couch on which to spend the night. Though Bob clearly could not take away the hurt that Tom felt that night, he provided an atmosphere within which Tom could express his feelings and share them with another person who cared. Tom will need to live with his hurt for a while before its eventual impact on his life is clear. That evening, however, he was provided support from a friend.

(b) Lethality was low in this case, precluding the need for directive action.

(c) Linkage to a helping resource was accomplished through the student counseling center referral. Marital counseling seemed the best approach to take to help Tom and Sue work through this crisis.

The extent to which the assistance offered will in fact facilitate coping cannot be judged until some time later. According to R. Lazarus's coping paradigm (1980), the question will be whether psychological first aid given that night assisted Tom in both managing his upset and in beginning the problem-solving process.

DIRECTIVE ACTION IN A SUICIDAL CRISIS

PRESENTING PROBLEM   Paul kept his gun in the trunk of his car. Until now the 22 rifle had been used for target shooting in the country near his boyhood hometown. Today, however, he was thinking it might serve another purpose. Although he didn't mention it on his visit to the University Counseling Center, Paul took some comfort in knowing that the gun might be a solution to his problem. It might slip out sooner or later, but Paul felt uncomfortable in saying straight out that he was thinking of shooting himself. He began, instead, by writing "depressed" on the information sheet he was asked to complete before seeing a counselor.

After about a 20-minute wait, Paul found himself sitting in the counselor's office attempting to respond to the offer to talk about "what is troubling you, and how might I help"?

Paul began haltingly at first, eyes turned away from the gaze of the counselor, preferring to look around the room, stopping now and then to see the expression on the counselor's face as the story unfolded. Paul's first words were about his parents, how prominent they were in their community, and how impossible it would be for them to accept what he now felt they suspected: that their 18-year-old son was a homosexual. The relationship between Paul and his parents had never been a smooth one, his father having had high expectations and ambitions for his son (athletic success, political career) which were quite different from Paul's own interests. His mother had always played the mediator role between the two, with very little success, especially in the past several years.

Paul moved from his small hometown to the state capitol to attend the state university six months ago, taking a room in a large dormitory. He had enjoyed the freedom of being away from home, found university life stimulating, and was a successful student. He had also developed a close intimate friendship with another young man, a relationship which in the past week or so had experienced considerable stress. Paul was reluctant to discuss his difficulties with his boyfriend, preferring instead to withdraw, which in turn led to increased frustration for both of them. Things had deteriorated so that the previous day his lover threatened to **PRECIPITATING EVENT**   break off the relationship.

It was shortly after this "fight" that Paul's parents stopped in unexpectedly while visiting the city on business. Paul managed to hide the source of his distress, though not the fact that he was upset. Jumbled conversation between Paul and his parents left no one very satisfied.

PSYCHOLOGICAL CONTACT   The counselor listened attentively as Paul spoke, frequently making reflective statements aimed at clarifying Paul's situation and his feelings about it. Whenever possible, and in as accepting a manner as he could, the counselor tried to help identify the feelings of frustration and anger (with the lover), anxiety (about dealing with parents), and depression (at there being no apparent solution) that Paul had experienced in the past two days

SUICIDAL CLUE   At one point early on in the hour, Paul said that he felt "it would be better if I were to end it all," a comment to which the counselor did not respond immediately. At a natural break in the conversation, however, the counselor came back to the comment, using Paul's own words:

EXPLORATION

Co: "Tell me what you mean when you say it would be better if you would end it all."

Paul: "Well, kill myself."

Co: "Do you want to die?"

Paul: "I just think that that might be the best thing all around. I can't deal with them (my parents). They can't know about this. It would destroy them. My father's career would be ruined. His political ambitions would be shot."

Co: "But what about you? How about your future, and what you want?"

Paul: "That doesn't matter either any more. I can't handle anything."

The counselor continued talking with Paul about the ideas which grew from his thought that he would like to end it all. Without arguing with him, he sought elaboration in a number of important areas. He distilled from the array of facts and

AMBIVALENCE feelings Paul's ambivalence about dying as a solution. Paul talked in terms of a part of him wanting to die, and another part wanting to live. Suicide might stop the intense emotional pain, though it would certainly not be a perfect solution. It would mean the end of a life that had many very satisfying moments, at least prior to this crisis. Paul had been a bright student, a talented musician, and had for many years envisioned a career as a concert pianist. As Paul and the counselor talked, it became increasingly apparent that Paul wanted more to end his depression, and to find some way of dealing with his current problem, than to end his life. The counselor also explored with Paul the angry messages (toward boyfriend

PREVIOUS and parents) implicit in the suicidal threat.

ATTEMPT The counselor inquired about previous suicide attempts, and found that Paul had once taken an overdose of sleeping pills in high school. His intention then was also not to die, but to get back at his parents, with whom he had had tremendous conflict. The situation was compounded by the fact that Paul felt isolated and left out by friends at school. His parents had found him unconscious in his room and had taken him to the local hospital emergency room to have his stomach pumped.

LETHAL In further inquiry about Paul's current suicidal thoughts, the counselor discovered

MEANS that Paul's plan this time would be to use his 22 rifle. It had been in the closet over the weekend, though Paul had moved it to the trunk of his car last night. Also, while standing alone in the parking lot late the previous evening, he had put the muzzle of the gun to his head, to check to see if he could reach the trigger with his hand.

POSSIBLE Paul and the counselor talked back and forth over several alternatives for dealing

SOLUTIONS with his most immediate concerns: confronting his parents, and resolving the difficulties with his boyfriend. Paul had never been a very assertive individual, and felt wholly inadequate at confronting either his parents or his boyfriend about his most intimate and, at times most troublesome feelings. He certainly felt unpre-

ACTION pared for talking to either of them right now. The counselor found himself coaching Paul on how he might confront his parents about his homosexuality when he felt ready to do so. The counselor also talked about dealing with parents as an especially important developmental issue for gay young people, one requiring considerable thought and, sometimes, support from others who had been through the experience themselves. The counselor told him of an organization of homosexual

SOCIAL men in the community which offered group counseling aimed at helping individuals
SUPPORT with this very task.

The counselor helped Paul look at the confrontation with his boyfriend as one which would need to be explored further before concluding that the relationship was necessarily at an end. They discussed the possibility of counseling sessions at the center for the two of them together. Paul was encouraged, then, to not draw too firm a conclusion about the eventual outcome of this conflict (for good or ill) until matters were explored further, and outside assistance utilized.

The counselor's immediate concern, however, was to reduce the probability of Paul taking his own life, and to establish some link for further work on the difficulties with the boyfriend and parents. The counselor therefore suggested having another session the next day, perhaps with Paul's boyfriend included.

Regarding Paul's talk of suicide, the counselor confronted Paul with a serious concern about the dangerousness of the situation: possession of lethal weapon, and rehearsal of killing himself the previous night, coupled with a previous attempt. The counselor drew heavily on the ambivalence that had emerged earlier in the conversation: both wanting to die and wanting to live. The counselor suggested at least postponing such a major decision until there was some time for things to cool off. He secured a commitment from Paul that he would not take his
REDUCE life in the immediate future. He also suggested that Paul not carry a loaded gun in
LETHALITY the trunk of his car right now, and offered to go with Paul to the parking lot after the session and transfer the weapon to the counselor's car trunk.

The counselor was also concerned, however, that at least one other person in Paul's immediate social network know of his intense depression and suicidal thoughts, and be available to Paul in the next several days. Paul was strongly against any contact with either his boyfriend or parents about his situation, so the counselor suggested the possibility of his (the counselor's) calling the resident assistant in Paul's dormitory. (Paul had earlier indicated that this was the only person he had really talked to since coming to the university.) Although Paul was
CONTRACT at first reluctant to include the resident assistant in all of this, the counselor convinced him that the potential gain in allowing this friend to help right now should outweigh Paul's desire to "go it alone." The phone call was placed to the resident assistant while Paul was still in the room. Paul agreed also to call the counselor
FOLLOW-UP should things take a turn for the worse in the next 24 hours (until the appointment with the counselor the next afternoon at 3:00). The counselor gave Paul his home phone number, and approximately one hour after the two first met they said good-bye, and agreed to meet again the next afternoon.

Comment

The help given Paul can be analyzed according to the five components of psychological first aid.

Psychological Contact

As identified in the headings in the left margin above, rapport was achieved primarily through reflective statements from the counselor. The counselor summarized, as accurately as possible, the events leading to the current crisis, and also identified Paul's unique reaction to each. By summarizing accurately what he was hearing and expressing empathy ("I can imagine how upsetting that must have been"), he communicated that he both understood and cared about what was taking place.

Dimensions of the Problem

The precipitating event for Paul's crisis was the encounter with his parents the previous day. His inability to cope in this particular situation grew from the fact that two seemingly insurmountable obstacles had been thrown in his path: an irresolvable conflict with his lover, and suspicions of parents about his homosexuality. Paul's inability to cope in this case was tied to his inability to deal assertively with his lover and parents. Thus, recent events had impinged directly on one of his skill deficits. Had the issue of suicide not arisen, the counselor might well have spent most of the time on this very issue, helping Paul to deal more directly with both his parents and his lover about his concerns.

The issue requiring immediate attention was Paul's suicidal ideation. The counselor judged the situation as highly lethal since Paul had attempted suicide previously, had a lethal and available means (gun) to take his life, and had poor contact with others in his immediate social network. The later issues uncovered by the counselor, which would be addressed in future therapy sessions, included: Paul's need for assertive skills in dealing with those close to him; whether or not and when to "come out" as a homosexual; his use (at least twice) of suicidal threats as a means of solving current difficulties. The counselor recognized that Paul's crisis had both situational (move to a new city and school six months ago) and developmental (identity, intimacy) components to it. For this first session, however, the main issues were offering support, reducing

the lethality of the entire crisis, and providing some link to a helping resource.

Possible Solutions and Concrete Action

The tactic adopted by the counselor throughout the session was to enlist Paul's cooperation in any maneuver made to reduce lethality. He began by listening and uncovering Paul's feelings about suicide as a possibility, attempting to frame the ambivalence in such a way that it could be used later in the negotiation process. While hospitalization, calling parents, or some other similarly controlling intervention would have been possible, the counselor elected (appropriately) to take a stepwise approach to reduce lethality, with each maneuver having the cooperation and consent of Paul.

According to the PFA flow chart in Chapter 6, the counselor took a directive stance characterized by both contractual negotiations with Paul (about the gun) and actively mobilizing other resources (resident assistant). By approaching it in this manner, trust was preserved and the therapeutic relationship between the counselor and Paul was maintained. Disposing of the gun and having Paul agree not to attempt suicide in the immediate future were the most direct means to reducing lethality. Setting up contact with the resident assistant in the dormitory and the counselor offering to be available by the phone that evening served to broaden the base of social support. The counselor's goal was clearly not to try to solve everything in that one session, but rather to set priorities, to buy time, and to take reasonable steps to insure that Paul would be alive to talk about the difficulty the next day.

The linkage to further helping resources dealt primarily with setting the appointment for Paul to see the counselor the next day, plus the contact with the gay community services group the following week. Again, the overall strategy was to broaden the base of support and assistance in as many ways as possible. The assumption was that Paul could profit from the support and guidance of other homosexuals who had confronted the issue of dealing with parents.

Another example of the directive stance taken by the counselor in this helping session was his coaching Paul on how to deal with both parents and roommate in the immediate future. Though he clearly could not teach Paul appropriate assertive behavior in one session, he was able to model the various possibilities, to demonstrate their potential usefulness, and add legitimacy to Paul's taking an assertive stance with his lover and parents around his current difficulties.

Follow Up

The principle mechanism for follow up was the appointment which was set for the next afternoon. The first session ended, then, with both Paul and the counselor knowing that there would be a specific time to check progress and/or make other arrangements to assist Paul.

The counselor's chief criteria in evaluating the effectiveness of his helping contact rested with whether he (a) provided support, (b) reduced lethality, and (c) made an appropriate linkage to another helping resource. In this particular case the counselor left the session with the impression that he had done each of these. Paul talked at the end about feeling somewhat better as a result of the conversation (the support); he agreed to give up his rifle and contact the counselor should the need arise that evening (lethality); and, he agreed to come in for a visit the next day (linkage to helping resource). When they went their separate ways after an hour's talk, the counselor had reasonable assurance that he had done as much as he could at that time.

At the follow-up session, the counselor planned to examine the outcome of his intervention by checking on Paul's reactions even further. He anticipated determining the extent to which Paul had in fact taken steps toward increased coping with the situation. The counselor would look for concrete indications that Paul was managing the subjective reactions (feelings of upset, anxiety, and the like) associated with the crisis, and that Paul was moving toward implementing the action steps (contacting the gay support group, talking to his lover, making decisions on how to deal with his parents) necessary to work through the crisis.

chapter eight

Second-Order Intervention: Multimodal Crisis Therapy

Crisis therapy picks up where psychological first aid leaves off by assisting the client in the process of rebuilding a life shattered by an external event, whether death of a loved one, loss of a limb, or any other situational or developmental crisis.[1] The uniqueness of crisis therapy lies not so much in its techniques (which, as we shall see, are borrowed from other broad spectrum therapies), but in the fact that everything the therapist does is aimed at helping the client to deal with the impact of the crisis event on each area of the client's life.

Crisis therapy attempts to help the client resolve the crisis, defined in Chapter 2 as:

> Working through the crisis event so that it becomes functionally integrated into the fabric of life, leaving the client open, instead of closed, to facing in the future.

This working through process is a much more extensive endeavor than psychological first aid, requiring more time, and a higher level of therapist training. We should remember also that not everyone who experiences a life crisis needs therapy to resolve it. Many individuals work through crises on their own, profiting from the advice of friends, lessons remembered from the past, or coping strategies learned without the aid of a therapist. Many

others, however, do not fare so well, and it is these who will come to the attention of counselors and therapists trained in psychology, psychiatry, nursing, social work, pastoral counseling, or some other professional specialty involving short-term therapy. For our purpose, the professional label is less important than the training and skills of the helper.

As described in Chapter 5, crisis therapy is most effective when it coincides with the period of disorganization (six or more weeks) of the crisis itself. Since some form of reorganization will invariably take place during this time, our intent is to offer assistance at that time to increase the probability that the re-

---

[1] Our expectation is that a therapist's/counselor's first contact with a client or patient will follow PFA guidelines, using the same checkpoints that an attorney or other nonmental health worker would. The main difference between counselor and, for example, attorney will be that the former will, by virtue of his/her knowledge of the crisis therapy assessment framework, be able to gather more detailed information under the second component of PFA, i.e., dimensions of the problem. For example, while the attorney will inquire about BASIC functioning for both pre-crisis and crisis time periods, the therapist will likely find out more about each modality, and client progress on the four tasks of crisis resolution, even during the PFA phase of the contact. Our intervention model expects both helpers to do PFA first, and then either refer the person for crisis therapy if that is required (as the attorney would do) or retain the client, and begin the crisis therapy assessment procedures either during the first session or the next (as the therapist would do).

organization is toward growth and away from debilitation. Therapeutic energies are geared toward helping the client to (a) physically survive the crisis experience, (b) identify and express feelings that accompany the crisis, (c) gain cognitive mastery over the crisis, and (d) make a range of behavioral and interpersonal adjustments necessitated by the crisis. These tasks will be the guide for the process of therapy. Every therapeutic strategy will be aimed at assisting the client to negotiate one or more of these tasks as it applies to the specific dimensions of the crisis. This chapter is devoted to the assessment, treatment, and evaluation components of crisis therapy.

ASSESSMENT The assessment and treatment framework used for crisis therapy in this volume was inspired by the work of Lazarus (1976, 1981) and others who have taken a multidimensional approach to psychotherapy (Hammond and Stanfield 1977; Horowitz 1976). While other crisis theorists (Burgess and Baldwin 1981; Halpern et al. 1979) have recognized the importance of assessing client functioning in several areas or subsystems (emotional, behavioral, cognitive), the crisis literature does not present a framework offering comprehensive assessment procedures tied directly to treatment strategies. The approach offered in this chapter is intended to fill this gap by applying a modified version of Lazarus's multimodal therapy to crisis situations.

The Five Person Subsystems: A BASIC Profile Table 8.1 lists each of the BASIC personality systems that become the focus of crisis therapy. The main differences between our BASIC personality profile and Lazarus's system are: (1) elimination of the drugs category, coding the taking of tobacco, alcohol, medication, and other substances as behavioral activities;

(2) including all physical functioning variables (including the sensations of vision, touch, taste, smell, and hearing) under somatic functioning (somewhat broader than Lazarus's sensation category); and (3) coding imagery and cognition dimensions under one heading (cognitive). (See also Chapter 2 for a discussion of Lazarus's (1976) system.)

The *behavioral system* refers to overt activity, particularly work, play, and other major life patterns, including exercise, dietary and sleep patterns, and the use of drugs, alcohol, and tobacco. In assessing a client's behavioral functioning, attention is given to excesses and deficits, antecedents and consequences of key behaviors, and areas of particular strength or weakness.

Affective variables include a full range of feelings that an individual might have about any of these behaviors, about a traumatic event, or about life in general. Attention is also given to assessment of the social appropriateness, or match between affect and various life circumstances. As with behavior, it is important to assess the conditionality of various feelings (antecedents and consequences).

Hammond and Stanfield (1977) have described four primary determinants of emotion. (a) Some emotions are best understood as conditioned physiological responses to environmental stimuli, for example, "butterflies" in the stomach. (b) Emotions can also be viewed as responses to internal stimuli such as cognitions, fantasies, or other mental images. The cognitive therapies (Beck 1970, 1971, 1976; Ellis 1962, 1974) regard the emotions as responses to environmental events mediated by thought processes. (c) Emotion is influenced by behavior; acting out an emotion intensifies affect (Hammond and Stanfield 1977). (d) Emotions can also be viewed as goal-directed operants that often function to manipulate the environment. Hammond and Stanfield (1977) offer the example of the client who makes negativistic self-statements, selectively focusing on unpleasant events in

TABLE 8.1   BASIC PERSONALITY PROFILE*

Modality/System	Variables/Subsystems
Behavioral	Patterns of work, play, leisure, exercise, diet (eating and drinking habits), sexual behavior, sleeping habits, use of drugs and tobacco; presence of any of the following: suicidal, homicidal, or aggressive acts.
	Customary methods of coping with stress.
Affective	Feelings about any of above behaviors; presence of feelings such as anxiety, anger, joy, depression, etc; appropriateness of affect to life circumstances. Are feelings expressed or hidden?
Somatic	General physical functioning, health.
	Presence or absence of tics, headaches, stomach difficulties, and any other somatic complaints; general state of relaxation/tension; sensitivity of vision, touch, taste, sight, hearing.
Interpersonal	Nature of relationships with family, friends, neighbors, and co-workers; interpersonal strengths and difficulties; number of friends, frequency of contact with friends and acquaintances; role taken with various intimates (passive, independent, leader, co-equal); conflict resolution style (assertive, aggressive, withdrawn); basic interpersonal style (congenial, suspicious, manipulative, exploitive, submissive, dependent).
Cognitive	Current day and night dreams; mental pictures about past or future; self image; life goals and reasons for their validity; religious beliefs; philosophy of life; presence of any of the following: catastrophizing, overgeneralizing, delusions, hallucinations, irrational self-talk, rationalizations, paranoid ideation; general (positive/negative) attitude towards life.

*Data sources for this table include the clinical interview, reports of family members, friends and referral source, questionnaires. (See Appendix B.)

his/her life until depression develops. The client's spouse may then respond by feeling guilty, which leads to nurturant and sympathetic behavior toward the client.

A client's *somatic functioning* refers to all bodily feelings, including sensitivity to touch, sound, sight, taste, and vision. Data on general physical functioning, including headaches, stomach difficulties, and general health are coded here. There is extensive published research regarding the contribution of physiological variables to psychopathology (Hammond and Stanfield 1977). In crisis situations, we are particularly interested in somatic correlates of psychological distress, and/or physical problems which may have precipitated the crisis. In many cases, a crisis will exacerbate existing physical problems or lead to behaviors which, if continued over long periods of time, can have a deleterious effect on health. Assessment of this modality leads directly to the first crisis resolution task, physical survival, which is discussed below.

The *interpersonal modality* includes data on the quantity and quality of social relationships between a client and family, friends, neighbors, and workers. Attention is given to the number of contacts in each of these categories, and to the nature of the relationships, particularly the role taken by the client with various intimates (co-equal, leader, passive/dependent, and so on).

Finally, mental processes are coded under the *cognitive modality*. Included here are images or mental pictures regarding goals in life, recollections of the past, and aspirations for the future, as well as relatively uncontrolled ruminations such as day and night dreams. Cognition is a label used to refer to the full range of thoughts and particularly self-statements that people make about their behavior, feelings, physical functioning, and the like. Drawing on recent trends in the cognitive therapies, this modality includes attention to catastrophizing and over-generalizing (Beck 1976), as well as various forms of irrational thinking (Ellis and Harper 1976). It is also the category within which the more traditional psychotic thought processes (such as paranoia) are coded.

It is important to assess both images or mental pictures (right hemisphere function of the brain) as well as verbal/concept thought processes (left hemisphere). Imagery has been found to play a profound role in psychopathology:

> For example, clients often picture images of feared catastrophies that may occur if they attempt to move toward a goal. These fantasies are generally a distortion of reality, but are perceived as valid by the client and lead to goal avoidance. To use a very common example, many men avoid revealing feelings to their wives lest they be perceived as weak or lacking in masculinity. This fantasy seldom has a basis in reality yet often contributes to aloofness and a lack of emotional intimacy in relationships. Another example is the wife who mentally pictures her husband with another woman when he is away on business. These images may stimulate and be associated with feelings of anxiety, fear, and resentment and later lead to responses of coolness, distrustful cross-examination, and verbal attack and accusation (Hammond and Stanfield 1977, p. 58).

Day and night dreams, or any mental pictures or images following a crisis event, often open the door to an understanding of what the event means to the client, both in terms of past goals as well as future hopes.

The second set of cognitive variables has to do with thoughts and particularly self-statements people make about their behavior, feelings, physical functioning, relationships, and events which occur through a lifetime. The central premise of the cognitive therapies is that our emotional reactions to life events will depend upon our cognitive interpretations, evaluations, and beliefs (Beck 1976; Ellis 1962, 1974; Mahoney 1974; Meichenbaum 1977). In Ellis's (1974) A-B-C paradigm of personality, an emotional reaction such as depression, guilt, or remorse (C) is caused not by an external event (A), but by the intervening thoughts (B) about the event. Shulman (1973) has suggested that our convictions about life serve as cognitive blueprints that guide both perception and behavior. A number of cognitive therapists have postulated cognitive errors, misconceptions, irrational ideas, and faulty beliefs which contribute to psychopathology. (Beck 1967, 1971, 1976; Ellis 1962; Lazarus and Fay 1975.)

The boxed insert lists common misconceptions frequently found in clinical populations (Hammond and Stanfield 1977). In crisis situations, many clients become aware that they have been functioning for years according to one or more of these misconceptions. The crisis provides an opportunity to examine the misconception and its relationship to recent stressful events, leading to subsequent changes in thinking.

Values and religious beliefs are also an important part of an individual's cognitive functioning. Although the methods used by behavioral scientists preclude assessment of a spirital dimension, an individual's stated beliefs, values, and overall philosophy of life are as available to the clinician as any other cognitive variables, and usually exert a powerful influ-

COMMON MISCONCEPTIONS ABOUT THE SELF, WORLD, GOALS, AND IDEALS
(Hammond and Stanfield 1977)

1. Distorted Self-Definitions
   a. I am a helpless, innocent victim. Unhappiness and what occurs in life is caused by outside circumstances or past events for which I am not responsible and have no control.
   b. I am not attractive, feminine, or manly enough.
   c. I am deficient (e.g., not smart enough), and therefore destined to fail.
   d. I am wicked.
   e. I am weak (and need to be led).
   f. I am so exceptional that I am entitled to my own way (narcissistic entitlement).
   g. I am undesirable and no one could love me.
   h. My worth is measured by my performance.
   i. I am worthless if my spouse (girlfriend, boyfriend, mother, father, child) does not love me.

2. Mistaken Assumptions About People and the World
   a. Life is a dangerous, dog-eat-dog, jungle. (People are hostile competitors.)
   b. Life doesn't give me a chance, and I'm destined to fail.
   c. Men (women) cannot be trusted.
   d. Life is chaotic and completely unpredictable.
   e. People are stupid, and one ought to take them for all he/she can.
   f. Other people are happy, "normal," and do not have feelings or problems similar to mine. In fact, some people have perfect marriages, perfect children, and so forth.
   g. Good looks, superior intelligence, athletic ability, money, and so forth, make one happy.
   h. People will look down on me as inept if I make or admit mistakes, admit limitations, and seek advice.
   i. Most things are either black or white, that is, good-bad, right-wrong, liked or disliked, clever or stupid, attractive or unattractive (Lazarus and Fay 1975, p. 85).

3. Mistaken, Self-Defeating Goals
   a. It is essential to be perfect, completely competent, and without flaw to be worthwhile. Don't make or admit mistakes.
   b. I must be loved and approved of (admired, liked) by everyone; I must never offend.
   c. I must find the perfect or "right" solution.
   d. I have to be the best, the first, or right.
   e. I must be the center of attention, the star attraction.
   f. I must be dependent on someone stronger to protect and lead me.
   g. I should retaliate and get even with the world.
   h. I must not let people know what I am really like (they may think less of me or use what they learn against me).
   i. I must ventilate anger whenever I feel it.
   j. I must be safe and secure at all times. I must be careful not to take any risks or chances.
   k. I must be completely self-sufficient and independent.

4. Mistaken Ideals
   a. The only thing worth being is a "star" (or genius). Nothing less is worth working for (Shulman 1973, p. 41).
   b. I should always be calm, cool, and collected and never lose control.
   c. I should always know the right answer.
   d. I should be the perfect spouse, parent, lover, employee, son, daughter, church member.
   e. A "real" man is a tough guy who never takes any guff from anyone.
   f. A "real" woman should always be feminine, nonoffensive, unassertive, and dependent.
   g. I should always have my own way.
   h. I have an easier/happier life when I avoid responsibilities and problems.
   i. I should be able to succeed and be happy without discomfort or struggle.
   j. I should always be unselfish, considerate, generous, happy.
   k. The purpose of life is to work hard and to be productive—not happy (Lazarus and Fay 1975, p. 65).
   l. If you try hard enough you can excel at anything and everything (Lazarus and Fay 1975, p.34).

[1] From *"Multidimensional psychotherapy: A counselors' guide for the map form"* by D.C. Hammond and K. Stanfield. Copyright 1977 by the Institute for Personality and Ability Testing. Reprinted by permission.

ence on every other dimension of personality.

Hammond and Stanfield (1977) remind us that early life experiences exert a powerful influence on the child's perception of the world, including expectancies about the future. When these expectancies and beliefs, with their accompanying interpretations and evaluations of events, allow the growing child (and later, adult) to manage life's circumstances along the way, then development is likely to occur without dramatic disruption or crisis. When, however, the childhood beliefs, values, and expectations cannot handle new data introduced at certain points, then crisis may occur. Under these circumstances, crisis therapy seeks to assist the client in re-examining the beliefs, shattered expectations, or cognitive errors/misconceptions in search of better replacements. The uniqueness of crisis (and, hence, crisis therapy) is that it is precisely during these times of tremendous upset and motivation to change that the diagnostic data about cognition is readily available ("I can't *believe* it!"; *Why* is this happening to me; I always *thought. . .*").

Assessment Assumptions

Though we have consolidated Lazarus's seven dimensions into five modalities, our assumptions about the assessment process are very similar. Assessment in crisis therapy is built on the following suppositions:

1. We must be able to assess the impact of the crisis event on all five areas of the person's functioning—behavior, feelings, physical health, interpersonal relationships, and cognition. To neglect one or more areas will lead to only a partial understanding of the crisis, and hamper subsequent therapeutic interventions.

2. The five BASIC subsystems, though assessed separately, are interrelated so that changes in one can be expected to lead to change in the others. The therapeutic challenge is to capitalize on this fact by assessing specific aspects of functioning in each modality (an unrealistic expectation about marriage in the cognitive modality) that can be dealt with directly,

leading to positive change in other areas (interpersonal changes in a marital relationship).

3. It is important to assess both strengths as well as weaknesses in BASIC functioning during the crisis, and whenever possible to mobilize the former to shore up the latter: for example, encourage a pattern of regular physical exercise (behavior) as a means of coping with the physical stress (somatic) accompanying a client's unexpected unemployment.

4. Assessment of an individual's crisis must include the contextual variables of family/ social environment, community, and culture. These suprasystem variables may be maintaining a current level of distress or may be a source of social support. Effective crisis therapy must account for the influence of these suprasystem variables early in the assessment phase, moving toward strategies which assist the client in either managing their negative influence or drawing on their positive support.

5. Assessment procedures must be organized to allow for evaluation at the end of therapy, and at various follow up points. This includes the need to track various personality variables from precrisis, on through the crisis and postcrisis periods as a means of measuring growth.

6. The goal of assessment is not to create a diagnostic label, but rather to provide a profile of BASIC crisis functioning in the context of a similar profile of BASIC precrisis functioning, both of which will yield concrete guidelines for selection of treatment strategies.

Data Sources

Assessment data can be drawn from several sources, the chief one being the clinical interview. Using the BASIC structure as a cognitive map, the clinician inquires about a client's functioning in each modality. Whether talking with the client alone, or with relatives and close friends, the clinician's main assessment task is to determine the impact of the crisis event on behavioral, affective, physical, interpersonal and cognitive functioning. In many cases it is feasible to have clients complete the Crisis Questionnaire (CQ), a fill-in-the-blank inventory that asks the crisis client to describe his/her BASIC functioning both before and after a crisis event. (See Appendix B.) The CQ can be used as an adjunct to a clinical interview during which the therapist elicits greater detail on issues in each subsystem.

Assessment Checklist

Table 8.2 offers a brief questionnaire which the clinician can use to summarize assessment data. The questionnaire can be used both as a guide for structuring the assessment interview, and also as a summary sheet to record information gathered from clients, family members, referral source, and others. Whether the clinician relies exclusively on the clinical interview or includes questionnaires, it is important that data be secured in each of the following areas:

1. Precipitating event(s);
2. Presenting problem;
3. Context of crisis;
4. Pre-crisis BASIC functioning;
5. Crisis BASIC functioning.

Precipitating Event

It is important to know what happened to touch off the crisis. Was there one major event such as the unexpected death of a loved one or was the precipitating event of the "last straw" variety, a minor incident occurring after an accumulation of stressors such as moving to a new community, a major shift in responsibilities at work, and the like. Particular attention is given to when the event occurred,

TABLE 8.2   CRISIS ASSESSMENT SUMMARY

Karl Slaikeu and Ruth Striegel-Moore (1982)

Name:_____   Age: _____ Sex: _____

Marital Status: _____   Occupation: _____

Name of Counselor: _____   Date: _____

Directions

This questionnaire may be used either as a guide for structuring a crisis intake interview or as a summary sheet to record information gathered from the client, family member, referral source, and others. When used as an interview guide, it is important to take a flexible approach, allowing the client to determine the sequence of his/her report as much as possible and to reorder questions in accordance with the client's readiness to discuss various aspects of the crisis.

I.   *Precipitating Event*
What event instigated the crisis?

_____

When did this event occur?

_____

Who else besides the client was involved?

_____

Describe similar events which have occurred before in the client's life?

_____

II.   *Presenting Problem*
What is the client's description of the problem(s) at the time therapy begins?_____

_____

_____

How does this differ from stated concerns of family and/or referral source?_____

_____

_____

What does the client want to accomplish as a result of therapy?_____

_____

_____

TABLE 8.2 (Continued)

III. *Contextual Issues*
Brief description of family members and their involvement in the crisis:

_____

_____

_____

_____

Neighborhood resources and/or stressors at the time of referral:

_____

_____

Job/office pressures on client, as well as identifiable sources of support:

_____

_____

_____

Community/cultural dimensions of the crisis:

_____

_____

_____

IV. *Pre-crisis BASIC Functioning*
For each developmental stage of the client's life, identify aspects of behavioral, affective, somatic, interpersonal, and cognitive functioning which bear most directly on the current crisis.

Childhood: _____

_____

_____

Puberty: _____

_____

_____

TABLE 8.2 (CONTINUED)

Adolescence: _____
_____
_____

Young Adulthood: _____
_____
_____

Middle Age: _____
_____
_____

Retirement: _____

V. *Crisis BASIC Functioning*
Examine the impact of the crisis event on each of the 5 modalities.
Behavioral Functioning: Find out how the crisis event has affected the client's behavior. For each of the following areas, indicate the impact of the crisis event:

No Impact	Change did occur	Specify
( )	( )	work: _____
( )	( )	exercise:_____
( )	( )	use of leisure time: _____
( )	( )	eating habits:_____
( )	( )	smoking: _____
( )	( )	drinking habits:_____
( )	( )	use of drugs: _____
( )	( )	sleep: _____
( )	( )	control of feelings (e.g. outburst of temper, frequent crying, etc.)

No	Yes	
( )	( )	indications of aggressive and/or self-destructive behavior:

TABLE 8.2 (CONTINUED)

_____

_____

_____

( )   ( )   Are there any specific behaviors or habits that the client wants to change?

( )   The client wants to learn a new behavior _____

_____

_____

( )   The client wants to do _more_ often _____

_____

( )   The client wants to do _less_ often _____

_____

( )   The client wants to stop completely_____

_____

_____

List 3 of the client's favorite activities: 1 _____

2 _____

3 _____

On the average, how much time does/did the client spend performing these activities:

Now   Prior to crisis event

1 _____ hrs/week   1 _____ hrs/week

2 _____ hrs/week   2 _____ hrs/week

3 _____ hrs/week   3 _____ hrs/week

Affective Functioning:
Examine the feelings that are most characteristic of the client at this time in her/his life. (Check as many as apply.)

Excited	( )	Overwhelmed	( )	Anxious	( )
Angry	( )	Tense	( )	Energetic	( )
Lonely	( )	Cheerful	( )	Guilty	( )
Happy	( )	Restless	( )	Comfortable	( )
Sad	( )	Afraid	( )	Bored	( )

TABLE 8.2 (CONTINUED)

"Numbed"   (   )   Jealous   (   )   Exhausted   (   )

Relaxed   (   )   Contented   (   )   Other   (   )

_____

_____

_____

_____

_____

_____

In what situations does the client feel most upset? _____

_____

In what situations does the client feel most relaxed? _____

_____

What situations/events/experiences might make the client happier? _____

_____

_____

What experiences could make the client angry? _____

_____

In what situation(s) would the client be most likely to lose control over his/her emotions? _____

_____

_____

What feelings would the client like to experience more often? _____

_____

_____

What feelings would the client like to experience less often? _____

_____

_____

Which feelings were characteristic of the client before the crisis event? _____

TABLE 8.2 (CONTINUED)

Somatic functioning:
Examine the impact of the crisis event on the client's physical well-being. Was the crisis caused by a physical loss (surgery, disease, loss of limb, etc.?

   (   ) No   (   ) Yes

If Yes, describe the exact nature of the loss and its impact on other bodily functions?

_____

_____

_____

Describe any physical complaints associated with the crisis event (e.g. headaches, stiff neck, stomach cramps, etc.).

_____

_____

_____

Which of these problems is a reactivation of previous physical complaints?

_____

_____

_____

Do these physical complaints necessitate treatment by a physician?

(   )   No

(   )   Yes _____ (name of physician)

Do these complaints currently necessitate changes in the client's life style?

(   )   No

(   )   Change of occupation

(   )   Change of exercise/recreational activities

(   )   Change of diet

(   )   Other _____

TABLE 8.2 (CONTINUED)

Evaluate the overall level of physical tension experienced by this client:

( )   ( )   ( )   ( )   ( )   ( )   ( )

completely relaxed   extremely tense

Is the client now taking medication?

( ) No

( ) Yes _____ (list drugs prescribed)

_____

_____

Other aspects of client's physical health prior to the crisis which were not discussed above:

_____

_____

_____

Interpersonal Relationships:
The following concerns important aspects of the client's relationships with other people. The primary focus is on how these relationships might impede or facilitate an adaptive crisis resolution.

Does the client have close family ties?

( ) No

( ) Yes (specify) _____

_____

Does the client have close friends?

( ) No

( ) Yes (specify) _____

_____

Is the client a member in a social organization (church, social club, etc.)

( ) No

( ) Yes (specify) _____

_____

TABLE 8.2 (CONTINUED)

Who is currently the most important person in the client's life?

_____

_____

What is the impact of the crisis event on the client's social relationships (spouse, children, friends, etc.)?

_____

_____

_____

Who in the social network can be approached to help the client work through the crisis?

_____

_____

Is the client open to accepting help from family or friends?

( ) Yes

( ) No. Why not? _____

_____

_____

Who in the client's network might hinder successful crisis resolution?

_____

Describe the client's interpersonal style during the time of crisis?

( ) withdrawn   ( ) aggressive

( ) dependent   ( ) assertive

( ) affiliative   ( ) independent

( ) rejecting

( ) other _____

_____

Overall, the client describes his/her interpersonal relationship as

	satisfying	acceptable	conflict-laden
parents	( )	( )	( )

TABLE 8.2 (CONTINUED)

siblings	( )	( )	( )
spouse	( )	( )	( )
children	( )	( )	( )
co-workers	( )	( )	( )
friends	( )	( )	( )
neighbors	( )	( )	( )

Was the quality of any of these relationships different before the crisis event occurred?

( ) No

( ) Yes (specify) _____

_____

_____

Cognitive functioning:
The next set of questions examines how the client perceives and interprets the crisis event.

False	True	
( )		The crisis event threatens the attainment of a highly valued life goal.
( )	( )	Specify _____
( )		The client verbalizes many "I should have" statements.
	( )	Specify _____
( )		The client feels responsible for the occurrence of the crisis event.
( )		The client ruminates excessively over the crisis event and/or its consequences.
	( )	Specify _____
( )		The client feels responsible for the occurrence of the crisis event.
	( )	"It is all my fault...
	( )	"It is not completely my fault, but I contributed to it."
	( )	"I am really confused. Maybe it was my fault."
( )		Since the crisis event, the client is experiencing nightmares.
	( )	Specify _____

TABLE 8.2 (CONTINUED)

( )　　　　Since the crisis event, the client has recurring destructive fantasies.

　　( )　　self-destructive

　　( )　　homicidal

　　( )　　abusive towards spouse

　　( )　　abusive towards child

( )　　　　As a result of the crisis event, the client has fearful thoughts/images about the future.

　　( )　　Specify _____

Examine the client's self-talk patterns. What self-statements are reported?

_____

_____

_____

Indicate the presence of any of the following:

　( )　catastrophizing

　( )　delusions

　( )　irrational self-talk

　( )　rationalizations

　( )　hallucinations

　( )　paranoid ideation

Has the crisis event touched off "unfinished business" (unsuccessfully resolved previous crises, repressed conflicts, etc.)? Explain.

_____

_____

How has the crisis affected the client's self-image? _____

_____

Describe any recurreng day and night dreams? _____

_____

What was the client's mental picture of life before the crisis? _____

_____

TABLE 8.2 (CONTINUED)

Now? _____

The future?_____

Describe any other client fantasies not mentioned above._____

_____

Other aspects of client's cognitive functioning prior to the crisis which have not been mentioned above: _____

_____

Rate the client's current level of overall life satisfaction:

( )	( )	( )	( )	( )
very satisfied	moderately satisfied	fairly satisfied	somewhat dissatisfied	dissatisfied

VI. *BASIC Summary:*

    A.　Area which gives the client the greatest difficulty right now: _____

_____

    B.　Problem which might be easiest to treat: _____

_____

    C.　Variable (e.g., thought, behavior) which accounts for most variance in overall client disorganization: _____

_____

_____

    D.　Systems noticeably unaffected by this crisis: _____

_____

_____

    E.　Areas of the client's life which have been strengthened by the crisis:_____

_____

_____

    F.　Most obvious personal resources or strengths of this client: _____

_____

_____

TABLE 8.2 (CONTINUED)

G. Most obvious social resources or strengths of this client: _____

_____

_____

H. Summary of interaction between precipitating event(s) and previously unresolved personal issues, major expectations,

or life goals: _____

_____

_____

VII. *Treatment Plan*
   Identify specific client activities under each heading:

A. Physical Survival

      _____

      _____

      _____

      _____

B. Expression of Feelings

      _____

      _____

      _____

      _____

C. Cognitive Mastery

      _____

      _____

      _____

      _____

D. Behavioral/Interpersonal Adjustments

      _____

      _____

      _____

and who was involved, as a backdrop for how the event interacts with the client's self-image, life structure, and life goals. Does the client view the event as a loss? Threat? Challenge?

Presenting Problem   This is essentially a summary of the client's difficulties at the time of the referral. What complaints does the client bring to therapy? What does the client *want* from crisis therapy? How does the client presently describe the difficulty, and what is the client's view of what he/she needs most at that time?

Context of Crisis   In exploring the context of the crisis, it is important to determine the effect of the crisis on the immediate family and/or social group. How might family members and neighbors be affected by the course of the client's crisis (physical threats)? How does the client as "identified patient" fit into the broader context of family dynamics at the time of the crisis? Are other family members' attempts to help the client actually exacerbating the situation? Is the client's crisis linked to some broader community issue such as unemployment tied to lay-off of large numbers of workers at a factory? To what extent is an individual's developmental crisis affected by community norms? How is the crisis perceived by the client's co-workers? Assessment of the context of the crisis looks at how the original crisis (for example, the diagnosis of cancer) is perceived by the community (employer, neighbors) and how this perception might possibly precipitate another crisis. What resources are available in the community to assist the client in working through the crisis?

Pre-Crisis BASIC   A brief developmental
Functioning   history is necessary in
                        order to fully appreciate the disorganization and disequilibrium

that follows a particular precipitating event, whether a single severe blow such as the loss of a loved one, or a relatively minor last straw after an accumulation of stressors. As Table 8.2 indicates, the primary concern is to identify the most salient aspects of the client's BASIC functioning during childhood, puberty, adolescence, young adulthood, adulthood, and retirement as they may relate to the crisis event.

Assessment of the person's BASIC functioning immediately prior to the crisis includes emphasis on the following:

1. Previous means of coping and solving problems (Caplan 1964; Lazarus 1980);
2. Most obvious personal and social resources (Caplan 1961);
3. Most noticeable strengths and weaknesses in BASIC functioning (Aguilera et al. 1974);
4. Unresolved conflicts or unfinished business which might be touched-off by the crisis event (Miller and Iscoe 1963);
5. Relative satisfaction or dissatisfaction with life;
6. Pre-crisis developmental stage (Erikson 1963, Danish and D'Augelli 1980; Stevenson 1977);
7. Excesses and deficits in any of the BASIC modalities (Lazarus 1976);
8. Life goals and life structure to achieve goals (Levinson 1976);
9. Goodness of fit between life style and suprasystems—family/social groups, community, society;
10. Other stresses before crisis event, for example, difficulties at work which might compound marital problems (Kraus 1979).

In sum, our concern is to determine how well the individual was functioning before the crisis event. While each of the variables listed is important, particular attention is given to determining previous coping patterns and unresolved personal conflicts. It is only by understanding these that we can appreciate how a particular event leads to crisis.

Crisis BASIC Functioning

Our chief goal here is to determine the impact of the precipitating event in all five areas of the individual's BASIC functioning. Crisis theory suggests giving particular attention to key dimensions in each of the five BASIC modalities:

Behavioral

1. What activities (going to work, sleeping, eating, and so on) have been most affected by the crisis event?
2. Which areas have been unaffected by crisis?
3. Which behaviors have been increased or possibly strengthened by the crisis?
4. What coping strategies have been attempted, and what was the relative success/failure of each. Are current strategies actually maintaining the present level of distress (Figley and Sprenkle 1978)?

Affective

1. How does the individual feel in the aftermath of the crisis event? Angry? Sad? Depressed? Numbed? (Horowitz 1976; Halpern 1973).
2. Are feelings expressed or kept hidden?
3. Does affective state give any clues as to the stage of working through the crisis (Caplan 1964; Fink, Beak, and Taddeo 1971; Horowitz 1976; Lindemann 1944)?

Somatic

1. Are there physical complaints associated with the crisis event? Are these a reactivation of previous difficulties or "totally new"?
2. If crisis stems from physical loss (loss of limb, surgery, disease), what is the exact nature of the loss, and what are its effects on other bodily functioning?

Interpersonal

1. Impact of person's crisis on immediate social world of family and friends.
2. Current social network and supports (Caplan 1964, 1976);
3. How well is help which is available from family and friends being used?
4. Interpersonal stance taken during time of crisis, for example, withdrawn, dependent, etc.

Cognitive

1. Expectancies or life goals violated by the crisis event (Taplin 1971; Levinson et al. 1976);
2. Current ruminations or intrusive thoughts (Horowitz 1976);
3. The meaning of the precipitating event in overall life (Tosi and Moleski 1975);
4. Presence of "shoulds," such as "I should have been able to handle this" (Perls 1969; Ellis and Harper 1961);
5. Illogical thought patterns such as inevitable outcomes ("she left me, therefore I'll never find another");
6. Current self-talk patterns (Meichenbaum 1977);
7. Day and night dreams (Lifton and Olson 1976);
8. Images of impending doom;
9. Destructive fantasies.

The cognitive modality captures the heart of the crisis experience since it focuses on the meaning of the crisis event(s) to the individual. Crisis theory suggests that it is critical to discover the individual's expectations, goals, and dreams that have been shattered by the crisis event (Taplin 1971; Levinson et al. 1976), and to assess current style of cognitive functioning, for example, blaming self, over generalizing, catastrophizing (Ellis and Harper 1961; Beck 1976). Perhaps more than any other, the cognitive modality is viewed by theorists as critical to understanding the crisis experience (Auerbach and Kilmann [surgery] 1977; [transition from one developmental stage to another] Danish and D'Augelli 1980; [psychological contact with home and family] Uzoka 1979; [cancer] Simonton et al. 1978).

Special emphasis should be given to "disruptions" in each modality when determining the impact of the crisis event on BASIC functioning. It is important to note that attention should also be placed on areas that have not been affected, or areas which might have been strengthened as a result of the crisis event. For example an individual might draw support from friends during a crisis, thereby strengthening interpersonal ties.

TREATMENT: FOUR TASKS OF CRISIS RESOLUTION   The initial task of treatment is to translate the BASIC crisis profile into task language. The data subsumed under each modality are

Table 8.3   Four Tasks of Crisis Resolution

Task	Modality	Client Activity	Therapeutic Strategies
Physical survival	Somatic	(a) Preserve life (prevent suicide, homicide).	(a) Offer psychological first aid (see Chapter 6, and Glossary re: establishing therapeutic relationship).
		(b) Maintain physical health.	(b) Consult with client about nutrition, exercise and relaxation (See Glossary re: autogeneic training, biofeedback, breath control, deep muscle relaxation, diet and nutrition, massage, pain control, physical exercise, yoga).
Expression of feelings	Affective	(a) Identify and (b) Express feelings related to crisis in a socially appropriate manner.	(a) Discuss crisis event, with particular attention to how the client feels about various aspects of the crisis (see Glossary re: active listening, establishing a therapeutic relationship, induced affect).
			(b) Educate client about the role of feelings in overall psychological functioning, and encourage appropriate forms of expression (see Glossary re: anger–control, expression, provocation; anxiety management; empty chair; meditation, stress innoculation training).
Cognitive mastery	Cognitive	(a) Develop reality-based understanding of the crisis event.	(a) Review crisis event and surrounding circumstances (see Glossary re: problem solving).

thought of not simply as representing the state of a particular subsystem but rather as a guide to client activity during the working through process, that is, the four tasks of crisis resolution:

1. Physical survival in the aftermath of the crisis,
2. Expression of feelings related to the crisis,
3. Cognitive mastery of the entire experience, and
4. Behavioral/interpersonal adjustments required for future living.

The guiding premise of crisis therapy is that in order for a person to grow through the crisis, to integrate the crisis event into the fabric of life and go on about the business of living, it is necessary for these four tasks to be accomplished. All therapeutic strategies are introduced with the view to helping a client negotiate activities in one or more of these areas.

Table 8.3 summarizes the client activities and possible therapeutic strategies associated with each of the four crisis resolution tasks. The strategies stem primarily from research in clinical psychology since the late 1940s. Congruent with Lazarus's (1976, 1981) multimodal perspective, this framework allows us to draw on such diverse approaches as Gestalt therapy, behavior therapy, cognition modification, and others, with each approach being ap-

TABLE 8.3 (CONTINUED)

Task	Modality	Client Activity	Therapeutic Strategies
		(b) Understand relationship between crisis event and client beliefs, expectations, unfinished business, images, dreams, and goals for the future.	(b) Discuss pre-crisis thoughts and expectation, plans, and impact of event in each of these areas (see also Glossary re: Rational Emotive Therapy.)
		(c) Adjust/change beliefs, self-image, and future plans in light of crisis event.	(c) Assist client in adjusting beliefs, expectations and self-talk (see Glossary re: bibliotherapy, cognitive restructuring, decision making, homework, guided self-dialogue, hypnosis, imagery, implosion, paradoxical techniques, self-help, thought stopping).
Behavioral/ interpersonal adjustments	Behavioral, Inter-personal	(a) Make changes in daily patterns of work, play, and relationships with people in light of crisis event(s).	(a) Review with the client changes that might be required in each of the main areas; utilize therapy sessions, homework assignments, and cooperation of social network, to facilitate change in each area. (see Glossary re: anticipatory guidance, assertiveness training, behavior rehearsal, family therapy, feedback, homework assignments, hot seat, interpersonal skills training, marital therapy, modeling, networking, paradoxical techniques, role-playing, self-help, systematic desensitization).

plied strategically to help the client accomplish a particular aspect of one crisis resolution tasks. A complete list of therapeutic strategies, including summary descriptions and references, appears as the Glossary (Appendix C). A summary of the main considerations under each of the task headings and the guidelines in treatment selection follows.

Physical Survival

The first task of crisis resolution is for clients to stay alive, and as physically well as possible, during the period of extreme stress and personal disorganization. Since suicide is one possible outcome of life crisis (see Chapter 2), steps must be taken early on in crisis therapy to assess possible suicidal tendencies and implement appropriate preventive measures. The main therapeutic strategy is the Psychological First Aid framework discussed in Chapter 6.

Beyond protecting against suicide or other physical harm, the client needs to regulate diet, exercise, and rest/sleep patterns in order to work on the other crisis resolution tasks. In case of extreme emotional distress (especially during the impact phase of crisis—see Chapter 2), a referral to a physician for medication to manage anxiety or facilitate sleep may be recommended. The disadvantage of medication is that it might interfere with expression of feelings and cognitive mastery, or lead to dependency if continued for long periods of time. Many clients will medicate themselves with alcohol or other drugs in an attempt to manage extreme emotional pain or physical discomfort associated with the crisis.

Most crisis clients experience disruption in eating and sleeping, and for some, poor eating habits and/or lack of physical exercise exacerbate their difficulties. For these clients, the therapist's recommendation of change in diet and/or exercise activities may mark the beginning not simply of immediate coping, but an improvement in daily care of the body that can last a lifetime. For example, clients may need to be taught principles of aerobic exercise, deep muscle relaxation, or yoga, as a means of coping with physical and mental tension accompanying a crisis, and facilitating better sleep at the end of the day. (See Glossary.) Most clients who are worried about lack of sleep can be told to expect that they will sleep poorly for a while, and that research on sleep suggests that its loss for temporary periods of time is not nearly as debilitating as the *worry* associated with losing sleep. Clients whose crisis involves physical injury of some sort, or those who have some pre-existing physical malady, or whose pre-crisis functioning has been characterized by extreme neglect of the body, will require medical consultation before engaging in any new exercise program.

Expression of Feelings

The central premise behind expression of feelings as a task of crisis resolution grows from psychotherapy experience with clients who have *not* resolved earlier life crises. At the heart of Perls's (1969) concept of *unfinished business* is the idea that emotions which were never fully understood, accepted, or expressed at the time they were first felt, will appear later as dysfunctional constrictions of thinking and behavior, as well as somatic complaints. Accordingly, the aim of the second crisis resolution task is to assist clients to express, in some socially appropriate manner, the intense feelings that accompany crisis, thereby freeing emotional energy to be used constructively in other aspects of life.

Before feelings can be expressed they must be identified. For example, many clients are angry and seem not to know it, often repressing anger for fear of what they believe it might mean about them if they were to express it ("I can't handle my problems," or "I'm going crazy.") Others are ignorant about what to do with anger, often fearing that its expression will of necessity lead to lack of control, and possibly physical violence.

The chief therapeutic strategy for identifying client feelings is *active listening* wherein the therapist listens both for what happened to the client and how he/she feels about the events. Heavy doses of empathic understanding by counselors can often serve to help clients admit to a range of troublesome and uncomfortable feelings. It should be noted that identifying feelings is more than a first step toward their expression. Feelings serve also as a reflection of a client's thought processes, which opens the door to the cognitive mastery task. Feelings serve further as a clue to the environmental situations that trouble the client most, an understanding of which is important for the behavioral/interpersonal adjustment task. Beck (1971) has suggested that the emotions of depression and sadness relate to a cognitive evaluation of loss of something positive, that anxiety grows from cognitive appraisal of threat and danger, and that anger is imbedded in a cognitive perception of injustice. By listening carefully to the verbalizations that accompany the expression of feelings, the therapist gains valuable information on specific explorations that will be necessary for the client in order to fully gain cognitive mastery over the crisis. Emotions give similar clues to anticipated behavioral changes, for example, a rape victim's panic at having to return to work because she does not know what (if anything) to say to her colleagues about the ordeal, and is fearful also of being attacked again while going to/from the office.

Table 8.3 lists possible therapeutic strategies that can be used to assist clients in expressing feelings. For many clients whose feelings are close to the surface, a therapist's empathic statements will be all that is needed for the client to cry, talk out anxieties and fears, or express anger. Others will need to be given "permission" to express feelings, to be reassured that feelings are normal, and that it is all right to be angry during the crisis, indeed that the anger or whatever feeling the client experiences at the time is a very natural reaction to the circumstances of the crisis. Some will need to be reassured that their extreme emotions (often entirely new to crisis clients, depending upon the history of stressful events in their lives) are *not* a sign of psychopathology, that "you are not going crazy, even though you might feel like it at times." Many of these strategies involve offering new cognitions or educating clients about feelings. This is especially true for clients who labor under common misconceptions about feelings: for example, that it is wrong, sinful, cowardly, unmanly, or a sign of weakness to feel (or be temporarily overcome by) sadness, hurt, anxiety, fear, remorse, guilt, and the like. As mentioned previously, clients may believe that to allow expression of a feeling, whether sadness or anger, will open the floodgates, leading to a loss of control. The therapist should look for client misconceptions and at times offer rules or guidelines for expression of feelings, such as the following:

(a) Catharsis can have both verbal (talking, screaming) and nonverbal (hitting a pillow, weeping) components; both are helpful;

(b) During a therapy hour, or when a client is alone, almost any means of expression of feelings is acceptable if it does not cause physical harm (hitting a human being) or property damage (breaking a lamp instead of hitting a pillow, or a handball).

It should be remembered by the therapist (and, in many cases, stated directly to the client) that there are many ways to express feelings, and that each person can find his/her own place, time, and company (or absence thereof) to do so. For example, there is nothing qualitatively better about a person's crying in a therapist's office as opposed to crying in bed in the middle of the night, or while at home listening to a particular song on the radio. The point to emphasize is that feelings are a psychological reality during a crisis (or at any time, for that matter) and deserve expression in some form or another.

The other techniques listed in Table 8.3 can

be introduced as appropriate by the therapist. During the therapy sessions themselves, the Gestalt "empty chair" technique, or variations thereof, can be particularly useful in facilitating expression of emotional material after a crisis. The therapist should be prepared for the expression of one feeling leading to another, for example, an estranged husband who begins by talking about the emotional sadness accompanying a separation, moving then toward intense anger at a spouse and her new lover. The link between sadness over loss and anger at injustice cuts across many situations, with different people in the client's life emerging as targets. The therapist's chief responsibility here is to assist the client in sorting through the various feelings, finding ways to identify and express them, and at the same time, finding out what they really mean to the client in terms of past experience, current expectations, and future plans, all as a lead-in to full cognitive mastery, the third task of crisis resolution.

Cognitive Mastery   The basic premise of the third task of crisis resolution is that cognitive factors are the mechanism by which external events turn into personal crises. This approach to crisis theory was first proposed by Taplin (1971) despite the fact that, with very few exceptions (e.g., Tosi and Moleski, 1975), the crisis literature has been slow to fully develop the applied implications of the cognitive perspective. This discrepancy is all the more striking since the emergence of the cognitive therapies has been one of the most important developments in clinical psychology in recent years (Beck 1976; Ellis and Harper 1961; Mahoney 1974; Meichenbaum 1977). The crisis therapist has numerous tested clinical strategies at his disposal to assist clients in gaining cognitive mastery over the crisis experience. As we have discussed earlier (Chapter 2), the cognitive perspective provides the clearest path for both understanding why an event leads to crisis (it

violates expectations about life, is discrepant with cherished life goals, shatters a particular self-image, etc.), and at the same time, what must be done in order for the client to move through and beyond the experience to deal with the future.

Our assessment framework elicits data on client images as well as thoughts in understanding why a particular event leads to crisis. Gaining cognitive mastery over the crisis involves use of data from both areas which is then focused on three sets of client activities.

(a)   At some point, the client must gain a reality-based understanding of the crisis event. The therapist asks the client to tell the story of what happened, what led up to the crisis, who was/is involved, the outcome(s), and other related details, listening all the while for gaps in information, possibly deliberate omissions, distortions, and so on. While people vary in their desire for concrete details, the premise is that in order for a crisis client to move through and past the crisis event, he/she must have some understanding of what happened and why. For example, a man whose thirty-eight year old wife files for a divorce (after 20 years of marriage, and raising three children into their high school years), will at some point need to answer questions such as: Why did she leave? In what ways was she dissatisfied with the marriage? Were there differences of opinion on division of household duties? Sexual difficulties? The willingness (or lack thereof) of her husband to assist her in developing a career outside the home as the children grew older?

A carpenter who loses a finger in an electric saw accident will need to confront the realities of whether the accident was due primarily to a faulty saw or to the carpenter's own negligence. The therapist's role is to serve as a reality check, much like a colleague on a research team might act in interpreting confusing data. The therapist helps the client to collect information, and to review the circumstances of the crisis event, as well as happenings before and after the event, as a means of laying groundwork for interpretation (discussed next) of what the event means to the client.

Many of the questions that clients need to explore are painful; anger, guilt, and a full range of emotional hurts emerge as the client reviews events. Indeed, the pain can be so strong for some clients that, left alone, they will avoid exploring the realities of the crisis event. The clinician's judgment is important here. In many cases, it is best to allow the client to retreat to some other aspect of the working-through process for the time being. Prolonged avoidance of a review of the event(s), however, may call for the therapist to gently, but firmly, confront the client with the avoidance: "How much do you really know about. . . . [why she left you, why they fired you, the circumstances of the accident, etc.]? I think that until you get some more information, you are going to remain stuck. You will actually limit your options for the future." While not wanting to force a client to review the realities of the event, this activity acts as an important step toward understanding, and, in some cases demythologizing the event, with a goal of eventually getting past the painful material.

(b) The second aspect of cognitive mastery is for the client to understand the meaning the event has for him/her, how it conflicts with expectations and cognitive maps, life goals/dreams, and religious beliefs. The best data sources here are the client's own words (which usually spill out freely in a crisis, without a great

deal of forethought) and a client's reported day and night dreams. The therapist should listen carefully for key thoughts, beliefs, and interpretations of events that lead to their being experienced as crisis. The injured carpenter may "picture" no future for himself now that he has sustained injury to his hand. The woman who has undergone a mastectomy following the diagnosis of breast cancer may view herself as unattractive, and think of herself as an unacceptable sex partner.

In listening for what the event means to the client, the therapist notes also any apparent cognitive errors (over-generalization, catastrophizing), misconceptions, or irrational beliefs. The therapist should avoid prematurely jolting the client with the therapist's own view of the cognitive mechanisms involved in the crisis, and instead use questions and reflective (clarifying) statements to draw the client's thought processes out for examination. Essentially, the therapist's questions shift from how-do-you-*feel*-about-that questions to how-do-you-*think*-about-that questions. For example: "How do you view yourself now that. . . .?" "What does it mean to you that she said. . .?" "You have said God must be punishing you; tell me more about what you think about that."

After noting unfinished business, expectations that have been shattered, beliefs that are discrepant with crisis data, or cognitive maps that are too limited to account for recent events, the therapist uses his/her clinical skill to relate this information back to the client. As most seasoned clinicians will attest, these interpretations run a far better chance of being accepted by the client when it is the client who first "discovers" them. The practical implication of this clinical wisdom is that the therapist should aim to generate considerable data about cognitions—overwhelming evidence, some might say—thereby increasing the probability of the client drawing the conclusions him/herself, or at least being receptive to the therapist's interpretation. Minimally, any interpretations should be based on data that both therapist and client have generated and reviewed together. Whatever strategy is chosen, the objective is for the client to gain some insight into why the event is experienced as a crisis. In most cases, some awareness of why (cognitively) things have fallen apart is considered a prerequisite for the rebuilding process.

It is important to note that emphasis on this seemingly intellectual aspect of crisis therapy does not mean that this therapy is restricted to what clinicians and researchers have called YAVIS clients (young, attractive, verbal, intelligent, successful) (Schofield 1964). All crisis clients—even very young children—have some cognitive understanding of the crisis event(s), and have some thought/image about what it all means to them in the future. Our key concern is with whether these cognitions are realistic, rational, and conducive to future growth and adjustment. A four-year-old boy who has been sexually molested by a relative, and threatened by the adult relative with punishment if anyone finds out, may believe that he (the child) is at fault for what happened, and simultaneously that he is in danger of being punished or rejected by his parents. Similarly, a six-year-old girl may be fearful of going to bed at night, having been told at her aunt's funeral, that, "she's just sleeping." The boy's belief that he will be rejected by his parents, and the girl's conceptual link between death as sleeping and sleeping at night will serve to guide their respective behavior in the months and years

to come. With children, or even adults with less than average intelligence, we need to identify the most salient cognitions and judge their adequacy, that is, are they true, and do they equip the person to deal with other life events in the future? It is especially important with children to give attention to whether their thoughts, interpretations, and so on are accurate, to the best of our knowledge. Whereas with adults our next step may be a rather complex process of cognitive restructuring, or some variation thereof, with children it may be as simple as offering another (truer) cognition to explain the data and allow the child to better understand some aspect of life. In the examples given, an adult will need to counter the child's inaccurate information, whether about culpability in the case of child abuse, or the nature of death and dying.

(c) The third cognitive mastery activity involves rebuilding, restructuring, or replacing cognitions, images, and dreams that have been destroyed by a crisis event. As we have emphasized throughout this book, this positive restructuring is a key ingredient of the growth potential in any crisis. The objective is to assist the client in developing new cognitions, perhaps amending an overall philosophy of life, and defining new goals/dreams that both square with the available data and equip the client to face the future. In some cases, as with the children just mentioned, this may be as simple as offering new information, though in other cases, the struggle for new beliefs, new self image, or a new dream or vision for the future will be much more intense, with false starts and stops along the way.

Table 8.3 identifies a number of strategies from the cognitive therapy literature that can be introduced at this point in crisis therapy. In addition to in-session activities such as cognitive restructuring, therapists can make use of external resources such as outside reading (see the Glossary), and referral to others who have either experienced a similar crisis (support groups for families of cancer patients) or who have special knowledge to assist in the cognitive rebuilding process (clergymen/women for adults whose religious faith is severely tested or challenged by a crisis). (See the Glossary of this volume, plus Hammond and Stanfield (1977) for summaries of cognitive therapy principles which can be used in crisis therapy.)

Behavioral/	The final crisis resolu-
Interpersonal	tion task is based on the
Adjustments	idea that behavioral

change is the "bottom line" for crisis resolution. In addition, well-timed, constructive action can make a person feel better (affective modality) and also improve self image and sense of mastery (cognitive). For example, systematically increasing activity levels can serve to combat depression, and has been found to correlate with adjustment following prisoner of war and hostage experiences (Segal 1982). Three out of four variables reported by Segal to be associated with psychological survival of hostages and prisoners of wars involve behavioral and interpersonal dimensions. The three include: (a) maintaining contact with others (even minimally, as in coded messages sent through POW camps); (b) taking steps to help others in trouble; (c) retaining some level of control over daily life (e.g., a hostage who invites his captors to sit down whenever they enter the cell, thereby exerting maximum control over both physical space and the interpersonal interaction). The remaining variable—maintaining confidence in one's own inner strength—is a cognitive variable wherein the prisoner reminds him/herself that there is an inner reservoir of untapped strength to draw on during times of severe stress.

Central to the fourth task of crisis resolution is the question of whether the person can eventually return to work, engage in play, and participate in meaningful relationships, in spite of the fact that any or all of these activities may have been brought to an abrupt halt or thrown into tremendous disarray for a period of time. Depending on what new behaviors are tried, and which ones become an integral part of the client's behavior repertoire, activities under this fourth task can signal the beginning of new skills associated with behavioral growth, or of constrictions associated with debilitation.

A comparison of crisis functioning in the behavioral and interpersonal modalities with pre-crisis functioning (see Assessment), will serve as a guide in identifying the specific client activities necessary to negotiate this task. This may include ground to be recovered (returning to work after an injury, reuniting with a spouse after separation), as well as new ground to be broken (finding an entirely new occupation, or learning to live as a single person, after being married for many years).

Some issues will require immediate attention, while others will stretch over a period of months. Similarly, the crisis client can be expected to be tremendously preoccupied with some behavioral and interpersonal changes ("I can't bear the thought of returning to the office after what happened this weekend"), and oblivious of many others (details of funeral arrangements for a loved one). The main consideration should be to help the client deal first with behavioral steps which, if neglected, will severely reduce options later on. For example, in the case described in Chapter 1 concerning the teacher who was a victim of an assault at school, it is predictable that the longer she waits to return to the classroom, the harder it may be to do so. Therapist and client should discuss these decisions together, with the therapist taking responsibility for raising the issues of priorities, as well as introducing strategies for change.

As Table 8.3 indicates, a wealth of behavior therapy techniques are available to the clinician in facilitating the positive behavioral and interpersonal changes required by any client's crisis. Quite often treatment will include other family members, as when a therapist or other health professional works with a rape victim and her husband/lover or with a family preparing for the return home of a heart patient whose exercise and diet patterns must be radically altered.

Helpers should also be alert to prevent friends and others in a client's social network from interfering with behavioral adjustments. For example, when a group of friends heard that a neighbor family's teenage son had killed himself with a gun, they took it upon themselves to remove all of the boy's personal possessions from his room (everything except the furniture) that afternoon. While the friends meant only to help, it is likely that by unilaterally taking away the behavioral demand of cleaning up the room and deciding what to do with the boy's belongings, they may also have inadvertantly interferred with the family's work on two other crisis resolution tasks: expression of feelings and cognitive mastery (the pain of confronting the blood stained room and the fact of the boy's death).

The crisis model suggests that each person connected with the boy's death—parents, siblings, and neighbors who want to help—will experience his/her own version of the same four crisis resolution tasks. Activities appropriate for one might be inappropriate or even interfere with activities for others, as when the neighbors' behavioral adjustment of doing something for the family, interferes with the family's own cognitive, affective, and behavioral tasks. A care giver with access to several parties in such a situation, for example, a minister/rabbi/priest, would use the four-task framework as a guide for counseling each of the parties so that their respective working through activities complement instead of conflict with one another.

DETERMINING PRIORITIES

The four-task guide for the process of crisis therapy is intended to serve as a cognitive map for the therapist, just as the five components of psychological first aid serve as a cognitive map for first-order crisis intervention. It is important to remember that each client will present unique problems and challenges, and that the order of task completion (and the amount of time required) will vary from one case to another. Our experience is that the therapist should assess task progress with each client during each therapeutic contact, and endeavor to make some progress (or lay groundwork) for each task during every session. Beyond this general guideline, the matter of which topics will be discussed and which adjustments begun should grow from a negotiation process between therapist and client. In deciding how to allocate therapeutic energies, the following should be considered:

(a) Determine which issues are most salient to the client at that moment. These might be nightmares about the crisis event, fears of the future, or behavioral demands from the environment. If in doubt, go to the area where the client is experiencing the most pain.

(b) Consider beginning with a crisis resolution activity that is the easiest to treat, that is, one that is most amenable to change. Beginning with a success can increase the client's self confidence and mobilize energy for working through other more difficult areas.

(c) Look for the crisis resolution activity that seems to account for the most variance in the client's overall disorganization. It may be that a faulty cognition can be dealt with directly, thereby opening the door for greater feelings of self-worth and rapid behavioral change. On the other hand, the client may need to make a behavioral change quickly, for example, finding a job, or confronting an employer, to pave the way for changes in other areas.

(d) Devote attention in the early sessions of crisis therapy to any activity which, if neglected, might reduce a client's option in subsequent weeks, months, and years.

EVALUATION OF OUTCOME

At follow-up, whether after several weeks of crisis therapy, at six months, or one or more years later, several key variables need to be assessed. The evaluation includes more than simply checking on the state of each of the personality modalities or subsystems, although this is where follow-up assessment begins. We want to look at the whole person, which, according to Gestalt psychology, is greater than simply the sum of the state of each of the five subsystems. Several issues are addressed:

1. Has there been a return to equilibrium, and a reorganization of the BASIC personality subsystems? While crisis theory indicates that such reorganization or return to a steady state will take place in a matter of weeks, the question at follow-up is (a) in what way, and (b) with what gains and losses? Has reorganization occurred in a direction of openness to the future, or has the person reordered life by withdrawing from life activities (behavior)? Has the reduction in unpleasant affect come about through increased cognitive mastery of the situation, or by settling into a narrow pessimistic view of life? By checking on the state of the various modalities, and their relationships with one another, crisis theory's constructs of equilibrium regained and openness to the future are examined.

2. Since the crisis state is caused by a breakdown in coping, we need to assess the extent to which coping capabilities have been regained. In particular, following Lazarus's (1980) paradigm, to what extent is (a) problem solving now possible and (b) subjective discomfort being managed? The former is assessed primarily by examining cognitive and behavioral functioning, and the latter by looking at the affective, somatic, and interpersonal modalities.

3. To what extent have any pre-crisis unresolved issues been worked through or finished at follow-up? Crisis theory argues that the crisis event might touch-off previously unresolved personality issues. At follow-up, we have an opportunity to check on resolution of these issues. Post traumatic stress disorder (PTSD) of war veterans, for example, can remain dormant for years until touched-off by some life event such as divorce or unemployment. At follow-up, the assessment is not only on resolution of the crisis, but also on whether progress has been made toward resolving the earlier conflict.

4. Has the event been integrated into the fabric of life? To what extent has the crisis event taken its place alongside other life events, no longer requiring intense attention?

5. Is the person open to facing the future, equipped and ready to work, play, and relate to others?

In sum, at follow-up, one examines the BASIC subsystems to determine the nature of crisis resolution. Has it been toward growth or debilitation, and in what ways? What have been the gains and losses in each area of the person's functioning: behavioral, affective, somatic, interpersonal, and cognitive? It is only by assessing the state of the individual's BASIC functioning at follow-up, along the same dimensions as assessed in pre-crisis and crisis periods, that we are able to say whether or not the crisis has been resolved, and in which direction.

CRISIS THERAPY RESEARCH Several theorists have pointed to the absence of research which links process variables with outcome in crisis therapy (Auerbach and Kilmann 1977). In an earlier chapter, we discussed the utility of the five components of psychological first-aid for research. Crisis therapy presents greater difficulties. For one thing, treatment takes place over longer periods of time—weeks to months—lending greater confusion as to what takes place to bring about specific changes, a constraint in all psychotherapy research. Our goal must be to define relevant variables as specifically as possible. The framework presented in this chapter has possibilities for research designs that specify treatment strategies, linking them to various outcome measures. Areas deserving the attention of researchers include the following:

1. Data using the BASIC personality profile needs to be collected to further refine our understanding of key crisis theory concepts such as disorganization/disequilibrium of the crisis state, breakdown in coping, utilization of personal and social supplies, resolution of crisis, and the like.
2. Lazarus's (1976) hypothesis that the durability of results can be predicted by the number of modalities treated needs to be tested in the context of crisis theory. It might even be possible, before collecting new data, to re-examine data from other crisis studies to extract information on a number of modalities treated through various strategies. (See Chapter 18 for an example with research on rape.)
3. While the multimodal format is not intended to arrive at a label, but rather at treatment strategies, it is possible to use this format in studying relevant diagnostic categories from DSM III (1980). The system might then facilitate the development of better bridges between diagnostic categories and treatment techniques.

4. A stronger empirical base is needed for one of the most intriguing clinical observations in crisis situations—namely, that crisis victims progress through certain stages or phases. The idea is provocative in the sense that if stages can be identified, it might also be possible to specify the treatments most appropriate for various stages. Horowitz (1976) makes a start in this direction. It would be important to collect BASIC personality profiles for crisis clients at various points in time, to see if stages emerge, and if so, what their characteristics are in terms of BASIC personality functioning. Another avenue would be to assume or hypothesize the stages (from Caplan or Horowitz) and to collect BASIC profile data for the various stages. The goal would be to specify the modalities most affected during each stage, which could then provide clues to treatment strategies that would be most effective during various stages. Which modalities, for example, are most affected at impact? Is denial a primary cognitive function? If so, which cognitive strategies might best be employed? Or, should other strategies (those which seemingly have an affective base) be applied to the primary cognitive process of denial?
5. It was noted earlier that many crises are resolved without the benefit of crisis therapy. Research that examines successful crisis resolution is needed to evaluate what environmental factors have been helpful in the working through process. By looking at adaptation in each of these modalities, our understanding of the mechanisms involved in coping might be enriched.

CONCLUSION This chapter represents a multimodal perspective on crisis therapy built on the model first developed by Lazarus (1976, 1981). The overriding assumption is that the assessment, treatment, and evaluation functions of crisis therapy (each important in any comprehensive approach) are greatly enhanced by looking at an individual in terms of the five BASIC subsystems or modalities. Essentially, we have taken Lazarus's format and asked various questions from crisis theory about each modality. Treatment is built on this assessment, but draws from a rich tradition in clinical psychology, medicine, and "holistic" approaches to health (emphasis on physical exercise and diet). These procedures take place within a general systems perspective in crisis theory which looks at an individual in the context of a family, social group, community, and culture. While there is a heavy treatment emphasis, the point was made that not all crises need to be resolved through therapeutic strategies; many crises are resolved in the natural environment. Further, many workers not trained in "therapy techniques" can facilitate positive crisis resolution by helping clients/friends to work through crisis in terms of the four tasks of crisis resolution. This environmental approach will have broad implications for consultation with key community caretakers such as clergy, employers, and school teachers who have access to a wide range of environmental resources which can facilitate or impede resolution of any individual's crisis. (See Section III.)

chapter nine

Multimodal Crisis Therapy: Case Examples

The two cases presented in this chapter illustrate the application of a multimodal framework to crisis therapy. The subheadings for each case cover the main dimensions discussed in Chapter 8.

Particular attention is given to how each client negotiates the four tasks of crisis resolution: physical survival, expression of feelings, cognitive mastery, and behavioral/interpersonal adjustments.

SURVIVING A PHYSICAL ASSAULT Physical assault, whether the result of a domestic quarrel or an encounter with a stranger, represents a class of situational crises which has become all too frequent in the past several years (Crime in the United States 1979). From the vantage point of crisis theory, physical attack represents a discrete event that can have a powerful impact on future psychological health, to say nothing of physical well-being. The case presented here highlights the most salient aspects of multimodal crisis therapy aimed at the psychological resolution of such crises.

PRESENTING PROBLEM AND PRECIPITATING EVENT Susan first thought someone might be following her when she was about a block away from her apartment. Though it was late at night (shortly after 11:00 P.M.), she stepped out into the chilly night air to make the short walk to a convenience store only three blocks away, knowing that she and her three-year-old son would need a quart of milk before breakfast the next morning. She heard footsteps. From the corner of her eye, she saw a man walking just behind her, though on the other side of the street. Quickening her pace, and at the same time trying to tell herself that there was no real danger, she kept walking down the street. With only 50 yards to go until she reached a lighted area in front of the store, Susan felt an arm around her neck. The next thing she knew she was being thrown behind bushes. Though much smaller than her assailant (5'5", 108 lbs. against 6'2", 200 lbs.), Susan began kicking and screaming for all she was worth. Her fear was that she would be raped, though, as it turned out, this did not happen. Her screams evidently saved her from sexual attack. The struggling stopped when her assailant hit her sharply across the front of her head with a blunt object, and quickly ran away. With blood pouring from her forehead, Susan stumbled to

151

the nearby grocery store where an attendant phoned for an ambulance to take her to the hospital emergency room.

Susan's wound to her head healed quickly. When it came time to remove the stitches, however, the nurse who spoke with Susan recognized that the potential harm went far beyond the physical wound alone. Susan reported being extremely nervous and anxious throughout the day and night. She frequently had nightmares about the attack, picturing her assailant coming after her. She was so frightened that the assailant might come back to get her that she would not walk out of her apartment alone, even during the daylight. This problem was further exacerbated by the fact that Susan felt she could no longer impose upon a neighboring girl friend to accompany her to work each day. She agreed to visit a clinical psychologist associated with her physician's family practice to discuss how to cope with the aftermath of the assault.

CONTEXT AND PRE-CRISIS FUNCTIONING From the first interview the therapist learned that Susan was a twenty-one-year-old woman who had been married three years, and separated from her husband for approximately ten months. She worked from 8:30 until 5:00 each day in an office building near her apartment. Though she had little trouble securing her soon-to-be exhusband's approval that she have custody of their child, frictions between the two parents were frequent, particularly around money matters. Susan was having a tough time making ends meet on her salary. The separation came rather unexpectedly from Susan's viewpoint, and at a poor time. The family had just moved to a community of 300,000 people, from their much smaller hometown over 600 miles away. Susan had found it difficult to leave family and friends, though she did so in order for her husband to take a promotion to a managerial position. Susan had not yet met many people in the new community during her 13 months of residence. Though she talked now and then with a neighboring couple in her apartment complex, she felt that she had no true friends in this town. She had taken her job just three weeks before the attack.

The previous 1½ years, then, had been a time of tremendous stress for Susan. Adjusting to a move to a new city, separating from her husband, financial worries, new job, few social supports. All in all though, Susan said that even though things had been very stressful, still she had been "making it" prior to the assault. She had been a strong-willed person. Though hurt and angry about the separation and the increased responsibilities thrown her way she was determined to "tough it out." She reported having had a difficult time understanding her husband's desire to end the marriage. She had thought things were going well, though he said they were not. He talked of having lost sexual attraction for her shortly after their baby was born. It was at this time that he began staying out later at night, drinking heavily, and fighting with Susan. In one sense, then, his moving out of the house 10 months ago actually alleviated some of the stress (i.e., fewer fights late at night), even though it added additional responsibility to Susan to care for her child.

MULTIMODAL CRISIS PROFILE Table 9.1 summarizes Susan's symptoms at the time of the initial interview. She reported having had behavioral difficulties such as inability to sleep, eat, and leave the house alone (even during the day). Her main affective symptoms included extreme anxiety and feelings of being "uptight" all the time, and a fear, bordering

TABLE 9.1   CRISIS PROFILE: SUSAN AFTER THE ASSAULT

Modality	Crisis State
Behavioral	Inability to leave house alone; difficulty falling asleep at night; poor appetite.
Affective	Anxiety, feeling "uptight"; fear of another attack; sadness.
Somatic	Headaches; stomach-aches; general physical fatigue.
Interpersonal	Isolated; reluctance to ask for help from friends; reliance on guilt inducing interactions with husband.
Cognitive	Day and night dreams about the attack; negative self-statements.

on terror, that she would be attacked again by the person who attacked her the first time. She reported headaches, stomach-aches, and a general physical weakness, due to the lack of food. For several days she had been existing on a diet composed mainly of diet cola. Interpersonally, she felt isolated from the rest of the world, talking only briefly to her neighbor friend (woman) about the attack as this person drove Susan to work each day (five blocks away). She had told her husband about the attack, particularly about the difficulties she was having in the aftermath, with a hint, as she told the story, of wanting him to know that he must bear some responsibility for what happened to her, that is, it was his fault that she lived alone in the first place. In the cognitive area, Susan's main symptoms were frightening day and night dreams about the attack. Since so many bad things had happened to her in the past year, Susan also ruminated on the fact that she would now never be able to "make it," on her own. The determination she had built up before seemed to have evaporated overnight.

Beyond the disruption in each of the five modalities, the most salient aspect of Susan's crisis was that it came in the context of her trying to cope with separation from her husband. It was very clear that Susan had not yet worked through her feelings about the separation, that she did not understand fully why it happened, and that she was bitter about the whole experience. She seemed to be taking care of herself, though she was reluctant to let her husband know that she could do so. The attack was seen as a "last straw" from Susan's vantage point, one which would surely show her husband what a mess he had made of her life.

Though she wouldn't let her husband know it, Susan did have real strengths which, if mobilized, could assist her in resolving the immediate crisis, and in making long-term adjustment to the attack as well as to life as a single parent. She had a strong will, evident in her attempts to handle things during the previous months, and in her fights with her husband (verbal) and with her assailant (physical). The question was whether this strength could be turned to her advantage, rather than being used solely for revenge against her husband.

Other resources or strengths for Susan included her job (which she liked, performed well, and, though low in pay, promised the opportunity for advancement during the next year), and the friendship of a neighborhood couple. While she had not talked a great deal with these two neighbors, they were available, and could be included as a source of support in the coming weeks.

TREATMENT   The initial agreement between the therapist and Susan was to do whatever they could to assist her in working through the crisis precipitated by the attack. In so doing, however, thoughts and feelings about Susan's current life situation—the unresolved separation experience—came to the surface and were discussed as well. Susan made the connection herself in statements such as the following:

"None of this would have happened if I weren't living alone."

Statements like these led to an exploration of the current crisis, the context in which it occurred, and other unresolved issues about the separation: feelings toward her husband, thoughts about whether she could "make it" as a single person, and what it meant to her to be a single person (a "one time" loser already!), and the like.

The treatment strategies employed can be summarized according to the four tasks of crisis resolution: maintaining physical well-being, expressing feelings, achieving cognitive mastery, and negotiating behavioral/interpersonal adjustments (see Table 9.2).

PHYSICAL   The chief difficulty Susan experienced physically, beyond the headaches, was
SURVIVAL   tenseness and an inability to eat and sleep. A mild tranquilizer was prescribed to be used as needed and Susan was taught deep-muscle relaxation (Jacobson 1974) to be used especially in the evening before bedtime. She was encouraged to begin a more well-rounded diet to regain energy, and to begin regular (though moderate) physical exercise (swimming at the YMCA with her neighbor friend). The therapist stressed the importance of improved eating habits in maintaining her physical strength in the aftermath of the crisis. Physical exercise would both help increase her sense of coping with the current situation, and make her physically tired enough to sleep at night.

EXPRESSING   Susan was encouraged to talk about her feelings concerning the attack. She
FEELINGS   spoke in detail about fears she felt at the time she was walking along the street, continuing through the attack, and the immediate days which followed. At one point she was encouraged to use a Gestalt "empty chair" technique to confront her attacker. It was striking how the dialogue using empty chairs moved from confrontation of the attacker to confrontation of all men, and then to Susan's husband. This was one of the early indications of how the marital situation was an important backdrop to the psychological impact of the physical assault.

COGNITIVE   Susan was also encouraged to talk about her day and night dreams (images) of
MASTERY   the attack, ruminations about how bad her life was, how the attack was the "final blow," and that things would be "downhill from here on in." After talking through the event, and having Susan interpret its various meanings (e.g., as a sign of her incompetence), the therapist helped Susan dispute these views, replacing them, instead, with more balanced language which emphasized Susan's strengths as well as weaknesses in the aftermath of the attack. Calming imagery was introduced as a replacement for the frightening recollections which continued to haunt her.

An essential component of cognitive mastery of the crisis experience was for Susan to understand it in the context of broader life experience, particularly the separation from her husband. Issues surfaced when Susan discussed her reluctance

TABLE 9.2 CRISIS RESOLUTION TASKS

Task	Objectives	Strategies
Physical survival	Control headaches, stomach-aches, and gradually increase physical strength/ energy	Medication; deep muscle relaxation; physical exercise (swimming); changes in diet
Expression of feelings	Express anger toward attacker (and men in general), and fear of another attack	Discussion of feelings with therapist; Gestalt "empty chair" technique
	Manage anxiety	Calming imagery to replace frightening recollections
Cognitive mastery	Understand the attack and its meaning to Susan in terms of self-image, separation from husband, managing life as a single parent	Guided discussion of the attack and Susan's thoughts about it; Gestalt dream work
	Adopt positive, more balanced concepts about her ability to cope from now on	Disputation of irrational self-talk; discussion of strengths as well as weaknesses
Behavioral/interpersonal adjustments	Make trips to and from apartment alone	In vivo systematic desensitization
	Work with police in identifying assailant's photograph	Behavioral rehearsal
	Ask for help from friends	Rational emotive therapy regarding managing everything alone.
	Begin single parent behaviors: e.g., take driver's license test to reduce dependence upon others, initiate social contacts, discuss child visitation with husband	Behavior rehearsal, assertion training, outside readings, referral to Parents Without Partners.

to practice the deep-muscle relaxation and to use the medication available to her. Susan suggested that, though she thought both would help her, she wanted her husband to "know how bad this was." Discussion of this issue opened up further the connection (in Susan's mind) between this particular crisis and the relationship with her husband. The issue became one of whether or not there were ways she could confront and deal with her anger toward her husband other than by destroying herself, hoping he would feel guilty witnessing her misery.

Her insight, as a result of these discussions, was that she had not yet been ready to break from the turmoil of the separation to a calmer, more manageable, more reasonable life on her own as a single parent. She had been resisting the idea of living on her own. A part of her wanted her husband to know how badly he treated her. Susan came to believe that, in a sense, much of her suffering had therefore been self-induced. Though in the long run she did not want to be just barely getting by, in the short run, there was some advantage in her husband knowing that she was suffering. Even though the guilt might not bring him back, it might at least keep him awake at night too!

Without viewing the attack as something she "asked for" or "wanted," Susan did recognize the ways in which she was trying to use the attack as a weapon in her struggle with her husband, and as evidence of her inability to make it on her own.

Throughout these discussions between Susan and her therapist, emphasis was placed on the fact that tremendous stress brought on by life circumstances (in this case, move to a strange city, birth of a child, separation, and physical attack), could bring about seemingly "crazy" thoughts and behaviors. The therapist encouraged Susan to talk about all of this in the context of coping and surviving, as opposed to "illness." Susan's "crazy" behavior served some purpose, and signaled her to make changes. Therapy at this time was an opportunity to reorganize her life. The assault touched off a period of serious reflection, which motivated her to make changes that would be necessary in order for her to live a full life in the years to come.

Finally, the therapist referred Susan to readings on divorce (Weiss 1975) to help her understand the conflicts of recently separated people and to realize that she was not alone in the struggles she faced.

BEHAVIORAL/ INTERPERSONAL ADJUSTMENTS   The first set of behavioral and interpersonal adjustment considered as a part of crisis therapy involved Susan's being able to leave home, go to work, and basically function outside her apartment. After extensive discussion of the reasonable precautions anyone would need to make in venturing outside the home alone at night, plans were made to enlist the cooperation of her neighbor friend for certain errands, and to take steps to "desensitize" her to being out of the home, first with a friend, and then alone. In vivo systematic desensitization was used to help her walk in the area near her apartment during the daylight hours.

Another behavioral step had to do with Susan's visiting the police station to look over photographs to help identify her assailant, followed by her identifying the man from a police line-up. As it turned out, Susan was ambivalent about whether to get involved in the process. She eventually chose to take this step, drawing some strength from assertively dealing with her attacker, even though she did not have to confront him face-to-face.

Perhaps the greatest gain for Susan came in a series of behavioral/interpersonal changes regarding her separation. Susan had been planning on taking the test to get a drivers license for some time, though she had put it off. She decided now, however, that she was ready to give up the dependent situation this placed her in, and make a move toward the greater freedom which the ability to drive a car would give her. She took steps to put herself in greater contact with others going through the separation/divorce process by joining a divorce adjustment group offered by a family guidance clinic in the community. She also planned to join Parents Without Partners in an attempt to establish contact with others who were coping with the difficulties of raising children alone. In addition, the therapist worked with Susan on becoming more assertive in dealing with her husband, especially regarding money, and visits with their son. Ever since the original separation, Susan had been dissatisfied with these arrangements. She had been reluctant to discuss the arrangements openly for fear that this would be interpreted as her accepting the separation and eventual divorce. Welcoming any opportunity for her husband to see that she was miserable, she had been content to just "muddle along." In deciding to give up this role, Susan and her therapist discussed ways in which she might assertively articulate what she wanted and needed from her husband regarding financial support for herself and her child, as well as visits between her husband and son. She had been particularly concerned that her husband had neglected the boy. She decided to make her requests clearer: for her son's sake she wanted the visits to take place regularly, and was willing to assist in making this possible. Anticipating that the couple might have difficulties in negotiating aspects of the divorce settlement, the therapist suggested that Susan consider divorce mediation through the family court as a means of working toward an agreement acceptable to both parties.

FOLLOW UP AND EVALUATION
At the end of eight weeks of therapy Susan reported having much less anxiety and fright about the physical attack. She reported that her eating patterns, ability to sleep, and freedom to leave the house had all improved. She still had "twinges" of fear about the attack, though she did not find them debilitating in any way. She was most reluctant to go out alone, though did so when necessary, and when reasonable care could be taken.

At follow-up nine months later, the attack and its aftermath had receded even further into the background of Susan's life experience. She reported having little difficulty in leaving the apartment alone, and enjoyed increased mobility now that she had a driver's license. Though still regretful about the divorce, she had accepted it and was effectively living the life of a single parent (dating, managing things at home with her child). She was also making appropriate use of social supports, for example, the singles' group at her church, and Parents Without Partners. Discussion of exspouse conflicts in the divorce adjustment group which she attended several months earlier had reinforced the assertion training she had received as part of crisis therapy. In retrospect, the attack appeared to be an event which provided the occasion for Susan making significant changes in how she was dealing with the process of separation, moving toward negotiating the adjustments necessary for life as a single parent.

Susan's crisis illustrates how an external event, in this case, the physical attack, can interact with, or touch off, other personal/social conflicts. The specific meaning given a precipitating event is all important in understanding the uniqueness of each person's crisis. Susan had been under a great deal of stress for a number of months: move to a new city, separation from husband, financial difficulties, beginning a new job. Though she had been "getting by" while separated from her husband, she was not adjusting well to the separation, and was playing manipulative games to make her husband feel guilty for the separation.

Whether or not he "should" have felt guilty, the games were not helpful to Susan. Even in the aftermath of the attack, she felt at times that the most important thing was to communicate her misery to her husband, instead of doing something to alleviate it.

The physical assault had the effect, in this case, of dramatically exposing her destructive coping responses. When things reached a breaking point it was no longer possible to hide her distress, and new means of coping were needed. In the final analysis this crisis, which began with a horrid physical attack, led to growth for Susan. She gave up dysfunctional patterns of behavior, and adopted more useful and gratifying behaviors appropriate for life as a single person.

DEALING WITH DAD'S MID-LIFE CRISIS

In most developmental crises, whether an adolescent struggling to establish an identity separate from parents, or a sixty-five-year-old executive worried about facing retirement, the turmoil of the person in crisis has a profound effect on family members. The case presented next offers a multimodal analysis of one man's mid-life crisis and its resolution, with special attention given to the impact of his crisis on the rest of the family.

PRESENTING PROBLEM AND PRECIPITATING EVENT Lewis visited a clinical psychologist at the suggestion of his family physician. His immediate concern was a "blow up" at work two days earlier. Lewis, who held a supervisory position in the safety division of a nuclear power plant, had bolted from a routine staff meeting, and then run out of the plant. He reported breaking into a cold sweat just before he and one of his subordinates were to discuss a routine safety test of the plant's emergency system that had been carried out the previous day. Though the drill was successful, Lewis had come to believe that the drill and the debriefing meeting had been engineered by a couple of people on his staff to show his incompetence.

After running from the plant, he called his wife from a nearby phone booth and asked her to pick him up to take him home. For the next two days he stayed at home (with his wife, who "called in sick" for him each day), brooded and nervously talked about how some of his co-workers didn't like him. As things got progressively worse, Lewis finally agreed to his wife's suggestion that they call their family physician, who then referred them to a clinical psychologist at a local mental health center. At the time of the initial visit, Lewis reported less concern about the plot, and more concern about the fact that he must somehow be "cracking up" under pressure at work. Why had all of this happened to him, he asked? How could he explain it to his colleagues? To his family?

CONTEXT AND PRE-CRISIS FUNCTIONING Lewis was 42-years-old, had been married 17 years, and was the father of two children, a girl 15, and a boy 12. Trained as a chemical engineer, he had worked seven years in a production job in a small plant, followed by 10 years of service with a large company whose primary product was fuel for nuclear power reactors. For the past five years, he had been supervisor of the plant's safety division, a position requiring both engineering knowledge and supervisory skills. Lewis' life had proceeded very much as planned: marriage, children, success in his career. In many ways, he had already achieved the goals that he had originally set for himself as a young man. He found little challenge in his present position, and at times longed for the days when he was doing chemical engineering work instead of "managing people," a task which caused him considerable anxiety. As a relatively unassertive individual, Lewis felt very much out of touch with his subordinates. He had delegated considerable responsibility to three employees, and felt increasingly removed from what they were doing, and consequently ignorant about the operations in his own shop. He was reluctant to ask about their work for fear that his questions might reveal his own ignorance and that his subordinates would take offense at his "checking up" on them.

In the aftermath of Pennsylvania's Three Mile Island nuclear accident (1978), considerable attention had been drawn to Lewis' company (and others in the southeast) by anti-nuclear organizations, and by previously "neutral" politicians and reporters. Lewis had therefore become even more concerned about the operations of the entire company, especially whether his division was capable of monitoring plant safety as it should.

With the exception of his wife, few others had any idea that Lewis was troubled. He was a loner at work. As a matter of fact, he felt uncomfortable in most interpersonal or social gatherings. Though he wanted to be "one of the boys," he felt far from it and envied others who could tell stories, have fun, and the like. Lewis was similarly reluctant to discuss his concerns with his wife Helen. His attitude was, "What good would it do anyway? Just getting her upset would make two of us worried."

Lewis had been a good provider for his family, and had a sterling work history (he could count the number of sick days taken on one hand). He was a "work horse" contributor to several civic groups, saying "yes" to chores that others did not want. His physical appearance was neat, and his life at work and at home was well organized. He applied his analytical training to most difficulties that came his way.

Lewis' wife, Helen, was a bright, vivacious, talented woman who had chosen long ago a career as housewife and mother. She was the complete manager at home, making lists of things to be accomplished, handling most of them herself, and delegating a few responsibilities to Lewis and the two children. She was quite active in a number of civic and volunteer groups, and worked very hard in each of these endeavors. All seemed to be quite well with Helen's life, though in the past year she had come to realize that her children were requiring less of her time, and she had talked about the possibility of taking a part-time job. The 15-year-old daughter, Cheryl, was independent, made good grades in school, and had many friends. Twelve-year-old Eric, however, had not quite lived up to his parents expectations as far as grades were concerned, seemed quiet like his father, and stayed pretty much to himself. Lewis had been concerned about the fact that his son did not seem to have many friends and that he might "turn out like me."

All in all, Lewis' family might be called typical American middle class: comfortable income, surburban home, public schools, a "full-time" mother, and a father with a "good job." If there were problems or concerns within the family, they were not apparent to neighbors and friends.

MULTIMODAL CRISIS PROFILE Lewis' report of what he called the "anxiety attack" at work included the following: cold sweat, tension in his stomach, horrible images that he would be asked questions in the meeting that he could not answer and that his ignorance would be exposed for all to see. He reported feeling that he simply "couldn't take it anymore," and so he literally ran away. He just had to get out of there. When he finally got home that afternoon, he felt some relief at being away from the office, though now he had new terrors to haunt him: What did they think of him at work? What would they do about him? What would he tell them now? What would his future in the company be? Would he be fired? Who would support the family?

These and other ruminations made Lewis almost immobile. He couldn't sleep and didn't feel like eating. He attempted to distract himself the first day at home by tinkering in his shop with Christmas presents he was building for his children, though to no avail.

Table 9.3 summarizes the state of Lewis's crisis two days after the scene at the office. Most salient characteristics were: inability to return to work, listlessness, depression and fear about the future, bodily tension and headaches, interpersonal isolation, and a series of frightening images and negative self-talk patterns.

Lewis's crisis had clear effects on other members of the family. A multimodal analysis of the various family difficulties associated with Lewis's crisis appear in Table 9.4. The children and Helen were nervous and emotionally upset at Lewis's agitated behavior. Somatic complaints, some of which had been dormant, re-appeared, for example, Helen's ulcer, Eric's stomach cramps. The family's reaction was for each person to busy him/herself more deeply in whatever activities had been taking place prior to the crisis. Helen worked hard to run the house as well as she could, hoping that a happy home atmosphere would somehow help Lewis's anxiety. Eric became even more withdrawn, watching TV, or staying in his room. Cheryl stayed away from home as much as possible. No one in the family talked directly about Lewis's episode at work; everyone seemed to handle one another with kid gloves, as if talking openly about things would make them worse. In the cognitive domain, no one could get a "handle" on what was going on. Though they would not admit it to one another, their fear was that their father was "sick," and that things could get very much worse. Helen, in particular, entertained thoughts that she had somehow failed as a wife because she could not be a good helpmate and assist Lewis in dealing with his work difficulties.

TREATMENT   The first problem faced in the therapy session was Lewis's concern about re-turning to work. Here the basic principles of psychological first aid were followed, namely, deciding what issues needed attention first, and what issues could be post-poned until later. Lewis's immediate concern was with what he would say to superiors, co-workers, and subordinates on the first day back at work. After talk-ing it over with the therapist, Lewis decided that he did not need to explain every-thing; indeed, he couldn't. For the time being, for those who needed to know, a

TABLE 9.3   MULTIMODAL CRISIS PROFILE: LEWIS

Modality	Crisis State
Behavioral	Inability to return to work; idleness (sitting around the house); inability to sleep; drinking too much alcohol
Affective	Depression; fears about future; anxiety about returning to work
Somatic	Bodily tension; headaches
Interpersonal	Isolation from co-workers; arguments with spouse; interpersonal distance between self and children
Cognitive	Negative self-talk ("I'm a failure, lazy, no good, etc."); catastrophizing; overgeneralizing; negative self-image (e.g., incompetent in face of emergency at the plant)

TABLE 9.4 MULTIMODAL PROFILE OF FAMILY REACTIONS TO LEWIS' CRISIS

Modality	Crisis State
Behavioral	Helen: increased housework activity Eric: More withdrawn; more T.V. watching; more time alone in room Cheryl: Time away from home as much as possible
Affective	Helen: Agitated, fearful, angry Eric: Worried, sad Cheryl: Worried
Somatic	Helen: Reactivation of ulcer Eric: Stomach cramps Cheryl: Slightly nervous stomach
Interpersonal	All: Silence, or hushed conversations (behind closed doors) about "the problem"
Cognitive	Helen: Self-blame: "It is my fault. I should have helped more." All: Catastrophizing: "This will get much worse." Children: Search for explanation: "He's mentally ill; perhaps I will be too."

statement that he had been under a great deal of stress and was now receiving medical assistance would suffice. The therapist also helped Lewis explore his fantasies about the terrible things which would come his way for having "lost it." He came to see that he would be able to survive what he felt would be the worst eventuality, namely, being fired, and that his chief concern now should be understanding what happened to him, what it meant, and what he should do about it. For the time being, Lewis would: (a) inform his boss that he was now doing something to help alleviate his concerns/worries about work, (b) keep his boss informed about his progress, and (c) request a meeting with his boss in two weeks to discuss the work situation.

The therapist questioned Lewis about his thinking regarding the other employees having "engineered" the drill and concluded that Lewis himself now felt this to be untrue, and no other evidence of thought disorder was present. The therapist concluded that Lewis was experiencing a severe stress reaction, not a psychotic episode.

Having "bought" two weeks time, Lewis and the therapist set out to explore the crisis, its meanings, and implications for his future. The therapist met with Lewis individually, and for several sessions with the family together. The chief treatment strategies used to assist Lewis and the rest of the family in working through the crisis are listed in Table 9.5. The main work on Lewis's crisis can be summarized according to the four tasks of crisis resolution: physical survival, expression of feelings, cognitive mastery, and behavior/interpersonal adjustments.

PHYSICAL SURVIVAL Each of the family members was having his/her share of physical difficulties during the crisis time. Though physical violence (fighting or suicide/homicide) was not a problem for this family, maintaining physical health was. They were told to expect that during the crisis, certain physical problems could be exacerbated, (re-

TABLE 9.5   CRISIS RESOLUTION TASKS: LEWIS AND FAMILY

Tasks	Objectives for Family	Therapeutic strategies
Physical survival	Manage headaches (Lewis), stomach cramps (Eric and Cheryl), ulcer (Helen)	Discuss stress reactions of family; teach relaxation techniques
	Reduce Physical tension (Lewis)	Encourage physical exercise
Expression of feelings	Identify and express fears/ worries about Lewis's condition (Helen, Eric, Cheryl), anxiety about work and future (Lewis), irritations about home life (Lewis)	Use active listening during family discussions of events and feelings; Gestalt "empty chair" (Lewis); Identify connections between thoughts and feelings; introduce anxiety management training
Cognitive mastery	Develop accurate understanding of recent events (Lewis's conflicts at work), and the family's reactions (everyone) Control catastrophizing (everyone), overgeneralizing (Lewis), and negative self-talk (Lewis).	Conduct reality based review of recent events in light of Lewis's past accomplishments, current strengths and weaknesses, and future plans Implement cognitive modification
	Discover accurate language and concepts to explain events and open the door for future change and growth (everyone)	Supply new labels for upsetting behaviors; discuss developmental perspective on crisis
	Stop self-blame (Helen)	Modify self-talk
Behavioral/interpersonal adjustments	Return to work, reduce dependence on alcohol, and sleep better at night (Lewis)	Conduct behavior rehearsal re: first day back on the job; reinstate daily exercise; teach deep-muscle relaxation
	Become more assertive at home and at work (Lewis)	Teach assertion skills
	Learn management skills (Lewis)	Refer to management training seminar
	Discuss job placement with boss (Lewis)	Encourage to talk to boss about career
	Spend more time with children (Lewis)	Coach Lewis on parenting skills
	Talk to one another about fears instead of retreating from one another (everyone)	Engage in family counseling re: communication skills
	Engage in physical exercise as an aid to stress management (everyone)	Offer guidance on exercise programs

activation of Helen's ulcer and stomach cramps for Eric). While simply discussing the family's problems helped somewhat, other measures were also introduced. Lewis was encouraged to begin his regular jogging routine again. Whereas several years ago, he had jogged regularly and reported feeling "great" physically, he had let it go in the past year and a half. The family was encouraged to accept exacerbation of physical difficulties as one natural accompaniment for this crisis, and to look toward physical exercise, diet changes, and deep-muscle relaxation (practice tapes borrowed from therapist) to assist in physically enduring these difficult days and weeks.

EXPRESSION OF FEELINGS Lewis was so agitated when he came to see the therapist that he had little difficulty talking about recent events. As he did, the therapist helped him express both the immediate feelings of anxiety and tension, and a number of worries, fears, and angers which had been kept hidden prior to the crisis event. As one who was not interpersonally assertive, one who kept things in most of the time, Lewis had accumulated a series of concerns that had built to a breaking point. He discussed feelings of loneliness, coupled with anger at the lack of understanding he felt from co-workers. He talked also about resenting superiors for putting him into a position where he might be the "fall guy" should an accident occur at the plant.

In family sessions, Helen, Eric, and Cheryl were encouraged to express their worries about what Lewis was going through, and what it might mean to each of them. This led to discussions of how the family had typically dealt with anger, hurt, and other unpleasant emotions in the past. Each had his or her own way of coping (retreating to a room, or leaving the house, or burying self in work), with none of the strategies including direct confrontation and discussion of feelings. The therapist was able to help family members confront one another with their fears directly at the time of the crisis, later pointing to the difference between this strategy and what they had been using before. Helen's initial feelings of worry and concern for Lewis turned later to anger that he had kept his concerns from her. Exchanges between Lewis and Helen in family sessions led also to the discussion of other issues which had been essentially buried for some time. These included Lewis's bitterness that Helen managed the family's finances, making him feel unneeded, and Helen's resentment that he had never said this to her, thus denying her the opportunity to unload some of the home pressure, or at least share it.

COGNITIVE MASTERY Everyone in the family needed assistance in understanding what had caused the particular breakdown Lewis experienced at work. In individual sessions, the therapist and Lewis examined closely the event which precipitated the crisis—a meeting at which Lewis and a subordinate were to report to their superiors on the recent test of one of the plant's safety systems. The therapist's tactic was to ask Lewis to describe in detail his reactions at the meeting. This discussion of feelings (anxiety) and thoughts ("I am unprepared, incompetent, etc.") led to an exploration of the background/contextual variables such as Lewis's training, skills, and approach to work. It became clear that Lewis had effectively put himself out of touch with his subordinates by his own unassertive style, and fear of looking ignorant to them. In reviewing the happenings prior to the crisis, Lewis also told of having read an article in the newspaper that morning about "the future of nuclear energy," which added to the pressures that he experienced that day. He became more and more uptight as the day progressed, and he had no outlet for his tension.

Lewis came to understand the interaction between his previous means of coping with stress, and the current crisis. His own words were, "something had to give." The combination of factors included: (a) a nonassertive personality style (keeping feelings to himself, fear of confronting others); (b) belief that to assert himself might lead to anger and rejection; (c) fear of this rejection since it fit with his already low self-image as one who was lazy, a failure, and incompetent. All of these issues were "forced" by Lewis's managerial status. In a sense, he had fallen victim to the Peter Principle, by rising to his own level of incompetence. A skilled chemical engineer, he was not emotionally suited to managing people. He could not yet deal well with rejection, which every boss must at one time or another face from subordinates, and he still needed to learn to assertively deal with people—particularly around personal evaluations.

Beyond these specific considerations about Lewis's personality, and the interactions with his job situation, the therapist encouraged him to look at this crisis as an experience in the context of a mid-life developmental transition. Lewis was presented with the idea (cognition) that most people "naturally" reevaluate their lives at mid-life, particularly concerning career, but also in relationships with spouses, family, and friends. In Lewis's case, there was discussion of the fact that he had pretty much achieved his goals set early in life, and that his satisfaction at this point was certainly not total. He felt out of place in his work situation, though he had risen to a respected position, and made good money. Similarly, in his home life, he and Helen had devoted primary energies toward creating a home situation within which to raise children, and had neglected their relationship with one another. Lewis talked of being dissatisfied with these patterns of living. Prior to the crisis he was actually bored with much of his life. The idea that the crisis could be made into an opportunity to really examine and change his life structure gave a new direction to the working-through process, that is, brought some encouragement to what had been to that point a totally confusing, frightening, painful experience.

Though most of the preceding exploration took place in individual sessions with Lewis, it was important that the developmental conceptualizations were shared in the family sessions as well, to assist the family in gaining cognitive mastery of the crisis. The developmental perspective was offered as a viable alternative to the idea that Lewis was sick, or mentally ill, or that he had some emotional disease. The transition of mid-life was discussed as one of several such transactions that "we all go through," though one not well understood by everyone, and one which can "sneak up on you, as it seems to have here."

Another important aspect of Lewis's cognitive mastery of the situation was a change in his self-talk patterns in the aftermath of the crisis. He was encouraged to replace negative, overgeneralized, catastrophizing statements about himself ("I'm a failure, and this proves it") with more balanced utterances ("My go-it-alone approach didn't work well in a management position. I should have asked for help. I will next time."). Instead of thinking of himself as a failure, and as lazy, he was taught to think of himself as a human being with strengths and weaknesses, varying according to the situation, though basically a worthwhile person. The relationship with the therapist was important in this regard, for he was able to affirm Lewis's worth, especially meaningful at a time when Lewis was feeling quite worthless.

BEHAVIORAL/ INTERPERSONAL ADJUSTMENT A series of adjustments were made by both Lewis and other members of the family during the crisis itself, and in the months following. The most immediate change for Lewis was his request to be transferred from a management position to a production position in the plant. After much thought and soul searching (and consultation with an in-house management consultant), Lewis decided that though it would be possible for him to seek additional training in management, he actually did not want to do this. He would much rather work in a production job than in the nontechnical supervisory role. While still recognizing that he would need to become more assertive in his interpersonal and work relationships, still, he felt that the job change would make his work life more satisfying in the long run.

As an outgrowth of the crisis therapy sessions, Lewis also bought several books on assertion skills, and enrolled in an assertion workshop conducted through the university. He had come to believe that, even if he were not in a management role, he would still need to learn to be more direct with others, keeping fewer worries to himself, than he had done in the past. The therapist coached Lewis on being more direct in dealing with co-workers (subordinates, peers, and superiors). As an adjunct to assertion training, considerable time was spent in therapy challenging Lewis's irrational belief that giving negative feedback to subordinates, for example, would lead to insurmountable interpersonal frictions.

At the same time, the family talked about how they might deal with internal conflicts from here on. As an aid, they decided to make such simple changes as not watching TV during the family dinner hour, allowing for more chances to talk with one another. They also planned weekly "family counsels" to discuss problems, as an adjunct to family activities that were oriented more toward external events (movies, ball games), and less toward discussion of family matters.

Since the analysis of family interactions revealed that Lewis and Helen had not had a vacation alone in more years than they could remember, nor evenings out just for the two of them, they agreed to work toward changes in this area as well. A number of other ideas were generated about changes in the family situation, ideas that had been on peoples's minds before that now seemed ripe for attention since things had "fallen apart," so to speak. Lewis, for example, had for some time wanted to talk to Eric about his concern that Eric did not have friends, though didn't know what to say. The two made a start on this in the family sessions, and followed up with more talk at home.

Perhaps one of the most significant family adjustments to emerge from Lewis's crisis experience had to do with Helen's career aspirations. When the idea of Lewis's crisis as a "developmental" transition was discussed, Helen began talking about taking stock of her own development. Though she had reported few regrets about her decision 17 years ago to devote full energies toward home and family, she had come to realize that they no longer needed her complete attention, and that her talents might well be used outside the home. The family members talked about how they would be affected if she were to take a part-time job, or go back to school to work toward an accounting degree. The therapist coached the family to think about adjustments each would have to make if Helen decided to do this. Interestingly enough, this possibility bore directly on Lewis's career shift since his future earnings in a production position would not be as great as if he had stayed in management. Though not fully explored at the time of these family sessions, the therapist raised the issue of how Lewis might feel with his wife working outside the home, moving him from the sole breadwinner role to one of partner in bringing in outside income. Lewis identified the pluses and minuses in the shift: he would like the extra income, though he would have to deal with cognitions developed early in his life that the man should "bring home (all) the bacon." By identifying this early cognitive "programming," however, he was able to open the way for new ideas and new possibilities which could be quite rewarding for him. This might, for example, allow him to become more actively involved in decisions on home management, decisions which could bring increased contact with his children, something he had desired for some time, though had not been able to change. Without pressing the point, the therapist suggested that something as seemingly simple as Helen's desire to take a part-time job outside the home would require "cognitive" shifts for everyone, even Helen. Would she, for example, be willing to "let go" of some of the home responsibility and share it with others in the family? The therapist sensed that though Helen might want this very much, she might also have difficulty giving up control in this area, or, living with less "perfection" on the home front than she had offered for the past 17 years.

FOLLOW UP AND EVALUATION   Individual and family sessions ran for just over three months. At follow-up one year later, Lewis was functioning well in his new production job, Helen had taken a half-time job outside the home, and several of the changes in family life (family counsel, more time spent between Lewis and children, etc.) had been accomplished. To use language from the crisis therapy chapter (Chapter 8), the crisis experience had been integrated into the fabric of Lewis's life, and both he and his family emerged with a sense of openness, or readiness to face the future. The major signs of growth for Lewis were his increased assertiveness at work and at home, and his increased involvement with his family. Lewis also reported further thought about a job change, something that would be new and give him even more independence. He liked the idea of going into business for himself (photography as the likeliest option), though he wanted to think about it some more, and talk also with Helen about her desire to go back to school. Though all of this had not yet been worked out at follow-up, it was clear that the two were thinking concretely about mid-life changes involving creative career alternatives. They looked at the crisis experience as an initially very difficult time which resulted in their looking at several new possibilities.

The case of Lewis' crisis at mid-life illustrates a number of theoretical considerations mentioned earlier in this volume. Lewis's crisis illustrates how a seemingly insignificant precipitating event (a work related stressor) can interact with a previously dysfunctional pattern of living (unassertiveness, ineffective coping strategies) to precipitate a crisis. The multimodal analysis highlights the pervasiveness of the crisis experience for Lewis, and for other family members as well. The fact that Lewis's crisis took place in the context of community controversy over nuclear energy, and was precipitated by the scheduling of a meeting at work, illustrates the importance of contextual variables in this crisis. Treatment needed to focus on the four crisis resolution tasks for both Lewis and the family. Attention throughout therapy was on all fronts at the same time: attention to physical needs, expression of feelings, cognitive mastery, and behavioral/interpersonal adjustments. In this particular case, work in the cognitive domain was critical, for example, offering a developmental understanding of the crisis events and individual reactions to them, allowing both Lewis and the family to reexamine dysfunctional patterns of living, and to redevelop newer, more adequate approaches for the future.

SUCCESS AND FAILURE IN CRISIS THERAPY

The cases reported offer illustrative data on the ingredients of successful crisis therapy. As all seasoned clinicians know, not every case works out so well. The author's experience is that outcome depends not only on therapeutic strategy, but also on a host of other variables, some of which are well beyond the therapist's control. Some clients are unwilling to risk new ways of thinking and behaving, even in the face of overwhelming evidence that previous means of coping no longer work. Most significant changes have concrete gains and losses associated with them, and often close family members are threatened by shifts from the old order to the new, which sometimes leads to a lack of support, or downright sabotage of client intentions. It is important, therefore, that therapists recognize the limits of their own power to influence crisis clients on a path toward growth and away from debilitation. The thrust of this point is not to soften our commitment to guiding the process and evaluating the outcome of crisis therapy according to the criteria outlined in the foregoing chapters, but rather to remind the reader that just as we always cannot take credit for a client's success (family, friends, other counselors, readings, and television all have access to clients during the reorganization process), so too, it is not always within our power to prevent failure.

PART III

SERVICE DELIVERY SYSTEMS

A basic premise of crisis theory is that workers in many community systems have a powerful influence on how individuals and families eventually resolve crises. Lawyers, police officers, emergency room personnel, and many others have opportunities to offer psychological first aid as a part of their regular duties, while referring crisis therapy cases to other mental health professionals. Other frontline workers such as school teachers and clergymen/women are members of systems that can track client progress over a period of months, and also mobilize other resources of the system to facilitate the working through process.

In Part III, we present crisis intervention by some of the most important of these professional and nonprofessional frontline workers: clergymen/women (Chapter 10), lawyers and legal assistants (Chapter 11), police officers (Chapter 12), health care practitioners (Chapter 13), emergency room workers (Chapter 14), telephone counselors (Chapter 15), school teachers and support staff (Chapter 16), and employers/work supervisors (Chapter 17). In writing this material, we have been guided by several service delivery principles. Since they apply to all of the systems discussed in this section we will summarize them here as a backdrop for issues specific to each setting.

1. Before adding crisis intervention to the job description of even one employee in the organization, it is important to understand the employee's day-to-day duties, the goals of the system, and the organizational structure. Organizational assessment should include factors that will facilitate (e.g., a supportive supervisory

network), as well as hinder (lack of time, presence of other job pressures), the employee's offering crisis services. Unless consideration is given to the context within which psychological first aid or crisis therapy will be accomplished (the specifics of the legal interview, or a teacher's schedule of classroom work, faculty meetings, and student conferences), then crisis services run the risk of being in conflict with other tasks, and therefore put aside, especially when resources such as time and money are scarce.

Our experience is that attention must be given to three major sets of variables in order to build crisis services into the overall system: organizational policy (including job descriptions), physical resources (work environment, telephone contacts with other services, transportation for clients), and personnel (both the selection of employees, as well as their training). The primary guideline for planning and also the main criterion for program evaluation is whether a system's policies, physical resources, and personnel are ready to offer clients psychological first aid and crisis therapy.

2. New services will be better received if they are understood as helping both clients in crisis and the system itself to accomplish its other work better or to solve some problem it faces. For example, our discussion of crisis intervention by lawyers (Chapter 11) offers the hypothesis that psychological first aid techniques can save valuable time, leading to more realistic decisions and more durable agreements when dealing with distraught clients. Similarly, crisis intervention in work settings has the potential for reducing absenteeism, poor work performance due to personal crises, and in many cases, the premature termination of valued employees, all reflected in monetary savings to business and industry.

Often the immediate gain for the helper from the use of crisis intervention techniques is readily apparent, for example, crisis intervention training as a means of reducing casualties to police officers during family disturbance calls. Sound program planning builds on these realities in working with practitioners to design services. Our premise is that in all of the settings described in this section, crisis intervention training can help employees to perform their regular duties more efficiently. In this sense, crisis intervention training need not be an extra duty, but rather a set of skills that enables an individual to deal better with situations faced every day.

3. Finally, a crisis service's chances of survival increase when the service is joined to some already strong (or growing) aspect of the existing system. A unit on crisis intervention, for example, can be included as a part of pastoral care courses in seminaries, or legal interviewing courses in law schools, and so on, as well as offered as part of continuing education seminars. Similarly, in our discussion of crises in work settings, we suggest linking training programs and consultation to a company's Employee Assistance Program, where one exists.

In organizing each of the chapters, we have first described general characteristics of the system, then reviewed the relevant literature on crisis intervention in the setting, and concluded with guidelines for applying the crisis model. In many chapters, we have offered specific guidelines on tailoring the psychological first aid and crisis therapy principles discussed in Part II to the unique work roles of key employees in each setting. In all chapters, the aim has been to present material in such a way as to facilitate building crisis services directly into each system.

chapter ten

Crisis Intervention by Clergy[1]

The idea that ministers, priests, and rabbis play an important role in the resolution of parishoners' life crises is well understood in both mental health and theological circles. Ryan's (1969) classic study of mental health services in the Boston area confirmed what many had long suspected, that the clergy were shouldering a significant portion of the city's counseling activity; the average minister saw as many people in counseling each year as an average psychiatrist in private practice. In an earlier study, Gurin, Veroff, and Feld (1960) surveyed 2,460 Americans and found that of 14 percent who had received professional assistance for psychological difficulties at some time in their lives, almost 42 percent sought help first from the clergy. Since the 1963 Community Mental Health Centers Act clergymen/women have been viewed as critical front-line community caretakers and, therefore, have been logical recipients of mental health consultation (Brodsky 1968; Haugk and Dorr 1976; Levenberg 1976; Slaikeu and Duffy 1979).

From the theologian's viewpoint, the clergy's counseling role is as old as Judaeo-Christian tradition itself. The twentieth century roots of modern pastoral counseling date back to the 1920s and the work of Anton Boisen, whose ideas were a striking foreshadowing of crisis theory as later developed by Lindemann (1944) and Caplan (1964):

Essentially he [Boison] recognized the increasing tension of inner conflicts, which were neither good or bad in and of themselves, but which comprised an intermediate stage that a person must pass through in order to reach a higher level of development. . . . without using the word "crisis," Boisen developed these ideas in detail in his classic and provocative book, *The Explanation of the Inner World*, in 1936. Here, in the context of the examination of the relationship between religious experience and psychosis, he reiterated the make-or-break nature of a high level of anxiety to the point of panic. . . . Even when there was a breakdown to the point of psychosis, it could be viewed as a problem-solving possibility, as a person sought "to assimilate hitherto unassimilated masses of life experience." The outcome, Boisen felt, was dependent "upon the presence or absence of an acceptable nucleus of purpose around which the new self can be formed" (Switzer 1974, p. 41-42).

There has been tremendous growth in the development of pastoral counseling as a discipline since Boisen's work. One of the most influential writers has been Seward Hiltner, whose early books broke new ground by applying Carl Roger's (1951) client-centered techniques to pastoral settings, and by defining the theological dimension of pastoral

---

[1] The author wishes to thank Susan deLoache for her assistance in preparation of this chapter.

counseling (Hiltner 1949, 1958). Other writers such as Howard Clinebell (1966) emphasized a wide range of counseling strategies, including family therapy, couple counseling, and crisis intervention. Outlets for published case reports and research were created through the *Journal of Pastoral Care* (established in 1948), *Pastoral Psychology* (1952), and the *Journal of Psychology and Theology* (1972). Two major organizations were established to provide clinical training for pastors and seminarians: the Association for Clinical Pastoral Education (ACPE), which offers clinical train-

ing based principally in hospital settings, and the American Association of Pastoral Counseling (AAPC), which provides supervised counseling training primarily in community-based counseling centers. Most seminaries now have courses in pastoral counseling skills through supervised field placements or hospital/clinic-based chaplain-training programs.

Survey data indicate that clergy view counseling not only as an important ministerial function, but one which consumes a considerable amount of time (Blizzard 1956; Brekke, Strommen, and Williams 1979; Hunt 1977;

**A WEEK IN THE
LIFE OF A PASTOR**

Pastors vary widely in their interests, skills, and attitudes. These characteristics, combined with the needs of the parish, lead pastors to devote quite different proportions of time to the major tasks of the pastor. In addition, each week is different because of seasonal emphases, more (or fewer) crises facing members of the congregation, and other factors. Thus there is no "typical" week in the life of a pastor. At the same time, a glance at a pastor's datebook, notebook, or log (diary, journal) might give an impression of the work of a pastor.

Sunday: Preached at the 8:30 and 11:00 worship. Planned to visit with the youth class at 9:45 but had to cut this short to fill in for the fourth-grade teacher who was absent. Met with the youth at 6:00 for snack supper, study, and recreation. Afterward Jack wanted to discuss how to help a friend who is on drugs.

Monday: Began plans for the next Sunday worship services, and prepared the "Pastor's Pen" column for the church newsletter. Planned to read some background studies on the Gospel According to Mark, but this was cut short when Mrs. Gibson came by to ask for help in finding a convalescent home for her eighty-six-year-old mother. After lunch, visited several members who are in the hospital. After supper met with the Council on Ministries to plan next month's details and set longer range plans.

Tuesday: At the hospital to be with Mrs. Jackson and Jim during Mr. Jackson's surgery. The family asked me a lot of questions about hospital procedures, death, and faith. This was my first opportunity to become better acquainted with this family. Returned to my church office about 10:30 and completed plans for the Sunday services. Gave information for the Sunday bulletin to the church secretary. Met for lunch with the committee working on ways to get tutor and counseling services to children who are not sufficiently served by the existing school services. Counseling appointments with a man wanting to change his career, a couple who is getting a divorce, and a teenager who thinks she is pregnant.

Wednesday: Completed most of the reading and outline for the sermon Sunday. About 10:00 Bill Anderson called to talk about what he might do to resolve a major conflict between several employees in his company. Lunch with the weekly noon study group composed of business persons who have agreed to study the Gospel According to Mark during their lunch hours. During the afternoon made seven brief calls to persons new to the community to welcome them to our church. At 7:30 met with the pre-school education task group to finalize plans for remodeling our pre-school rooms and make them more attrac-

Schuller, Strommen, and Brekke 1980). In a study of ministry in America surveying 5,000 clergy, lay persons, church leaders, theological professors, and seminarians in 47 denominations, Schuller et al. (1980) note that:

> Even though all the content of the minister's role remains communal, involving a group in workshop or learning, the point of focus is on the individual. Much ministerial specialization in the last 20 years has involved increasing personal skills in counseling. To a great extent, the work of ministry has involved individual contact in crisis situations (p. 6).

THE CLERGY'S UNIQUE ROLE

Ministers are ideally situated to do crisis counseling for a number of reasons. Stone (1976) views ministers as "natural" crisis counselors whose unique advantages include the following:

1. Most parishoners in crisis will contact their minister before they will seek out other mental health professionals. "When an individual in suffering finally seeks out the counsel of a psychiatrist or other mental health professional, it is usually because the clergy or

---

tive and serviceable as well as to minister to our younger children and their parents. We will have to find some special gifts to have enough money for this project.

Thursday: Met in the morning with the other pastors in our district and checked on several important special offerings, plans, etc. Afterward, five of us met for about two hours to share problems and discuss how to do a better job with persons facing crises. Studying actual cases (with no personal identification) is really a help. Received word about 1:00 that Mr. Young had died. The funeral will be Saturday afternoon, and I am to conduct the service. When I arrived at their home, Mrs. Young and the children were very upset. It's remarkable how much just being present with the family is supportive to them. I spent most of the afternoon with them. Met for supper with our teams of visitors who go to visit in the homes of new residents, visitors to the church, and homes that have sickness. The enthusiasm of this group is tremendous.

Friday: During the morning completed preparations for Sunday and also for the funeral on Saturday. Margie and Bob called to set up the series of premarital counseling interviews since they plan to be married in about six months. They are a very fine couple.

Saturday: Visited Mr. Young's family in their home briefly before the funeral this afternoon. Helped her to contact some agencies to arrange some financial help and other matters related to adjustments after the funeral. Will want to see them several times after the funeral. About 10:30 Mr. and Mrs. Simmons called and wanted to meet immediately with me to talk about their son who was arrested. I met with them, but this situation will require some longer-term family counseling.

Family and Personal Time: Usually Friday afternoon and Saturday are reserved for my time with my family. The funeral Saturday took some of this time, but we were able to go on the overnight camping trip we had planned. I usually assist our children with some of their homework; and when evening meetings are scheduled, I help the kids as much as possible before these meetings. We always manage to have some family time, usually a full day off every week as well as my own personal time for a game of golf or tennis. We have a varied and flexible schedule; and when pastoral duties and family activities conflict, we can usually arrange for suitable changes.[2]

[2] Source: R.A. Hunt, *A Christian as Minister*. Nashville, Tennessee: Board of Higher Education and Ministry, The United Methodist Church, 1977, pp. 32-33.

other natural interveners, such as family and friends, have failed to relieve the distress. The minister is often among the first persons to be sought out when crises arise. . . ." (p. 6).

2. Ministers are expected to "go where the people are," which means they often take initiative in reaching out to those in crisis, instead of simply waiting for parishoners to come to them. There is nothing unusual about a minister hearing from a member of the congregation that "Mr. A is going through a rough time right now—lost his job, trouble at home, etc.," and following up with a pastoral visit. With almost all of the situational crises identified earlier in this volume, pastoral and parishoner expectations give pastors greater freedom than other mental health professionals to help or intervene by reaching out.

3. Ministers preside over a range of religious rituals, many of which accompany developmental transitions bearing crisis potential. Clinebell (1966) notes that rituals of baptism, confirmation, marriage and funeral serve to reduce the anxiety associated with major life transitions, and provide a structural framework for adjusting to changes. Ministerial leadership at the time of death, for example, can facilitate crisis resolution. As Clinebell (1966) states:

> An important purpose of the funeral is to facilitate emotional release. The service should emphasize, among other things, the reality of the loss and the appropriateness of mourning. It should use familiar hymns, prayers, and scripture which may help to release dammed-up feelings. A funeral meditation on a text such as "Blessed are those who mourn" may help to facilitate mourning. Nothing should be said which suggests that stoicism in the face of grief is a Christian virtue or that one whose faith is genuine will not experience penetrating grief (p. 169).

4. The minister's continued contact with individuals and families allows "tracking" of crisis resolution months and years after the crisis event. The minister knows, for example, what Mrs. J was like before the crisis of divorce, physical injury, or loss of a loved one, *and* will be able to observe Mrs. J's progress in working through the crisis in the months and years thereafter. Through a myriad of interactions—church school classes, social functions, business meetings, home visits—the pastor has access to data far richer than that available to clinic and hospital-based therapists who might see Mrs. J on a weekly basis for one or two months.

5. By virtue of their congregational contact, ministers can mobilize networks of social support to help individuals and families in crisis. Whether the need is for food and shelter immediately after a crisis event, or for increased social contact months later, the minister can call upon elders, church school teachers, members of women's/men's groups, pastoral care teams, and others to help individuals and families work through life crises. By contrast, secular therapists have no such source of committed individuals to rely upon. Church members who call or visit persons in crisis offer assistance as well as a sense of belonging that can offset loneliness and isolation.

6. Since the crisis state is usually accompanied by feelings of anxiety, helplessness, depression, worthlessness, and lack of hope, it is the minister as "symbolically God's representative" that can offer faith as a counterforce to these feelings (Stone 1976, p. 72).

7. Since cognitive mastery—one of the four tasks of crisis resolution—often deals directly with religious beliefs, ministers are uniquely prepared to facilitate this aspect of crisis resolution by virtue of their theological education. In ministers' work with victims of bereavement, unexpected physical injury, terminal illness, or divorce, for example, questions such as the following are often an integral part of the crisis client's thinking: "Why is this happening to me?" "Is God punishing us?" "How

can a loving God take my child?" "Is this divorce God's will?" Clinebell (1966) suggests that to parishioners in crisis the minister symbolizes the "dimension of ultimate meaning" in life:

> In many cases crises confront people with the emptiness of their lives, the poverty of their relationships. Reflecting on his death camp experience Victor Frankl declares, "Woe to him who saw no more sense in his life, no aim, no purpose. . . . He was soon lost." In the crisis ministry the clergyman's role as *awakener of meanings* is crucially important. His unique function is to help crisis-striken people to rediscover the ultimate meaningfulness of life in relationship with God, whose steadfast love is real and available even in the midst of tragedy (p. 158).

In the crisis model presented in this book, theological questions are viewed as important issues to be addressed as the crisis client gains cognitive mastery over the crisis experience. Though the answers to questions such as the ones just mentioned would certainly vary from one religious tradition to another, most ministers are in a much better position than other mental health professionals to help crisis clients explore these issues and, in many cases, to revise/amend theological beliefs in light of the crisis experience.

CRISIS COUNSELING STRATEGIES

Several pastoral counselors have written about the specific crisis counseling functions of clergy (Clinebell 1966; Pretzel 1970a; Stone 1976; Switzer 1974). Two of the best-known books on the topic (Switzer 1974 and Stone 1976) present Jones's (1968) ABC model as a guide for pastoral interventions in crisis situations:

A Achieve contact with the client;
B Boil down the problem to its essentials; and
C Cope actively through an inventory of the client's available resources.

This approach is congruent with first-order crisis intervention as described earlier in this volume, and includes some elements of second-order crisis therapy. The remainder of this chapter will be devoted to ministers' use of both psychological first aid (PFA) and crisis therapy techniques in pastoral care and counseling.

First-Order Crisis Intervention by Clergy

Kadel (1980) has suggested that pastoral counseling must be designed for use in a number of different social and environmental situations, not just office settings. A glance at any minister's diary reveals that crisis counseling can occur in numerous settings: parishioner's home or place of work; pastor's office; parking lot; hospital waiting room, hallway/corridor, patient's room, etc.; or over the telephone.

Psychological First Aid as outlined in Chapter 6 of this volume can be offered by the pastor in any of these settings. Though the basic framework is the same as for other counselors, some features change as a result of the pastor's unique role as representative of the church/synagogue.

I Making Psychological Contact

This first component of PFA has a great deal in common with Hiltner's (1949) pastoral counseling model. Anything the pastor already knows about client-centered techniques (Rogers 1951), and the use of reflective statements or active listening (Gordon 1970) will assist in making psychological contact in crisis situations. Many parishioners report that the very presence of the pastor in time of need (death of a loved one, sudden illness, marital or work crisis) is a source of comfort in itself. It is important for pastors to develop their own combination of verbal and nonverbal messages that communicate understanding, acceptance, and support during crisis situations. In any case, the sort of empathy, understanding, acceptance, and caring taught in most pastoral care programs will equip the pastor for making the contact required in first-order crisis intervention.

II Examining Dimensions of the Problem

In addition to inquiring about the precipitating event, previous coping attempts, lethality, and so on, it is important for ministers to give special attention to theological issues that might have been raised by the crisis event. Remembering that crises ensue when an individual's expectations or cognitive maps of life have been violated in some major way, ministers should listen for both individual expectations ("I must be a perfect husband/breadwinner, capable of handling all stresses thrown my way") as well as theological beliefs ("An all-loving God would not take my son from me, cause me to be ill, allow my wife to divorce me, etc.") that might be a part of the crisis. By listening to the verbal flurries that often accompany the crisis experience—many times, expletives thrown at the minister as God's representative during moments of panic and fear—the minister is able to get his/her first clues about why this is a crisis for this particular person. This insight lays the groundwork for subsequent discussion of shattered beliefs and hope. In some cases, the "growth" which results from a crisis relates directly to the exchange of a childhood view of God for a more mature, adult theology.

Attention should also be given to what the parishioner "wants" from the minister at that particular time. Since ministers wear many more "hats" (preacher, administrator, counselor mediator, etc.) than clinic-based counselors, it is not always clear why a parishioner brings his/her problems to the minister in the first place. Does the parishioner who calls his pastor want a message of hope from the Scripture? Support for his/her side of an issue, as in a marital crisis? Someone to help talk the problem through? Emotional support? While many experienced pastoral counselors are adept at inferring answers to this question, there is no substitute for simply asking the crisis client what he/she most wants from the pastor—to do something such as intercede with a member of the parishioner's family, or to listen/talk the matter through, to pray, etc.

III Exploring Possible Solutions

The most important addition to the procedures in Chapter 6 for this component (enlisting the client's cooperation in generating solutions, building on his/her strengths, etc.), is the minister's introduction of church resources to facilitate coping. Whether the immediate need is shelter for the weekend, food, the physical presence of another person, or someone to follow up with a telephone call or home visit, the minister looks for ways to use congregational support networks during major life crises. Following PFA principles, the tactic is always for the client to do as much for him/herself as possible, and, for the counselor continually to test (not impose) possible solutions. Very often parishioners in crisis will "accept" help they are too upset or embarrassed to "ask for," (friends bringing food for the weekend, a Sunday School teacher's taking small children to the park, or an elder providing transportation).

IV Assisting in Taking Concrete Action

One of the most useful components of the PFA model as applied to pastoral counseling is the decision-making structure (based on lethality and the ability of the crisis client to act on his/her own behalf) which assists the minister in determining just how involved he/she should become in the crisis and its resolution. The theological mandate of the Judaeo-

Christian tradition is to care for others (even being "all things to all men" according to the apostle Paul, I Corinthians 9:22). Ministers working with clients in crisis therefore face difficult decisions as to how much to do to assist parishioners. It is not at all uncommon for a minister to receive a phone call at 12:30 A.M. from a distraught parishioner who wants the pastor to "come over right away" or for a parishioner to tell a minister, "You've got to talk to my husband/wife/child/parent. . . ." If the minister says "yes" to all of these requests, he/she might fulfill the theological mandate to care, but the result would leave little time to do other pastoral work. In addition, practitioners' work with crisis clients attests to the fact that very often the "solutions" elected in the heat of the crisis (for the minister to visit the home in the middle of the night, or intercede with a family member) prove later not to be the best direction at all. The PFA model outlined in Chapter 6 requires that solutions chosen be based on a thorough examination of the dimensions of the problem and selected from a range of alternatives, all in the context of a "first things first" approach. Though many late-night phone calls begin with a request for direct action on the part of the pastor, the use of PFA techniques will often lead instead to a 20 to 30 minute problem-solving telephone conversation, which is followed by an office visit the next day. On the other hand, if the pastor's assessment is that lethality is high, or that the "best and next step" cannot be taken by the parishioner at that time, then more directive action might be needed. In any case, the assessment criteria for concrete action in the PFA model can help the pastor in making these decisions.

V Follow Up

Follow up by pastors is essentially the same as for other community care-givers, with one exception: follow up is a more natural function for clergy since continued pastoral care over time is well accepted and expected as a pastoral responsibility. In addition, the pastor can give some of the responsibility for follow up to the parishioner by asking that he/she call back with information about progress. By putting the responsibility on the shoulders of the person in crisis to "check back," an implicit message is given that the minister cares that things work out and that the minister feels the person in crisis has the strength/energy/capability to stay in touch with those who care.

Crisis Therapy by Clergy

There are at least two ways that pastors can use the crisis therapy approach described in Chapters 8 and 9. First, ministers with extensive graduate training in counseling, and whose daily job descriptions include a counseling case load, will offer crisis therapy in a matter analogous to other mental professionals. The major difference will be that these pastoral counselors will likely be better equipped than some other professionals to deal with religious questions that arise during crisis. Depending upon the nature of their counseling training (use of cognitive, behavioral, Gestalt, and other techniques described in the Glossary) other aspects of pastoral counselors' crisis therapy may be very similar to that of secular counselors.

Second, parish clergy for whom one-to-one counseling is only one of several important duties can use the crisis therapy model as a guide in counseling sessions and as an aid in allocating congregational resources to facilitate crisis resolution. Building on the minister's "natural advantage" as a crisis counselor—ongoing relationships with entire families, and access to the physical and social supports available through congregational networks—the minister can use the four tasks of crisis resolution as a guide in matching resources with a person's/family's needs.

Physical Survival   Once a minister has determined a need for life saving precautions, such as constant contact with a suicidal person, or other measures to maintain physical well-being, such as food, shelter, exercise, or medication, he/she can draw on a pool of natural helpers in the congregation. The food brought to homes after a death in the family is one example of how parishioners can facilitate the first task of crisis resolution. Offering the use of a spare bedroom to a runaway child or an estranged spouse is another. In many cases, the "observation" required for a potentially suicidal person can be provided by a member of the congregation planning to spend time with the person over the weekend. One minister who knew that regular exercise was a critical ingredient for a cardiac patient's recovery arranged for his pastoral visits to include long walks with the parishioner/patient. Two other church visitors did the same, thereby encouraging the man to stay with his exercise routine.

Expression of   Many people in crisis
Feelings   are very reluctant to admit feelings of hurt, guilt, anger, confusion, and remorse. For some, the reluctance is embedded in a belief—erroneous or not—that the feelings are wrong in the eyes of the church. In most crisis situations, parish ministers, unlike their counseling colleagues who work exclusively in clinical settings, have several opportunities to legitimize expression of feelings. Sermons, church school lessons, and words spoken during pastoral visits can have considerable impact on whether parishioners will be able to express some of the painful feelings that accompany life crises. Due to suggestibility during crisis episodes (Taplin 1971), many parishioners will look to their minister for guidance on how to handle the emotional turmoil. Even though words spoken, for example, at the funeral or grave site service might not have an effect at

that moment, they will often be remembered months and years later. In many cases, the pastor's influence on the person in crisis is indirect through family and friends. To help children in crisis, the pastor can coach parents, other relatives, church school teachers, and the like on the importance of modeling the expression of grief and allowing the same—indeed, encouraging it—in children suffering a loss.

Cognitive Mastery   As suggested earlier in this chapter, the minister's approach to helping parishioners gain cognitive mastery of a crisis will often include a discussion of theological problems. Beyond attention to the issues raised in Chapter 8 (what happened, how and why it happened, who is responsible, what can be learned from the crisis, and so on), parishioners can be expected to ask a minister questions such as: "Is this God's will?" "Am I being punished?" "How can a loving, all knowing, all powerful God allow. . . ?" Sometimes anger toward God is taken out on the visiting minister. In the aftermath of tragedy, more than one minister has been made to feel unwelcome, as if he/she represents one who could have prevented all of this, but did not!

Cognitive mastery in this context involves three steps:

1. Understanding the realities of the crisis event (what happened, etc,);
2. Examining what the person in crisis believes/thinks about the event, "I never thought I would be a widow at such a young age. I can't go on without him/her. If God really cared about. . . , then He wouldn't have . . . .";
3. Discussion of beliefs in light of the realities of the crisis, resulting in confirmation of the beliefs, significant changes in them or, in some cases, replacement of shattered beliefs with new ones.

Any secular counselor can help a crisis client through the first two steps, although ministers are better equipped to help in the task of either refining/amending shattered theological beliefs, or replacing them with new ones. The central focus, of course, is on developing beliefs/thoughts/images which are capable of handling the data of the crisis itself. A psychological test of the new beliefs is first whether they square with available data (sufficiently explain what happened, who bears what responsibility, and so on) and, second, whether they allow the person to put the event into historical perspective and go on about the business of future living. Most experienced ministers have observed positive and negative outcomes of parishioners' attempts at cognitive mastery of crises. Some lose their faith and leave the church altogether after tragedies or extreme setbacks. Others report that it was at the time of crisis that they felt the presence of God most keenly, or that they were forced to throw off simplistic theological understandings for more mature beliefs.

Behavioral/ Interpersonal Adjustments   The value of congregational resources is especially apparent in considering how ministers can help parishioners with the fourth task of crisis resolution. Once physical survival is assured, feelings have begun to be expressed, and intellectual understandings of the crisis have emerged, it will be important for the person in crisis to make changes in behavior and interpersonal relationships. Having identified the changes needed, the minister can ask others in the congregation to assist in this difficult aspect of crisis resolution. A widow left with children to raise, for example, faces a range of such adjustments, most of which have to do with managing *alone* tasks which had previously been the exclusive responsibility of her husband (possibly finances, keeping cars in repair) or had been shared (disciplining the

children). She will also eventually face the difficulties of re-entering the social world where she is now a single woman, no longer a member of a couple. Ministers sensitive to the need for behavioral and interpersonal adjustments can marshal congregational resources to assist. Beyond counseling the widow on how to cope with certain difficult social situations, they can coach those who set up church functions on how to best relate to a widow in the process of re-entering the social world. As one widow put it:

> The worst thing you can do is to "invite" a new widow to a party or other church function. You cannot imagine how hard it is to decide whether to go in the first place, and then to get ready, and then finally to drive alone across town at night. The very thought of all this, plus images of entering the room, dealing with awkward greetings, and then leaving alone later, is too much to bear—it makes you want to stay home instead. Far better for a caring person to say something like: "Our class is having a party Saturday night. I'll pick you up at 7:30 p.m. Okay?" The added directiveness—almost like taking charge, for the moment—can be enough to get me involved in something that will be good for me in the long run, though hard to initiate on my own (Author's Files).

For our purposes, it is sufficient to note that the minister is in a position to offer counsel such as this to members of the congregation as they assist widows and widowers in adjusting to life as single people. A moment's thought about other crises and congregational resources reveals many other strategies. One pastor, for example, was concerned about a ten-year-old boy whose eight-year-old brother had been killed in a freak drowning accident in the spring of the year. The pastor knew that church summer camp (June) was coming up soon, and would present a choice point for the boy and his family—to go or not to go. Hearing that the boy's parents were not quite sure what to do, and knowing that the camp experience (which, under normal circumstances, the boy would not have missed for anything) would help him get back into the stream of living normally again, the minister talked first to the parents, and, with their approval, asked the boy's Sunday School teacher to pay him a visit, encouraging him to come to camp. The attitude that the minister suggested was one of "expecting" that the boy would go—"Looking forward to having you at camp this year"—instead of acting as if the business of living must surely stop indefinitely (months, years) now that the tragedy of the brother's drowning had occurred. The minister also prepared the teacher (who would be at camp as a sponsor) not to shy away from talking to the boy about his dead brother, and to be ready for possible tears, anger, guilt, or whatever, as a spin-off of some activity at camp. After all, this would be the first time he had gone camping, played ball, gone canoeing, and so on *without* his brother. Though the boy should not be pushed beyond his will in these activities, those around could help by communicating an expectation that he would participate, by tilting the ledger toward participation whenever the decision was close, and by facilitating talk of the missing brother, thereby allowing expression of feelings as they arose.

Pastoral intervention such as this one (which involved, incidentally, only one visit to the parents, and a phone call to the church school teacher) are possible with many other life crises. Very often instead of the minister getting members of the congregation to "do something" for parishioners in crisis, the roles are reversed: behavioral adjustment is enhanced by having the person in crisis do something to help someone else. One couple, gratified at having weathered a severe marital crisis, wanted to repay the pastor for his help by offering some service for the church. The pastor wasted little time in setting them up as sponsors of a youth group, knowing full well that not only would the children benefit, but that this par-

ticular couple, whose emotional and physical distance over the past several years had played a strong role in their recent marital crisis, could profit by this shared activity. It is well known that many mental health workers—professional as well as volunteer—are first motivated to "help others" as a result of having gone through times of tremendous need themselves. As an overseer of an entire congregation, a minister has the opportunity to match these resources in ways that benefit everyone concerned.

A LOOK TO THE FUTURE

A close look at crisis theory in the context of parish ministry yields several directions for future training and research. First, instruction on predictable life transitions/crises that parishioners face (see Chapters 3 and 4) would undoubtedly be an important training component of any seminarian's preparation for parish work. Second, supervised pastoral counseling training should include both first- and second-order crisis intervention for cases that arise in parish (as opposed to institutional) settings.

While many seminaries have courses (or portions thereof) on crisis counseling, the chief settings for supervised counseling experience are clinics, hospitals, and other institutions. Parish-bound seminarians and pastors seeking to increase their counseling skills are usually directed to hospital-based clinical pastoral education (CPE) programs where they receive intensive supervision with hospitalized patients, or to counseling centers where their client load is again made up of persons who have sought professional counseling assistance. The disadvantage of such an arrangement is that it does not give the minister experience in dealing with the crises that will confront him/her in parish settings, namely crises that have not yet come to the attention of therapists/chaplains in hospitals or clinics. In addition, counseling training in an institutional setting gives a pastor no experience in using the "natural advantage" ministers have as crisis counselors—ongoing relationships with families and the use of congregational resources. To maximize learning on how to use these resources, there needs to be a closer link between counseling training and field work. Instead of restricting intensive counselor supervision to clinical/hospital interactions, it should be geared toward what Kadel (1980) calls the numerous "pastoral conversations" of crisis work—brief telephone contacts, visits at home, after church meetings, in the emergency room of a hospital, over luncheon meetings, and the like. Similarly, supervision should assist pastors in making judicious use of congregational resources as an aid in helping people work through the four tasks of crisis resolution. Whatever approach to training is chosen, the aim should be to give the pastor experience with cases which emerge in parishes as opposed to institutional settings.

Third, considerably more research is needed on the number and kind of life crises which present themselves to ministers, and further, on the best strategies for dealing with them. Griffin (1980) contends that studies such as Hiltner and Colston's (1961) research two decades prior marked the end instead of the beginning of systematic investigations on the nature of pastoral counseling. One reason for this might be that the counseling models "borrowed" from psychology (e.g., Rogers (1951) client-centered therapy) were not comprehensive enough to capture the richness of pastoral counseling. It is possible that the multimodal perspective which we have applied to crisis therapy could fill this gap, particularly since it specifically includes theological issues (described under the cognitive modality) and looks at the role of the religious community in the resolution of parishioners' crises.

SUMMARY

The crisis model can help ministers to develop a clearer identity of themselves as helpers, especially as they compare themselves with other mental health counselors and psychotherapists. Since the beginning of pastoral counseling as a discipline, ministers have viewed themselves far too often "adjunct" or "second class" therapists. However, a proper understanding of ministers' natural advantages as crisis counselors suggests just the opposite. Given proper training, parish ministers can and should be the primary caretakers in crisis situations. Their usefulness should extend well beyond early detection and referral, and should rest ultimately with the application of broad based crisis therapy strategies to individuals and families in the natural environment where crises occur.

chapter eleven

Crisis Intervention by Attorneys and Legal Assistants

de Rosset Myers,Jr.
Karl A. Slaikeu
Diane W. Slaikeu

When meeting with a criminal defendant for the first time. . . .you've got to realize that you are dealing for the most part with a psychologically debilitated person. . . .If you were suddenly to be accused. . .you're arrested, you're handcuffed, you're subjected to that sort of indignity, you're photographed, fingerprinted, pushed into the system. . .You begin thinking in terms of the shame and ignominy you've brought upon your family and, when you come to the lawyer, you're a psychological basket case. . . .

Richard "Racehorse" Haynes
on the Dick Cavett Show, January 8, 1980

This description of what happens when a defendant enters the criminal justice system highlights the potential emotional consequences of the legal process in criminal cases. Haynes' description has a ring of truth to it: Being thrown into jail is a frightening and dehumanizing event. The client exercising his right to legal counsel demands more than legal advice. His attorney may be the first ally he sees after being locked up. It is not easy, however, to meet client demands in the rushed, confined conditions typically found in jailhouse interview rooms. How can lawyers deal with clients' emotions in such situations? What can a lawyer do with a tearful, bitter client who wants revenge against an unfaithful husband? What about the businessman who seems determined to sacrifice the economic interests of his business by suing a partner whose behavior may have been personally or ethically reprehensible, but legally circumspect? How about the client who calls her attorney at home asking for immediate protection from an abusing husband? Or the terminally ill and frightened grandparent who does not know how he wants his estate set up but objects to every legal suggestion and seems troubled about the fact that his children are already jockeying for advantage in dividing his estate?

In each of these situations, the attorney may find the legal path that would be most productive blocked by emotions which seem sometimes irrational, often excessive, and almost always frustratingly counterproductive. These emotions can transform otherwise insignificant details in the settlement of property in divorce cases into battlegrounds where anger, vindictiveness, and bitterness destroy weeks of careful negotiation between attorneys. They are the enemies of good legal advice and are probably partially responsible for the fact that domestic cases are frequently channeled down the hierarchy in large firms.

Price and McCreary (1976) argue that many clients contact lawyers for reasons other than the need for legal assistance. Some clients mistake problems that are essentially psychological in nature for legal problems. Others have limited access to mental health services because they lack time, money, transportation, or even an awareness that these resources exist. These authors view many so-called "problem" clients as being caught up in fear, confusion, ambivalence, and ignorance about what to do to help themselves. Also, emotional difficulties can emerge around particular legal issues such as estate planning (Bernstein 1977a; Sprott 1973), drawing a marital contract (Bernstein 1977b), divorce proceedings (Emerson and Messinger 1977; Sabalis and Ayers 1977), personal injury (Preiser 1979; Rosenthal 1974) and probate (Rosenfeld 1980), to name a few.

Attorneys devote from 30 to 80 percent of their time counseling clients (Shaffer 1976), yet they receive almost no formal training in how to handle their frequently difficult and emotionally upset clients. (Freeman 1964, 1967). They must rely on undergraduate psychology courses of questionable practical utility, common sense, and their ability to slow the process down until time, and possibly assistance from mental health professionals, can cool emotions. Unfortunately, taking time for clients' emotions to cool delays dealing directly and effectively with the important legal issues. Also, many attorneys have no interest in dealing with clients' emotions, contending that they didn't go through years of legal training in order to end up holding hands with crying divorcees. For others, confronting a client in crisis precipitates a type of crisis for the lawyer as well, particularly if failure

to help is seen as a threat to the attorney's professional competence (Schoenfield and Schoenfield 1981).

Courses in legal counseling are now more frequently part of law school curricula than in the past, but they are generally given low priority (Freeman 1964, 1967). The interest in these courses grew in part from Chief Justice Burger's criticism of attorneys' lack of technical expertise (Goldstein 1979a). Although many law schools have attempted to provide more practical training in substantive legal areas, the development of interviewing and counseling skills that lie near the core of the day-to-day work of many attorneys still has not received adequate attention (Goldstein 1979b).

There are no simple solutions to the complex human problems faced by lawyers. What follows will not be a "how to" cookbook promising the impossible. There is much we do not know about human behavior and each case is different. What we shall do is present crisis theory as a tool for understanding and dealing effectively with clients under extraordinary stress. We shall outline how the steps involved in crisis intervention, and particularly in psychological first aid, can be useful to attorneys in dealing with clients in crisis.

As we shall see, many of the components of crisis intervention have been suggested in books and articles on legal interviewing. We shall attempt to weave the most promising strands from the literature into the fabric of crisis intervention and to apply the product within the context of legal interviewing. Finally, we shall frame the questions that need attention in future research. The view taken in this chapter is that (1) attorneys and their assistants are key "frontline" workers who have contact with people in crisis. (2) Crisis intervention is compatible with the more comprehensive models on legal interviewing. It is *not*, however, a method of training junior psychologists or psychiatrists, something that the legal profession clearly does not desire

(Freeman 1967; Schoenfield and Schoenfield 1981). (3) Effective use of crisis intervention strategies can reduce rather than increase the time needed to reach satisfactory settlements. By recognizing and defusing intense situations, helping clients clarify priorities (including postponing major decisions until turmoil abates), and establishing linkages to other helping resources, crisis intervention can allow attorneys to do their legal work more quickly, effectively, and efficiently. (4) Crisis intervention can be taught in law school and continuing education workshops in relatively little time—probably as a 15-hour intensive course.

LITERATURE REVIEW

Most authors of legal interviewing texts and articles emphasize the inevitability of lawyers having to engage in some form of counseling with their clients (Binder and Price 1977; Rosenthal 1974; Preiser 1979; Shaffer 1976; Schoenfield and Schoenfield 1981). Freeman and Weinhofen's (1972) *Legal Interviewing and Counseling* casebook for law students provides the most comprehensive overview—through specific case narratives and critiques—of the range of legal issues (marital–family to business–financial) which immediately thrust the attorney into the role of counselor.

In considering the role of the attorney, several legal scholars and counselors have suggested that it properly includes the provision of empathy and guidance, resembling what we have called psychological first aid (Chapter 6) (Kahn and Cannell 1965; Simons and Reidy 1971; Benjamin 1981). In their introductory text, Binder and Price (1977) suggest a relatively straightforward approach to legal counseling. They outline a three-step process designed to help the attorney facilitate disclosure of relevant information and formulate a strategy for providing help. The client is first encouraged to express concerns and emotional reactions. The attorney assists in

this process by allowing the client to describe the situation as he/she conceptualizes it. Through empathic responses and active listening techniques, the attorney helps the client to acknowledge emotions. Having done this, the attorney obtains a chronological overview of the problem, encouraging the client to describe specifically what happened, and when. Finally, the attorney begins to develop and verify theories based on what has been learned. The first two steps correspond directly to "making psychological contact" and "assessing dimensions of the problem" in administering psychological first aid.

Particularly important to the process which Binder and Price describe is the attorney's ability to help the client evaluate alternatives in dealing with the problem. They argue that both attorney and client must attend to the social and psychological, as well as the legal, consequences of each alternative.

Shaffer (1976) argues that legal counseling should provide maximum freedom and information for the client, though this is rarely done. He notes, for example, that lawyers generally do not allow clients to participate in decisions about how to handle their automobile liability cases even though data suggest that clients who are involved in the decision-making process win larger settlements than those who are not. (See also Rosenthal 1974). To maximize a free flow of information, the attorney must work to develop a personally equal relationship between him/herself and the client. Obviously, the attorney is the legal specialist who can and should lay out legal options; but before doing this, the attorney needs to develop trust and a clear sense of how the client feels about what has taken place and what might happen. The attorney must practice "active listening," which involves being sensitive to feelings and exploring them by responding to the feelings rather than focusing only on the objective facts. Shaffer suggests that feelings *are* facts and are equally as important as the specific details of a case. In a sense, they are the guideposts which allow the lawyer to begin to understand the importance of the objective facts. The attorney's role is, therefore, to establish rapport with the client. Rapport must be developed, and feelings explored, before any other progress can be expected.

The lawyer must also be constantly attuned to what is referred to as the "process" of the interview. Content aside, is the attorney setting him/herself up as the expert, the final arbiter, the parent? If so, constructive rapport will not develop, and, though the client will probably agree to good advice, he/she is unlikely to follow it. Finally, the lawyer needs to be a good problem solver who is able to explore alternative courses of action with the client, bring legal expertise to bear where it is appropriate, and help to evaluate outcomes. Shaffer emphasizes the importance of encouraging the client to do as much as he or she can to solve the problem, legitimizing, and responding to feelings, and using a problem-solving strategy in coping with the client's difficulties.

The Lawyer in the Interviewing and Counseling Process, by Andrew S. Watson (1976), is written to serve as a text for a law course in interviewing. It provides a good example of what must be learned by the lawyer if he is to develop adequate interviewing skills from a psychoanalytic perspective. Several assumptions are made: The client may appear confused but unconsciously knows what he wants. The task of the attorney is to expose this unconscious material. To do this he must understand the motives, unconscious thoughts, and personality structure of the client. In so doing, he can anticipate having to cope with both transference and countertransference. Transference refers to the client's tendency to react to the counselor as if the counselor were someone about whom the client has powerful, disturbing feelings. Those feelings are transferred to the counselor rather than directed at the appropriate person. Counter-transference takes place when the counselor reacts to the

client as if he/she were another important person (to the counselor). In this model, emotions are to be dealt with directly, and events are to be seen from the client's perspective in order to overcome the client's resistance to seeing events and emotions as they actually are. Dysfunctional behavior is seen not as a result of some event but, rather, as a consequence of personality factors and unconscious motives that cause the client to interpret events in certain ways. In this model, attorneys are taught to understand unconscious motivations and deal with the problems posed by transference. By virtue of its psychoanalytic assumptions, this interviewing model adds considerable complexity to the legal interview— more, it would seem, than the average lawyer would want or have time to learn.

Schoenfield and Schoenfield's (1981) primer on interviewing and counseling for lawyers includes a section on crisis intervention and the legal interview. Beginning with the discussion of the general dynamics of communication, the authors present methods for structuring an interview, followed by a discussion of crisis intervention techniques. The authors list of counseling approaches in crisis situations includes:

1. Communicating effective concern;
2. Allowing the client to express feelings;
3. Exploring the precipitating event;
4. Examining past coping efforts;
5. Focusing on the immediate problem;
6. Helping the client to develop a cognitive understanding of the problem;
7. Seeking practical solutions;
8. Structuring a plan for action;
9. Making referrals.

These dimensions cover points included under the five components of psychological first aid described in Chapter 6, though the list is not organized according to a general problem-solving model. The authors present a number of practical suggestions for understanding the nature of client distress, and responding effectively during the legal interview.

Though there are differences in these approaches to legal interviewing, each is predicated on the belief that, from the lawyer's point of view, it is both practical and efficient, in the long run, to deal directly with the emotions which clients bring to him. The time saved by sticking to the "objective" legal facts is likely to be lost if the client confuses facts with feelings. The client may feel alienated from the legal process and fail to carry out suggestions made by the attorney. If the client's feelings are not taken into account, the client may be difficult to reason with, or likely to sabotage even the most carefully laid plan. Overall, this drains both the lawyer's and the client's time and emotional energy.

PSYCHOLOGICAL FIRST AID IN THE LEGAL INTERVIEW

Psychological first aid in the context of the legal interview incorporates many of the ideas from the literature just reviewed. The procedures are designed to help clients deal with what seem to them to be overwhelming events, and are described fully in Chapter 6 of this volume. What follows is a discussion of the application of these principles in the context of a legal interview.

I Making Psychological Contact

This is both the easiest and most difficult of tasks for the attorney. Both facts and feelings need to be addressed. Lawyers tend to be highly skilled at gathering the important objective facts and weaving them together into an intelligible whole. They are frequently less familiar and comfortable with the feelings which accompany facts—the rejection, rage, and desolation felt by parties to a divorce, or the humiliation and sense of failure experienced by the bankrupt businessman. As frightening and threatening as they are, these feelings frequently float near the surface during legal interviews. If ignored, the client is likely to present facts poorly and cooperate reluctantly, if at all. They need to be expressed if the client is to move beyond his preoccupation with them. While it is hard to resist the temptation to shut feelings off by dismissing ("You shouldn't feel that way") or ignoring them, this tends to exacerbate the client's discomfort. Once expressed, emotions can begin to burn themselves out and the client can begin to provide information about which facts are especially important.

A number of strategies for encouraging the appropriate expression of feelings are outlined in Chapter 6 and in the literature we have reviewed. Clients in distress relay how they feel both in what they say ("He has taken away the reason I had for living") and in what they do (downcast eyes, quivering voice, flushed face). It is often helpful to verbally recognize the feeling ("I can appreciate how disappointed and hurt you must feel...") and then give the client a chance to respond. Active listening and empathic responses are approaches that help both the client and the lawyer to get a feel for the client's reactions to the facts. Both techniques direct the interviewer's attention to the feelings underlying the content of the client's statements.

II Exploring Dimensions of the Problem

Lawyers seem to function best at this stage of psychological first aid since it parallels so closely their skills in gathering background information for relating specific cases to the law. In listening to the client's story, the lawyer should consider how the event(s) may have disrupted the client's life goals or life structure (Levinson 1978). To understand how a proposed legal action might be related to a client's life structure, the attorney should listen for what the event (divorce, bankruptcy proceedings, change in will) means to the client, how he/she interprets what has happened. It is important to know, for example, how a bankruptcy action will affect a client's view of his/her financial and leadership responsibilities towards spouse and family.

Attorneys and their assistants should assess lethality when a client gives clues to destructive behavior. Chapter 6 offers guidelines for making decisions on what to do in these situations.

III Examining Possible Solutions

Appeal to the legal system through an attorney represents an attempt at coping with crisis. The continuous failure of other solutions to problems (appeals to friends by unhappy spouses, repeated pleas for a little more time from creditors) exacerbates the sense of desperation generated by the problem itself. Under these circumstances, any solution is likely to look good no matter how weak or inappropriate. Inadequate strategies may be eagerly grasped only to backfire or simply be abandoned, frustrating the attorney and wasting time. It is more productive, in the long run, to generate several possible solutions to current problems, and then evaluate each solution.

The attorney needs to know about available community resources (clergy, marital counselors, women's shelters, social agencies which provide emergency funds, self-help groups such as Alcoholics Anonymous, etc.) in order to help clients generate solutions to their multifaceted problems. It is frequently helpful for the attorney to keep a list of resources that have proved useful in the past. It is likewise helpful to know about referral specialists in the community. Several states have begun to implement program and service assistance systems accessible by telephone.

IV Taking Concrete Action

Most lawyers are action oriented, and they prefer to flesh out the

relevant facts in a case, decide what needs to be done, and do it. Acting too quickly, however, can be counterproductive in the long run. It is often best for clients in crisis to decide to "do nothing," especially in the heat of the moment. Once the dust has settled, the problem may well assume different dimensions demanding different solutions. Inappropriate solutions waste time and energy in the long run.

Crisis theory suggests encouraging clients to do as much for themselves as they can. The flow chart in Chapter 6 can guide attorneys in how directive to be in any particular case. Gathering background information, talking to a friend, checking with relatives about short-term financial assistance, finding a temporary shelter, exploring immediately available employment opportunities are all examples of concrete client actions which might be discussed during the legal interview.

V Following Up

In crises where the stakes are high and the client's coping skills are low, it is important to know whether or not the plans and agreements made during the interview have been carried out. Follow up need not take a good deal of time. Frequently, a quick call from the client or the person whom he/she planned to contact is sufficient to confirm that plans have been implemented. Team work can further dissipate the burden of follow up: Secretaries and legal assistants can help by phoning to see that the client, for example, made an appointment with an emergency mental health worker or moved into a shelter for battered women.

Legal solutions are likely to have their intended effects only if the client's needs are clearly understood and he or she is motivated to cooperate with the attorney. The five components of psychological first aid provide the lawyer with a cognitive map that is useful in conceptualizing what is happening with the client and what needs to be done. It can help in establishing rapport and trust, and in setting priorities so that the client will be willing and able to follow through with the necessary legal moves as time passes. Finally, used as a cognitive map by the attorney, it flags certain information and suggests certain responses which can be spliced into the more traditional legal interview.

FUTURE TRENDS

There are several obstacles to the implementation of crisis intervention training for attorneys. There is little enough time during law school for the legal content courses, to say nothing of adding training in areas such as crisis intervention. Many view training in crisis intervention as an "extra," to be included only when the "real" legal material has been mastered, an attitude which, if left unchallenged, nearly insures that this material will never reach most lawyers. Several points need to be emphasized in dealing with obstacles which preclude use of the crisis model in legal interviewing.

1. Crisis intervention training needs to be presented as a set of strategies useful as much to the lawyers themselves as to their clients. It is not enough to point out that crisis clients need to be understood, listened to, and/or referred for psychological counseling when needed. An equally important point is that in the long run, knowledge of psychological first aid will save time and money. No attorney relishes late night (or early morning) calls from a distraught divorcee, or vacillation, intransigence, etc., in response to a rational agreement. Psychological first aid can be viewed as a "tool" for dealing with problem clients.

2. Training packages, whether as part of a law school course on legal interviewing or in a continuing legal education seminar, should be time limited (10 to 20 hours), and should emphasize the compatibility of psychological first aid with existing legal interviewing models. Courses at the University of Texas at Austin and University of South Carolina schools of law, for example, have used Slaikeu's (1978) videotape training program, *Defusing the Distraught Client*, as a part of broader legal interviewing training.

3. Crisis theory (see Chapter 2) should be presented as a useful alternative to the language of psychopathology with which most lawyers are familiar by virtue of undergraduate courses in abnormal psychology, or trial experience with sanity pleadings. Crisis theory offers a conceptual framework that not only sheds light on individual and family dynamics present at divorce, arrest, estate planning, probate, and the like, but also offers guidelines about what the attorney can do to help clients to successfully negotiate these life transitions. Training programs for attorneys should give particular attention to the four tasks of crisis resolution as a backdrop for understanding significant changes in client thoughts, feelings, and behavior as a legal case reaches settlement (Chapters 2 and 8).

4. In line with the idea of integrating the crisis model into daily law practice, training in psychological first aid can be useful for receptionists and paralegal assistants, since they usually have direct contact with clients. The ability of these individuals to deal effectively with emotionally upset clients can contribute a great deal to the overall effectiveness of a law practice.

5. Mental health practitioners, whether part of an outreach program in a community mental health center, or in private practice, can offer brief consultation (most likely over the telephone) to attorneys who need assistance in dealing with crisis clients. As suggested in Chapter 6, since the psychological first aid model is built on a problem-solving base, it can serve as a useful framework for mental health consultation.

SUMMARY While the crisis literature supports the program directions outlined in this chapter, there is still a need for systematic investigation of the psychological components of clients' legal problems. A step in this direction would be to explore the fit between the symptoms of clients and those predicted by crisis theory. Other studies are needed to rigorously test our hypothesis that proficiency in crisis intervention will actually save time in working with distraught clients. In any case, it is clear that many attorneys experience considerable difficulty in dealing with the emotional or psychological aspects of their clients' problems. Our hope is that the ideas in this chapter will serve as a stimulus for researchers and educators to look closely at the crisis model as a framework for increasing lawyer effectiveness in the legal interview.

chapter twelve

Crisis Intervention by Police

Jeffrey B. Luckett
Karl A. Slaikeu

A frantic mother calls for help; her husband is choking their teenage daughter. Family Crisis Intervention Unit officers arrive and find the father hostile, the mother weeping in the kitchen. While his colleague unobtrusively looks over the situation elsewhere in the house, the other officer removes his hat, sits down on the couch, and begins talking directly to the father. The officer agrees that disciplining children is necessary, yet difficult. He gradually draws the man away from his immediate and explosive concern and into a more general discussion. Before long, the father has unclenched his fists and lost his hostility; he and the officer agree that choking is an ineffective means of discipline. Meanwhile, the second officer has arranged for the daughter to spend the night with a friend and has given the wife information she requested about procedures for obtaining a possible divorce. In half an hour the situation is defused and the husband shakes hands with the officers as they leave (Blanton, 1976, p. 61).

Although the police are best known for their crime fighting responsibilities, only about 10 to 20 percent of a typical officer's time is spent identifying and apprehending criminals or in other aspects of crime control. The remaining 80 to 90 percent of the average officer's time is spent in order maintenance activities, many involving crisis intervention. These noncrime activities include social conflict calls such as family fights, calls to help mentally disturbed or intoxicated citizens, suicide attempters, victims of accident, assault, rape and other offenses (Goldstein et al. 1979; Reiss 1971). The high percentage of interpersonal police work is especially significant in light of surveys which indicate that only 10 percent of an officer's training involves human relations (Jacobs 1976).

Citizens often turn to police when confronted with extremely disruptive, sometimes bizarre, situations. Wallace and Schreiber (1977) suggest that communities depend heavily on police assistance in crisis situations because police can be called at any hour of the day or night by telephone, they respond quickly, they are prepared to provide assistance at the scene, and they are able to handle situations involving violence. Most police officers, however, do not welcome family crisis calls. One officer put it succinctly: "It's the worst call a car can get" (Wallace and Schreiber 1977). Another stated, "I'd rather face a mugger than a family fight" (Hamilton 1973).

Traditionally there has been resistance to the concept of counseling as a part of the police function. Often police do not see family disturbances as a real police matter, but feel because citizens ask for help there is a legal responsibility to respond (Burnett et al. 1976). Professional rewards—promotions, increases in salary, and so on—are linked with criminal activities and not resolution of family crises (Mann 1973). At the same time, however, studies show that police are daily thrust into crisis situations, each one potentially explosive, unpredictable, and with a high threat to personal safety (Horstman 1974). In each case, the officer works with limited community resources, does so on a twenty-four hour a day basis, and works with clients who many times neither recognize their need for help nor desire the officer's assistance.

This chapter reviews the most relevant literature on police crisis intervention and then discusses how the crisis intervention model can be used by police. Our view is that: (1) police are strategic frontline workers who deal with people in crisis; (2) the crisis intervention model is compatible with police procedures; and (3) effective use of crisis intervention strategies can reduce the time spent on non-crime related activities. Our aim is to provide a practical tool for police which provides both sound assistance to citizens in crisis and offers the least possible threat to the officers' personal safety.

LITERATURE REVIEW

Since the late 1960s a number of articles on crisis intervention by police have appeared in the police and behavioral science literature. Most are descrip-tions of training programs, though some have reported evaluative data, and a few have offered step-by-step instructions for training police in crisis intervention. Our review will begin with a summary of findings on the nature of police crisis calls, followed by evaluative studies, and training models.

Police Crisis Calls

Patton (1973) has described six aspects of disturbance calls. Family disturbances to which police are summoned are:

1. Citizen invoked, meaning that the person initiating contact has a vested interest in the type of resolution that officers may provide;

2. Time consuming, since clarification and even temporary resolution requires gathering extensive information;

3. Ambiguous, since there is rarely a clear statement of events leading to the call, and the responsibility for the conflict is often difficult to determine;

4. Dangerous, since each call has a potential for violence;

5. Anxiety producing, due to the ambiguity and potential dangerousness of the situation; and

6. Unevenly distributed among the general population, with more calls coming from economically disadvantaged families and neighborhoods.

Beyond these general characteristics, disturbance calls usually involve a wide range of participants, for example, husbands, wives, children, in-laws, grandparents, neighbors and friends (Reid 1975). This means that the responding officer is never quite sure of the situation or of the people he will encounter. Two aspects, however, are predictable (Goldstein et al. 1979). First, calls will almost always involve citizens who are emotionally upset. Aggressive feelings and behavior are usually present during family disturbances, anxiety and depression during suicide attempts or accidents, hysteria or shock in the aftermath of rape and assault, and cognitive confusion and agitation with mentally disturbed or intoxicated citizens.

Added to these psychological characteristics of citizens in crisis is a second feature of most disturbance calls: the high danger to the officer's personal safety. The FBI Crime Report for 1979 reveals that 18,743 law enforcement officers were assaulted while responding to disturbance calls during that year, a figure making up 31.7 percent of the total number of police assaults. Furthermore, between 1975-1979, of the 532 police officers killed, 16.7 percent were killed on a disturbance call assignment.

Explanations of data on the dangerousness of disturbance calls focus on both police and citizen contributions to the problem. On the one hand, citizens whose psychological/family problems reach the police often do not want outside help. Liberman (1969) compared people whose psychological problems are brought to police with those whose problems are brought to medical/psychiatric personnel and found that 71 percent of the former group thought that they did not need outside help, while only 11 percent of the latter resisted the idea of outside intervention. Added to this is the fact that police are the only community helpers with the legal authority (and weapons) to enforce change during a crisis. Though the presence of police weapons may be assumed to facilitate control in some situations, in others it may invite resistance and thereby increase the dangerousness of the situation. Horstman's (1974) analysis of assaults on police officers concluded that the probability of assault varies directly with the officer's skill in human relations, and appropriate use of the authority inherent in his/her role. In sum, the literature offers consensus on the extreme difficulty, and the very high stakes involved, in family disturbance calls, which demands crisis intervention techniques capable of rapid assessment and action of the kind not usually required of other community helpers.

Evaluative Studies   Though most police officers have learned to handle disturbance calls by on-the-job training, a number of federal, state, and municipal training programs on police theory and tactics now include training in crisis management (Reid 1975). Perhaps the best known work in this area is Bard's (1970) training of New York City police to handle family crisis situations. Eighteen officers were selected to provide 24 hour a day, 365-day a year crisis intervention services for a residential area encompassing 85,000 mostly lower class and lower middle class families. The 18 patrolmen underwent five full days of intensive training each week for one month, including lectures, audiovisual and role play demonstrations, human relations exercises, and the like. In addition, each officer was assigned a consultant to provide weekly consultation and on call aid.

Bard evaluated the project along six dimensions. It was hypothesized that in comparison with a control precinct, the demonstration project precinct would show a reduction in: number of family disturbance complaints, number of repeat interventions needed, homicides, assaults, homicides among family members, and injuries to policemen. Contrary to expectations, Bard found that results on four of these criteria were opposite of those originally predicted. The demonstration project had three times more disturbance complaints than the control precinct, more repeat cases, and increases in overall homicides, as well as family homicides. There were, however, fewer assaults found in the demonstration precinct than in the control precinct, and there were no reported injuries sustained by members of the demonstration project. During the same time period, three patrolmen from the control precinct were injured at the scene of the disturbance call.

Bard suggests that increased diligence in filing reports by the demonstration officers accounted for their greater number of disturbance complaints and repeat interventions, though concluded that the operation of the crisis trained patrolman failed to effect any change in overall homicide incidence. Others have pointed to the shortcomings of crime statistics, for example, variation within samples, susceptibility to influence of extraneous variables, in evaluating the impact of police crisis intervention, implying that homicides may have been reduced even in the Bard study, though the overall rate increased due to other variables (racial unrest during the summer of 1967) (Driscoll, Meyer, and Schanie 1973).

Driscoll et al.'s (1973) study was designed to measure the immediate effects of crisis intervention training on police performance. Twelve officers in the Lewisville Police Department were given five to six hours of training, five days a week, for five weeks, after which they were assigned to their regular duties. The effects of training were measured by telephone interviews with families who had been the recipients of police interventions, and by questionnaires given to the officers themselves four months after the training had ended. Questionnaire responses from officers indicated that they had an increased understanding of family problems, and were more accepted by citizens, who were also more receptive to the officer's suggestions. In addition, officers reported a decrease in the use of force, and a belief that their overall effectiveness in family disturbance calls had been increased as a result of the training. Telephone interviews with the families themselves corroborated these officer perceptions. Family members rated trained officers as demonstrating greater rapport between themselves and the citizens in crisis and as being more involved with the citizens, which resulted in increased overall satisfaction by the citizens, as well as an increase in regard for the police.

Many others have followed the lead of Bard and his colleagues in training police officers in crisis intervention (Burnett et al. 1976; Henderson 1976; Phelps, Schwartz, and Liebman 1971; Wallace and Schrieber 1977; Walsh and Witte 1975; Valle and Axelberd 1977). Though these articles do not report evaluative data based on followup of citizens' crises, they all demonstrate the feasibility of training police in crisis intervention and point out noticeable improvements in relations between police and both citizens in crisis and also other social service agencies (Cesnik, Pierce, and Puls 1977).

Training Models There is considerable variation in the police crisis intervention literature on the presentation of details for training programs. Some articles emphasize training methodology (extensive use of simulations and videotape feedback by Bard 1970, and Driscoll et al. 1973), or broad procedural guidelines (Blanton 1976; Cesnick et al. 1977), and a few offer detailed instructions for police to follow during crisis situations (Goldstein et al. 1979; Loving 1981a, 1981b). A consistency that runs through crisis training models for police is that attention must be given to the best use of the officer's authority to calm intense situations, and that officers must above all take steps to reduce physical danger (Bard 1970; Blanton 1976; Burnett et al. 1976; Driscoll et al. 1973; Goldstein et al. 1979; Henderson 1976; Mann 1973; Phelps et al. 1971; Phillips 1975; Reid 1975; Wallace and Schreiber 1977; Walsh and Witte 1975).

One of the clearest step-by-step guides for police crisis intervention has been developed by Goldstein et al. (1979) for the Syracuse Police Department. Police behavior is structured around four main tasks: oberving and protecting threats to the officer's safety, calming the situation, gathering relevant information, and taking appropriate action. Officers are taught how to apply these four steps to a wide range of crisis situations including family disputes, mental disturbances, drug and alcohol intoxication, rape, and suicide.

Blanton's (1976) training model is similar to the Goldstein et al. approach, though adds a decision structure to assist police officers in deciding *what* action strategy to select. The first three steps of Blanton's model—observing the scene, defusing the situation, and fact finding—closely parallel Goldstein's approach. According to Blanton, following a judgment about whether a crime has or has not been committed, the officer can either arrest the violator, or choose from three other strategies: mediation, referral, or separation of the disputants.

The psychological first aid model presented in Chapter 6 can also be used as a framework for police crisis intervention. It includes many of the elements found in Goldstein and Blanton, though it gives additional guidance for officers when it comes to choosing action steps, that is, how directive/controlling a stance to take during a crisis situation.

PSYCHOLOGICAL FIRST AID BY POLICE

This section assumes that the reader is familiar with the five components of psychological first aid as outlined in Chapter 6. By adding the strategies suggested by Goldstein et al. (1979), we will focus on the specific application of the psychological first aid (PFA) model to police crisis intervention. The five components of psychological first aid are intended to serve as a cognitive map for dealing with the full range of police crisis calls.

Approaching the Scene

Goldstein et al. (1979) stress the importance of an officer's preparing himself mentally before entering a crisis situation. This involves recollections of prior experience on similar calls, anticipating that the unexpected might actually happen on this particular call, and formulating a tentative plan of action. This "psyching up" for the call is actually a preventive measure, since crisis calls for police represent a potential threat to the officer's safety.

As the officer approaches the scene, the first step is to observe and neutralize threats to safety. As stated by Goldstein et al.:

> By this we mean not only removing the obvious weapons such as guns and knives, but also removing or neutralizing the heavy and throwable objects (ashtrays, folding chairs, etc.), scissors, kitchen utensils, boiling water (in a pot on the stove, or in a coffee cup), and the like. We would also recommend routinely and immediately separating disputants; placing yourself away from windows and staircases; avoiding turning your back on any of the disputants; and, both knowing where your partner is, and if possible, actually having him in view—even when each of you is with a different disputant in a different room (p. 13).

Making Psychological Contact

The immediate objective of making psychological contact in family disturbance calls is to reduce tensions, and lend calm to the situation. Goldstein et al. suggest that the officer create a first impression of "non-hostile authority," which again highlights one of the major differences between crisis intervention by police and by other community helpers. While other counselors usually avoid, at least in the early stages of crisis intervention, taking the role of authority, police officers do not have this option. Uniformed officers are, by definition, in a role of authority and the central issue then becomes how the authority will be used.

> . . . it is important to avoid being either too soft or too harsh. The officer who too gently asks the individual to do such and such will

often fail to achieve his purpose because he's neither gotten the person's attention to a sufficient degree, nor made the citizen feel sufficiently secure or reassured by his presence. The officer who opens his arrival at a crisis call by being too harsh, by leaning too hard on the people involved, may also fail to achieve his purposes of calming the scene and resolving the crisis. In fact, just the opposite may occur. The disturbance level may actually increase, and threats to the officer's safety may actually become more possible (p. 15).

Goldstein et al. offer several procedures that have potential for calming a distraught citizen.

Showing Understanding This is the empathy that is central to psychological first aid, that is, letting the person know by the helper's words, tone of voice, and facial expressions that he/she has an understanding of what the person is feeling at the time. Reflective statements such as the following might be used: "I can see how angry you are," or, "I can imagine how frightening that was to you." The objective is to avoid taking sides by supporting one party more than the other, or saying that an individual's position is *right*, but instead to show that the officer *hears* what the person is saying and feeling at the time.

Modeling Calm Behavior Since people in crisis often gauge their own feelings, and the seriousness of the situation, by the way others react—particularly someone new on the scene, such as a police officer—it is important that the officer model a calm approach to the intense situation. This includes not only what is said, but also tone of voice, facial expressions, and gestures. Simply removing his/her hat, and sitting down to speak with disputants in a normal conversational tone of voice can contribute a calming influence to a crisis situation.

Reassuring This takes the calming influence one step further; beyond acting calm himself, the officer gives the person in crisis reasons why he/she should also feel calmer. The officer can express confidence about the eventual outcome ("You can work this out"), the ability of others to help ("The ambulance workers will know how to handle this"), as well as the officer's competence ("I've handled many like this before").

Encouraging Talking Because it is difficult to be yelling, crying, fighting, etc. in an emotional manner while at the same time attempting to answer a series of questions, asking questions and encouraging talk is often effective in calming the crisis victim. The officer should learn to recognize those times when it is useful to encourage talking about the crisis itself (ventilation) versus encouraging the individual to talk about matters other than the crisis (diversion). This decision can be made after noting the effect discussing the crisis has on the individual. If the person is encouraged to talk about the crisis and becomes more upset, the officer can divert the person's attention to background information which is needed for his formal report.

Using Distraction An effective means for calming emotional persons is to divert their attention in ways other than asking for background information. Some methods of distraction are: (1) asking for a favor ("May I have a glass of water?"); (2) asking a question irrelevant to the situation ("Can you tell me where you got that lamp?"); and (3) offering an observation irrelevent to the crisis situation ("I've got the same brand of T.V., but we've been having trouble with it lately."). Obviously distracting comments and questions have only a temporary effect, therefore the officer should be prepared to follow them with other calming procedures.

Using Humor   With some citizens, humor can be effective in helping gain a more accurate and less serious perspective of their current circumstances. This behavior can communicate to the citizen that the officer is not overly upset by what is happening and it can often cool emotions in a crisis characterized by aggressive feelings.

Goldstein et al. (1979) consider the first six calming methods outlined as *conversational* methods. By showing understanding, modeling, reassuring, encouraging talking, or using distraction or humor, the officer attempts to calm the individual by words or deeds designed to have a quieting effect. In addition to these six methods, there are four other calming techniques which can be employed with the emotional citizen. When the conversational methods have proven unsuccessful it may be necessary to employ two *assertive* methods for calming emotional citizens.

Repeating and Outshouting   Often individuals in crisis are so angry, anxious, depressed, or confused that they are tuned in to only their own feelings. These persons may be unresponsive to others' feelings, communications, and even presence. The officer may have to repeat himself several times to "get through" to the citizen. When the emotion is anger, an officer may have to outshout the citizen to be heard. Other actions such as slamming a clipboard or other object often have an immediate quieting effect.

Using Physical Restraint   When all previous calming methods have failed, including repeating and outshouting, or where considerations of physical danger exist, it may be necessary to subdue the aggressive citizen. The officer should employ only enough force as is neces-sary to accomplish this goal and avoid excessive force. It should be noted that in family disputes it is not uncommon for a complainant wife to turn on the officer and attempt to resist her husband's arrest even though it was her complaint that brought the police in the first place.

There will be crisis in which calming the individuals is best handled by means other than the conversational or assertive methods.

Using Trusted Others   An officer may request another individual to calm the citizen. This person could be another police officer, family member, neighbor, etc.; whomever is trusted by the individual in crisis could be used. This action may prove necessary if the crisis situation has a high risk of lethality; when there are too many upset citizens involved for the officer to deal with; when the person is fearful of police; if the individual speaks a foreign language; and when conversational and assertive methods have been unsuccessful.

Temporarily Ignoring The Person   The officer may be placed into a crisis situation where he/she will use none of these procedures but decide to deal with the emotional citizen by temporarily ignoring him. Circumstances that could promote this action include threats to an officer's or other's safety, emergency aspects of the situation (i.e., a bleeding child), securing the premises from further harm, etc.

Finally, it should be noted that only through experience can the police officer know which one(s) of these methods are best employed with each crisis. The officer should be familiar with each one of these calming procedures and remain flexible in the attempt to match the best method with the different types of crises and people encountered.

Examining Dimensions of the Problem In the psychological first aid (PFA) model, problem exploration by the helper aims at determining which issues need immediate attention, and which can be postponed. The helper determines also (a) whether lethality is high or low, and (b) whether the client is capable of taking care of him/herself at that time, in order that the helper can gauge how directive an action stance to take. Police officers must add a third dimension during the problem exploration or fact finding phase: (c) whether or not a crime has been committed. Goldstein et al. (1979) summarize a range of types of questions and statements officers can use in gathering information. Each approach yields somewhat different information. Nondirective procedures include:

Open-ended Questions These are similar to the who, what, why, where questions of PFA. In addition to generating considerable data, they allow the individual to let off steam, thereby defusing the situation.

Listening Not only must the officer listen, he/she must also give the citizen signs that he/she is doing so: eye contact, head nods, verbalizations such as "I see what you mean," or "I can understand that."

Closed-ended Questions Questions that can be answered with yes or no or with a brief reply are closed-ended questions. They are a necessary part of the interview though should not be used where open-ended questions would be preferable.

Restatement of Content (Paraphrasing) This procedure consists of saying back to the citizen, in words different than his/her own if possible, the essence of the message. This serves to show the individual that the officer is paying attention and encourages the person to continue talking.

Reflection of Feelings Whereas restating content involves repeating the facts of the person's statement, this action focuses on expressing the citizen's main feelings. Therefore, to accurately grasp what the individual is communicating the officer must pay close attention both to what the person is saying and how he is saying it. When people feel they are understood, they are more likely to continue to provide information and this technique can facilitate such disclosure.

Selective Inattention and Use of Silence Often an excited or anxious person will deluge the officer with details. Sometimes this information is irrelevant to the officer in the quest to take appropriate action or it may be relevant but it is more than the officer needs at the time. When faced with a citizen who talks too much and is difficult to keep on track, simply failing to pay attention to irrelevant or excessive comments is often an effective means of quieting the verbal barrage.

Encouragement and Use of Specific and Implied Invitations Often people under extreme stress will become confused and disorganized in their speech and thinking. Under these circumstances simple questions like "What happened here?" can produce wandering, erroneous answers. The officer therefore needs to make questions very concrete. The overall approach should be one of a patient listener, questioner, and reflector, who builds the interview one question at a time. Combining this method with appropriate calming procedures is likely to reduce the citizen's confusion and yield more accurate information.

Self-disclosure and Use of Immediacy People tend to disclose more about their thoughts, fears, feelings, and backgrounds when others reveal similar information about themselves. Often the police officer will be called into crisis situations where self-disclosure can be a useful interviewing technique. Goldstein et al. stress, however, that there is an important distinction between private self-disclosure and public self-disclosure on the part of the responding officer. Private self-disclosure in which the officer reveals private, personal information about himself (the officer's own marital history, depressive episodes, etc.) is not considered an appropriate interviewing procedure. Experience indicates this type of self-disclosure tends to diminish the officer in the eyes of the citizen and fails to increase further self-disclosure by the citizen. However, public self-disclosure in which the officer may usefully relate public experiences he/she has had which are relevant to the crisis interview (places visited, types of people dealt with, etc.) is an appropriate technique.

The use of immediacy refers to the effects of positive officer comments on further disclosure by the citizen. An example of immediacy would be "I can tell from what you've said that you're really trying hard."

Confrontation Confrontation can be an interviewing technique in which the officer points out discrepancies between two statements the citizen has made (content-content discrepancy) or between something the citizen has said and the way he/she said it (content-feeling discrepancy).

Demanding If the citizen is very hostile, resistive, or if lethality is judged to be high, the officer may be required to employ this technique. *Demanding* requires the officer to firmly instruct the citizen what is to be done and to do it immediately.

Exploring Possible Solutions Assuming that the police officer has been called because previously attempted solutions have failed, it is important to ask both disputants what has been tried, and to get citizens to generate possible options for resolving the crisis. Whether talking with disputants separately or together, a central question is, "What do you want to do/have happen here?" and "What are some possible solutions?" Alternatives suggested/imposed by the officer will usually be resisted unless the citizens have had a chance to offer their own ideas. Also, by putting the matter of solutions back on the citizens, the officer gives an implicit message of confidence in the disputants, reinforcing their decision making capabilities, which may seem well hidden in the heat of the crisis.

Taking Concrete Action If (a) lethality is low, (b) the citizen is physically and psychologically capable (not incapacitated by drugs, alcohol, or psychosis), and (c) no crime has yet been committed, then the officer takes a "facilitative" stance with the citizen(s) in crisis. While the generic PFA model (Chapter 6) calls for a range of helper behavior from discussions/verbal support to advice, for police crisis intervention this range is redefined as mediation, on the one hand, and negotiation or counseling, on the other (see Table 12.1).

Mediation The central principle behind mediation as an action strategy is that people are more likely to abide by solutions they create than by those imposed by someone else. The basic approach for the officer is to assist the disputants in reaching their own solution to the problem. A pair of officers might speak first with each of the disputants separately, and then together. The goal is for the disputants to generate solutions, to discuss them back and forth, and finally arrive at a mutually agreed upon action step (or several). These steps might include a suggestion about where one party will spend the night, a decision to seek marital counseling in the morning, agreement about how money will be spent in the next several days, and so on.

Quoting from a Florida crisis intervention seminar,[1] Goldstein et al. suggest several guidelines for conducting mediation:

1. If possible, use mediation as your first approach to crisis intervention.
2. Inform the citizens that you cannot solve their problems, that they must do so themselves.
3. Avoid suggesting solutions.
4. Elicit suggestions from the citizens as to how their problem can be solved.
5. Check each proposal with the other disputant, until there is acceptance or compromise.
6. Avoid criticizing the citizens' solutions even if you do not agree with them.
7. Offer encouragement for them to follow through.

Negotiation   As a procedure that is somewhat more directive than mediation, negotiation involves suggesting solutions or compromises and actively assisting citizens in selecting a direction. As with mediation, the officers might talk with each party separately, and then bring the two together for a negotiation session. Each officer assists the spouses in negotiating, following Goldstein, Sprafkin, and Gershaw's (1976) steps of successful negotiation:

1. State your position.
2. State your understanding of the other person's position.

3. Ask if the other person agrees with your statement of position.
4. Listen openly (not defensively) to the response.
5. Propose a compromise.

Counseling   As the most directive of the facilitative stances an officer can take, counseling includes not only assisting disputants in understanding their feelings and expectations, but also offering suggestions and giving advice on what the disputants can do to resolve the problem. "Counseling" as defined by Goldstein et al. merges with "giving advice" in PFA, and is offered when mediation and negotiation strategies fall short in helping disputants take appropriate action.

If lethality is judged to be high, if the person is physically or psychologically incapable of taking care of him/herself, or if a crime has been committed, then the officer takes a directive stance in psychological first aid. As Table 12.1 indicates, the initial strategies, called "actively mobilizing resources" in the PFA model, involve referral to other agencies. Referral takes place only after the problem has been identified, and its success rests on the officer's familiarity with community agencies. Goldstein, et al. (1979) offer the following guidelines to increase the probability of police referrals being successful:

1. Let the citizen know that you understand his crisis problem and his feelings about it.
2. Tell the citizen that the chances are good that the agency to which you would like to refer him can be of help regarding the crisis problem.
3. Give the citizen, in writing, the appropriate referral information, and make sure he

---

[1] Office of the Sheriff., *Crisis intervention seminar*, Jacksonville, Florida, 1975, in Goldstein, *et al.*, 1979, pp. 29-31).

TABLE 12.1   PSYCHOLOGICAL FIRST AID BY POLICE[a]

APPROACHING THE SCENE

Reflect on prior experience on similar calls
Anticipate the unexpected
Form tentative action plan

CONTACT	DIMENSIONS OF THE PROBLEM	POSSIBLE SOLUTIONS
Showing understanding Modeling Calm Behavior Reassuring Encouraging talking Using distraction Using humor Repeating and outshouting Using physical restraint Using trusted others Temporarily ignoring	Open-ended questions Listening Closed-ended questions Restatement of content Reflection of feelings Selective inattention and use of silence Encouragement Self-disclosure and immediacy Confrontation Demanding	Possible attempts at solution Successes and failures Possible alternatives

ACTION STEPS

If:
- Lethality is low;
- Person can act on own behalf; *and*
- No crime committed,
Then *Facilitative* stance, which ranges:

From: To:
Discussion/verbal   Advice (Negotiation,
support   Counseling)
(Mediation)

If:
- Lethality is high;
- Person cannot act on own behalf; *or*
- Crime committed,
Then *Directive* stance, which ranges:

From: To:
Actively mobilizing   Control
resources
(Referral)   (Arrest, Hospitalization,
                                              Arbitration)

FOLLOW UP

Name, phone number, address of disputants

Agreement that citizen will call back, or
that officer, mental health worker, etc.
will call back

[a]This table represents a combination of the generic psychological first aid model (Chapter 6) with training procedures (Goldstein et al. (1979) for police crisis intervention.

understands it. Use an "emergency telephone numbers" referral card.

4. Deal with any citizen resistance to the referral, e.g., most agencies take people at all salary levels.

5. If possible, have the citizen call the agency when you are still present.

6. If the citizen is too upset or otherwise unable to call the appropriate agency, get his permission for you to make the call, and do so.

7. If circumstances make it inappropriate for either you or the citizen to telephone the agency at the time of your crisis call, obtain a commitment from the citizen (or other person at the crisis scene) that the agency will be contacted at the earliest possible time (p. 32).

In more extreme situations, the officer takes steps to ensure a particular outcome, or to control the situation. Strategies here are adopted only after everything else has been found to be inadequate—mediation, negotiation, counseling, referral. At this point, the officer can engage in arbitration or physically take steps to control/protect the citizen(s) by making an arrest, or driving a person to a hospital emergency room for assessment and possible hospitalization. Arbitration involving a third party making decisions for disputants. In the crisis context it means that when previous measures have proven inadequate, the police officer reviews the situation (strengths and weaknesses of possible solutions), consults with his/her partner, makes a decision, and authoritatively tells the citizen what to do. Goldstein et al. point out that arbitration is the least desirable of the action alternatives available since it makes for a high percentage of return calls, is likely the most dangerous of the approaches available, and therefore should only be used as a last resort.

A directive approach that goes even beyond arbitration is for the officers to settle the dispute by taking steps to physically control the environment of the citizen, for example,

putting the person in jail, or in a hospital. Violation of the law is a prerequisite for the former, and "imminent danger" to self or others for the latter (Chapter 6).

Following Up   As with all PFA contacts, the aim of followup in police crisis intervention is to find out whether the action steps set in motion during the intervention had the intended effect in subsequent days. While police officers themselves will usually not have the time to conduct follow up, they can still close each PFA contact with the expectation that follow up will occur. If the dispute has been successfully resolved via mediation or negotiation, for example, the officer might ask the disputant(s) to call back the next day to let the officer know how things are going, and in particular, if a referral worked out as expected. This procedure need not take much of the officer's time; simply checking for messages on the appointed day can allow him to make recontact by telephone to check on progress. Depending upon the nature of liason with other community agencies, these other workers might conduct follow up after police family disturbance calls.

CONCLUSION   Though there is consensus in the literature that police officers need to have crisis skills, the idea that crisis calls are not "real" police matters is still prevalent in some departments and can hinder the development of a successful training program (Bard 1970). Our view is that the success of any training program will depend not simply on *what* officers are taught but also on the extent to which trainers address a number of interdepartmental variables.

1. To counter the idea that crisis work is "extra" duty, it can be included as a

component of every police officer's training instead of being restricted to special units (Driscoll et al. 1973). Minimally, every police officer ought to have enough of an understanding of life crises to not be surprised by the erratic behavior of citizens/families in crisis. Similarly, every officer, whether he/she spends a great deal of time or not in working with citizens in crisis, should be aware of how the tactics outlined earlier in this chapter can be used to defuse intense situations. By including a rigorous and well-defined component of crisis training with training in other areas, such as use of weapons, it is possible to minimize the nonpolice aura of crisis work.

2. All levels of police management systems should have input into training programs on crisis strategies. Police officers themselves should be involved in implementing training programs instead of relegating crisis training to mental health personnel from outside the department. Much of the success of the training programs mentioned in this chapter rests with the fact that police officers were intimately involved in their design and implementation.

3. In planning crisis services, emphasis needs to be placed on the rewards inherent in effective crisis management. Officers need to understand that effective use of crisis strategies during family disturbances calls, for example, can reduce, instead of increase, the amount of time spent on these matters, thereby freeing them to pursue other crime related cases. Similarly, the fact that crisis intervention training is aimed not just at helping citizens, but also at reducing police casualties, should be an impetus for crisis training. Finally, by revising criteria for promotions in police departments, it should be possible to build in rewards for effective crisis work.

Beyond these intradepartmental considerations, for police crisis intervention to be suc-

cessful, there will need to be mutually rewarding working relationships with other mental health and social service agencies. The experience in many communities is that police officers and mental health workers can help one another though a fair amount of liaison work and dialogue is necessary to define precisely how this will take place. Cesnik et al. (1977) created a police position of Social Service Coordinator to serve as a liaison between the police department and community mental health agencies. Other considerations include the following:

1. Each community should have a place, besides the city/county jail, where police officers can take citizens for assessment and possible short-term hospitalization. It is unfortunate that in many communities the public hospitals are not equipped with holding rooms for psychiatric observation, and that officers must put citizens who require hospitalization into jail instead.

2. Telephone linkage—911 systems—can serve as a connection between police, twenty-four hour telephone hotlines, and emergency rooms, thereby coordinating services for citizens in crisis.

3. Mental health centers can offer consultation to police officers on handling crisis calls though coverage will need to include nights and weekends, times when many mental health facilities are not in operation. Rotating schedules, often using social service personnel placed in hospital emergency rooms, is one way of maintaining twenty-four hour support for police responding to crisis calls.

4. One of the most useful services which community mental health centers and other social services could provide to police officers is assistance in follow up of crisis calls. At hotlines, for example, there are usually slack periods during the day when few people are calling, times during which counselors could make follow up phone calls to families recently involved

in crises. In this way, police disturbance calls can lead naturally to outreach by other mental health agencies. Besides helping the families in crisis, this cooperation is a step toward nurturing good relationships between the police and social service agencies.

Finally, there are a number of opportunities for further research on police crisis intervention. Evaluations of training programs are possible using the research framework outlined in Chapter 18 of this volume. Telephone follow up with citizens after police intervention can measure both current functioning and also citizen evaluation of officer performance along various specific dimensions. (See Chapter 18 for discussion of outcome questions following psychological first aid.) In addition, various elements of Bard's (1970) and Driscoll's et al. (1973) important research need to be replicated, for example, that crisis training can reduce the frequency of officer injury during disturbance calls. Confirmation of these hypotheses could further strengthen the case for devoting resources to crisis intervention training for police.

chapter thirteen

Crisis Intervention by Health Professionals

David S. Siegel
Karl A. Slaikeu
Gordon M. Kimbrell

Physicians, nurses, and other health professionals have a direct impact on how their patients' resolve life crises in at least two ways. First, as discussed in Chapter 4 (Situational Crises), health professionals have ready access to individuals and their families who are struggling with crisis reactions associated with physical injury and illness. In most cases, it is the nurse or physician who first informs the patient about the existence and the long range implications of illness or injury. It is at this point that psychological first aid may first be offered. Physicians, nurses, and other members of health care teams (social workers, physical therapists, speech therapists, vocational counselors, and hospital chaplains) have continued contact with patients during the course of an illness and are therefore in a unique position to track the process of crisis resolution and to make important interventions.

A second point of contact by health professionals involves the somatic correlates of all crises, whether they begin with physical injury or illness or not. Physicians involved in primary care can attest to the high percentage of patients who present physical symptoms (and ask for "medical" treatment) related to critical life events. [See Chapter 2 regarding the relationship between life events and physical illness (Holmes and Rahe 1967).] The challenge for the health care team in these instances is to properly diagnose the relationship between the physical symptoms and life crises (divorce, unemployment, migration, or whatever) and to make treatment recommendations or referrals for crisis therapy that are congruent with principles of effective crisis resolution.

It is unfortunate that the progress of the past several years in understanding the relationship between psychological problems and physical illness has not been accompanied by a corresponding increase in training health professionals from all aspects of the health care system to deal with their patients' crises. Nurses and social workers usually receive at least some theoretical training in crisis intervention while in graduate school; yet, many other hospital staff members have not been trained adequately and do not feel comfortable dealing with patients undergoing reactive crises. In addition, as Zind (1974) has reported, attending to and dealing with the emotional component of patients' problems is not always viewed as a high priority in the hospital system. It is the technical and task-oriented aspects of staff work that are often more highly scrutinized. Consequently, the angry, criticizing, demanding, or crying patient may be purposefully excluded or avoided by staff. Thus even in cases where staff members are trained, the hospital system may interfere with their adequately taking on the role of crisis intervention.

We will first review the growing literature on crisis intervention surrounding problems that begin primarily as medical concerns, including a section on chronic disability. We will follow this with suggestions for future research, as well as general guidelines and suggestions for use of the crisis model by health professionals treating the complete range of situational and developmental crises.

LITERATURE REVIEW

Critical Illness or Trauma in the Intensive Care Unit

There are many types of intensive care units (ICU) that are specialized to provide highly technical care to severely ill or traumatized patients. The patients admitted to these units are invariably in the midst of a multifaceted crisis. The core of the crisis is the confrontation with the threat to one's body—loss of function, disfigurement, even death. This overwhelming insult to sense of body image is also accompanied by intense feelings of helplessness, dependency, and humiliation.

Many writers have pointed out that the very environment of the ICU can become an emotional hazard for the patient (Kuenzi and Fenton 1975; Rosen 1975; Schnaper and Cowley 1976; Williams and Rice 1977). The impact of such an environment has been well described by Hay and Oken (1972):

> Initially, the greatest impact comes from the intricate machinery, with its flashing lights, buzzing and beeping monitor, gurgling suction pumps, and whooshing respirators. . . . Desperately ill, sick and injured human beings are hooked up to that machinery. And in addition to the mechanical stimuli, one can discern moaning, crying, screaming, and the last gasps of life. Sights of blood, vomitus, and excreta, exposed genitalia, mutilated wasting bodies, and unconscious and helpless people assault the sensibilities (p.110).

Obviously, this is usually a frightening and stressful experience for the patient as well as the family. Sometimes patients find themselves in an ICU after having been comatose or semiconscious. Other patients have been medicated so that their perceptions of what is happening to them and around them is distorted. Still, other trauma patients awaken and are amnesic about the events associated with hospitalization (Schnaper and Cowley 1976). Various psychological sequelae to trauma and serious illness in the ICU have been reported (Crupie 1976; Keily 1976; Schnaper and Cowley 1976; Sund 1976; Weisath 1976). These range from states of agitation, anxiousness, fear, delerium, and depression to psychotic-like reactions including delusions and hallucinations. It is very likely that environmental effects of the ICU, such as overstimulation, sleep deprivation, sensory deprivation, and loss of perceived diurnal variation can play a role in precipitating these sorts of reactions.

Family members of the ICU patient are also likely to be in crisis, and the ICU environment can be expected to add to their stress as well. Faced with the possible loss of a loved one, the family may also be scrambling to adapt structurally to the absence of a significant member (Minuchen 1974). As Williams and Rice (1977) point out, the resulting disequilibrium in the family system constitutes a major crisis. Family members must deal with a host of health professionals who are busy responding rapidly and technically to complex life or death situations. They find themselves in an extremely tense environment surrounded by equipment and people performing tasks that are only vaguely, if at all, understood.

Kuenzi and Fenton (1975) have presented some general principles of crisis intervention for nurses dealing with patients in the ICU. These principles emphasize the importance of communication:

> The patient should be given frequent information about his status and progress. All activities of nurses and other health personnel which directly or indirectly affect the patient should be adequately explained. Statements made by any personnel, including physicians, which are directed to, or even just overheard by the patient should be explained. The use of all equipment and its purpose should be explained and all questions answered (p. 832).

Kuenzi and Fenton (1975) also suggest that nurses take an active role in discussing various concerns with the patient regarding death, body disfigurement, the conditions of other patients nearby, and the recovery process.

Intervention with families of ICU patients have also been described (Epperson 1977; Kuenzi and Fenton 1975; Williams and Rice 1977). Epperson (1977) reports that families typically undergo a six-phase recovery process before regaining equilibrium: high anxiety, denial, anger, remorse, grief, and reconciliation. These phases are similar to those reported by Kuenzi and Fenton (1975) in their work with families of trauma victims in which a typical sequence included denial, shock, disbelief, anger, depression, and resolution.

Williams and Rice (1977) have encouraged social workers to employ techniques to help family members understand and accurately perceive events in the ICU, ventilate feelings, cope more effectively, and mobilize support systems. It is very important to establish effective lines of communication between families and staff. Social workers can play a vital role by interpreting physicians' discussions with families and by preventing or correcting misinterpretations about the patient's condition.

Family members cope with their feelings in different ways. The ICU staff needs to understand that family members may vent anger towards them, and must accept the fact that this will be one of the ways the family deals with fears for the patient's life, and the family's own helplessness. Crisis interveners can be instrumental in helping and allowing members to express these and other difficult feelings.

Surgery

Patients who have been hospitalized in order to have surgery usually experience anxiety before and after the procedure. Because of this, and because surgery (as a stressor) is often a predictable event, efforts have been made to intervene with patients in order to facilitate coping. Crisis intervention with surgical patients has generated a large number of clinical reports and empirical investigations.

Several reports have focused on interventions administered to patients in the hospital before their surgery (Auerbach and Kilmann 1977; Wise 1975). For example, Wise reported on pre- and post-operative interventions with an eight-year-old girl who underwent cardiac surgery. Before any interventions with the child began, the nurses assessed the family's potential for coping with the impending surgery. Interventions with the child were seen as falling into two categories: anticipatory guidance and ego support. Anticipatory guidance involved clearing up any misconceptions or misunderstandings about the impending event, providing information about what to expect post-operatively, and facilitating the expression of feelings. At one point, the child became very anxious about having injections in her upper thigh. When the dimensions of this problem were explored, it became apparent that the girl had been accustomed to having injections in her buttocks and believed that, when delivered to the thigh, they would cause paralysis. The nurse handled the situation by giving support and reassurance, and encouraging her patient to take some concrete action to test out her misconception: the girl was encouraged to move and walk around after the thigh injection. At another point, the girl was given a pre-operative visit to the ICU where she observed and handled cardiac monitors, mist tents, Foley catheters, and other gadgetry that would physically support her later. Post-operatively, the child showed pride in knowing about all the equipment's uses and functions, and seemed to have gained a degree of mastery in the ICU after her surgery.

Under ego support, Wise included activities such as allowing the child to be dependent initially and then gradually encouraging her to increase her independence and responsibility for recovery. The child knew that she could exert some control over the recovery process if she actively assisted in post-operative turning, coughing, deep breathing, and other painful procedures, and was supported and praised for doing so. She seemed to have been well prepared for surgery and its aftermath, having been helped by the professional interventions to minimize the unexpected, the unfamiliar, the stressful, and the frightening.

The impact of surgery often does not end when the procedure has been completed. The aftermath is frequently associated with considerable stress, and the recovery period itself may be fertile ground for life crises. Postsurgical stress has been investigated by Lewis, Gottesman, and Gutstein (1979). They compared two groups of patients: one group which had undergone exploratory surgery for a possible malignancy and another group which had less serious surgery. Both groups took a number of psychological tests including the Spielberger State-Trait Anxiety Scale, the Wakefield Self-Assessment Depression Inven-

tory, the Internal-External Locus of Control Scale, the Rosenberg Self-Concept Scale, and the Halpern Crisis Scale. The tests were administered four times, on the night before surgery and thereafter at 3-week intervals. The cancer group showed more psychological distress on each test over eight weeks after their surgery. Other follow-up data suggested that the patients may have been in crisis as long as 28 weeks afterwards (Belfer, Mulliken and Cochran 1979; David and Barrit 1977).

Sanchez-Salazar and Stark (1972) have described a program of crisis intervention delivered by a speech pathologist and a social worker to laryngectomy patients. They identified four critical events from the time laryngectomy is recommended through the weeks after post-operative discharge. The first stressful event occurs when the patient is told that he/she has cancer of the larynx and needs a laryngectomy. The shock of having a malignancy and the threat of death may overshadow the realization that a lifelong means of vocal communication must be given up. The second stressful event occurs after surgery when the patient is confronted with the impact of actual voice loss and altered breathing patterns. Another set of adjustments occur when the patient is faced with discharge from the protective confines of the hospital. The patient and family frequently have concerns about whether the cancer has been completely removed, and whether they can adequately deal with health maintenance at home with no immediate assistance. Finally, the patient faces stressful adjustments in the following weeks of convalescence. By this time, the patient has begun to react to the interpersonal impact that the disability has on others. In addition, family and friends may become less attentive and concerned.

In the Sanchez-Salazar and Stark study, interventions were delivered at each of these critical points. In addition to pre- and post-surgical interventions which provided support and information, post-discharge contact was maintained in a number of ways. A home visit was made by a nurse two or three days after discharge in order to give the family support, assess potential psychosocial problems, and make certain equipment was being used properly. If emotional problems arose, a social worker made additional visits. The patient also began an outpatient schedule of speech therapy lessons, and was invited to attend meetings of the "Lost Chord Club" (a group of laryngectomees who gave support and encouragement, and shared their experiences with the new members). In addition, for those patients who had a particularly hard time adjusting, short-term group interaction therapy was provided in conjunction with individual speech therapy. The social worker and speech therapist served as co-therapists. Patients were encouraged to attend these sessions along with their families. The "Lost Chord Club" illustrates a way in which patients' range of social support can be broadened. The Club provides patients with a new and valuable role model of a patient who has "made it" and can now help others.

Witkin (1978) has reported her experiences in working with women who have undergone mastectomies. The major post-operative issue confronting these patients concerned their sexual self-concept. Concerns in this area were ususally more important than fear of death. Witkin found that the attitude of the patient's husband or lover was critically important to the recovering woman, and that most men were eager to participate in outpatient counseling with their partner. Post-operative psychosexual counseling was viewed as being an extremely important aspect of the total treatment of the mastectomy patient.

Langer, Janis, and Wolfer (1975) found that getting patients to involve themselves in a particular cognitive strategy (such as thinking about positive aspects of surgery) was more effective than simply giving them specific information about surgical procedures or no information at all. Melamed and Siegel (1975) found that children who were shown a film conveying specific pre-surgical information about impending procedures adjusted better pre- and post-operatively than children who viewed a film with content unrelated to hospitalization.

Andrew (1970) and DeLong (1971) evaluated the role of individual differences in patients' preferred mode of handling stress, and how these differences influence the impact of pre-operative information on the recovery process. In both studies, patients were divided into three groups: (a) "copers" who preferred vigilant or sensitizing defenses, (b) "avoiders" who preferred denial or avoidant defenses, and (c) "nonspecific defenders" who showed no preference for either style of defense. In their review of this research, Auerbach and Kilmann (1977) concluded that avoiders tend to respond poorly when confronted with information regarding surgery, and adjust better when not exposed to this information. On the other hand, copers adjust relatively well when exposed to specific information about surgery, but poorly when not given such input. Nonspecific defenders seem to recover well regardless of whether they receive this sort of information. These results show that crisis intervention techniques need to be tailored to the individual. In some studies, the no-intervention control groups adjusted well to having surgery; that is, some groups recovered well without intervention (Auerbach and Kilmann 1977). This suggests that crisis intervention may not be necessary for all patients and need not be indiscriminately administered to all.

The Birth of Defective Children

A number of reports have appeared concerning the crises of parents who have experienced the birth of a defective child (Farrell 1977; Hancock 1976; Parks 1977; Spink 1976; Stanko 1973). The literature in this area has been comprehensively reviewed by Bahr (1980).

The experience of pregnancy and the prospect of entering parenthood is a developmental transition that can become a crisis for some people. Parks notes that even with normal birth, there can be a discrepancy between the child who the parent has "expected" and the real infant. Parents are expecting a celebration at the birth of a child. With the birth of a defective baby, the parents are hurled into an overwhelmingly shocking situation for which there has usually been little, if any, preparation. They must mourn the loss of their idealized perfect infant, and reorganize their lives around caring for a handicapped child.

Researchers have observed that parents react to the birth of a defective child in a series of stages (Hancock 1976; Parks 1977; Stanko 1973). Combining these authors' observations, Bahr (1980) suggests that the typical sequence includes denial, shock or protest, despair or depression, and finally, attempts to deal with the realities of having a defective infant. Hancock indicates that a period of anger may also appear in the reactive emotional sequence.

Hancock describes interventions conducted with the parents of a newborn infant who was the victim to toxoplasmosis. Initially, the physician in charge of the case was reluctant and uncomfortable in telling the parents about their infant's mental retardation. Instead, the physician minimized this fact, and focused the discussion on the child's visual impairment. As Hancock reported, "He held the opinion that if he discussed retardation with them, they would reject the baby, and she would not benefit from parental warmth; he felt it would be better to let the parents believe she had normal intellectual functioning until they discovered for themselves or from another pediatrician at a later point that she was damaged" (p. 426).

The parents began to make plans based on their fragmentary understanding of their daughter's condition. In response to this, the social worker emphasized that more tests were being conducted, and that they should not make decisions and plans too hastily. The

peak of the crisis came when the physician leveled with them about their infant's retardation and spasticity. The social worker's interventions at this point involved encouraging the parents to express their thoughts and feelings. As Hancock describes, "Both parents felt that she might soak up their love and sap their energy like a sponge, giving little or nothing in return; this was felt as a threat to the family . . . The issue that emerged was whether it was better for the parents and/or the baby to grow to love and then lose each other or never to love each other at all" (pp. 428-29). Instead of letting them become overinvolved in the "right" decision, the social worker helped the parents formulate various possibilities for the child's future and to consider both positive and negative aspects of each. After recognizing their options, the parents decided to have the baby live with them temporarily, and to plan placement outside of their home eventually. After the ordeal of considering options and arriving at a decision, the parents felt a sense of closure and felt that they had an accurate, realistic picture of the future. There was a new sense of closeness between these parents and a sense that they had tapped new-found resources in themselves.

Parks (1977) also emphasizes the importance of encouraging parents to express their emotions about their defective children. In order to realistically begin to accept the defective infant, the parents must often "detach" or withdraw themselves from their expected, wished-for, idealized child. The parents may endure a period of sadness and despair before withdrawal from the idealized child occurs. Because this process comes very close to rejecting the defective newborn, parents may not reveal these undesirable feelings unless the crisis intervener encourages and legitimizes them.

Stanko (1973) describes her own personal experience as a mother of a defective newborn and recalls that people around her discouraged her from seeing her child. Whenever doctors, nurses, interns, etc. discussed the child, they focused on the defect and painted a grotesque picture of the infant. Eventually, she demanded and was reluctantly given permission to visit the baby. The experience was truly positive in that it affirmed her as a mother and gave her assurance that her child was being well cared for and loved.

The issue of withholding information or protecting the parents is addressed by both Stanko and Hancock. It is important to consider the possible motives of health professionals who are reluctant to provide parents or patients with the true picture. Are they afraid of the parents' reactions and feelings, and of possible harm to the infant? To what extent are they protecting themselves instead of the parents? These articles provide examples of why it is important for health professionals to be at least minimally skillful in dealing with these emotional issues. If the physician or nurse is not comfortable in dealing with emotional issues, the patient or parents should at least be provided the option of access to someone who is trained to deal with these issues.

Elderly Inpatients

There has been increasing interest in applying crisis theory and crisis intervention techniques to the problems of hospitalized elderly patients (Burnside 1970; Grauer and Frank 1978). Hospitalization of the elderly person is particularly traumatic because the threat of functional loss or death is compounded by other physical problems such as hearing loss, memory loss, etc. Such infirmities increase the stress involved in adapting to the hospital environment. In addition, the process of leaving the hospital can be just as traumatic as entering, since the patient may have great difficulty adjusting to the discharge setting.

Oradei and Waite (1974) have described short-term group intervention with patients recovering from stroke. As might be expected, the patients' psychological reactions often interfere with the rehabilitation process which is aimed at bringing patients to their highest possible functional capacity. To deal with these psychological problems, Oradei and Waite organized a group for stroke patients to give them assistance and provide the opportunity to ventilate their feelings and discuss their problems. The patients were reported to have had a number of benefits from the group sessions. Patients became more involved with each other on the ward, thus extending one another's social support system. The ventilation of anger and depression over their losses was viewed as a necessary step toward successful coping. In addition, alternative methods of coping were frequently discussed. Patients often had the opportunity to try out new behaviors at home on weekend passes, before their actual discharge from the hospital occurred.

Terminal Illness

Crisis theory and crisis intervention have become widely accepted as ways of understanding and helping terminal patients and their families. The application of crisis concepts to this area has been given impetus by the work of Kubler-Ross (1969). Her framework for viewing the dying person and those close to him/her is consistent with crisis theory.

A number of reports have appeared in the literature describing the crisis of terminal illness for the adult patient and family, and have illustrated the use of crisis intervention by health professionals (Capone et al. 1979; Cohen and Wellisch 1978; Giacquinta 1977; Grady 1975; Kopel and Mock 1978). With recent advances in the treatment of various types of cancer, the patient's life expectancy has often been significantly prolonged. However, along with the increased months or years can also come a decreased quality of life (for instance, because of chemotherapy effects) and the looming threat of a renewed malignancy.

Cohen and Wellisch have illustrated the kinds of family problems that can arise during this terminal cancer treatment period. Their crisis therapy approach is modeled after Minuchin's (1974) structural family therapy. One of their case descriptions concerns a man who was referred for depression, problem eating habits, and general agitation. As therapy with the patient and his wife progressed, it became apparent that the eating problem

> was deeply woven into the fabric of the marital relationship as well as into the couple's cognitive conceptions of Mr. S's disease. Mr. S. was desperately trying to please Mrs. S. by eating copious amounts of the food she prepared as it symbolized his acceptance of her love and efforts. Mrs. S. felt blocked in any way she tried to help Mr. S. and food became the only area where she could do something for him in her estimation. For both, loss of weight meant that the cancer was 'getting the upper hand'. They reasoned that if one lost weight, death would surely follow; and if one gained weight, somehow one had bested the disease and held death at bay (pp. 568-69).

Interventions decreased Mr. S.'s anxiety about eating and his compulsive weighing of himself.

At a later point in Mr. S.'s illness, when he was visibly dying and in great pain, another problem developed. Mrs. S. was controlling interactions with her husband in such a way that he did not ask for pain medication when he clearly needed it. It became apparent that the wife was dealing with her husband's approaching death "via a tightly interwoven logical chain: (1) If he doesn't need pain medicine his disease is better; (2) if his disease is better he won't die; (3) if I don't give him the pain medication so readily and he can live without them, his disease is better and he won't die" (p. 570). Therapy at this point involved getting Mrs. S. to confront her denial, the result being that constraints on her husband's access to pain medication were removed. After her husband's death, Mrs. S. was

seen for two therapy sessions and was assisted in her mourning process.

A weekly group for families and friends of hospitalized tumor patients has been described by Kopel and Mock (1978). The purpose of the group was to provide a setting in which the participants could share feelings and experiences, and provide one another support. Information was also given concerning the system of operation within the ward. If certain members of the group seemed particularly overwhelmed, referrals for individual therapy were arranged.

Family members in the group were assisted in expressing and understanding very complex blends of emotions. In addition to their grief, family members experienced feelings of intense anger and guilt for a variety of reasons. They frequently were reacting to being "abandoned" by their partner, who up until his/her illness was the dominant one in the relationship. They also were reacting to the massive burdens imposed upon them by the ill member. Some experienced guilt because they felt like they had not done enough for their partner, had not lived the desired sort of life with him/her, or because they sometimes wished that she/he would hurry up and die.

A number of examples of these sorts of issues are provided by Kopel and Mock (1978). One woman was emotionally and physically exhausted by having to drive a round trip of 60 miles each day to keep up with the visitation demands of her hospitalized husband. With help from other families in the group, the woman's choices were increased. She was invited to stay with another person who lived in town, thus making her trips unnecessary. Another woman was terribly hurt, upset, and bewildered by her husband's angry abuse whenever she visited him. She helplessly began to feel that something about her behavior was producing these responses. However, the group assisted her in exploring the dimensions of the situation and helped her formulate alternative explanations for her husband's behavior (such as, that it might relate to his resentment of being dependent rather than to her inadequacies). Ultimately, alternative strategies to be used in dealing with her husband's behavior were discussed.

Parents who have a terminally ill child face an unquestionably tragic and emotionally taxing experience. A series of crises confront the parents (and, of course, the child) from the time they are informed of the diagnosis to the time following the death (Lascari 1978). Since the physician is the person who informs the parents of the diagnosis, he/she has the responsibility of helping them deal with the news. Avoiding the issue of the child's death and not providing the parents with factual information about the disease, its course, and its treatment can only add to the already overwhelming problems which the parents must face (Powers 1977).

Interventions with individual families (Lascari 1978) and with groups of families having a terminally ill child (Heller and Schneider 1978) have also appeared in the literature. Assistance can be provided by the child's physician or by another health care provider working collaboratively with the pediatric service. Lascari (1978) believes that interventions with the family should be continued throughout the course of the child's illness and beyond the time of death. When the diagnosis is presented, the facts of the disease should be thoroughly discussed. The parents frequently react with guilt, stemming from feelings that they are somehow responsible for the child's situation. They need a great deal of support during this time and may not absorb portions of the facts presented to them. The interim period between the time when the diagnosis is presented and the time of the child's death presents additional problems. The parents may withdraw emotionally from each other, or one may align with the child in a coalition, excluding the other parent. Also, anger may be directed at the physician (who was the bearer of unwanted

news) or toward the child (because of the torment the illness brings). In addition, the parents invariably are faced with problems of how to treat the child: how to discipline and how to answer questions.

The physician's role during this period is to maintain contact with the parents, to accept their feelings of anger and to help them understand their emotions. If the parents feel guilty about looking forward to the end, the physician can help them accept the fact that their child's dying is an anguishing experience and that it is normal for them to look forward to the time when the child, and they, no longer have to suffer. The physician at this time can also be instrumental in helping the parents examine all of their options concerning issues such as discipline, where the child will die, etc.

Hoffman and Futterman (1971) have also described the emotional tasks required of parents having a leukemic child. These tasks are often contradictory and extremely stressful. For example, parents must maintain investment and hope in their child's welfare and survival while also preparing for the possibility of death (a process called "anticipatory mourning"). Success with leukemia has dramatically increased in the last 10 years. Fifty percent now survive at least 5 years. To retain emotional investment is to become more vulnerable to the pain of loss, and may lead to self-protective withdrawal. On the other hand, to begin mourning for the child before death can become associated, in the parents mind, with killing him/her, and may cause considerable guilt. While many families can function with a "life as usual" attitude in their daily activities, efforts to avoid the impact of terminal illness are likely to be highly strained under the stress of treatment and periodic visits to the outpatient oncology clinic.

Hoffman and Futterman directed their interventions to the oncology clinic setting. In order to facilitate coping with the clinic visits themselves, a play program (involving story telling, playing with toys, etc.) was started in the clinic waiting room. The two therapists involved in the program (an occupational therapist and a psychologist) had a hidden agenda. Although the intervention was aimed at improving coping with the immediate clinic situation, the hope was that the altered emotional climate in the clinic would have a more general therapeutic impact on family coping.

Before the play program was begun, the atmosphere in the waiting room was tense and depressed. Parents interacted very little with each other or with their children. Little spontaneous play was observed. However, the atmosphere, changed dramatically after the program began. With their children occupied, parents were given the opportunity to "get away" and interact with each other as well as with the therapists. As this happened, they began to express feelings and concerns which they had kept to themselves in the child's presence. The therapists encouraged them to ventilate and to investigate the coping mechanisms of other parents, leading to interaction and involvement in one another's situation. They became attached to other parents' children and in a way "adopted" them psychologically. Subsequently, they underwent some amount of mourning when these children died. Mourning the loss of another's child indirectly contributed to mourning for their own at a level more easily endured (anticipatory mourning). As a result of increased interest and involvement of parents with one another, a parent group was initiated in the outpatient clinic, affording these families the option of more intense exploration of concerns. It is likely that by hearing how others were coping, and by serving as problem solvers and providers of support, the parents were able to increase their own choices and coping options. By actively assisting others in coping with their mourning, a parent might further the work of anticipating the death of his/her own child. Providing support to others was also a concrete way of compensating for feelings of helplessness and inefficiency brought on by facing the fact of terminal illness.

Death of a Family Member

The death of a family member, a sibling, a spouse or one's child, is typically followed by a predictable pattern of grief and mourning. Bereavement is a time of tremendous stress and life change, and may carry with it the possibility of a chronic decrease in global functioning (Defrain and Ernst 1978; Lindemann 1944; Parkes and Brown 1972; Tietz, McSherry and Britt 1977). Defrain and Ernst have reported that unassisted families take about eight months to regain their previous level of organization after the sudden, unexpected death of an infant (sudden infant death syndrome, SIDS). It would be expected that the family's bereavement would be particularly difficult since SIDS makes it impossible for any anticipatory grieving or coping to take place. Parents interviewed by Defrain and Ernst required an average of about 16 months in order to regain their previous level of marital happiness. These figures are probably biased because 60 percent of the parents in the sample had moved away and could not be located at the time that the questionnaires were mailed. However, the fact that so many had moved may in itself be an indicator of severe disruption.

Franciosi and Friedman (1977) have emphasized that the reactions of siblings to SIDS should not be overlooked. These authors' view is that the resulting family turmoil may serve as a precipitant to significant personality and behavioral problems since siblings may be poorly prepared intellectually and emotionally to deal with the situation. This appears to be an area ripe for the application of crisis intervention techniques with family members.

There have been attempts to demonstrate empirically the efficacy of crisis intervention with the recently bereaved (Raphael 1977; Williams, Lee and Polak 1976; Williams and Polak 1979). Raphael conducted crisis intervention with a group of 31 widows within three months after their husbands' deaths, and compared outcomes with a control group which received no contact. Outcome was assessed via a validated general health questionnaire mailed to the widows 13 months after the husband's death. Scores on the questionnaire led to categorizing subjects as having either a positive or negative outcome. The results showed that a significantly greater number of subjects in the treatment group proceeded to a positive outcome than in the control group (21 to 27 as opposed to 12 of 29). The no-contact subjects were characterized as having more symptoms of various sorts: painful joints, general aching, sleeplessness, back pains, rheumatism, shortness of breath, appetite loss, weight loss, increased smoking and alcohol consumption, stopped menstruation, and depression.

Other researchers have obtained more tentative results (Williams, Lee, and Polak 1976; Williams and Polak 1979). These researchers tried to investigate the general hypothesis that preventive crisis intervention following the sudden death of a family member would decrease the risk of subsequent physical, psychological, and social dysfunction. Random selection of treatment and no-contact control groups was arranged through the Denver County coroner's office. Crisis team members accompanied the coroner's representative to to the place of death. If the families agreed to participate, they received from 2 to 6 sessions of therapy over a period of from 1 to 10 weeks (Vollman et al. 1971). Intervention was aimed at increasing the effectiveness of the family in coping with feelings, decisions, and subsequent adjustment related to the death. Outcome measures were collected after a six-month period in areas of medical illness, psychiatric illness, family functioning, crisis coping, and social cost. The overall results did not support the contention that the intervention had the desired impact on post-bereavement adjustment, although six months may be too short a period of time to measure changes in health status, given the significance of the stress which these patients endured. Williams and Polak reported that at six months post-death, the treatment group showed higher concern for work, family, socioeconomic well being, and had greater monthly expenses. The group also tended to be slightly more depressed and expressed more need to seek help.

The authors reported that the service providers felt as though they were "intruders" into the lives of those they were trying to help. There was some concern that they might have actually interfered with the families' normal grieving process and with natural support systems, although this certainly was not anticipated. Perhaps this points out the need for crisis intervention to be naturally associated with one of the systems in which a death occurs, so that contact with relevant family members can be pre-established. If the place of death is a hospital, nurses, social workers, and physicians might be the most appropriate interveners since they are likely to have already established psychological contact with families before their loved one's death occurs. If the patient dies at home, but had outpatient involvement with a clinic prior to death, then perhaps relevant clinic staff would be the most appropriate interveners.

Renal Failure   Just as advances in the treatment of cancer have extended the lives of cancer patients, other medical advances have lengthened the lives of patients suffering from chronic renal failure. However, these patients and their families are placed under severe stress which often precipitates a continuing series of life-threatening crises. The patient's concern with the acute threat of death shifts to a concern with the prolongation of life by artificial means. End-stage renal patients who undergo hemodialysis must endure a number of psychological stresses: (a) conflicts between needs for dependency vs. independence; (b) a relationship with an inanimate object (the dialyzer); (c) ambivalence over life vs. death (is life with the dialyzer worth living); and (d) interpersonal conflicts related to the dialysis unit personnel and the dialysand's spouse (Abram 1970).

Drotar and Ganofsky (1977) and Levenberg, Jenkins, and Wendorf (1978) have presented case reports illustrating the use of crisis intervention with renal patients and their families. Drotar and Ganofsky detail childrens' reactions to dialysis and transplantation including severe anxiety, depression, and isolation of the patient by the family. The authors report a case of a seven-year-old boy who seemed to be reacting well to the prospect of dialysis. He seemed to have a positive attitude and listened intently to the brief explanation given to him of the dialysis procedure and its purpose. However, at the point of actually inserting the needles, the child unexpectedly panicked. It was necessary for someone to be physically present with him during the actual dialysis to offer support, hold his hand, talk to him and shield him from seeing the needles. Gradually, however, he gained mastery over the situation by integrating the experience into his play at home, and by repeatedly offering verbal explanations of the procedure to other patients and to new staff. There may be value in introducing such children beforehand to other children who have successfully mastered the procedure, having new patients watch the experienced child as he/she undergoes dialysis and simultaneously explains what is happening.

In another case (Drotar and Granofsky) involving an adolescent whose family had emotionally withdrawn from her, crisis-oriented therapy had two goals: to help manage her depression by dealing with her anger toward her family, and to help her independently manage diet, medications, and stomach bag care. She was also actively encouraged (against her parents wishes) to return to school even though she had a catheter and stomach bag in place. She reportedly adjusted well to school and gradually began to be treated in a more normal way by her parents.

Levenberg et al. (1978) have presented a number of case studies showing how crisis intervention has been utilized with hemodialysis patients and their significant others. Home dialysis requires considerable cooperation between the patient and his or her partner. Marital problems in the couples' relationship before renal failure occurred often become crystalized and magnified under the demands and stress brought on by home dialysis. Using short-term systems family therapy (Haley 1976; Minuchin 1974) and behavioral techniques, intervention was directed at making the smallest system change necessary for minimally successful dialysis to be carried out. Although dysfunctional marital patterns were often observed, interventions were not directed at alleviating them.

Abortion   Social workers, nurses, and other health care practitioners who conduct problem pregnancy and abortion counseling commonly view their work as crisis intervention (Boekelheide 1978; Gedan 1974; Kaminsky and Sheckter 1979). The maturational crisis of pregnancy and motherhood is compounded by a situational crisis when it is an adolescent who becomes pregnant unexpectedly (Gedan 1974). The pregnancy occurs then in the context of negotiating the adolescent developmental task of striving for emotional and social maturity. Extreme emotional reactions associated with adolescence are often accompanied by unrealistic expectations about bearing children. Gedan helps her clients explore the dimensions of her problem: the girl's own highly charged feelings, fantasies about what her parents will do, attitudes about her behavior, expectations of what it might be like to have an infant, and the choices that she believes are available to her. Gedan also tries to involve the girl's parents directly in order to handle the possible family crisis which might result. She then presents to the girl all the possible solutions open to her (along with accurate information concerning the benefits and drawbacks of each). The girl is then encouraged to take responsibility in making her choice of action and is assisted in carrying out the solution.

Although descriptions of psychological sequelae to elective abortion have been reported (Blumberg 1975; Payne et al. 1976), no research has been conducted assessing the extent to which abortion counseling reduces the risk of negative aftermaths. The one experimental study conducted at an abortion clinic concerned the effects of some components of crisis intervention on the anxiety and attitudes of men who accompanied women seeking abortions (Gordon 1978). Men in the clinic waiting room were invited to participate in a two-hour "rap session" while their partners underwent the abortion. Intervention procedures involved helping them clarify their own feelings, and providing support and empathy. Pre- and post-measures were taken on the Spielberger State-Trait Anxiety Inventory and on certain attitudinal measures as well. Results from the treatment group were compared to those obtained from a no-contact control group. State anxiety (anxiety induced by the situation rather than anxiety stemming from predispositional traits) decreased, and attitudes toward the clinic and toward the abortion were more positive as a result of treatment. Interestingly, however, the group's ratings of their own feelings were more negative after the intervention. As mentioned by the authors, it remains an empirical question as to whether this sort of emotional release increased or improved the clients' coping abilities.

Chronic Disability

As medical care and treatment have advanced, the corresponding proportionate gain in health has not been realized. Recently there has been greater attention turned toward the lasting psychological effects of illness. It is now recognized that many patients are emotionally or psychologically crippled or incapacitated by illness far in excess of the extent of the physical incapacitation of the disease.

This excess disability is well documented for a variety of disorders such as cancer, coronary heart disease, renal disease, multiple sclerosis, and physical disability and is referred to as the chronic disability syndrome. The syndrome appears independently of type of disease and mode of onset (accidental, emergency, or progressive). [See Alger 1978, Byrne and Whyte 1979, Croog and Levin 1977, Garrity 1976, and Miles 1979 for a description of the syndrome and its seriousness in terms of medical treatment.]

Many careful investigations demonstrate that the disability syndrome is psychosocial in nature and that the degree of disability is not related to the degree of physical impairment (Albrecht and Higgins 1977; Fordyce 1976; Lavey and Winkle 1979; Mayou, Foster and Williamson 1978; O'Malley, et al. 1980; Susset, Vobecky, and Black 1979; and Wooley, Blackwell, and Winget 1978). These patients do not respond to traditional medical or dynamically oriented psychotherapeutic treatment. They develop a constricted maladaptive lifestyle which centers around the illness (Fordyce 1976).

Various treatment programs (largely behavioral) have demonstrated that excess disability can be viewed as being learned behavior, and that the reinforcement of wellness and independent behaviors (and extinguishing sick role or dependent behaviors) can reduce the disability or modify specific symptoms which interfere with normal living (Fordyce 1976; Wooley et al. 1978). Such programs have been almost entirely inpatient intensive treatment programs conducted with willing patients who have already established a degree of disability sufficient to prompt such intensive treatment. A serious limitation of such intensive inpatient programs is that the new behaviors may not be retained in the natural, home environment.

If the "well" behaviors are not reinforced in the home environment, patients are likely to relapse back to their "sick" behaviors. It is too early to assess the long-term effects, but the short-term gains indicate that chronic disability behavior is at least amenable to treatment.

To date, no adequate studies have been conducted in the area of prevention of the chronic illness syndrome. McFarlane et al. (1980) and Kupst and Schulman (1980) report that such studies have been started. Kupst and Schulman report beginning a five-year study of the patterns of coping behavior in families in which a child is diagnosed as having leukemia. They hope to identify the factors that predict good coping, and to test the effectiveness of an intervention plan that is intended to promote effective coping.

Long-term studies on the impact of illness have generally made some attempt to determine pre-illness variables on the basis of demographic factors or the use of retrospective questionnaires about life events or styles of coping. Such retrospectively obtained data are always suspect, as the illness itself may alter the perception of previous life. The chronic illness syndrome does not seem to be associated with any particular form of life style (Croog and Levin 1977; Wooley et al. 1978) but research may support the hypothesis that the individual's pre-illness style of coping with stress may be a useful predictor.

Much of the literature available has been based upon time-limited clinical observations, impressions of process and reaction, and/or has placed too much reliance upon retrospective data. Systematic prospective studies of the normal course of adjustment to illness are needed in order to adequately understand the etiology of the chronic illness syndrome and thus lead to the development of more effective means of intervention.

The prevention of chronic illness syndrome is an area of special interest to crisis therapy. In as much as crisis therapy makes extensive theoretical and clinical use of the patient's natural environment (support groups, resources, etc.), and takes into account stage of development, it seems especially suited to the development of intervention within the medical illness context in order to promote better medical care and better psychological health.

Several studies concerning post-illness psychosocial adjustment have been conducted on substantial numbers of patients and indicate several areas where crisis intervention is likely to be particularly effective in altering the long-term psychological disability associated with illness and in obtaining improvements in the patient's physical health as well. Croog and Levin (1977) in a one-year study of over 300 patients who had experienced their first myocardial infarction, found that the psychological and social factors affecting rehabilitation were enormously complex. There was wide individual variation in both good and bad patterns of adjustment.

Some of the major findings concluded that the way in which the family copes with the interruption and alteration of life style is critical to the subsequent psychological and physical status of the patient. How the patient copes with his family's distress (or his perception of such distress) is important. Patients who reported that their families were supportive and helpful fared better physically. A small percentage reported positive improvements in marital life attributable to the crisis surrounding the myocardial infarction episode.

Mayou et al. (1978) conducted a more detailed study for one year with 100 first-time myocardial infarction patients. While Croog relied almost exclusively on retrospective questionnaires, Mayou employed periodic structured interviews conducted prior to release from initial hospitalization, at two months and at one year. The findings generally support those of Croog. Mayou found a small percentage of patients who were able to identify the myocardial infarction as having set the stage for improvements in the marital relationship. There was a high and significant correlation between the patient's physical and psychological adjustment and the psychological adjustment of the spouse. It was also found that a high percentage of patients were not following medical advice about what to do physically and that, overall, approximately 50 percent of the medical advice had become garbled and vague. Better adjustment and better adherence were correlated.

While such data are helpful, it is not known whether the "better adjustment of the spouse" existed prior to the illness or whether it was developed post-illness. What is striking from these studies and others is that the impact upon the families, in terms of psychological distress, is often as great or greater than that upon the individual patient (Byrne and Whyte 1978; 1979; Eiser 1979; and Susman et al. 1980). Further, the manner in which the family copes with the impact of the illness is closely related to the way in which the patient copes and, thus, is also related to the patient's subsequent physical status.

The finding clearly suggests that significant improvements in both the physical and psychological aspects of chronic illness might be obtained by family interventions oriented toward coping with the crisis, a view supported by research from various areas (Alger 1978; Blackburn 1978; Hackett and Cassem 1978; O'Malley et al. 1979; and Stern and Pascale 1979). Wooley et al. (1978) reported the results of a behaviorally oriented, chronic illness treatment program (over 300 patients), in which one particularly effective treatment modality was family therapy. Patient progress in the program was related to family therapy that was instrumental in supporting the behavioral interventions constituting the main focus of treatment. Treatment success at one year after release from the hospital program was related more to the presence or absence of an intact family than to any other variable. Thus the family is a critical support element. Where families are not intact or where they

are unable to provide the critically necessary support, interventions have to be developed that provide substitute support groups or that lead to their development.

The venerable concept of "denial" is currently being employed in crisis theory in a nonunitary fashion (not as an unconscious defense mechanism) with evidence accruing that denial can have a specific adaptive as well as maladaptive function (Horowitz 1976). This view of denial is also consistent with modern formulations of coping theory (Roskies and Lazarus 1980). Denial of some aspects of illness has been shown to be highly adaptive in managing the immediate crisis-produced anxiety (Johnston 1980; Phillip et al. 1979; Tyrer, Lee, and Alexander 1980) and to be predictive of long-term recovery (Beisser 1979; Burchfield 1979; Miles 1979; O'Malley et al. 1979; Soloff and Bartel 1979). It would also follow that maladaptive forms of denial might also apply to the pre-illness period in that such individuals might be prone to follow "health harmful lifestyles" and/or not seek medical treatment at opportune times.

Beisser has discussed the "flight into health" phenomenon as based upon maladaptive denial of illness. Likewise, the "flight into illness" which is germane to our investigation of chronic illness is seen as resulting from the maladaptive denial of health. Intervention efforts need to strengthen the "affirmation of health" as well as the adaptive aspects of "denial of illness."

In Summary   It seems apparent that when serious illness strikes a family it is almost certain that a psychological crisis state will result. The chronic illness syndrome is likely to be one of several outcomes of such a crisis. The individuals who will likely not develop chronic illness syndrome are those who, along with their families, are able to make effective use of denial, turn the focus of their attention toward other issues, provide adequate support, continually develop effective means of coping with various after effects of the illness, and enjoyably engage in the pursuit of life as modified, but not dominated by, illness.

A number of authors have pointed out ways in which both negative medical and psychological outcomes of illness may ensue from focusing too much on the illness, its negative aspects (such as the certain untimely death of a child affected with cancer), or the family's presumed inability to carry on, while giving too little attention to other developmental life issues (Hamera and Shontz 1978; Kling 1980; Miles 1979; Susman et al. 1980). Since the important breakthroughs in the treatment of certain forms of childhood cancer, various writers are turning away from an almost exclusive preoccupation with the child's views of impending death and the family's pre- or post- death bereavement and more toward exploring the area of how to best help the family cope with the distress, how to develop the ability to help the child deal with it, how to ensure that the child receives the best available medical treatment, and how to maximize the child's opportunity for as normal a life as possible (Eiser 1979).

Broad-based comprehensive crisis therapy (see Chapter 8) seems to be ideally suited for preventing maladaptive life-styles. Such crisis therapy could also be applicable in strengthening patients' acceptance of responsibility for treatment and recovery, strengthening their ability to act independently (Wooley et al. 1978), and, through effective use of denial as a coping mechanism, helping to decrease the focus on symptoms or negative aspects of illness develop (or resume) a satisfying style of life.

The notions of independence (to act in spite of the illness) and responsibility were found by Wooley et al. (1978) to be critical ingredients in reducing the disability due to the chronic illness syndrome. Studies on the perceived locus of control lend support to this finding. It has been found that those patients who have an internal locus of control (or can develop one) adjust better to rehabilitation regimens than do patients who have (or develop) an external locus of control (Finlayson and Rourke 1978; Poll and DeNour 1980; Pritchard 1979). It is possible that locus of control is related to coping style with internals adopting denial of the futile or disabling aspects of the illness so that they free up the resources needed for participation in the often painful and arduous rehabilitation program.

CRITIQUE AND LOOK TO THE FUTURE

All of the studies cited in this chapter describe procedures that are congruent with one or more aspects of our comprehensive intervention model. For example, the work of Kuenzi and Fenton (1975) and Williams and Rice (1977) with ICU patients and their families illustrates components of what we call psychological first aid, or first-order intervention. Efforts are directed early on to making psychological contact with patients and families. The patient is continually provided with accurate information, which not only serves to let the patient know that she/he has been heard and listened to, but also provides a basis for altering inaccurate perceptions, and thus increases coping ability. Kuenzi and Fenton explicitly state that they attempt to assess all the other potential hazards impinging upon the family (that is, they explore the dimensions of the problem). After this step, they are in a position to help the family set priorities, pose solutions, and carry out actions to deal with situational difficulties. For example, who in the family will carry out its most pressing functions? Who will stay with the patient, visit later, take care of the children, act as decision maker, etc.?

Similarly, Wise's (1975) report of pre- and post-operative interventions with a young girl illustrates aspects of both psychological first aid and crisis therapy. What Wise terms "anticipatory guidance" and "ego support" can be viewed as second order interventions involving cognitive restructuring, and behavioral adjustment (use of desensitization, and reinforcement techniques which assisted her recovery). Data on the girl's problems included the behavioral, affective, and cognitive dimensions of the BASIC personality framework described in Chapter 8.

Few of the studies reviewed, however, describe interventions that cover all of the psychological first aid components, or all four crisis intervention tasks. As we look to the future of crisis intervention in health care settings, our view is that both research and service delivery can be improved by structuring interventions according to the comprehensive model described in Part II of this volume. Within the model as applied to the work of health professionals, we can make several other suggestions for future research and training.

RESEARCH ISSUES

It is clear from the review of the literature, that most of what has been published concerning crisis intervention by health professionals has been of the case study or program description variety. Clearly, more well controlled research studies are needed to determine the effectiveness of crisis intervention in inpatient and outpatient settings. Research on crisis intervention with surgical patients has been the most sophisticated in terms of methodology (see Auerbach and Kilmann 1977). Certain studies in this area (Andrew 1970; DeLong 1971; Langer, Janis, and Wolfer 1975); can be used as models for future research. There is a need for more carefully controlled studies that employ adequate contact-control groups. Without these groups to compare with those receiving the experimental treatment (crisis intervention), there is no way to determine whether any positive effects observed in the experimental group are due to other factors

such as attention, expectancy, placebo, or to the intervention itself.

All research in this area could profit from clearer definition of process and outcome variables. (See the discussion of this topic in Chapter 18.) The following appear to be some of the more fruitful directions for further investigation:

1. As with surgical preparation, the efficacy of first-order crisis intervention in the intensive care unit (Kuenzi and Fenton 1975) should be empirically investigated. We would hypothesize that ICU patients provided with ongoing emotional support, accurate information, and other aspects of first-order intervention would show speedier recoveries, more positive physiological indices, greater psychological adjustment, and more positive behavioral ratings than patients given the same amount of staff contact but none of the critical components of crisis intervention.

Bunn and Clarke's (1979) study of intervention done with families of critically ill or injured patients is a good first step, but needs to be expanded. Subjects were encouraged to identify their feelings and were given accurate information and opportunities to express their feelings. Future research might include other components of first-order intervention in the treatment regime: helping families formulate possible solutions to their immediate needs, and assisting them in taking concrete action to implement them. In addition, psychological and physical health measures might be administered at various follow-up points, months afterwards, to assess more long-term effects of the treatment.

2. The use of crisis intervention with mothers who have given birth to defective children needs more empirical support to increase its usefulness. Follow-up studies of mothers who have and have not received first-order intervention at the critical time following the birth would be an important step for-

ward. We would expect that mothers and fathers receiving intervention would show improvements in psychological adjustment and physical health months after hospital discharge when compared to appropriate control groups.

3. Oradei and Waite (1974) have described a short-term group for patients recovering from stroke. It would be possible to expand this into a study in which the treatment group's adjustment would be compared with a contact-control and a no-treatment group. We would hypothesize that the treatment group would demonstrate improved recovery, speedier hospital discharges, and higher levels of overall functioning upon follow-up months later.

4. Sanchez-Salazar and Stark (1972), as reported earlier, have described post-discharge interventions with patients who had undergone laryngectomies. Interventions included individual staff follow-up visits with the patient and family, encouragement to participate in the Lost Chord Club, and short-term therapy (if deemed necessary). A follow-up study should be done assessing the recovering and adjustment of these patients as compared with those not receiving some or all of the interventions. In addition, a contact-control group (in which patients would receive none of the post-discharge interventions but an equivalent period of staff contact and interaction) would greatly increase the strength of the experimental design.

5. As we reported earlier, a number of descriptions have appeared concerning the use of crisis intervention with families and couples where one member is terminally ill (Cohen and Wellisch 1978; Hoffman and Futterman 1971; Kopel and Mock 1978). Research needs to assess the effectiveness of these treatments on family coping. The fundamental question is whether crisis intervention with families prior to the anticipated death leads to greater

psychological and physical health than in families receiving the same amount of staff attention but no crisis intervention. The effects of Kopel and Mock's group intervention might be subjected to an experimental design. Patients could be randomly assigned either to a crisis-intervention group, a didactic contact-control group, or to a no-contact control group.

Hoffman and Futterman have described a number of interventions in the patient waiting room of a pediatric tumor clinic aimed at decreasing the stress and anxiety associated with the visits. Their ultimate goal was also to help families cope more adaptively outside the clinic by getting them to engage in anticipatory mourning. If this concept could be better operationalized and defined behaviorally, it might be possible to assess the value of this sort of coping. A longitudinal study (with appropriate control groups) assessing the post-death coping of parents and siblings who have engaged in anticipatory mourning via crisis intervention would be an important step forward.

6. Research on the aftermath of sudden infant death syndrom (SIDS) needs to be extended. No research has been conducted which assesses the effects of first-order and second-order crisis intervention on the later adjustment (for instance, one year post-death) of families, couples, and siblings. This sort of research would be very valuable, especially since SIDS creates a situation in which the family has had no warning of the traumatic event.

The reports by Williams, Lee, and Polak (1976) and Williams and Polak (1979) raise some important issues, not the least of which is to infuse some caution about the effectiveness of crisis intervention in certain situations. We need to closely examine the possible factors that might have contributed to their findings. Could it have been that the way in which the crisis team gained access (via the county coroner's representative) into the family systems affected their ability to intervene effectively? What if the interveners had been health professionals who had gained access to families because of prior contacts with them in the hospital or clinic? Would the interveners still have felt like intruders? We do not know, but clearly more research is needed assessing the ways in which crisis interveners enter family systems.

7. Research needs to be conducted in the area of crisis intervention and abortion. Although psychological sequelae to abortion have been described, and descriptions of crisis-oriented abortion counseling have appeared, no studies were found that linked intervention procedures to a lowered incidence of subsequent psychological and physiological difficulties. Studies assessing the impact of both pre-abortion and post-abortion crisis intervention would be valuable.

TRAINING IN CRISIS INTERVENTION The distinction between psychological first aid and crisis therapy brings with it concrete implications for the training of health professionals in crisis intervention. First, there will continue to be a need for crisis therapists whose formal academic preparation may be in fields such as psychiatry, psychology, nursing, social work, pastoral counseling, or rehabilitation counseling to assist victims of physical illness/injury in working through the crisis experience. As suggested in the literature reviewed in this chapter, crisis therapy by these practitioners (according to the guidelines presented in Chapter 8) has the potential of reducing greatly the number of patients who slowly fall victim to patterns of chronic disability. The primary candidates for this form of crisis therapy will be those patients whose personal and social resources are inadequate for crisis resolution in the natural environment. The availability of broad spectrum crisis therapy would not only

reduce the probability of further disability (and increase the probability of growth in certain areas of BASIC functioning) but also serve to reduce health care costs in a way that we expect will become increasingly apparent to insurance companies.

In addition to the direct availability of crisis therapy through health care settings (both inpatient and outpatient), we believe that all health professionals, by virtue of their immediate and continued contact with patients, need to be skilled in psychological first aid procedures and familiar with how to use the four tasks of crisis resolution as a guideline for the medical treatment and possible referral of patients in crisis, as well as for brief consultation to patients on what the patient can do to work through the crisis on his/her own. To train health professionals for this role, the material in Chapters 6 and 8 can be used in both graduate courses for physicians, nurses, social workers, etc., as well as continuing education workshops and seminars for these professionals and health care support staff (volunteer aids). Our experience in consulting with health professionals suggests that in addition to the principles outlined in these earlier chapters, consideration should be given to the following in order to tailor the general principles to the unique features of health care settings.

Helping in Seemingly Hopeless Situations One of the most difficult aspects of crisis intervention by health professionals is that they are often the bearers of bad news to their patients. Most crisis work brings with it the stresses of dealing with intense client feelings, but the interaction becomes even more difficult when the helper is also the first one to inform the patient about a diagnosis of life-threatening illness or impending death. It is not uncommon for a physician or nurse who has worked to prevent the occurrence or spread of disease to view the terminal illness of a patient as a personal failure. Some practitioners have not thought through their own views (including religious/philosphical beliefs) about death, which makes them reluctant to discuss the matter openly with dying patients and families. Others are simply ignorant of the psychological dynamics associated with physical illness and injury and therefore are ill-equipped to assist patients in working through the crisis components of these physical problems. At the same time, however, many health professionals seem naturally suited to dealing with psychological crises, whether by previous life experience, training in counseling, or learning through feedback from patients about the importance of expressions of human concern and caring during medical treatment.

In order to assist patients in coping with life crises, especially those precipitated by medical illness/injury, it is important for health professionals to explore their own feelings and thoughts (personal reactions) to their patients' crises. Questions such as the following can be asked: "What are my characteristic reactions to patient anger/sadness/anxiety/panic? Do I view the death of one of my patients as a personal failure? How realistic is this view? How am I likely to react (what will I say, do, think) when confronted with the task of telling a patient about terminal illness? If I avoid this responsibility, or run through the motions quickly, why is this the case?"

One avenue to professional preparation in this area is for practitioners to use the four tasks of crisis resolution (Chapter 8) as a framework for dealing with their own feelings, thoughts, and behavior when working with patients in crisis. For example, the intensity of crisis work requires that health care practitioners must attend to their own physical well being, for example, appropriate exercise as an ingredient of stress management (physical survival). They must also find ways to express feelings of frustration, depression, and sometimes despair in the face of intense human pain and suffering (expression of feelings). Health professionals must develop an accurate understanding of their own professional limitations, and learn to make assessments of realistic client goals, as well as develop their own life philosophies/theologies in the context of crisis work (cognitive mastery). Finally, practitioners must implement strategies to improve their own competencies, whether through enrolling in continuing medical education seminars, engaging in reading, or consulting with colleagues (behavioral-interpersonal adjustments).

Each professional must find his/her own specific answers to these challenges. Sharing various strategies can be made a focus of continuing education seminars on crisis management. For example, in one of the author's seminars a nurse noted that in the face of the certain death of one of her patients, she reminded herself (cognitive strategy) that the patient's immediate family members were also potential patients later on, depending upon how they began coping now with the loss of their loved one. This new challenge—how to assist them in beginning the crisis resolution task—served to counterbalance the loss she felt at the impending death of her patient, and led to a richer contact with the entire family.

Psychological First Aid in Health Care Settings

Our view is that the full range of health professionals and support staff in hospitals as well as outpatient clinics should be familiar with the basic principles of psychological first aid, just as they should be able to offer cardiopulmonary resuscitation when necessary. The five components of psychological first aid (Chapter 6) can be taught in graduate courses in medicine, nursing, and the like, as well as continuing education seminars. In addition to the principles outlined in Chapter 6, the following should be emphasized in health care settings.

*Making
Psychological
Contact*

Our experience is that this component of psychological first aid captures a great deal of what both patients and practitioners mean when they talk about a physician's or nurse's bedside manner. One of the chief needs of patients is for those involved in medical treatment to take the time (often a few minutes can do wonders) to listen to the patient's concerns. Active listening wherein the practitioner communicates an understanding of the patient's view of the situation, including fearful feelings, is the primary ingredient in both PFA and a caring bedside manner.

*Examining
Dimensions of
the Problem*

Beyond the areas identified under this component in Chapter 6 (focus on immediate past, precipitating event, how the client views the situation, and impending decisions), particular attention should be given to lethality, especially as this may be affected by prescribed medication. Since crisis patients may call their physicians to obtain medication, the physician is in a unique position to pick up clues to self-destructive ideation and behavior. Attention should be given not only to immediate requests, but also the possibility that a patient has in his/her possession pills from previous prescriptions. Beyond these considerations, the rules for assessment and intervention are the same as those described in Chapter 6.

*Exploring
Possible
Solutions*

One impediment to psychological first aid in medical settings is the idea (believed by both patients and some medical personnel) that it is the role of the patient to describe symptoms, and the exclusive role of the physician to recommend or prescribe treatment. As emphasized earlier, it is important that patients in crisis do as much as they can to help themselves, including actively sharing in a search for solutions to immediate concerns. Our best counsel to health professionals is to view the exploration of possible solutions as a truly joint venture wherein both patient and professional have something to offer. The patient has information about his/her history, and inclinations, and the physician or other member of the health care team has expertise on common crisis reactions, possible medical indications/contraindications, and solutions that have worked for other patients. It is important to draw on both sources of information in generating possible solutions for each patient's immediate concerns.

*Assisting in Taking
Concrete Action*

As with exploring solutions, patients may too quickly cast responsibility for the action component of crisis on the physician or professional. While the psychological first aid guidelines clearly specify that directive action is sometimes necessary, health professionals should remember that in most cases the "best next step" will be taken by the patient him/herself. Every effort should be made to build on the patient's strengths, with the helper taking the least directive intervention possible. As discussed in Chapter 6, the purpose of this is to increase the probability that the patient will emerge from the crisis with a sense of responsibility (and some credit given to him/herself) for having weathered the storm. The cognitive set of the health professional should be toward a negotiation process with the patient around how much the patient can do by him/herself, and which steps the professional should implement (talking to a relative about the patient's condition, initiating hospitalization and the like).

Following Up To
Check Progress
Large case loads often seem to preclude follow-up of crisis patients by medical staff. Our chief suggestion is that practitioners be innovative in ways to structure this important component of psychological first aid into the operation of clinic or hospital. As suggested in the chapter on crisis intervention in emergency rooms (Chapter 14), it is possible for support staff to make follow-up calls to patients during nonpeak hours. Another approach is to elicit commitments from patients to call back to report progress, particularly on completion of referrals. The chief point is that eliciting a commitment (and specifying some straight forward procedure) is the best single way to increase the probability that the patient will follow through on any plan agreed to by both helper and patient.

Using the Four Tasks
of Crisis Resolution
as an Adjunct to
Medical Treatment
Knowledge of the four tasks of crisis resolution—physical survival, expression of feelings, cognitive mastery, and behavioral/interpersonal adjustments—is perhaps the most useful component of the crisis model for medical personnel involved in primary care. The fundamental issue for physicians, nurses, physician's assistants, and others who have regular contact with patients struggling to cope with physical injury, or who bring physical symptoms related to divorce, unemployment, and the like, is: How can I assess patient progress in working through the crisis, and how can I determine whether the crisis has been finally "resolved"? The most direct answers to these questions grow from the crisis therapy framework described in Chapters 8 and 9. Our suggestion is that health care teams assess patient progress according to these four tasks during the resolution process, and that the crisis therapy bottom line—integration of the crisis event into the fabric of life, and openness/readiness to face in the future—be used as a gauge for determining whether or not the patient (and family) should be referred to a psychotherapist. As a courses, as well as continuing medical education seminars, these practitioners can play an instrumental role in guiding and making concrete suggestions to patients on how to negotiate these tasks. Beyond the guidelines outlined in Chapters 8 and 9, the following considerations apply to suggestions made by health care practitioners:

Physical Survival
Health professionals are uniquely trained to counsel patients on this crisis resolution task. Patients who present somatic complaints accompanying a major life crisis may be unusually receptive to ideas about changes in both nutrition and exercise as a means of physical survival. Others will request tranquilizing medicine to deal with anxiety, or other medication to aid in sleeping. The dependence that might result from prolonged use, and the potential side-affects, are the two chief drawbacks to reliance on medication for physical survival during a crisis. We should remember that over time (weeks to months) our concern is that medication not interfere with the other crisis resolution tasks, particularly expression of feelings, and cognitive mastery. While there may be immediate physical relief in medication, every attempt should be made to keep it from interfering with the other aspects of the working through process described in Chapter 8.

Expression of Feelings
Many patients are ignorant—or labor under false assumptions—about their own feelings, first road to intervention, physicians, nurses, and their colleagues involved in primary care can assess the extent to which patients are physically surviving the crisis, expressing feelings, developing appropriate understandings of the event and its meanings for the future, and making behavioral changes appropriate to

the circumstances. Our view is that by training primary care staff through graduate for example, thinking it is "wrong" to feel anger, sadness, etc., or believing that intense feelings such as these are signs of mental illness. The health professional has an opportunity to give permission or to legitimize the expression of feelings by a patient. In so doing, the practitioner makes constructive use of the authoritative power vested in his/her role by the patient in instructing the patient that it is natural to experience intense feelings during a crisis, and that it is appropriate/ helpful/healthy to give vent to these feelings in socially appropriate ways. (See Chapter 8 for further discussion of this task.)

Cognitive Mastery   In addition to the general considerations about cognitive mastery described in Chapter 8, it should be emphasized that the health professional can often draw very accurate inferences about the relative adequacy of the patient's cognitive mastery simply by listening to the way he/she describes current reactions as well as worries/fears about the future. In many cases, the physician or nurse can have a considerable impact on cognitive mastery simply by providing clear and accurate information about the patient's condition and prognosis for the future. In other situations, the practitioner must be alerted to distortions the patient makes about the situation, and particularly its meaning for the future. For example, a patient who had one testicle surgically removed, needed information from his physician about the impact the injury would have on future sexual functioning. In most cases, as the practitioner listens to a patient describe fears about the future, it is possible to distill from the narrative specific beliefs or thoughts on which the future fears are based. The physician can then inquire further about these, correct them if the patient is open to hearing alternative views (especially from a "professional"), or refer to a therapist if further work

is necessary, for example, if the misconceptions or fears about the future are imbedded in more deeply rooted, unfinished personal issues from the past.

In addition to these considerations, it is important for physicians and their colleagues to remember that most physical injuries and illnesses will have some impact on self image, either as a patient makes judgments about him/herself being helpless during an illness, or as the patient feels threats to self-image in the future. With surgical procedures such as mastectomies, physicians can expect that patients will need to re-develop a positive self-image if the crisis is to be resolved.

The practitioner's role can parallel the guidelines for this task in crisis therapy, beginning with assisting the patient in developing a reality based understanding of the crisis situation and implications for the future. In many cases, brief input from the physician or nurse can also help the patient make the adjustments in thinking required by the crisis event, while in other cases the patient may need to be referred to a mental health specialist. To prepare for both situations, health professionals should be familiar with the principles of cognitive mastery described in Chapter 8.

Behavioral/Interpersonal Physicians, nurses, and
Adjustments   other health professionals involved in the direct treatment of illness and injury should be able to identify the adjustments necessary for an individual suffering from a particular physical injury based on their experience with patients and their acquaintance with the crisis literature. As described in Chapter 8, particular attention should be given to changes in work, play, and relationships with people. The practitioner is then in a position to inquire about whether patients are thinking ahead to prepare for adjustments in these areas, or whether they are likely to stumble into them unprepared.

A behavioral adjustment directly related to many injuries and illnesses is what has been referred to as "compliance" with a medical regimen, whether it is the taking of medication, following a particular dietary pattern, or engaging in physical exercise. Beyond finding a new job, or learning to relate differently to people, many patients experiencing crisis associated with physical illness or injury must engage in regular exercise, change eating habits, and/or take medication regularly if they are to survive. Whether people follow doctor's orders in these areas is often a complex issue that has a great deal to do with the doctor-patient relationship, the patient's beliefs/images about getting well, the nature of family and social supports, and the relative adequacy of the behavioral plan adopted. (See Chapter 8 for a summary of behavioral strategies useful in crisis revolution.)

In summary, the literature cited in this chapter provides considerable support for incorporating crisis intervention into health care systems (Bartolucci and Drayer 1973; Conroe, Cassata, and Racer 1978; Dressler 1973; Kales and Kales 1975; Klein 1971; Langsley 1978; Lindenburg 1972; Llinas 1976; Miller 1977; Shields 1975; Smiley and Smiley 1974; Weiskopf and Binder 1976). In order for crisis intervention to become an integral part of health care systems, however, changes will need to be made in the training of various health professionals, including expanding the curricula of many professional training programs. One advantage of the crisis intervention model described in this volume is that the same principles used by mental health professionals to treat patients can also serve as a guide for consultation with professionals involved in primary health care. This shared model and language can result in clearer communication and therefore greater cooperation across the disciplines involved in health care, providing in the long run an increase in both the efficiency and quality of health care.

chapter fourteen

Crisis Intervention in Hospital Emergency Rooms

Sheri I. Leff-Simon
Karl A. Slaikeu
Karen Hansen

An ambulance brings a man who has been shot in a neighborhood dispute to the emergency room of a city hospital. While a medical team attends to his injury, the patient's wife, his child, and three neighbors pace nervously in the waiting room.

An 18-year-old girl who has been raped sits in a state of shock in an examining room waiting for a physician to arrive. She can hardly respond to the police officer's questions about her assailant. It appears, however, that she has no family, and few friends, and is fearful of having to return to her empty apartment alone.

A young father, whose 4-year-old son just died of injuries sustained in an automobile accident, angrily explodes, throwing over a scale, and cursing a nurse, saying "You killed him! Why didn't you do something!"

Going to a hospital's emergency room is not always associated with a traumatic event or a life crisis. Many people routinely visit the emergency room for quick medical treatment, for example, to get an allergy shot, or to receive medication for a common cold. For many other patients, however, a visit to a hospital's emergency room is an event tied closely to a major life crisis.

The illnesses or injuries that bring patients to emergency rooms often strike suddenly and unexpectedly, and are sometimes life and death matters. Psychological crisis associated with serious illness or physical injury is often related to the perceived threat to important life goals and potential loss, resulting in feelings of helplessness and an inability to handle the situation using customary problem-solving mechanisms. The emergency room visit itself comes when the crisis is first felt by the patient and his/her family. Shock, anger, hysteria, and even physical violence are not uncommon symptoms of emergency room patients in crisis. By virtue of their presence at the onset of crisis, emergency room workers have the opportunity to spot potential future adjustment difficulties, and refer patients to mental health facilities.

The capability of emergency rooms to handle the psychological concomitants of physical emergencies varies widely. Traditionally, emergency rooms have been set up to offer medical, life saving treatment, with little attention—in terms of physical space, staff training, and administrative policy—given to the psychological problems of patients and families. In this chapter, we will review the most important literature on this topic and then offer guidelines, based on the crisis model described in this volume, for the inclusion of crisis services in hospital emergency rooms.

LITERATURE REVIEW

From 1960 to 1970, the overall use of emergency rooms doubled, while psychiatric use tripled (Zonana, Henisz, and Levine 1973). This increased use of emergency rooms for psychiatric problems has been attributed in part to the implementation of the Community Mental Health Centers Act (U.S. Congress 1963) which de-institutionalized many patients from state hospitals (Bassuk and Gerson 1979). The emergency room has been a haven for many expatients who have had adjustment problems. The increase in usage is also attributed to a general trust in the conventional medical model, the social stigma of seeking help at mental health centers (hence a preference for "medical treatment"), emergency rooms' 24-hour availability, and insurance reimbursement requirements (Bassuk and Gerson 1979, Watson 1978). Paradoxically, while use of emergency rooms for psychiatric emergencies has been on the increase, many emergency rooms have not been prepared to offer the services expected of them. In order to maintain its "readiness-to-serve" capabilities, many emergency rooms use a triage system that screens those patients with nonurgent conditions and sends them out to other community facilities (Bassuk and Gerson 1979).

In addition to the increased use of emergency rooms for strictly psychiatric emergencies, many emergency patients present combinations of somatic and psychological complaints (McCarroll and Skudder 1960; Palarea 1965). These mixed complaints often lead to improper diagnosis, and ultimately, to improper treatment. With so much research indicating an inverse relationship between healing and stress, it is especially important to attend to *both* the physical and emotional factors of an emergency, which is often a difficult task for staff oriented toward providing medical treatment only (Soreff 1978).

Several researchers have noted that medical residents staffing emergency rooms are often ill-equipped for providing psychiatric care. Residents have been known to dislike emergency room work, responding with anxiety, poor performance, and even phobic avoidance (Amdur and Tuder 1975; Beahan 1970; Blane, Muller and Chafetz 1967; Knesper, Landau, and Looney 1978; Linn 1971; Spitz 1976). Such reactions lead to meaningless diagnoses, under-referral of psychiatric illnesses (Jacobsen and Howell 1978; Spitz 1976; Summers, Rund, and Levin 1979), turning patients away (Satin 1972; Soreff 1978), and even failure to treat physical problems once a psychiatric label has been assigned (Amdur and Tuder 1975).

These failures to provide adequate care have been attributed primarily to two factors: ignorance on the part of emergency room staff, and inappropriate hospital organization (Bassuk and Gerson 1979; Jones, Jones, and Meisner 1978; Knesper, Landau, and Looney 1978; Summers, Rund and Levin 1979). For example, Spitz (1976) evaluated a Cincinnati emergency room and found that the physicians working there were the most inexperienced physicians in the hospital, and that they were rotated out just as they were getting accustomed to the rigors of the emergency room.

Patients were treated by staff who had neither the training nor the experience necessary for meeting patients' nonmedical needs. For training purposes, emergency rooms will always have to utilize rotating staff members, but many authorities advocate changing hospital policies so that a permanent staff is maintained as well. This permanent staff can then accrue the experience necessary to help train the rotating personnel.

Maintaining a permanent staff offers other important advantages such as providing opportunities for developing liaisons with other hospital services and community referral sources (Ianzito, Fine, Sprague, and Pestana 1978; Spitz 1976), and making follow-up on each patient more feasible. Follow-up is necessary for insuring the well-being of each patient as well as for giving emergency staff feedback on the adequacy of their services and referrals (Hoehn-Saric 1977). Hankoff et al. (1974) point to several factors that hinder the development of psychiatric services in emergency rooms:

1. The staff is usually oriented toward dealing with definable medical emergencies;
2. Patients must move through rapidly to make room for others;
3. Emergency services are not geared for following up on patients;
4. Rapid assessment does not allow for histories to be taken;
5. Overuse of the emergency room for nonmedical emergencies has caused overcrowding, which leads to numerous referrals to mental health facilities; and
6. Relatives are viewed as being a time-consuming burden.

A review of the literature on emergency rooms reveals several programs aimed at overcoming these barriers.

Innovative Staffing Patterns

Many innovative "comprehensive" emergency room programs have varied staffing patterns which include both volunteers, students, and paraprofessionals, as well as nurses, social workers, consultants, psychologists, psychiatrists, psychology interns, physicians, residents, and multidisciplinary teams. Though the programs, staff, and the type of service delivery may vary, the intent remains the same: to use available community resources to provide comprehensive care to patients in crisis.

Social Workers

Grumet and Trachtman (1976) describe a program utilizing psychiatric social workers in a Rochester mental health center tied to a general hospital's emergency room. Experienced psychiatric social workers (M.A. and 3 years clinical experience) were the only on-site mental health staff in the emergency room. They assisted physicians with the evaluation and disposition of psychiatric patients when the mental health center was closed. The social workers were backed-up by a psychiatrist and supervised by a social work coordinator and director of psychiatric emergency services. There are some advantages in the use of social workers: they are alert to family and social complexities, familiar with community resources, not intimidating to patients, and they can continue with a client while physicians necessarily get transferred to the next case. Mendel and Rapport (1969) suggest another advantage of using social workers in the emergency room, namely that they tend to hospitalize less because they are less tied to the medical model and more aware of the community resources. Grumet and Trachtman were careful in their recruitment of workers, looking primarily for individuals who were cooperative and flexible, and therefore capable of minimizing conflict with physicians. They report that after a short resistance period, the social workers became valuable staff members and even helped change many physicians' originally unsympathetic attitudes toward drug abusers, alcoholics, suicidal patients, and psychotics.

Groner (1978) describes the delivery of clinical social work services in a Los Angeles emergency room. Social workers deal directly with medical and psychological crises, and can call on a psychiatric consultant when needed. They provide follow-up services and make referrals to agencies. These workers serve as an important liaison to community agencies, and are in a good position to know which community resources are successful in meeting patients' needs. They are also capable of dealing with a wide range of emergencies, such as family members reactions to the death of a loved one; anxiety reactions associated with minor medical disorders; medical home-care arrangements; and, child abuse and neglect.

Nurses Pisarcik et al. (1979) argue that psychiatric nurses best fill the need for psychological services in the emergency room because they are familiar with the hospital setting and are comfortable working in a health care environment. Pisarcik et al. describe the role of nurses who cover a Boston emergency room on a 24-hour basis and have four main functions: assessment, direct patient care, coordination and collaboration, and teaching and consultation.

Whitehead (1978a) also recommends the use of psychiatric nurses in the emergency department. To establish effective psychiatric emergency service in outpatient departments, Whitehead recommends including crisis intervention services that provide help in the home and community through a walk-in clinic in the emergency department. He suggests using psychiatric nurses to provide this round-the-clock service, backed up by an on-call consultant psychiatrist. Whitehead rejects the training of regular emergency room staff in psychiatry because of their lack of interest and frequent staff turn over.

Multi-Disciplinary Teams Several researchers advocate employing permanent "medicopsycho-social" teams in the emergency room (Bartolucci and Drayer 1973; Burgess and Johansen 1976; Frazier and Moynihan 1978; Spitz 1976; Weissberg 1979; Whitehead 1978b). Bartolucci and Drayer suggest that the psychiatric nurse-psychiatrist-social worker combination leads to more prompt and adequate intervention than when only one service specialty is used. A variety of combinations are possible. The principal advantage of the team approach is that it fosters interdisciplinary collaboration (Weissberg), and thus facilitates information exchange among the staff members, improving treatment, referrals, and the co-ordination of diverse services required, as, for example, in rape cases (Frazier and Moynihan).

Outside Consultation Amdur and Tuder (1975) observed that emergency room staff react with anxiety to psychiatric patients because they cannot rapidly categorize or prescribe treatment. Staff members then cope with this anxiety by denying the existence of emotional problems. Therefore, Amdur and Tuder suggest that psychiatric consultants should take on the tasks of staff education and supervision to help staff members recognize and deal with their responses to these anxiety-provoking patients.

Soreff and Elkins (1977) describe a community mental health center's consultation services in a general hospital that uses two psychiatrists and three case aides. Since the service is part of the mental health center, it works closely with the other divisions—inpatient and outpatient care, child psychiatry, psychology, day treatment, and community psychiatry. The divisions meet together weekly to discuss referrals. They are also connected with many additional community resources. For the emergency service, the consultant meets with the family, patient, physicians, nurses, etc., recording background information, complaints, psychological and medical history, and mental status, and then provides a diagnosis and recommendation. The authors describe this program as being integrated into the medical emergency service of the hospital, allowing the hospital to provide comprehensive services to emergency patients.

Paraprofessionals   Several authors have reported on the use of trained student and community volunteers who provide crisis intervention services while under the supervision of psychiatrists, social workers, or clinical psychologists (Getz et al. 1977; Getz, Fujita, and Allen 1975; McCombie et al. 1976; Robinson, Oldham, and Sniderman 1975; Schuker 1978). Getz et al., for example, developed a program which employed two part-time supervisors, and utilized undergraduate and graduate students with academic majors in the human services (social work, nursing, educational psychology, clinical psychology). The students took part in weekly seminars in which cases were presented, readings assigned, and theoretical concepts discussed. The students developed their treatment skills and obtained college credit, while the community received low-cost crisis services.

The program was located in an office adjacent to the emergency room where workers provided 24-hour in-person and telephone counseling for patients as well as the patients' relatives and friends. The service delivery process included the following steps:

1. The patient was screened and referred by the attending physician.
2. The counselor interviewed the patient.
3. The counselor consulted with the supervisor to discuss the case and outline a treatment plan.
4. The plan was discussed with the physician.

5. The plan of action was presented to the patient, and an agreement for the follow-up interview was made.

In an evaluation of the program, Getz et al. found that the emergency room patients rated their friends, relatives, and spouses as being the most helpful during the crisis, and the counselors as being the next most helpful. Apparently, these paraprofessional counselors were successful in their efforts to mobilize the patients' own resources.

The authors cite many advantages of this program over traditional emergency room programs, primarily that the physician has the opportunity to screen and refer incoming patients, which then frees the physician for other emergencies.

Special Services   A theme common throughout the literature on rape is

Rape   that early crisis intervention is critical to the future well-being of the victim. (Burgess and Holmstrom 1973; Frazier and Moynihan 1978; Lefort 1977; McCombie et al. 1976; Schuker 1978). The American College of Obstetrics and Gynecology has acknowledged the need for emergency care for all rape victims and has published guidelines for this care (ACOG, 1970).

Development of special services for rape victims is not easy. There is much community and hospital resistance to recognizing rape as a legitimate health issue in need of medical and psychological services (McCombie et al.). The multidisciplinary makeup of the hospital staff, however, makes the emergency room a good place for comprehensive physical and emotional care (Adelman 1976; Frazier and Moynihan 1978; McCombie et al. 1976). Abarbanel (1976) developed a model rape treatment program in a Santa Monica Mental Health Center that offers medical treatment and sensitivity education for the medical staff, follow-up medical care, supportive services for victim, family, and friends, 4–6 months of continued support from a social worker, information on legal rights and options, and interagency coordination.

Similarly, Burgess and Holmstrom set up a 24-hour crisis intervention service for rape victims in a Boston city hospital emergency room. In addition to providing medical treatment and counseling to rape victims, family and friends received counseling services as needed, with follow-up calls made during the first two days following the rape, and then weekly, as needed.

Drug Abuse   Though they frequently turn up in emergency rooms, drug abusers are often neglected in terms of emotional support and appropriate referral (Bozzetti and Kane 1978; Kinsella and Africano 1977; Yowell and Brose 1977). In addition, drug abusers are susceptible to physical abuse: for example, in an eight-month study of 250 emergency room drug-related cases, Duncan (1977) recorded staff reactions ranging from verbal abuse to punitive stomach pumping. These negative reactions were traced to:

1. Overworked staff who resent dealing with people who self-inflict injury.
2. A conviction that drug abusers are hopeless.
3. A conviction that drug abusers are difficult, uncooperative, and ungrateful.

Duncan advocates re-educating emergency room staff members to sensitize them to the special needs of drug abusers, and to teach them how to attend to those needs.

Patients' Families   Several authors have reported on the development of services to benefit the indirect users of emergency rooms (Hankoff et al. 1974; Sherman 1977) since these indirect users (family and friends) are best able to offer future aid to the patient, and early intervention might prevent future maladaptive family functioning. Bloom and Lynch (1979) describe a program in which social work students meet with families in an emergency waiting room to provide emotional support, information on access to services, screening and referral. Hankoff et al. describe another program in which nurses administered crisis counseling to families, resulting in an increase in referral completion rate for patients. Bunn and Clarke (1979) found that brief supportive counseling with relatives reduced otherwise high levels of anxiety. They emphasize the importance of managing relatives' anxiety in order to enhance future recovery of the patient.

Follow-Through   Though a referral system may be set up in *Referral Completion*   an emergency room, clients frequently fail to follow through with their referrals. Several studies have linked patient characteristics such as age, sex, social class, ethnic background, and diagnosis with the rate of referral completion. (See Bassuk and Gerson 1979, for a review.) For example, lower completion rates have frequently been associated with patients who are younger than 40-years-old, male, from lower socioeconomic groups, black, or diagnosed as psychotic, while higher completion rates have been associated with people over 40-years-old, female, from working classes, or diagnosed as being neurotically depressed.

Nevertheless, some researchers suggest that the referral techniques employed may have more effect than patients' predispositions (Chafetz 1968; Rogawski and Edmundson 1971). Rather than dismissing referral noncompliance as a function of patients' deficiencies, noncompliance can be viewed as a reflection of deficiencies in the treatment program. When the counselor, acting as liaison, contacts the referring agency, or provides for transportation, referral completion rates increase dramatically over mere recommendations that the patient go to the agency (Bozzetti and Kane 1978; Craig, Huffine, and Brooks 1974; Jellinek 1978; Rogawski and Edmundson 1971; Ungerleider 1960). Spitz (1976) found that referral attempts are useless without cooperative contact between agencies. Completion rates also increase when there are no waiting lists and when the facility is immediately accessible and familiar to the patient (Bassuk and Gerson 1979; Craig et al. 1974). To increase referral effectiveness, Soreff (1978) recommends that the emergency room liaison be an integral part of the community mental health treatment network.

Bassuk and Gerson note that many emergency room patients are seeking immediate relief through human contact rather than referral for long-term treatment. Lazare et al. (1972, 1976) suggest, therefore, that it is important to understand what the patient wants, and to negotiate a suitable treatment plan. Jellinek found that high rates of referral completions corresponded with the counselor understanding the individual patient's goals and negotiating the treatment plan, while noncompleters characteristically were more vague in defining their goals and complaints. Jellinek concludes that, for increased referral success, physicians must go beyond diagnosis in order to clarify patients' problems, identify individual needs, communicate these perceived needs to the patient, and work with the patient in developing a treatment plan.

Repeaters

Groups of patients who repeatedly return to the emergency room have been identified. Wilder, Plutchik, and Conte (1977) report that these people view the emergency ward as their "primary physician." Bauer and Balter (1971) found that repeaters have a distinct symptom profile, which includes high levels of depression, anorexia, suicidal thinking, and psychomotor retardation. They are predomi-

nantly females who are separated, divorced, or widowed, and are often labeled borderline personality with long-standing chronic problems (Bassuk and Gerson). Bassuk and Gerson suggest that these repeaters do not benefit from traditional evaluation and referral, and call for increased attention to these patients' special needs.

Feedback

Traditional emergency room systems have not included feedback components and, consequently, emergency room workers have not been able to judge their own effectiveness. Some authors suggest that follow-up services can improve patient care by providing staff members with feedback, which allows them to monitor the progress and care of each patient. Burgess and Johansen (1976) suggest that follow-up responsibilities help make counselors more accountable for the care they provide. In addition, Spitz (1976) suggests that a change in emphasis from mere disposition to the establishment of goals for patients and families will help increase staff morale, which in turn should benefit the patients.

SERVICE DELIVERY GUIDELINES

The literature reviewed indicates that it is clearly possible to offer crisis services as a part of the ongoing work of an emergency room, though concrete guidelines on the most important considerations in designing these delivery systems are missing. The following suggestions grow directly from crisis theory and the intervention model presented in this volume:

1. Since physical illness and injury are often precipitants of psychological crisis (Chapter 4), emergency rooms should be equipped to offer crisis intervention services to patients as well as to their close family members or friends.

2. Since emergency room visits occur so soon after the precipitating events themselves,

psychological first aid, as opposed to crisis therapy, is the treatment of choice.

3. Three chief systems components—administrative policy, personnel training, and physical space—should be designed so that the objectives of psychological first aid can be met (providing support, reducing lethality, and linking to helping resources).

Administrative Policy   Each hospital must decide which personnel will be engaged in offering aspects of psychological first aid. The literature on emergency rooms suggests that the use of multidisciplinary teams, with social workers and other nonmedical staff as members, available for twenty-minute to several hour-long conversations with persons in crisis, is the most cost-effective approach since it frees medical staff, (residents, nurses, etc.) to treat medical problems. At the same time, since the disorganization in behavior, thinking, and affect during crisis will likely be expressed to almost anyone working in the emergency room, all staff should be trained in offering psychological first aid. For example, while a resident or nurse might not devote the same amount of time in talking with a patient in crisis that a psychiatric social worker or chaplain might, still he/she should know techniques for making psychological contact to defuse intense emotions and should be able to recognize clues to suicidal or homicidal behavior. (See Chapter 6.) A comprehensive administrative policy will also designate a portion of emergency room staff time for conducting follow-up interviews to check on whether referrals have been completed and also to inquire about crisis resolution. Administrative policy might involve, for example, allocation of a social worker's time to include both "front line" as well as follow-up services and liaison work with other agencies. Since emergency room work is very demanding, Spitz recommends work shifts of 5 to 6 hours duration with about 25 hours of front-line duty a week,

and the rest of the time being spent in follow-up, checks on admitted patients, educational activities, and visits to community centers. However staff time is allocated, the various intervention roles must receive administrative legitimacy by being written into in the job descriptions of emergency room staff.

Staff Training   Many emergency room workers will have received crisis intervention training as a part of their graduate school education (social work, psychiatric nursing), though others will need in-service training to learn effective crisis skills. Brief programs, taking anywhere from a few hours to a full day, can be developed by drawing on the material in Part I of this volume and the psychological first aid model in Chapters 6 and 7. It would be possible also to videotape an entire training sequence for the orientation of all new employees. Everyone on the staff, from receptionists to physicians should be familiar with how physical illness or injury can precipitate life crisis of the kind described in Chapter 2. They should understand the often erratic, threatening, and even dangerous behavior that can be a part of the crisis experience. All employees should also be trained to recognize signs of lethality, and to use psychological first aid techniques in providing support, reducing lethality, and setting up linkages for further help. Training programs should focus also on identifying which parts of the psychological first aid model are most important for each group of employees. For example, receptionists would not be expected to take steps to completely assess and reduce lethality, but they can be expected to make threatening information known to nurses and other staff. They should also be trained to use the "contact" part of the psychological first aid model (judicious use of empathy statements) to allow patients to talk, as a means of defusing emotions at any point during the emergency room visit.

Physical Space

The third systems variable that must be manipulated to allow for the provision of crisis services is physical space, including waiting, examining, and interviewing rooms. Waiting rooms should be comfortably furnished and large enough to accommodate family and friends accompanying the patient. Private interviewing rooms should be available so that social workers, chaplains, psychiatric nurses, and others can talk with patients and family members away from the gaze of other patients and staff.

Coordination With Other Service Delivery Systems

In planning crisis services for hospital emergency rooms, other resources in the hospital and the community should be identified so that the emergency system can make best use of these other services, and so that these other resources can, in turn, utilize emergency room services. In the hospital itself, referral to psychiatry, chaplain's office, a stress clinic, bereavement counseling, etc., should be as straight forward a matter as a referral to x-ray, cardiology, or pathology. Similarly, the emergency room should maintain regular contact with community services outside the hospital such as crisis hotlines, ministers, police, mental health centers, social service, and the like. These contacts are a necessary ingredient for both linkage to other resources, and follow up —two of the three objectives of psychological first aid.

Evaluation

Evaluation strategies for crisis services in emergency rooms follow directly from the design considerations just mentioned. First, the readiness of an emergency room to deliver crisis services is determined by assessing whether or not the policy, personnel, and physical plant systems are in place to allow staff to administer psychological first aid to patients and families. This is the first avenue of program evaluation for crisis services in emergency rooms. The next level is to measure outcome by determining the extent to which the three objectives of psychological first aid are being achieved with particular sample(s) of patients and families visiting the emergency room. Following the research framework offered in Chapter 18, data can be collected at the end of the psychological first aid contact (just before the patient leaves) and then later, during telephone follow up, when staff members check on whether referrals have been completed and whether the patient and family are successfully coping with the crisis. The crisis therapy framework (Chapters 8 and 9) can provide a guide for assessing patient progress—assessing the extent to which the patient is regaining equilibrium, integrating the crisis event into the fabric of life, and appearing ready to go on with the business of living. By making telephone follow-up a part of an emergency room's ongoing operation, meaningful evaluation can be conducted at relatively low cost. Telephone follow-up serves both to assist the individual patient (referring to further help when needed), and to allow for a broader program evaluation of emergency room services. Direct front-line contact with patients in crisis is exhausting work for social service personnel assigned to emergency rooms. By using a portion of staff time for telephone follow up, the hospital offers a break in the routine for staff, and also makes program evaluation possible.

The literature cited attests to the fact that crisis service can be integrated into the ongoing operation of an emergency room. However, constraints of time, staff resources, and physical space mean that great care must be given in determining which services should be offered and by whom. Our hope is that the guidelines offered in this chapter will assist planners, administrators, and trainers in deciding on the best allocation of resources for individual hospitals.

chapter fifteen

Crisis Intervention by Telephone[1]

Karl A. Slaikeu
Sheri I. Leff-Simon

Levine and Levine (1970) have documented the idea that helping services are influenced, if not shaped, by the social and economic conditions of the times. This has been no less true of the "hotline" or telephone counseling movement than of other social services. Modern telephone crisis intervention, which began in the late 1950s, became the backbone of the suicide prevention movement, and grew rapidly in the context of social activism in the 1960s. Although it was not the first twenty-four hour telephone counseling service (New York City's National Save-A-Life League established one in 1906), the Los Angeles Suicide Prevention Center is credited with first developing techniques on how to use the telephone to perform life-saving interventions (McGee 1974).

The Los Angeles Center's use of volunteer personnel, around the clock (every day) coverage, and training institutes on how best to counsel distressed callers over the telephone laid the groundwork for the rapid development of centers across the country. While many of the smaller centers that were developed in the heyday of telephone counseling folded after a few years, most survived, and a steady rise

in this total number of centers was seen through 1980. A national survey of suicide prevention and crisis services in the United States and Canada found over 500 known centers, compared with less than 50 in 1965 (Haywood and Leuthe 1980).[2]

Beyond the increase in the number of centers, the seventies saw the development of new programs (Motto 1979) as well as a rapid expansion in the telephone counseling literature (Auerbach and Kilmann 1977). The net result has been to underline the important role telephone counseling can play in comprehensive crisis service delivery systems. In this chapter, we will first discuss the unique

[1] The authors wish to express their appreciation to Dr. Charles Haywood, Director of Crisis Intervention Institute, Buffalo, New York, for providing information concerning Crisis Services, Inc., and for his helpful comments on an earlier draft of this paper.

Portions of this chapter are taken from Slaikeu, K.A. "Crisis intervention by telephone." In L. Cohen, W. Claiborn, and G. Specter (Eds.) *Crisis Intervention: Second Edition.* New York: Human Sciences Press, 1983.

[2] This figure does not include the large number of college-based counseling services, youth oriented hotlines, and religious counseling hotlines.

features of telephone counseling, then look at how to use the psychological first aid model over the telephone, followed by an examination of research issues and future trends.

THE UNIQUENESS OF TELEPHONE COUNSELING

The most distinguishing feature of telephone counseling is that the help offered to a person in crisis takes place without the benefit of nonverbal cues such as facial gestures and body language, and relies exclusively on the words spoken between helper and caller (content) and how they are spoken (noncontent) (Blumenthal, Tulkin and Slaikeu 1976; Slaikeu 1979).

Lester (1977) summarizes the most important characteristics of telephone counseling, citing the increased client control associated with telephone contact. In face-to-face counseling, a client generally takes a place in the waiting room, perhaps fills out forms or psychological tests given by a receptionist, is ushered into a therapist's office, sits down, and begins talking, all at the guidance or instruction of another person. The length of the contact is usually set, with termination being initiated by the therapist. In telephone counseling, this power differential is equalized, giving more to the client. The client not only begins the therapeutic or helping interaction whenever he/she wants to, but is also free to terminate it at any time.

A second feature of telephone counseling is that it preserves client anonymity. The possibility of shielding identity is believed to facilitate greater self-revelation and openness on the part of many callers.

Third, counselors are also anonymous, a fact that facilitates positive transference. Visual cues being absent, there is greater opportunity for the counselor to live up to the caller's fantasy of what the ideal counselor would be than in a face-to-face situation.

Fourth, telephone counseling reduces the dependency of a caller on an individual counselor, and transfers it to the clinic or counseling service. Most callers are asked only for a first name, and dependency on a particular counselor is discouraged.

Fifth, telephone counseling is unique in its accessibility. Most people have a telephone (or ready access to one) and the cost for its use is low. Accessibility is critical for crisis clients, especially those who are suicidal or homicidal, and for those unable to leave their homes (elderly or physically disabled).

Finally, telephone counseling is available at any time, day or night. Most services are open twenty-four hours a day, year round, which means that assistance is available with the bare minimum of waiting time. (See Miller 1973 for other properties of telephones pertinent to their use in counseling.)

The chief characteristics of hotlines as service delivery systems have been described by several writers (Bleach and Claiborn 1974; Delworth, Rudow and Taub 1972; Haywood and Leuthe 1980; McCord and Packwood 1973; McGee 1974; Motto 1979). While the minimum requirement for a telephone counseling service to function is one telephone line, most have several lines, often advertised under different names through newspaper personal columns and the telephone directory. Two of the best descriptions on how to set up a hotline (Delworth et al. 1972 and McGee 1974) suggest that there should also be a separate business line that is not listed as an emergency line, but used primarily to call volunteers, other agencies, rescue units, and so on. Other aspects of typical ongoing telephone counseling operations include:

1. Primary use of nonprofessional, volunteer counseling staff to work on the phones (McGee 1974; Rosenbaum and Calhoun 1977).
2. Taping of calls to assist in supervision and research.
3. Accurate record keeping to allow for

agency accountability (number and type of calls during each month) to facilitate planning during peak times, and as an aid to improving services for repeat callers (McGee 1974).

4. Cultivating networks with other community agencies to facilitate referral of callers (Hoff 1978; McGee 1974).

5. Follow up of callers several days after the call to the center. It was found that over half of the centers responding to an international survey engaged in follow up of callers (Motto 1979).

The two most striking changes in the operation of telephone counseling centers through the 1960s and the 1970s were the shift "away from the earlier passive role of waiting for the person in crisis to call, toward a more active case-finding approach with greater visibility and the availability of programs" (Motto 1979, p. 182), and the use of the telephone counseling operation as a central link giving citizens access to all human services in a community (Haywood and Leuthe 1980).

From a survey of 70 suicide prevention centers around the world, Motto describes innovations in both the target populations served and in procedures used.[3] Based on an analysis of calls received, centers have designed specific intervention programs for the elderly, for victims of crime (rape, mugging, sexual abuse, battering), and have developed programs geared toward crisis in such diverse settings as schools, jails, and pop and folk musical festivals. The main procedural changes in telephone counseling operations have dealt with community education, the development of specialized training programs for other community workers, such as police and jail personnel, and the use of outreach and home visits as an adjunct to telephone counseling. Many of these programs follow McGee's (1974) description of outreach as a logical compliment to a telephone operation.

ONE TOWN'S HOTLINE: BUFFALO (N.Y.) If you need help for a personal or family problem, call *Crisis Services* any time of day or night, seven days a week. The number is 834-3131.

Crisis Services provides confidential problem-solving by phone; information about 500 helping agencies; direct counseling for personal distress and family discord; assistance for victims of rape and sexual assault, and access to comprehensive mental health and mental retardation services. Workers are on duty 24 hours a day to respond to suicidal calls, crisis situations and mental health emergencies.

This advertisement which appears frequently in the *Buffalo Evening News* sums up quite succinctly the chief features of *Crisis Services, Inc.*, a comprehensive system that includes a telephone counseling operation, outreach, and concrete linkage to a complete range of other community resources for the benefit of callers. Originally named the *Suicide Prevention and Crisis Service (SPCS)* in 1968, the organization was established to meet a need for 24-hour crisis counseling and also to facilitate closer coordination of public and volunteer services in the Buffalo and Erie County area. In the late sixties, SPCS had four telephone lines (advertised separately in the phone book and "personal" columns of the newspaper): *Suicide Prevention, Drug Hotline, Problem of Living Line,* and *Teen Hotline,* staffed by 80 volunteer telephone counselors. The volunteers were trained by a professional staff made up of clinical psychologists, social workers, and psychiatric nurses proficient in telephone crisis intervention. An emergency outreach service (crisis intervention in homes, bus depots, and the like) was added in 1973, the year in which SPCS was changed in both name and function. As *Crisis Services, Inc.*,

---

[3] See Motto 1979, p. 175 for a listing of programs and the centers at which they are offered.

the center shifted away from a suicide and crisis focus to a life stress and crisis counseling approach (Haywood 1977). In addition, the center became a central interchange between citizens and 500 organized human service agencies in the Buffalo area. The life stress and crisis counseling operation is staffed by 150 nonpaid phone counselors who receive training and supervision from a paid professional staff. Through its telephone function, *Crisis Services* provides the only constant and reliable link between the full range of human service agencies in the Buffalo area. (In the blizzard of 1977, *Crisis Services* was the only service that could remain open to help citizens suffering from the psychological stress accompanying this natural disaster.)

Crisis Services has a number of other key characteristics:

(a)   The problem-solving help given to crisis callers is viewed as taking place in the context of a "stress modulation and health maintenance" framework (Haywood 1977). The model emphasizes a holistic approach to human functioning, based on clearly articulated human values (diminishing social alienation and sharing responsibility for problem solving in the community), aimed at building life skills for stress reduction and coping.

(b)   *Crisis Services* views its work with callers as both prevention of psychopathology and enhancement of the quality of life by facilitating growth through resolution of life crisis.

(c)   Innovative services (a Night People Program for alcoholics, a Care Ring Program for shut-ins, Hospice Services for the terminally ill, and others) are "spun off" as soon as they are ready to stand on their own. Many of these programs grew from assessment of citizens' needs through the center's telephone operation. This approach fits with other "clinical-community" strategies where preventive community programs are developed as a direct result of information gleaned from clinical work (Slaikeu 1977).

(d)   Volunteers are still the mainstay of the service, although they are now more appropriately called "nonpaid staff."

(e)   Every attempt has been made to increase the accessibility of services. For example, anyone walking on the street in the Buffalo area can pick up a telephone from a police box and be put into direct contact with *Crisis Services*.

(f)   Calls are routinely tape recorded for supervision and research purposes.

(g)   Callers are routinely called back in approximatley two weeks to check on problem resolution and appropriateness of referral (if any).

PSYCHOLOGICAL FIRST AID BY TELEPHONE

The psychological first aid model presented in Chapter 6 is a generic model for use across a number of community settings, and can be readily adapted for telephone counseling. It was originally designed to capture the most important ingredients of other telephone counseling training models (Fowler and McGee 1973, Knickerbocker and McGee 1973; Walfish et al. 1976) though in a consolidated form. Those interested in applying the five components of psychological first aid to telephone counseling should first familiarize themselves with the description of each of the five components in Chapter 6, and the case material in Chapter 8. When using the model for telephone counseling, the following considerations should be kept in mind:

Making Psychological Contact

It is important to remember that in telephone counseling the main vehicle for achieving contact with a client is the counselor's voice, which includes not only what the counselor says, but how he/she says it. To achieve the objectives of this first component of psychological first aid, namely, for the crisis client to feel understood, accepted, or for an air of calm to begin to replace the turmoil and confusion of the crisis state, the counselor's tone of voice needs to be calming and reassuring. Telephone counseling trainees should listen to tape recordings of their own voices, and also receive feedback from other trainees on the impact of voice tone, speed, and the like when talking to a crisis caller. Instead of becoming caught up in a caller's panic (often reflected in high pitch and rapid rate of speech), trainees must learn to counter with attentive, calm, and controlled speech.

In addition, attention should be given to the different role played by silence in telephone counseling as opposed to face-to-face discussions (Blumenthal et al. 1976; Slaikeu 1977). Without nonverbal cues such as facial gestures and bodily movement in a chair, for example, silence over the telephone is much more ambiguous for both counselor and caller. Does a silence mean that the caller is thinking productively about what has been said or, that he/she does not know what to say, or how to say it? Callers reluctant to talk might be helped by a worker's brief, reflective, empathic utterances that demonstrate caring and a desire to understand the situation. For example:

> "It must be hard to put some of your feelings in words."
> "I can imagine how upsetting that must be to you."
> "Take your time, and talk when you are ready."

Beyond these considerations, the strategies for making contact over the telephone follow the procedures outlined in Chapter 6: listen closely for events and feelings, and make use of reflective, empathic statements to let the caller know that the counselor hears, understands, and accepts what the caller is saying.

Examining Dimensions of the Problem

Since most telephone counseling contacts involve callers who are not previously known to counselors, there is usually little background information to facilitate understanding of the caller's problem. This means that the helper must rely on the caller's narrative description of the problem, coding each part according to the categories described in Chapter 6 (immediate past, present state of crisis callers' BASIC functioning, lethality, strengths and weaknesses, resources, impending decisions, and so on). A useful tactic is to ask open-ended questions such as: "*What* has been happening recently to make things so difficult for you right now?" or, "Tell me more about what has been troubling you recently." These and other *who, what, where, why, when* and *how* questions can be asked in a nonthreatening manner and have the potential for eliciting information on the dimensions of the caller's problem.

One of the advantages of telephone counseling is that since counselors are not seen by the callers, they can make written notes as the conversation proceeds. Coding sheets based on the topics covered in Table 6.1 (especially *Dimensions of the Problem*) can be used, as a guide to the counselor on important areas to be covered.

Exploring Possible Solutions

The very fact that an individual calls a hotline or a telephone counseling service gives some clue about difficulties in arriving at solutions to the crisis. Callers have often exhausted their personal and social resources (Caplan 1964; Speer 1976), or somehow believe that those available to them (family, friends, coworkers) do not understand or for some other reason should not be involved in the problem at that time. A telephone contact, then, provides an excellent opportunity for the counselor to ask about the various avenues that the caller has tried, to explore the obstacles that were met (including, quite often, the caller's own cognition that "he wouldn't understand," or "I could never say that to her"). Many times the telephone counselor's tactic is to get the caller to reconsider a solution that has been tried only feebly or rejected too soon. The objective is to generate as many potential directions as possible in order to act on the *immediate* needs identified earlier.

Assisting in Taking Concrete Action
The distinction between facilitative and directive interventions is especially important in telephone counseling, since it gives guidelines for whether or not the telephone counselor will involve other parties (family, friends, other agencies) in the caller's crisis. If lethality is low, and if the caller presents him/herself as one capable of taking the agreed upon next steps in re-establishing coping, then the counselor devotes energy toward helping the caller take action. Should directive involvement be required (high lethality, or caller incapable of acting on his/her own behalf), then the telephone counselor's access to other community resources is critical. The directive action might range from the counselor's calling a family member, to having an outreach team visit the caller in a home, or sending a rescue unit to a home in the aftermath of a suicide attempt.

Follow Up
In the early days of telephone counseling, it was assumed that the anonymity which people sought by calling these services would preclude follow up. This turned out not to be the case, however, Slaikeu, Lester, and Tulkin (1973) and Slaikeu, Tulkin, and Speer (1975) found that telephone volunteers could elicit from the caller at least a first name and

telephone number to allow for subsequent call back. The most important considerations are for workers (a) to explain to callers the reasons for follow up, and (b) to take steps to protect the confidentiality of the telephone contacts. Statements such as the following can be made: "I/we care about you, and want to know how things work out. Could I call you back tomorrow evening (or some other time, after an agreed upon action step would have been completed), or could you call me here at the center, to let me know how things work out?"

In most cases, nothing more than a first name and a telephone number is needed for follow up. Confidentiality can be protected if the caller gives either a time to call (when other family members, roommate are away), or if the caller agrees to call the center at a particular time.

Procedures such as these need to be an integral part of agency policy. Follow up serves ultimately to benefit the caller and can also be a boost to the morale and motivation of telephone workers in the form of feedback on how their help has been received.

RESEARCH ON TELEPHONE COUNSELING
Over the past two decades, researchers have turned their attention to several important aspects of telephone counseling: characteristics of volunteer telephone workers (Pretzel 1970; Resnick 1968); selection criteria for telephone workers (Evans 1977; Gray, Nida, and Coonfield 1976; Jamison and Johnson 1975; Otten and Kahn 1975; Schoenfeld et al. 1976; Tapp and Spanier 1973); the relationship between training and worker performance (Carkhuff 1969; Evans, Uhlemann, and Hearn 1978; Genthner 1974; Hart and King 1979; Lister 1976; Schinke et al. 1979; Walfish 1981); training models for telephone workers (Dixon and Burns 1974; D'Augelli et al. 1978; Fowler and McGee 1973; Knicker-

bocker and McGee 1973; Lister 1976; McCarthy and Berman 1971; Walfish et al. 1976); characteristics of callers (Greer and Weinstein 1979; Lester 1970; Morgan and King 1977); problem contents of calls (Preston, Schoenfeld, and Adams 1975); and the outcome of telephone counseling contacts (France 1975; Slaikeu et al. 1973, 1975; Slaikeu and Willis 1978; Walfish et al. 1976).

The consensus of major reviews of this literature is that far too few studies have investigated the relationship between the *process* of over-the-phone counseling (what happens during the telephone call) and *caller outcome* (what happens to the caller later) (Auerbach and Kilmann 1977; Rosenbaum and Calhoun 1977; Slaikeu et al. 1975). In their detailed analysis of crisis intervention outcome studies, Auerbach and Kilmann noted that many of the outcome studies had reported only on the outcome of training programs, answering the question of whether workers performed on the phones as they had been trained to do. Few studies had collected data on the outcome for the caller in the days, weeks, and months following the call, and even fewer had attempted to establish a link between process variables (in call) and outcome variables (after the call).

This means that we still know very little about the impact that telephone counseling has on how callers resolve their crises. This gap can be filled because telephone follow up of callers has been found to be possible (Murphy et al. 1969; Slaikeu et al. 1973). By training workers to ask for a first name, a phone number, and a convenient time to call back, follow up data can be collected to find out how the crisis that led to the initial call is being managed in subsequent days and weeks.

While data for both process and outcome are available (analyses of taped calls and call back of callers), there is still a need for greater precision on what process variables to investigate and what outcome questions to ask. One of the most frequently used process coding systems, *Clinical Effectiveness*, (Knickerbocker and McGee 1973) continues to present problems in terms of inter-rater reliabilities, and *Technical Effectiveness* (Fowler and McGee 1973) and the *Walfish Crisis Contract Scale* (Walfish et al. 1976), though quite high in reported inter-rater reliability coefficients, still capture only a part of what crisis workers are supposed to be offering callers during a crisis call. (See Auerbach and Kilmann 1977 and Slaikeu et al. 1975, for a more detailed critique of the first two systems.) The five-component model presented in this volume— Psychological First Aid—has the potential for telephone counseling process research since it covers the main worker behaviors described in training manuals, and is specific enough to yield high inter-rater reliability.

Outcome categories for telephone counseling research need to be similarly refined. As outlined in Chapter 18, crisis is assumed to involve a breakdown in coping mechanisms (Caplan 1964); therefore, follow up should check on whether there has been any improvement in the caller's ability to cope with the crisis after the phone contact. According to R. Lazarus's (1980) theoretical framework, this means that follow up should access (a) the caller's ability to manage the *subjective* aspects or feelings associated with the crisis, and (b) the caller's ability to take steps toward solving the immediate problem(s). Studies that have investigated the referral process (France 1975; Slaikeu et al. 1973, 1975) are examples of how to use follow up to see if the action steps agreed to during the call were or were not helpful.

Outcome needs to be considered at (at least) three points: the end of the call, several days after the call, and six weeks or so following the phone contact. In the first case, the goal is to determine whether the telephone conversation has been of immediate assistance. In the psychological first aid model presented earlier, this is judged by whether: (a) support has been provided; (b) lethality reduced; and

(c) linkage to other helping resources accomplished. In the second case (a few days later), assessment of the caller's coping ability is made (according to R. Lazarus, 1980), checking specifically on action steps agreed to in the initial call. In the third case (several weeks later), crisis theory suggests examination of the nature of the reorganization that is taking place (Caplan 1964; Viney 1976).

A LOOK TO   The trends for tele-
THE FUTURE   phone counseling in
the late 1970s offer clues to the direction of service delivery in the 1980s. For example, Motto's (1979) survey highlighted changes in both *programs* and *procedures*. The chief trend in programs was toward individualized services for such groups as: victims of crime (including rape, battering, sexual abuse); the elderly; grieving families; persons with venereal disease; and single parents. Procedural innovations included technological changes such as the addition of telephone tapes as an adjunct to telephone counseling at the University of Texas at Austin (Iscoe et al. 1979), and a "tele-link" system for group interaction in Brisbane, Australia (Motto 1979). The main program changes, however, have been the addition of activities that go beyond traditional telephone counseling and referral to include outreach services, community education regarding life crises and suicide prevention, and the training of staffs of various community agencies in crisis intervention. Similarly, Haywood and Leuthe's (1980) survey of 500 centers found that those which had survived the longest had multiple funding sources, and served a coordinating function for other community services.

The most important implication of these findings is that the future of telephone counseling centers might well rest with their ability to meet the needs both of consumer groups and of other agencies in the community.

For example, the Cleveland, Ohio Suicide Prevention Center serves as a 24-hour center for evaluation and referral of psychiatric emergencies for the county emergency medical service, and also handles all emergency telephone calls on nights and weekends for several mental health centers. The Montreal Tel-Aide Center is used by Parents Anonymous and other community groups who are then relieved of the burden of having to set up their own 24-hour service.

Our view is that when hotlines meet the needs of other agencies in this way, the end result is much more than mere cooperation. This approach serves also to form a political base which will be necessary to maintain funding in the 1980s. In an era of reduced federal spending, human services will have to rely even more on local and state resources. Iscoe's (1974; 1977) maxim that human services recognize "political realities" suggests that hotlines should work toward making themselves indispensable to other agencies (handling their night time and weekend emergency work, offering 24-hour coverage for "nine to five" agencies, generating referrals, and the like) in addition to meeting the needs of various consumer constituencies. As funding decisions are made on the local and state level, it will become increasingly important for services such as hotlines to have allies ready to support the budget requests that will be scrutinized all the more carefully in an era of diminishing resources.

In addition to these political considerations, it will be necessary for centers to demonstrate an impact on how callers resolve crises. As suggested earlier in this chapter, the ground work for a solid outcome research has been laid although many questions remain. The challenge of the next decade will be to conduct studies linking process and outcome (based on caller follow up) that will refine our understanding of the key ingredients in effective telephone counseling.

chapter sixteen

Crisis Intervention in the Schools

Elizabeth R. Nelson
Karl A. Slaikeu

Schools are unique settings for crisis intervention for at least two reasons. First, schools are the only public institutions sanctioned by society to have daily contact with children, usually six or more hours per day, for at least nine months during each year. Children spend at least as much time with teachers and classmates at school as with their own families. This means that school personnel have ample opportunity to notice that a child is in crisis and, by virtue of their continued contact with the child, to assist him/her in working the crisis toward resolution.

In addition to physical proximity, and the opportunities for intervention that go along with it, there is a striking compatability between the goals of educational institutions and those of crisis services: both aim at growth and development based on learning. According to crisis theory, each crisis in the life of a child represents opportunities for learning that may never come again. Instead of viewing crisis intervention as an extra duty of school personnel, it can be viewed instead as a special opportunity for teaching. When a child cannot cope with a situation, whether it be the divorce of a parent, the death of a close friend,

or moving to a new community, he/she will be, for a time, vulnerable as well as highly suggestable, as if looking for new ideas, new ways of conceptualizing (understanding) what is going on, and new skills to manage the disruptive feelings and behavior. It is at these points that those who have daily contact with the child—teachers, coaches, guidance counselors, school social workers, office personnel, administrators, support staff—have an opportunity to facilitate learning that might be very difficult, if not impossible, to achieve when things are more "normal."

Crises that emerge in school settings cover almost the entire range of situational and developmental events outlined in Chapters 3 and 4. It is not uncommon for teachers to have children in their classes who are coping with the divorce of parents, the unemployment of a father, the death of a parent or a sibling, or the psychological upset occasioned by physical illness. Similarly, from preschool through high school, children are engaged in the process of attempting to master developmental tasks which will allow them to proceed from one developmental stage to another (see Table 3.1). Even teachers untrained in crisis theory can recognize the symptoms and disorganization of life crises: absence from school, inability to concentrate, emotional upset, drop in academic performance, withdrawal from others, aggressive behavior, cognitive disorientation, etc. What is not as readily apparent to teachers is what they can do to assist children in working through these events in such a way that growth, instead of debilitation, is the outcome. It is our premise that all employees in a school system, everyone on the organizational hierarchy from janitors to the principal, can play a role in both the recognition and treatment of the crises faced by students. We also believe that knowledge of crisis theory and use of crisis skills need not be a *new* burden to already overworked teachers, but can be an aid to dealing with problems that are already there, will not go away, and can be addressed in the context of regular classroom activities and periodic conferences with students and parents.

Over the past 20 years, there has been a growing literature on crises that emerge in school situations and how various teachers, social workers, guidance counselors, school psychologists, and administrators have dealt with them. We will first summarize the literature, pointing out some of the most interesting and provocative reports of crisis intervention with school children. We will then propose guidelines that can assist in the application of the crisis model through the entire school system.

LITERATURE REVIEW

The literature on crisis intervention in school settings can be divided into three areas: articles offering a theoretical framework, program descriptions, and case studies. We will summarize representative selections from each group.

Theoretical Articles

Perhaps the most significant theoretical treatise on crisis intervention with children is that of Caplan (1964).

As discussed earlier, Caplan views the prevention of mental disorders as a function of whether or not children have adequate physical, psychological, and cultural supplies for dealing with life's stresses. Children who cope well with life crises are seen as having not only personal and psychological strengths, but also the social supports necessary for enduring disequilibrium and making appropriate changes. Caplan's "mental health consultation" for teachers and other school personnel was a logical extension of crisis theory.

Klingman (1978) has developed a theoretical-typological model for helping children cope with either natural or manmade disasters. Based on an analysis of the needs of the Israeli children following the 1973 Yom Kippur War, Klingman's model rests on Caplan's distinction between primary prevention (aimed at heading off crisis events or teaching people to cope with them *before* they occur), secondary prevention (assistance given in the immediate aftermath of a crisis event), and tertiary prevention (treatment given long after the crisis event, aimed at rehabilitation of casualties). A second theoretical component is Glass's (1959) five-stage behavioral model for phases of reaction to a disaster: pre-impact, warning, impact, recoil, and post-impact.

Figure 16.1 applies these ideas to crises in school systems. The five sections in the graph represent (I) Caplan's 3 stages; (II) the target populations involved; (III) Glass's stages of disaster; (IV) the target population as conceptualized from a mental hygiene viewpoint; and (V) the intervention strategies themselves. Primary prevention focuses on the school as a social organization, and takes place during a pre-impact period, targeting nomal populations (children who have not yet undergone any stress), and dealing with anticipatory guidance, or, teaching coping and problem-solving skills for difficulties that have not yet arisen. Secondary prevention focuses on individuals, groups, and others who are undergoing a current crisis (or experiencing Glass's warning, impact, or recoil periods in reaction to disaster), and involves crisis intervention strategies like those outlined in this book. Tertiary prevention in this model focuses on individuals, groups and institutions well after the crisis event has taken place (Glass's post-impact), when dysfunction is already apparent, and aims at restorative intervention or rehabilitation.

The advantage of this approach is that it focuses sharply three sets of intervention strategies: teaching, crisis intervention, and rehabilitation. According to Klingman, a school system should devote resources to each.

Program Descriptions The literature on crisis intervention in the schools includes a number of reports on programs developed for assisting individuals in dealing with particular crises. Klein and Lindemann (1961), for example, developed crisis groups to assist children dealing with the transition from home to a school setting. Winters and Modione (1975)

trained high school volunteers to operate a hotline for fellow students during school hours. Neills's (1977) crisis counseling project in a California school system combines elements of peer counseling, parent education, and a hotline, all aimed at helping students who are "out of control." The program emphasizes teacher training in crisis counseling techniques (for university credit), as well as coordination between the school program and various community services. Kaplan (1979) describes a series of group sessions offered in six-hour blocks for six to twelve students, all having experienced a recent loss (of a loved one, a valued personal relationship, a pet, a limb, etc.).

Training Programs developed by Morse (1972) and Cochrane and Myers (1980) teach crisis intervention principles to teachers as an aid in dealing with disruptive classroom behavior. These models use the crisis concept in a more general sense, that is, behavior disruptive to classroom functioning (and therefore a prob-

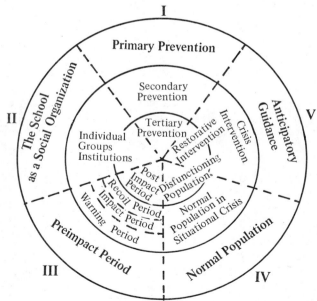

FIGURE 16.1
STAGES OF EDUCATIONAL-PSYCHOLOGICAL INTERVENTIONS FOR CRISIS SITUATIONS

Source: "Children in stress: Anticipatory guidance in the framework of the educational system" by A. Klingman, *Personnel and Guidance Journal*, 1978, 57, 22-26. Reprinted by permission.

lem for the teacher), as opposed to the disorganization and upset experienced by a child as we have described it in Chapter 2.

Bower (1964) suggests that school systems should design "stress-immunity" programs to assist children in negotiating predictable transitions such as school entrance, birth of a sibling, change of schools, and so on. He describes one such program at the junior high level. Students attend a study class and also work two and a half days each week at a childcare center run by the school district. Each student in the class is assigned to a different child and given an initial observation guide for study. Structured discussion in the social studies class (which includes the teacher and various assistants such as a psychologist and a social worker) helps students to understand not only the children in their care, but also their own development. Class discussions focus on questions such as: What did you feel you did best with the children? Why? What did the children like about you? What didn't they like about you? Which child did you find most interesting? Though Bower does not present data on effectiveness of such programs, the article has considerable heuristic value since it demonstrates how one can use developmental markers from crisis theory (Erikson 1963; Caplan 1964; Danish and D'Augelli 1980) as a beginning point in designing interventions.

Case Studies

A number of case descriptions offer rich clinical material on how crises manifest themselves in school settings. Bryant's (1978) article on "Teacher in crisis: A classmate is dying" offers concrete suggestions for teachers on how to deal with children facing terminal illness. An example highlights the choice points for teachers and other school personnel:

John's sister had leukemia. She was a year older than he and went to the same school. Everyone in John's second-grade class knew who his sister was, even those who didn't know her name. Her name was Anne, but everyone recognized her as the girl who was sick. The children didn't know the name of the disease Anne had, but they knew it was something terrible because no one was supposed to talk about it. John didn't know many details about the disease, but his mother always told him everything was going to be fine. John was confused, however, because she told him with tears in her eyes and a voice that caught in her throat.

One morning, over the loudspeaker, the principal announced a change in the bus schedule and a cub scout meeting. Then he said that he was sorry to tell everyone that Anne Bradbury had died.

The children were stunned at this news. Mrs. Russell, John's teacher, said it was a terrible, terrible thing. She asked them not to mention Anne's name to John when he returned to school because it might upset him. The children wondered to themselves: How did she die?

Had she hurt? Where was she now? Stealthily, masking the intensity of their feelings, they slipped a few questions into the beginning discussions of the day. What disease had Anne had? Could they get it? What happened at a funeral? What would happen to her body? How would John act? Mrs. Russell said she wanted all this talk about death stopped; it was time to get on to pleasanter things.

But the discussion did not stop. It simply moved from classroom to playground, where what few facts were known were altered by gossip and speculation.

Meanwhile, in an effort to insulate John from further pain, his parents immediately sent him to visit friends in another state. John perceived that his parents loved Anne more than him. They didn't even want him around! When he asked about Anne's death, he was told that God had chosen her to be with Him. John felt panic. Would God want him, too? John couldn't wait to return to school and feel normal again.

But John didn't feel normal at school at all. There was a barrier between him and his classmates. Rather than risk saying something inappropriate to John the children simply avoided him. Mrs. Russell and John's other teachers were sympathetic but unsure as to the best way to approach him. They told him life would get better and to try to think about happy things. Three months later, when John's grades had slipped and his mood had darkened, Mrs. Russell said he would just have to get his "chin up" and "buckle down" to work. In the hope of protecting John, Mrs. Russell had isolated him.

John couldn't buckle down to work because his life was in chaos. He could not forget that throughout much of his sister's illness he had wished her dead. Was he responsible for her death? He continued to worry that God would take him, or at least, punish him. He also knew that things were not right at home; his mother had moved into Anne's room.

Mrs. Russell visited John's mother to express sympathy. With tears in her eyes, John's mother went over the story of Anne's death. She added that she feared that she could not hold up and that she and John's father had no real married life any more. Mrs. Russell was deeply concerned for John's mother and her family, but was also embarrassed and at a total loss as to how to handle the situation. Feeling completely inadequate, she said she was sure that everything would be all right in time and left.

Mrs. Russell wrote in John's file that there might be problems ahead for this family. And there have been. John's parents are separated; John drifts aimlessly through school. For some time, John and Anne's classmates were fearful of hospitals, terrified of leukemia, and anxious about death. When they think about Anne and John, they remember not the human qualities and shared experiences, but forbidden fascination and speculation that surrounded Anne's death (p. 233-234).

In the absence of an opportunity to secure concrete information about Anne's death, the students were left to their own fantasies and fears about what her death implied for them. The task of the teacher is to assist the children, and the parents of the dying child as well, in grasping the reality of the situation, dealing with feelings which it provokes, and taking the behavioral steps necessary to work through the crisis.

Keith and Ellis (1978) studied six cases where children, teachers, and school administrators were forced to deal with the death of a student. The project covered approximately one year during which the authors conducted open-ended clinical interviews with students from the deceased's classroom. In five of the situations, the death was of an elementary school child, with the sixth being a 30-year-old teacher. Seven-year-old Ted had walked away from the school playground to an "off limits area" and was killed when he fell to the ground from a high ledge. Eight-year-old Laura was killed in an automobile accident in which her father was the driver. Brad, 8-years-old, was also killed in an automobile collison, though his death did not have the impact of the others since he had just moved to the area and was not as well known to the children. Jamie, a 9-year-old fourth grader, was accidently shot by a neighbor boy (also known to Jamie's classmates). The fifth subject, 8-year-old Steve, slowly died of leukemia. The sixth subject, a 30-year-old single and dedicated teacher, died suddenly of pneumonia complications. Her pupils had seen her in class on Friday, only to learn on Monday that she had died over the weekend.

The results of the authors' case analyses indicated two principle methods of coping with deaths: dealing directly with the death of students/teacher, or ignoring it completely. Ignoring the death entailed the following:

> . . . the general procedure was to avoid any mention of the death. The official reason for ignoring the death was that discussion would keep the children stirred up. In the case of Jamie, where the child's death was ignored, officials abruptly removed the dead child's belongings, including the desk. The rest of the childrens' reactions to the event was fear. No questions were asked. A book, which belonged to the dead child, was accidentally opened by one of the children in the classroom. The child who opened the book saw the dead boy's name, screamed, and dropped the book. Even though

most of the materials of the dead boy had magically disappeared during the night, the classmates carried his memory with them. The students spoke of Jamie's disappearance and the rumors of death they had heard. During snack breaks, recess, and other times, the children would gather and talk about the boy who had disappeared. The reactions of the adults appeared to communicate that Jamie's disappearance was a magical, terrible event, an event so horrible that no one could speak of it. The classroom effect consisted of restless behavior, an inability to concentrate, and a slight decrease in learning.

The counselor requested a series of interviews with the teacher who gradually acknowledged that she was having trouble helping her class master the death of their classmate. She related her personal, painful experiences with death and how upset she had felt upon learning of the death of the child in her class. As they talked, she became more upset; the death of this child apparently made her relive previous personal experiences in which she had had to face the loss of important persons in her life. This teacher's repression of her feelings had sufficed until she was faced with the death of her pupil (Keith and Ellis 1978, p. 231).

The author's account of the reactions to ignoring this particular death highlights several important issues. (a) Just because the children were not given the opportunity to talk about the death did not mean that their interest in the matter lessened. They sought out their own opportunities to discuss what had happened, to gather information, and to attempt to put the matter together themselves. (b) The death of a child has an impact not only on other classmates, but on teachers as well. The nature of this particular teacher's crisis fits with theoretical conceptions mentioned earlier (Caplan 1964; Miller and Iscoe 1963) wherein a life event (here the death of a student) touches off previously unresolved conflicts for the person in crisis. The child's death stirred up repressed feelings about the loss of other important persons in the teacher's life.

This background was necessary to understand the teacher's inability to help her class "master" the crisis. On the positive side, the crisis gave the teacher an opportunity to work through the earlier losses, this time toward a different end.

Dealing directly with the death of the school child meant participation by all involved.

The participation began with the principal, or at least his approval and included teachers, special personnel, and the dead child's classmates. The professionals met often as a group and planned a course of action. The principal, in one case, sent out a brief memo to all the school personnel informing them of the tragedy. Teachers were prepared for their classes to be upset and disrupted following the death. Each class was usually told of their classmate's death at the beginning of the day. Questions were encouraged and answered by the teacher. General discussions followed the death announcement, and the decision of what to do with the dead child's belongings was discussed by the class, as a prelude to making a group decision. The involvement of the children in the performing of active and mastery-oriented acts was considered important. The purchasing of flowers, signing a sympathy card, or planting a tree were all active symbolic gestures that were used to express grief. These were considered concrete actions in which the children could participate (Keith and Ellis 1970, pp. 231-232).

Based on the interview data, the authors concluded that the reactions of pupils to a classmate's death depend a great deal upon the behaviors of the adults involved, a powerful influence being that of the classroom teacher. If the teacher denies the child's capacity to deal with the death and is afraid to deal with the painful feelings surrounded by the death, then his/her attitude can prevent the children from working through the grief process. The authors recommend the following guidelines dealing with the death of a pupil:

1. Immediately upon receiving the news of the pupil's (or teacher's) death, a meeting of the principal, teachers involved, and a school counselor should be called to discuss how to deal with the situation, including the reactions of peers and parents.

2. One or more of those present at the meeting should then be designated to discuss the death with the dead pupils' classmates and to answer questions. If the person who knows the class best, the teacher, is unprepared for such a meeting, then he/she could be present while another person (principal, school counselor, or whomever) leads the discussion.

3. One outgrowth of the discussion should be a plan of action for removal of the dead pupil's belongings, sending a message of condolence to the family, and some sort of memorial for the deceased student. Ideally, the pupils should have major input into the design of the plan. The plan should be simple and allow for closure within a reasonable period of time.

4. In the immediate aftermath of these activities, the teacher should have administrative approval to respond to individual and group requests to discuss death either in terms of the deceased pupil or as a more general phenomenon. This has the potential for providing a learning experience for pupils and also for providing an opportunity for the teacher to observe students' progress in resolving the loss.

5. The principal and/or school counselor should continue follow up with the teacher to check on how the class is progressing, to resolve any further issues concerning further contact with the family regarding the death, and to check on other effects the death might have on classroom activity.

One of the most valuable case studies in the crisis literature involves the work of a psychiatric consultant to an elementary school in the aftermath of the homicide of a teacher (Danto 1978). The teacher was shot to death by her estranged husband as she stood before her class of 30 first-grade pupils. Danto's detailed report (the entire November 1978 issue of the *School Counselor*) describes the range of symptoms experienced by the pupils in the days and months after the tragedy (somatic disturbances, clinging and dependent behavior, bedwetting, academic difficulties, and other regressive behaviors) and step-by-step strategies taken by the school administrators, counselors, police, and attorneys in working with the children through the trial, during which several of them testified. At the heart of this analysis is the idea that by reacting thoughtfully and deliberately, school personnel were able to maximize the opportunities for learning and growth of the children occasioned by this. The crisis following the homicide was a time of great potential danger to the children (regressive behavior might continue, children might emerge with beliefs which would make them more fearful of the future), but one which also presented opportunities for learning. Danto identified the four basic learning needs that guided their work with the children in the aftermath of the shooting:

1. Assisting the children in learning about death, e.g., answering their questions about death precipitated by the shooting.

2. Learning about how totally unacceptable violence is (dealing with the conflict between the real shooting that took place in the classroom, and the television violence to which they had been previously exposed).

3. Learning about one's responsibility as a citizen to insure that wrongdoers are brought to trial (assisting the children in cooperating with police and other investigators in bringing the accused husband to trial).

4. Learning that punishment is a consequence of violent action (exposure to the workings

of the criminal justice system which in this case found the defendant guilty).

The intervention involved a series of meetings with parents, the pupils themselves, police, and school personnel (teachers, guidance counselor, principal, administrators), all aimed at assisting the children in understanding what had happened, in expressing feelings, and in dealing with immediate tasks such as talking to police and testifying in court. Danto describes issues of cognitive mastery of the crisis:

> While not emphasizing the trauma of the experience, the children needed to explore and understand why some persons became violent, what death entails, and they needed to look at the positive as well as the negative traits of their teacher so that she would not become defied. (p. 72).

Parents needed assistance in dealing with children who developed fears of returning to school, began clinging to their parents, and who displayed somatic symptoms such as stomachaches, nausea, headaches. The author needed to coach parents on why children needed to work through the experience, cautioning them against trying to get the children to forget the event too quickly:

> I explained that even if a child is taught to forget, he in fact does not forget; the knowledge is repressed. Thus, he keeps the trauma intact, never learning to cope with it. Only by facing the situation directly and dealing with it openly, can he learn to cope with it. And if he doesn't talk about it, he also gets the message that talking itself is dangerous and he never learns to verbalize what he feels (Danto, p. 73).

Though the article does not provide hard data on the children's progress over time, the author reports that the impressions of teachers and other school personnel was that the interventions were helpful to the children and their parents.

Danto's suggestions for others involved in organizing a school system's response to tragedies such as these parallel those of Keith and Ellis (1978):

1. All school staff should be involved, in addition to competent outside consultants skilled in the application of crisis intervention techniques, thanatological principles, knowledge of forensic psychology, and experience in working with the police and the court system.
2. Parents should be a part of the decision making process at each stage, including decisions on how to deal with the press, the police, and the court system.
3. The consultants should be with the children and parents at the time of the trial, particularly when they may have to testify in court.
4. By way of conclusion, the author underlines the view that situational crises such as this one should be viewed as events that force people in a system to confront major life issues.

> . . . we learned that not all the anxiety expressed was solely related to this one event. We found that there were recurring worries evoking recurring questions. The questions mainly involved anxiety concerning death and mourning. These concerns did not just develop at the time of the McDonald killing—they were there all along (Danto, 1978, p. 88).

The challenge for school systems is to respond to these individual events in such a way that discussion of these anxieties leads to constructive learning instead of debilitation.

As the literature indicates, many school personnel are sensitive to the life crises which emerge for both children and teachers, and a number of program ideas—many grounded in crisis theory principles—have been implemented. A major deficiency in the literature, however, is that lack of evaluative data on the various programs and ideas proposed. Similarly, there is a need for greater clarity on the guidelines that teachers might follow in various crisis situations. It is to these deficiencies that we now turn our attention as we outline directions for future service delivery and research.

TAILORING CRISIS INTERVENTION TO SCHOOL SETTINGS

The unifying theme from the literature on crisis intervention in schools is that crises present teachers and their colleagues with unique opportunities to teach. For example, there is no time during the school year when a teacher has the undivided attention of his/her class as when discussing the death, illness, or injury of a student or another teacher. By emphasizing the important learning that takes place during a crisis, with dramatic implications for future growth and development of students, crisis intervention in schools becomes not an extra duty or responsibility, but rather an important aspect of comprehensive curriculum planning. The training challenge then becomes one of preparing all school employees for their contribution to facilitating crisis resolution for each child or group of children as the need arises. Building from this theoretical link between crisis theory and the overall mission of schools, we can offer guidelines for use of the crisis intervention model (Chapters 5, 6, and 8) in school settings. We will begin with systems issues, a discussion intended primarily for planners and school administrators. This will be followed by suggestions for training, intended primarily for teachers and counselors who work in school settings.

Designing Service Delivery Systems

The chief components of any service delivery system, whether a school, mental health clinic, hotline, or other human service are:

The written *policy* of what to do when a crisis occurs; the *physical resources* to carry out the policy, and the trained *personnel* to implement the service.

The objective in planning for appropriate crisis intervention in schools, therefore, is to orient the school policy, physical resources, and personnel so that objectives of both psychological first aid (PFA) and crisis therapy can be achieved. (See Chapter 5 re: distinction between these two aspects of crisis intervention.)

Administrative Policy

It is important for administrators to include crisis services in the job descriptions of teachers, counseling personnel (guidance, school psychologists, social workers), and administrative personnel (including secretaries and office staff, as well as principals, deans, and others in higher administration). It needs to be agreed beforehand that when a crisis occurs, the school policy will be to temporarily put aside the regular curriculum in order to give necessary attention to the survival and learning objectives associated with the crisis, whether this involves class discussions, group meetings, or individual conferences. This is not to negate the value of "keeping up" routine duties such as daily classwork, after-school activities, sports, and the like during a crisis. The aim is to strike a balance in which business as usual accomodates itself to the learning opportunities of the crisis. Some employees will be more involved than others. Social workers and guidance counselors, for example, might have as a part of their regular job description home visits, allowing for short term crisis therapy with students and families. Teachers, on the other hand, might be expected to meet with some students on a one-to-one basis after class, or to put aside a day's lesson, so that a class discussion can be held on, for example, the death of a class member, the class's response (e.g., attending the funeral, preparing a memorial), and the like. In all cases, there needs to be administrative support for both PFA and crisis therapy as legitimate parts of the job description of various school personnel.

A major theme running through all of the case presentations summarized earlier in this chapter is that teachers, full-time school counselors, and administrators need to work closely with both parents and other community workers (police, attorneys), if they are to maximize their effectiveness in helping children work through crises. For situational crises such as unexpected death, parents need the same crisis services as the classmates of the deceased pupil. For many situational crises which strike a large group of children at the same time, the target of intervention should be not only the children, but other family members as well.

In a similar vein, the effectiveness of crisis services offered by the schools depends in large part upon coordination with other community resources (police, social services, courts, churches) who have contact with the children. Quite often the school representatives, whether school psychologist, social worker, guidance counselor, or teacher, can serve as the focal point for clarifying communication and for planning action steps in the aftermath of a critical event. Schools can make arrangements with mental health centers, for example, to provide consultation on crises which affect large numbers of students. In crises such as these, meetings which include parents, school personnel, social service workers, police, and the like, should be the rule rather than the exception.

Physical Resources Most schools are already equipped with the physical or environmental supports necessary for providing crisis services. For PFA, this means that teachers and counselors need the physical space (private) to talk one-on-one with a student when this is needed. Phone contact between a teacher and family may also be needed to monitor the progress of a family dealing with a life crisis. Schools might also help teachers maintain the sort of helpful contact recommended by Bryant (1978) by providing a travel allowance for home visits. In the main, however, by virtue of the compatability of various educational strategies and crisis intervention, most school systems are already equipped with the physical resources necessary for offering crisis services.

Trained Personnel The final systems component for comprehensive crisis services is the network of school employees available to work with students. Various groups of individuals will need to know how to offer psychological first aid and/or crisis therapy in a manner compatible with other aspects of their respective duties. Since one of the primary qualifying criteria for offering psychological first aid is accessibility to individuals in crisis, this training should be included for virtually all school employees. The aim is for anyone who might have contact with a student in crisis to be able to use the five components of psychological first aid to provide support, reduce lethality, and link the person to some other helping resource.

In addition to PFA, school personnel should be trained to use the four tasks of crisis resolution as a guide for continued contact with pupils in crisis, and for assessing progress over time. School counseling personnel, whether school psychologists, guidance counselors, social workers, or others, can offer crisis therapy as a regular part of their counseling activity. The multimodal approach presented in Chapters 8 and 9 can be made a part of graduate educational curricula in these professions, as well as continuing education workshops for professionals already working in school systems. The focus is for a counselor to have contact with the child and the family, directing counseling activity toward helping the crisis client to negotiate the four tasks of crisis resolution: physical survival, expression of feelings, cognitive mastery, and behavioral/ interpersonal adjustments. School counselors have the advantage (shared by some other community caretakers) of having contact with many elements of the crisis client's (child's) environment, such as school classroom, after-school activities, sports, and family. This means that counselors can design interventions that use these social networks to help the child achieve these four tasks.

Evaluating Crisis Services

The structure for the design of crisis services in schools also provides a framework for evaluation. The central issue is whether the system components identified above (policy, resources, trained personnel) are in place and whether they work, that is, achieve the desired outcome. Specifically, program evaluation is oriented around the following questions:

1. Is the provision of crisis services a part of school policy? Are specific activities written into job descriptions of teachers, administrators, counselors, support personnel?
2. Are the physical resources (space, transportation) available for offering both psychological first aid and crisis therapy to students when needed?
3. Are the appropriate school personnel trained in the techniques of psychological first aid and crisis therapy?

Program evaluation oriented around questions such as these can pinpoint deficiencies in a service delivery system thereby making it possible to offer training where it is needed most.

Another phase of evaluation has to do with whether or not the services offered are effective in helping students work through life crises. Using the research model proposed in

Chapter 18, it is possible for studies to be conducted to determine both *immediate coping* (objective of PFA), and *crisis resolution* (objective of crisis therapy) as a function of a school intervention program. For example, the four tasks of crisis resolution—physical survival, expression of feelings, cognitive mastery, and behavioral/interpersonal adjustments—are a systematized version of the clinical case reports presented by Bryant (1978), Danto (1978), and Keith and Ellis (1978), to name a few. It is possible, for example, to use the crisis therapy framework to investigate the impact of *ignoring* as opposed to *dealing directly* with the death of a classmate (Keith and Ellis 1978). The crisis intervention model described in Chapters 5-7 provides a structure for data collection in schools on both process variables (class discussion oriented around the four tasks of crisis resolution) and outcome variables (students' learning following a crisis experience and readiness to move on to other aspects of living). (See Chapter 18 for further discussion of research possibilities using these variables.)

Training Teachers and Counselors

The description of procedures for PFA and crisis therapy in Part II can be used as a model for training school personnel in crisis intervention. The remainder of this chapter will be devoted to suggestions for applying the PFA and the crisis therapy models to school settings. This discussion is intended to compliment the description of the intervention process in Chapters 6 and 8. Though the comments that follow identify teachers in the primary helping role, the principles apply to anyone offering PFA or crisis therapy in school settings.

Psychological First Aid

It is important to emphasize that the objectives of psychological first aid are limited. The expectation is not that teachers will take on the added responsibility of counselors, but rather that in talking with a child on the playground, in the classroom after class, or on the telephone, the five components of psychological first aid can be used as a cognitive map, a guide for helping the student take steps toward coping with a crisis situation. In addition to the procedures outlined in Chapter 6, the following emphases apply to PFA in school settings:

Psychological   The primary aim of
Contact   psychological contact
                       with children is to
counter the sense of aloneness and fear which children often experience during a crisis. Many books on relating to children deal directly with adult behaviors that fit with this first component of psychological first aid (Ginott 1965; Gordon 1970). This involves listening carefully to how the child describes the situation, imagining oneself in his/her "shoes," giving particular attention to how the child feels at the time (upset, angry, afraid), and then finding some way to indicate to the child one's appreciation/understanding of the situation.

The newness, strangeness, unfamiliarity of the crisis experience will apply especially to young children. A child who is extremely sad, angry, anxious, or frightened may believe that he/she is the only one who feels that way, and, absent feedback from a trusted other person, come to believe that something is "wrong" with the emotional reaction. A sensitive teacher can be especially helpful to such a child by listening to the child's story, and recognizing (thereby legitimizing) the feelings present.

Dimensions   Beyond the parameters
of the   of this component
Problem   which are listed in
                       Table 6.1, teachers
should give special attention to possible development issues touched off by any crisis event.

As a part of learning psychological first aid principles, teachers should familiarize themselves with the major developmental stages listed in Table 3.1, and particularly the developmental tasks and possible crisis events associated with each. While the teacher may not discuss these issues directly with the child during a PFA talk, in many cases they will illuminate dynamics of the particular crisis, and lead to a sound referral for further help later on.

As discussed in Chapter 3, a critical event can represent a loss, threat, or challenge to a child in crisis. The helper should ask: "Which of these might apply to this particular child?" Danish and D'Augelli (1980) suggest that some developmental transitions turn into crises because children lack either information, skills, or willingness to take risks in moving from one developmental stage to another. The teacher might ask him/herself: "Which of these deficits might be present with this child, and how might they be remedied?"

The guidelines for dealing with suicidal and homicidal threats outlined in Chapter 6 apply in school settings, with one addition. Teachers often have direct access to a student's suicidal ideation through written term papers, poems, and even classroom discussion. Without over-interpreting these verbal cues to destructive thoughts/plans, an alert teacher will note blatant suicidal/homicidal themes and look for an opportunity to either talk with the student or have some other trusted person (guidance counselor, or coach) do so. The inquiry itself will follow the steps suggested in Chapter 6 (intentions, plan, previous attempts, and use of outside help).

Possible   The maxim that crisis
Solutions   clients should be as
and Concrete   involved as they can be
Action   in generating their own
                       solutions to problems
applies to children as well as adults. A child's

sense of mastery over the crisis is increased insofar as he/she actively generates alternatives, weighs the pros and cons of each, and then (with the help of a caring other person), picks a "best next step." It is a mistake for an alarmed helper to take over too quickly, thereby robbing the child of an opportunity to sort through feelings, thoughts, and behaviors, and elect a course of action that is acceptable to the child. The best guideline is to aim for assisting the child in doing as much for him/herself as is possible, even if the options are as narrow as choosing who, for example, should make a phone call, deliver a message, or carry out some action step.

The decision structure for action during PFA, which rests on an assessment of lethality and whether the person can act on his/her behalf, can be especially useful for a teacher in deciding how far to go in involving other people in the helping process. (See Table 6.1.) In many cases, the teacher's action stance will be primarily *facilitative*, dealing mainly in active listening and possibly giving advice about what the student should do next. In other cases, however, the teacher will take a *directive* stance and refer the student to a guidance counselor, school social worker, school psychologist, or someone outside the school system such as a minister/rabbi/priest or physician. An advantage of PFA in schools is that the teacher can get help from many other colleagues, each of whom usually has had some kind of contact with the student in crisis. Training programs in PFA in schools should emphasize use of these networks in carrying out the directive action steps described in Chapter 6.

Follow Up

The last component of PFA is usually easier to accomplish in school settings since teachers see their students on a daily basis. This puts them in a position to briefly inquire about how things are going, particularly regarding whether agreed upon action steps have been taken. When the student is absent following a PFA talk between teacher and student, a telephone call or possibly a home visit can achieve follow up objectives. In all cases, by simply indicating that the teacher wants the student to check back after an agreed-upon time interval, he/she further communicates concern and interest in the student.

Crisis Therapy in Schools

With one major exception, the crisis therapy offered in school settings is no different from that offered by other counselors/therapists in clinic and hospital settings. Accordingly, the guidelines for assessment and treatment described in Chapter 8 and 9 can be used by school psychologists, social workers, guidance counselors, psychiatric nurses, and others who serve a direct counseling/psychotherapy function with children, and in many cases, their families.

Professionals who work in school settings, however, have a unique advantage in crisis therapy which is not readily available to their counterparts in community clinics. By virtue of their daily contact with a child's teachers, they have access to a wealth of information on how the child is coping with a crisis, and, depending upon the quality of the collegial relationship, the counselors and teachers can design classroom activities to influence how a child works through the crisis.

Our discussion of crisis therapy in Chapter 8 identifies helper and client behaviors for each of the four tasks of crisis resolution—physical survival, expression of feelings, cognitive mastery, and behavioral/interpersonal adjustments (see summary in Table 8.3). When applied to crises in schools, it is important that all "helper activities" include the resources of both professional counselors *and* classroom teachers and aids. As the literature reviewed earlier in this chapter illustrates, a teacher's classroom discussion following the death or

---

TEENAGERS CARRY   MERCER ISLAND, Wash. (UPI) At lunch time or after school, Jason, 16, and
OUT SUICIDE PACT[1] Dawn, 15, would lead their friends in long talks about suicide and reincarna-
                         tion. No one knew how serious they were.

No one knew, that is, until early Monday when Jason and Dawn stole a 1972 Chevrolet Camaro, roared at top speed across the North Mercer Junior High parking lot and smashed through the concrete wall of the school's gymnasium.

Jason, behind the wheel, was killed instantly. Dawn, who apparently had a change of heart and dived under the dashboard at the last second, was hospitalized in serious condition.

The doctor at the Medical Examiner's office said a note, signed by Jason and found in the car, was "sufficient evidence" the cause of his death was suicide.

The tragedy stunned the teenagers of the affluent suburb, particularly the couple's close friends, who said they had "jokingly" discussed detailed suicide plans with them many times.

"It was a game. It was just a big game," a friend, 15, said, shaking her head and on the verge of tears.

"They took the idea too far, I think," said another friend, 16.

Sheryl, a blond junior high student with braces on her teeth, said she, Jason, Dawn and two other teenagers began talking about reincarnation months ago after Dawn read the book *Illusions*, by Richard Bach.

"We're hoping to get Richard Bach to just talk to Dawn when she comes out of it," she said.

In a fantasy hatched by the group, Sheryl said, Jason and Dawn were supposed to steal a red Italian sports car. They would die in a flaming crash at their old junior high school and move to a "higher plane of existence."

A year later to the day, Sheryl and another teenager would kill themselves in the same way, except in a green sports car.

Instead of a red Ferrari or Maserati, Jason and Dawn took a car belonging to Dawn's sister, Diane. They crashed into the school shortly after 5 a.m.

---

[1] From "Teenagers carry out suicide pact" in *The Columbia Record*, May 14, 1980, United Press International. Reprinted by permission.

---

illness of a student, for example, can have a powerful impact on eventual cognitive mastery of the crisis for each student. Our view is that inservice training and college courses for teachers should include exposure to the four tasks of crisis resolution and the role of various classroom activities on how the child negotiates each. When used in this way, the crisis therapy model offers a shared set of constructs and language for both mental health professionals and their teacher colleagues in schools. What follows are a few suggestions on how teachers and counselors can work together in helping children in crisis to work through the four tasks of crisis resolution.

Hopefully this will serve as a stimulus for discussion during training sessions with school personnel on how to design treatment plans for individual students.

Physical   By virtue of their daily
Survival   contact with students,
                        classroom teachers are
in an excellent position to evaluate whether a child is maintaining his/her physical health during a crisis. A brief conversation after class can determine whether disruptions in eating, sleeping, and exercising are contributing to physical fatigue in class. Consultation with

a school nurse and/or health education teacher can lead to suggestions to the child about how to manage somatic concerns during a crisis. Creative ideas may emerge on how a child's peers and other school personnel can encourage positive exercise and eating behaviors during a crisis, such as assertively encouraging a withdrawn child to play outdoors after school, instead of continually retreating to his/her room to watch TV.

Expression of Feelings   A review of the discussion of this task in Chapter 8 should generate numerous ideas from teachers on how classroom activities can facilitate the identification and expression of feelings during a crisis. The richness of the school environment is that reading, art work, music, and sports all have a potential for tapping feelings of sadness, fear, anxiety, anger, guilt, and the like which may reside just below the surface during a time of crisis. Following brief conversations with a child, or as a result of information offered by others who know of a child's situation, a teacher can encourage activities which may facilitate release of these feelings. Consultation between teachers and school counselors can lead to coordinated efforts and the creative use of the numerous avenues available in school settings as an adjunct to counseling sessions with one of the school counselors. As emphasized in Chapter 8, the objective is not to force the expression of feelings, but rather to find appropriate ways to educate the child about how to identify and express feelings in his/her own way.

Cognitive Mastery   The third crisis resolution task includes activities that are already familiar to most school teachers, and represents another area where classroom activities can have a powerful impact on the eventual outcome of the crisis. As discussed in Chapter 8, the objective in working with children is to identify their interpre-

tation of events (by listening closely to how they describe what happened, current difficulties, and thoughts about the future), to judge the accuracy of their perceptions, to assist (when necessary) in making up cognitive deficits by providing information and/or alternatives interpretations of the crisis event(s) and its implications for the future. In some cases, the teacher can simply provide information through a class discussion, and in others he/she will assist the child in finding answers through readings or discussion with knowledgeable others such as ministers, physicians, and counselors. The aim for teachers and counselors who consult with them about a child (or the entire class) will be to identify, early on, opportunities for learning which are inherent in the particular crisis. The key questions are: what does the child need to know to eventually master and grow through this experience? What can we do, using classroom resources as well as counseling sessions, to facilitate this learning?

Behavioral/Interpersonal Adjustments   The first step in planning for this crisis resolution task is for teachers and counselors to share their knowledge about the child and the specific crisis in order to identify impending behavioral and interpersonal demands that might be made on the child. The parameters of the predictable developmental transitions (Chapter 3), and the major situational crisis (Chapter 4) can be helpful in identifying specific tasks such as attending a funeral following the death of a classmate, talking to a police officer following a crime in a school, and so on. As with the other tasks, teachers and their counselor colleagues can then draw from a full range of in-school activities to help a child achieve the specific behavioral and interpersonal adjustments required by a crisis. The activities may be as varied as a sixth grader arranging for a memorial for a deceased classmate, an eighth grader writing a research paper on stresses associated with moving from one town to another, or a high school senior visiting the library as a step toward making career plans.

SUMMARY

There can be little doubt that schools are a powerful socializing force in human development. The fact that children spend so many of their waking hours in school puts teachers, administrators, counselors and support personnel in a critical role in helping children negotiate major life transitions. When situational crises such as divorce, death, sudden illness, crime, or other acts of violence occur, childrens' individual reactions are evident to teachers immediately. Provocative case analyses such as the ones summarized in this chapter offer a challenge to school administrators to develop crisis services.

Even though the literature weighs heavily on the reports of situational crises in schools, it should be noted that half of the crises addressed in this volume—the developmental types—are the main charge of school systems, from preschool and kindergarten on through high school. The challenge of the future will be for training and research to explore applications of comprehensive crisis intervention (including psychological first aid and crisis therapy) to both situational and developmental crises in school settings. Our hope is that the ideas presented will stimulate collaborative efforts between mental health professionals, teachers, and administrators aimed at maximum use of school resources to facilitate adaptive crisis resolution in children.

chapter seventeen

Crisis Intervention on the Job/ In the Office

Jonathan Simons
Karl A. Slaikeu

An assembly-line worker asks to see the boss about a personal matter. Almost as soon as the worker is in his office, the manager sees that something is very wrong. The worker is visably anxious, with eyes darting continuously around the room. His palms are sweating and he dries them on his pants often. The manager is somewhat frightened of the worker's behavior, but asks how he can help. The worker starts to talk but has trouble making sense, beginning with bits and pieces of the story, and acting as if he may burst into tears at any moment. Then he abruptly tells his boss that the previous evening his house burned down, killing his brother and leaving the family destitute. The manager is at a loss. Though concerned for the worker, he doesn't know how to begin helping. He doesn't know if he should concentrate on calming the worker's emotional state, which appears to be almost psychotic, or if he should concentrate on the practical problems of sheltering and caring for the family. Either way, the manager feels inept, since he knows nothing about psychotherapy or even community resources. The manager offers financial help and suggests getting in contact with a local church. The worker thanks him and leaves, but the manager doesn't feel like he's really helped much. He wonders whether the upset worker really heard his advice. Will he follow through on the suggestions? Does the worker have any sense of comfort as a result of the meeting? These questions remain unanswered for the manager and leave him with feelings of frustration, guilt, and anger at having had to take on a role he was not prepared for.

This true story, told to the authors by the manager of a small factory, highlights the central premise of this chapter: managers and supervisors will be confronted with their workers' crises, and are an important resource in helping employees to cope with these crises. Crisis intervention training could have given focus to this manager's comments, increasing the probability of securing the needed assistance for the employee. In this chapter, we will offer a theoretical and practical rationale for developing crisis intervention strategies in the workplace. We will propose training in both white- and blue-collar settings, since the life crises discussed in this book cut across socio-economic classes. We will begin by discussing "work" in general, its demands and rewards, and the psychological and social aspects of job settings that touch almost everyone for the greater part of their adult lives. We will then turn to a review of the most important literature on crisis intervention in the workplace, and conclude with a summary of implications for training and research.

WORK SETTINGS

Work plays an important part in almost everyone's life as evidenced by the fact that most people spend more time at work during their waking hours than any other place. Work can be thought of as a way of making a living and, for most people, as a reflection of personal identity. "What do you do?" or "Where do you work?" are frequent questions following the exchange of names when people are first introduced. When work is satisfying it enhances feelings of self-worth and purpose in life. On the other hand, poor working conditions and fluctuations in income can be a source of dissatisfaction, frustration, and worry.

While each work setting is unique, there are commonalities that help us understand how a worker will experience a job, whether police work, construction, teaching, management, or anything else. Neff (1977) suggests that we understand each work setting as a subculture whose values, norms, and expectations can be described along five dimensions.

The first dimension, *physical setting*, refers to the fact that work takes place in a special environment, separate from our homes. Unlike our personal places of residence where we can, more or less, create a comfortable atmosphere according to personal taste, the workplace of-ten requires that people adjust to external demands, often beginning with the requirement that workers travel long distances in automobiles, crowded buses, and trains to get there. The process of going to work may involve pleasant or unpleasant experiences. For the less fortunate worker, getting to work is stressful and contributes to the overall level of stress that work possesses. Once on the job, the worker must adjust further. For many, the workplace offers comfort, as in plush offices, or well-designed shops and buildings. Others are exposed to dangerous machinery, environmental pollutants, and discomforts in the form of poor lighting, temperature extremes, and the like.

The second dimension of Neff's work subculture involves *privacy*. Most jobs require more visibility than is expected at home. For example, it is expected that the employer has the right to know what workers are doing with their time, which means that a worker's behavior is often scrutinized and evaluated more than in other settings. Rules, regulations, and expectations influence dress, language, smoking, eating, drinking, etc. In short, work is often a place where one's personal life-style, habits, and need for privacy must be temporarily suspended.

Work can also be *impersonal*, which is Neff's third dimension. In many job settings, the ultimate concern of management is productivity, efficiency, and dependability. Workers may often feel like a "cog in the wheel," especially when the job is repetitive, boring, and seems unrelated to the final product. The impersonal effects of work vary tremendously among different types of jobs, but many workers experience some sense of depersonalization.

Almost every employee either has a boss, or a supervisor, or is one him/herself, which leads to Neff's fourth dimension of work systems, the *authority* relationships. Workers have to learn how to handle being told what to do, and telling others what to do. A worker in a position of authority has responsibilities that are often greater than those encountered with home and family. On the other hand, a person who exercises a great deal of authority at home may be in a subordinate position at work. Dealing with authority often places people in conflict between their needs to be assertive and expressive, and their desire to keep their jobs. There are also conflicting demands for autonomy and dependency. That is, one is expected to be able to function without constant help and attention from a supervisor, but also to know when to consult the supervisor before starting something new or trying a different approach.

The final dimension of work settings involves *peer-relations*. New workers must adjust to the norms of the existing work group, which includes both performing adequately, so as not to bring discredit to the work group, but also limiting performance to prevent the rest of the group from appearing inferior. Depending upon physical proximity and the nature of job descriptions, relationships between co-workers can be close and positive (including possible sexual liaisons) or filled with conflict. The quality of these relationships can have a powerful immediate impact on productivity, as well as overall job satisfaction.

McLean (1967) has noted that performance on the job is a function of an interaction between personality variables and environmental variables such as those described by Neff. Just as lines of authority vary from job to job, so there are clear differences in workers' capabilities to deal responsively with superiors, peers, and subordinates. As we shall see from the literature, how an employee resolves a life crisis may be intimately tied to one or more of the five dimensions of the work subculture.

LITERATURE REVIEW

The relationship between work and crisis intervention has two parts. First, work can precipitate a life crisis. This can come about through an on-the-job injury, through an accumulation of job pressures until they reach a breaking point, or through a dramatic setback (being passed over for a promotion, or being fired). A second connection between the world of work and crisis intervention lies in the unique opportunities inherent in job settings for assisting workers in crisis. Levy (1973) suggests that naturally occuring systems can be of greater benefit to troubled individuals than formal systems such as psychological clinics. Help which occurs "naturally" at work is usually given earlier in the crisis and also serves to preserve the individual's sense of competency and mastery since the worker perceives him/herself as capable of functioning and carrying out expected duties despite the crisis.

Work as a Cause of Crisis

Numerous studies have explored the psychological dangers associated with employment and with specific jobs (Martindale 1977; McLean 1967; Rose, Jenkins, and Hurst 1978). The life-event stress scale by Holmes and Rahe (1967) identifies a significant number of work-related items, such as promotion, retirement, job loss, and transfer as sources of stress. (See Chapter 2.) Most of the other literature in this area deals with two main categories: high stress jobs, and job change as a crisis.

High Stress Jobs

Certain jobs have been shown to be particularly stressful, both physically and psychologically. For example, Martindale and Rose, Jenkins, and Hurst have reported on the stress of air traffic controllers who monitor radar and communications systems and are responsible for maintaining safety in the crowded air space above airports. The job requires intense concentration and quick thinking. A wrong decision or instruction could result in the loss of many lives. The tremendous responsibility and decision-making pressures of such jobs can lead to psychosomatic disorders such as ulcers and heart disease. As Holmes and Rahe have found, the pressures associated with high-responsibility jobs can accumulate until a crisis occurs. Many workers, of course, forestall crisis with a variety of stress management techniques, many of which can be debilitating in themselves (abuse of alcohol and other drugs).

Jobs that hold the possibility of immediate danger for the worker such as police work and firefighting represent, perhaps, the most obvious examples of how work can precipitate crisis. Central to the stress associated with these jobs is the possibility of serious injury or death. An injured employee must cope with financial, physical, and psychological burdens. (See Chapters 4 and 13 for a discussion of the factors leading to crisis in medical situations.) Survivors of workers killed in the line of duty are often in need of crisis intervention. Most employees in dangerous jobs escape serious disability, though the more subtle casualties such as divorce, drug abuse, and emotional breakdown are common.

Another high-stress job that has been investigated by mental health workers is that of the inner-city teacher. Bloch (1978) studied 253 teachers from Los Angeles inner-city schools referred for psychiatric evaluation by physicians, co-workers, lawyers, and union representatives because of various psychological and physical problems associated with stress at school. He considers these patients to be victims of the "battered teacher" syndrome that involves a combination of stressors including physical assaults and threats, sustained high levels of fear and anxiety, little support from administration, and insufficient training in dealing with problem situations. Bloch hypothesized that the teachers' reactions were similar to those found among some soldiers involved in combat. Factors associated with both combat neurosis and battered teachers syndrome were: severity of the traumatic event; chronic nature of the stress; lack of pleasant

stimuli to offset the unpleasant, the unexpectedness of the event; and impaired morale. It was found that these factors correlated with the severity of physical and psychological disorder in the teachers, a relationship previously noted among patients suffering from combat-related neurosis. It is significant to note that only 28 percent of the teachers had been actually assaulted and that most assaults caused only minor injuries. The more indirect stressors in the school environment were potent in bringing about psychiatric problems in the majority of the sample. Bloch recommends activity in three areas to prevent or decrease the severity of reactions to inner-city school stress. First, teachers should be prepared for the physical and psychological dangers of inner-city schools through a program involving education and role-play. Second, teachers need to sustain morale through discussion groups and administrative support. This support should come in the form of transferring violent students following an attack, rotating teachers out of problem schools after a few years, and a generally open attitude on the part of administration, reflected in acknowledging the problem, listening to complaints, and actively trying to make changes. Finally, Bloch recommends that a crisis intervention team be assigned to each school district. The team would consist of teachers with some mental health training who would be supervised by a psychiatrist or clinical psychologist. The team would act through discussion groups to diffuse crisis situations where teachers and students are in conflict, and also offer crisis counseling for teachers. A teacher-oriented walk-in clinic would aid, as well, in dealing with crises.

Feldman (1979) describes a hot-line that helped teachers deal with nonacademic concerns. Originally designed as a service for students, the hot-line became a resource to teachers for finding help with problems such as conflict with administrators, discipline problems, fear of poor ratings, and general emotional difficulties. The service included private consultations,

Saturday workshops and lectures, as well as telephone counseling. The staff of the service consisted of teachers who had worked for a minimum of three years in the school system.

Job Change as a Crisis

A number of studies have investigated the psychological impact of changes in job status such as transfer, promotion, firing (out-placement), and retirement (Broussard and DeLargey 1979; Hirchowitz 1974; Jones 1979; Kinzel 1974). Each of these changes—whether sudden and unexpected, welcome or dreaded—represents a shift that requires adjustments in an individual's daily routine, relationships, and self-image. As with developmental transitions, these changes have potential for long-term benefit for the worker (even if it may not look like it at the time, as in getting fired), or long-term harm (if, for example, the worker and his family do not adjust well to the new circumstances).

Hirchowitz describes some of the emotional dangers involved in job change. The transitions can result in growth and mastery, but also have the potential for disorganization and debilitation (depression, alcoholism, physical illness, and even cardiac death). This author describes job change as "crisis in transit" and compares it to the experience of loss and mourning for a loved one, identifying a three-stage process. (a) At impact, the person may appear to be in a state of shock, which can last several hours to several days. (b) The recoil-turmoil phase is a period of disorganization lasting one to four weeks, followed by (c) adjustment, which is characterized by problem solving and adjusting to new roles and responsibilities.

Hirchowitz's presciption for dealing with the stress of a job change emphasizes providing information as the most effective weapon against maladjustment following this transition. He further advises employers to provide: support and reassurance that supervisors care and recognize the worker's contributions; guid-ance in helping the worker adjust to new roles, relationships, and the demands of a new physical setting; and finally, the opportunity for workers to express throughts and feelings about the change.

Jones discusses the problems of involuntary career change in terms of grief and crisis theory. A review of the work of a number of investigators led to the conclusion that the grief experience in involuntary career change is similar to the grief reaction most people experience at the loss of a loved one. Jones identifies the person grieving over a job loss as one likely to be in a crisis state, and advocates fostering coping through planned organization, activation of resources, and an emphasis on strengths.

Kinzel advocates programs to counsel executives faced with early retirement. He characterizes the reaction to early retirement as a process involving a deterioration of planning abilities due to panic. Executives' most pressing needs include financial counseling, assistance in "filling the time gap," as well as attention to concerns about self-respect. A similar approach is suggested by Lamberson (1978), who presents a five-point plan for retirement counseling: (1) financial counseling where specific questions regarding taxes, pensions, government benefits, etc., are answered; (2) health consultation on issues such as proper insurance coverage, changes in physical abilities, etc.; (3) legal consultation on matters like equal opportunities for older people; (4) housing advice; and (5) family relations consultation, where important concerns such as the changing relationship of the retired person to his or her family are explored. Lamberson describes a project that included an advisory board made up of employees 50-62 years of age as well as others who had already retired. The use of the advisory board provided for constructive feedback from a group made up of people at various stages in the retirement process.

Another job transition service is outplacement counseling which seeks to minimize the negative effects of firing or laying off workers. The dynamics of a group outplacement workshop are explored in a study by Broussard and DeLargey (1979). After discussing the rationale and basic preparations for outplacement counseling, the authors present the important issues, concerns, and group dynamics involved in such a meeting. The workshop is offered as an extension of the job being left, which has certain advantages and disadvantages because of the association with the former employer. Hostility toward the leader as a representative of the employer will undoubtedly be the first obstacle to overcome. The leader must process the group's feelings and direct these away from him or herself and emphasize the constructive potential of the group. The members are encouraged to use the experience to build a cohesive group from which they can learn and receive continued support throughout the job-seeking process as they share feelings, ideas, and behavioral strategies with one another.

Help Offered Through Work Settings A number of articles report on programs aimed at alleviating the personal problems of workers, some focusing on specific problems such as alcoholism or bereavement, with others taking a more generic approach. Traditionally, companies have been more direct in their treatment of alcoholism than many other problems (Filipowicz 1979). The automobile industry has been especially concerned with "substance" abuse, as exemplified in a program at General Motor's Oldsmobile Division (Campbell and Alander 1975). The program included supervisory staff as the first line of interveners. They were taught to identify workers who might be overusing drugs or alcohol. Employees were then referred to the plant physician, who in turn offered referral to one of several community services for treatment. Throughout the entire project, an attempt was made to maintain a supportive communication link between supervisors and troubled employees. The authors reported that one of the most positive features in the program was its cost-effectiveness. A control group of untreated substance abusing workers was significantly less productive than the "treated" group. The increase in productivity of the treated workers more than compensated for the cost of the program.

Sager (1979) presents a review of some causes of alcoholism in industry and the current state of affairs of alcohol treatment programs in the workplace. Programs at the United California Bank, International Telephone and Telegraph, and Corning Glass Works are among the most successful described. Rehabilitation is usually measured in terms of increases in job performance, and reductions in absences and accidents. Recovery rates of 60–80 percent are consistently reported. Most articles concerning industrial alcoholism emphasize the need for confidentiality, informed written consent by workers, and specific corporate policies concerning alcoholism when a company decides to start a treatment program (Sager 1979).

Lawrence and Steinbrecher (1979) report that the number of such programs jumped from 500 to 2,400 in the five years preceding their report. These programs have received a great deal of support from the National Council on Alcoholism, the National Institute on Alcohol Abuse and Alcoholism, and the Senate Alcoholism and Drug Abuse Subcommittee. These authors also describe a recent American Society of Personnel Administration-Bureau of National Affairs (ASPA-BNA) survey that ranked alcoholism as the second most prevalent employee problem, affecting almost 5 percent of professional and managerial workers and almost 8 percent of production or service personnel.

Bereavement counseling is another form of help that has been offered through work settings. The process of mourning is one that touches all people at some point in their lives. A program designed to help company employees during the difficult period of mourning was instituted in a metropolitan personnel department (Crowder, Yamamoto, and Simonowitz 1976). Eight nurses in the occupational health service of the department were trained in crisis theory with special emphasis on the mourning process and identification of pathological reactions to loss. Notices concerning the availability of the bereavement counseling programs were posted, sent to supervisory staff and included in employee newsletters. Of the 84 names given to the counseling service during its first year, 49 were contacted, and 31 participated in counseling. Results presented are anecdotal, but generally positive, supporting the idea that in addition to churches/synagogues or hospitals, counseling through work settings may be a useful service for bereaved employees.

A company's singular focus of its helping resources on either alcoholism or bereavement runs the danger of ignoring a host of other worker problems. Filipowicz (1979) argues, therefore, for a broad-spectrum approach to worker problems, with a decreased emphasis on alcoholism. While it is estimated that the annual cost of alcoholism in business and industry is 5 billion dollars, the estimated cost for "emotional" problems is 17 billion dollars (Filipowicz 1979). Similarly, Lawrence and Steinbrecher's (1979) survey of workers' problems found alcoholism to be the second most prevalent problem among workers, but that the most prevalent worker problems involved a "personal crisis situation" involving marital, family, financial, or legal concerns.

An alternative to specialized, in-house interventions (whether for alcohol abuse, or for bereavement) are the more general employee assistance plans (EAPs) which rest on contracts with outside agencies and consultants. These firms usually serve a large number of people and can therefore afford to provide a wide range of services for many problem areas. It has been suggested that EAPs can provide more confidentiality than in-house programs, which might then lead to more people using them. An

executive, for example, might be less willing to talk to a company's physician about a personal problem than he would to a caseworker from the outside. In the latter case, the executive avoids having to discuss a personal problem with someone who holds a lower rank in his/her organization.

Many corporations now make use of Health Maintenance Organizations (HMOs) in their benefit package for workers. HMOs provide services directly to the corporations and includes a full spectrum of physical and mental health services, with opportunity for prevention as well as the treatment of disorders. Sank (1979), for example, describes an intervention carried out by the psychology department of an HMO following the release of hostages held at B'nai B'rith's Washington D.C. headquarters in 1978. To prevent possible psychological debilitation in the former hostages, the psychologists undertook a massive crisis intervention effort. They encouraged former hostages to participate in group meetings where they could discuss the ordeal in a supportive atmosphere, and receive assistance in dealing with specific problems such as returning to work, dealing with nightmares, and the like.

Beyond direct contact with troubled employees, mental health professionals can serve as consultants to company supervisors on how best to deal with troubled workers. Reardon (1976) describes a program instituted in the Southern Connecticut Gas Company which employed less than 600 people. Company supervisors were trained in one three-hour session regarding their role in the company's EAP. They were taught to help put troubled workers in touch with the personnel office, which then referred them to the local family service agency of the United Way. Bosch (1979) describes another program with similar goals and methods, though utilizing union instead of supervisory personnel in the key referral role. The AFL-CIO's Union Counseling program offers training for rank and file workers and union personnel in a six-week course.

Participants are instructed in interviewing techniques and use of referral sources within the community. Workers who are in crisis or are experiencing difficulties are thus identified and counseled by co-workers, thereby avoiding management's knowledge or intrusion.

FUTURE TRENDS

Though few of the studies reviewed made direct use of crisis theory in planning research or service delivery, it is noteworthy that many of the strategies used bear a striking resemblance to crisis intervention principles outlined earlier (Bloch 1978; Crowder et al. 1976; Feldman 1979; Greenbaum, Rogosky, and Shalit 1977; Martindale 1977). Other studies demonstrate how crisis theory can be useful in conceptualizing employee job difficulties (Broussard and DeLargey 1979; Hirchowitz 1974; Jones 1979; Kinzel 1974; Lamberson 1978).

The future use of the crisis model in planning psychological services for business and industry will depend on the results of research on the nature of life crisis in work settings. There is a need for investigations to answer the following questions:

1. Of the work-related psychological problems reported to supervisors, company physicians, and personnel departments, what percentage fit the categories of developmental and situational crisis (Chapters 3 and 4), as opposed to more long-standing or chronic personality problems?
2. Do co-workers or supervisors become aware of difficulties (and therefore have an opportunity to help) significantly earlier than physicians, ministers, and other groups who have been traditional targets of crisis intervention training?
3. Can crisis intervention training for key groups such as supervisors be shown to be cost effective according to such traditional outcome measures as reduced absenteeism and increased productivity, as has been the case with alcohol treatment programs?

4. Where in work systems is help best placed? It would seem, for example, that programs sponsored by a union might be better received by some blue collar workers than help offered by management, though at present there are no data to support this.

Data on these questions (especially cost effectiveness) could do much to advance the use of the crisis intervention model in work settings. Even before such studies are conducted, however, the existing crisis literature offers guidelines for those involved in planning mental health services in work settings. Combining a knowledge of the nature of life crises (see Chapters 2, 3, and 4) with the nature of work settings (Neff 1977) leads to suggestions for (a) education, (b) training, and (c) referrals.

Education

Through whatever means available (articles in company newspapers, training programs for managers, etc.), workers should be made aware of the psychological concomitants of the predictable transitions associated with employment. By anticipating the adjustments in living arrangements, finances, self-image, and family life associated with such developmental markers as transfer, promotion, termination, and retirement, workers stand a greater chance of maximizing whatever personal gain might be associated with each, and minimizing the danger to themselves and their families. Brief articles could be written for company newsletters, and training modules developed based on the four tasks of crisis resolution (see Chapter 8). The aim would be to use brief, focused educational efforts to offer workers a cognitive framework which would help them master the predictable transitions associated with their jobs.

Training

Frontline employees—those in a position to first notice that a worker needs help—should be taught the principles of psychological first aid (Chapter 6). Limited goals should be emphasized, with supervisory efforts aimed at helping the worker to re-establish coping. Training would revolve around learning the five components of psychological first aid described in Chapter 6—making psychological contact, examining dimensions of the problem, exploring possible solutions, assisting in taking concrete action, and following up to check progress—tailoring each to the unique job requirements of the helper. Since the same PFA framework applies over the telephone, in the office, or standing in a corridor, it is ideally suited to the challenges presented by crises in work settings. Training should include role-play situations tied to the employee's work situation to facilitate transfer to each employee's day-to-day tasks. The psychological first aid principles can be taught along with physical first aid in orientation programs for supervisors and managers. Beyond immediate psychological assistance, workers should be made aware of the other helping resources available for referral, both in the company itself and in the community. Throughout the entire training process, emphasis should be on understanding and dealing directly with the extreme disruption and disorganization associated with situational and developmental crises, whether due to a work-related matter, or a divorce, sudden illness, death in the family, or something else.

Referrals   All companies, whether large or small, should have a referral network available for workers who need short-term therapy in order for them to adequately resolve life crises. Depending upon company resources, these could be in-house professionals, or therapists who work on a contract basis as part of an employee assistance plan. From the vantage point of crisis theory, the treatment available should be a broad spectrum approach that assists both the worker and his/her family in negotiating

the four tasks of crisis resolution—physical survival, expression of feelings, cognitive mastery, and behavioral/interpersonal adjustments—in such a way that the individual can rejoin the ranks of productive fellow workers as soon as possible (see Chapter 8).

Mental health professionals serving as a part of EAPs and HMOs, for example, can use the crisis model presented in this volume—PFA and crisis therapy aspects—as a guide for both the treatment of troubled workers, and for consultation with supervisors, managers, and personnel departments having daily contact with employees in crisis. When used in this manner—as a model for both treatment and consultation—the crisis intervention model can be used to both strengthen informal "on the job" helping networks, and to facilitate referral for outside treatment when necessary. Training programs for consultants could draw on material from Chapters 10 (Clergy) and 16 (Schools) which offer examples of how to mobilize systems resources to help individuals negotiate the four tasks of crisis resolution.

One clear advantage of the crisis model in work settings is that it utilizes nontechnical language, thereby facilitating communication between work supervisors and mental health consultants. In addition, the crisis model's focus on positive coping, mobilizing strengths, and growth through difficult times is entirely congruent with current emphases in business and industry on health enhancement. The future will likely see increased recognition by insurance companies and employers that crisis intervention services can not only reduce health care costs (see Chapter 1), but also increase productivity and overall job satisfaction, and therefore should be included as an integral part of any company's comprehensive health maintenance services. Hopefully the material in this chapter will help consultants and employers as they plan the introduction of comprehensive crisis of services in work settings.

PART IV

RESEARCH

Throughout this volume we have emphasized the need for further research on both the nature of life crises and also the effectiveness of various intervention strategies. Though our primary focus has been to explicate an intervention model, directions for future research have been summarized in almost all of the earlier chapters. We now conclude with a discussion of a research paradigm congruent with our comprehensive crisis intervention model. This section will be of interest to practitioners who want to critically evaluate their own work with crisis clients, and also to behavioral scientists and their student colleagues who wish to conduct formal investigations on the course of life crises and the intervention process.

chapter eighteen

A Model for Crisis Intervention Research

A review of the crisis literature published since Lindemann's (1944) early work following the Coconut Grove Nightclub fire reveals far more case reports, theoretical treatises, and "how to" articles than systematic research studies. In their extensive review of crisis intervention outcome research, Auerbach and Kilmann (1977) noted that (a) "crisis" as a construct had no established core of meaning or theoretical base, and (b) crisis intervention techniques were too broad and loosely organized to be called a coherent treatment system. After reviewing studies from suicide prevention programs, psychiatric settings, and surgical settings, these authors concluded that in order to increase our knowledge of life crises and the utility of various intervention techniques we will need a comprehensive model to organize data and guide research efforts.

> Such a model should: (a) specify operationally the criteria for classification of stressors as crises, and for classification of individuals as being in a state of crisis, (b) account for the pattern of emotional arousal and development of interference behaviors for different classes of crises and for different types of individuals, and (c) specify appropriate points of intervention with those techniques for given persons/crises which will maximize coping ability and minimize emotional distress. Hopefully, data relevant to these areas will continue to be obtained in settings where some degree of experimental

control can be imposed, and the findings will begin to be applied to naturally occurring crisis events and crisis intervention in applied settings (Auerbach and Kilmann 1977, p. 1213).

This call for model building in the crisis area needs to be examined in the broader context of the process of behavioral science investigation. In Gottman's (1979) report on systematic study of marital interaction, four phases of investigation are outlined:

1. description of real life phenomena (e.g., how married couples interact in clinical vs. nonclinical situations, or life crises as they emerge in various community settings);
2. parsimonious presentation of the phenomena described in terms of a "model";
3. testing of the model to see that it not only describes existing data, but also allows prediction of future behavior; and,
4. formulation of a "theory" which both explains and predicts.

The crisis model presented in this book serves two purposes. Its immediate function is to summarize existing knowledge in such a way that frontline community workers and therapists can deal with their clients' life crises in as clear and straightforward a manner as possible. At the same time, the model represents phase two of Gottman's behavioral science paradigm, and thus sets the stage for investigations which will further test and refine the model. The crisis intervention model described in Chapters 5, 6, and 8 grew from descriptive studies and clinical practice in crisis situations, and its formal characteristics were designed to address the needs articulated by Auerbach and Kilmann (1977) and others (Butcher and Koss 1978; Korchin 1976). The multimodal diagnosis of crisis (Chapter 8) allows us to classify individuals as being in or out of crisis, to track the crisis experience (in terms of five BASIC subsystems) over time, and to specify appropriate treatment strategies. The model thus offers a general framework for categorizing a wide array of both situational and developmental crises, and also for investigating the relationship between specific treatment strategies and various outcome measures. Two lines of inquiry are important in future crisis interven-

TABLE 18.1 POST-CRISIS FUNCTIONING: LONG-TERM IMPACT OF RAPE[a]

Modality	Variables[b]
Behavioral	Change in sleep pattern (49%, 10), (51%, 11)[c]
	Turning on radio or TV when alone (8)
	Absent from work for at least 2 weeks (21%, 11)
	Change or abandonment of job within 6 weeks (43%, 5)
	Change of residency (76%, 11), (48%, 4)
	Change of phone number (4)
	No intercourse within 6 months after the assault (38%, 6)
	Frequency of intercourse:
	no change: 19% (6)
	decrease: 30% (6)
	increase: 7% (6)
	Change in eating habits (57%, 4), (70%, 11)
	Suicide attempt or abuse of drugs and/or alcohol (22%, 5)
	Suicide (7%, 9)
Affective	Elevated scores for trait and state anxiety (8); specific fears:
	fear of being alone
	fear of being awakened at night
	fear of going out with other people
	Traumatophobias (4):
	fear of indoors
	fear of being alone at home (40%)
	fear of crowds
	fear of people behind her

[a] From *Women in crisis: A reformation of the rape trauma syndrome,* R. Striegel-Moore and K. Slaikeu. *Unpublished manuscript,* Copyright R. Striegel-Moore, 1982. Reprinted by permission.

[b] Sexuality variables have been included under each of the five modality headings, depending upon the way data was coded, e.g., decrease in "frequency" of intercourse (listed under Behavior), "pain" during intercourse (listed under Somatic). When a symptom appears to fit under more than one heading, its most salient characteristics are used to decide the modality under which it best fits (e.g., decrease in "initiating" intercourse listed under Interpersonal).

[c] First number = percentage of subjects with the symptom;
second number = author(s) (listed below).

References: (1) Bart 1975
                    (2) Becker, Abel and Skinner 1979
                    (3) Burgess and Holmstrom 1973

tion research: studies investigating the nature of life crises using a multimodal framework, and investigations that link process and outcome variables.

THE NATURE OF LIFE CRISES

Chapters 2, 3, and 4 include research sections highlighting some of the most promising directions for future

studies on the onset, development, and resolution of life crises, with or without formal outside intervention. As we have stressed throughout, however, in order for knowledge to increase, data must be collected covering all of the relevant person subsystems—behavioral, affective, somatic, interpersonal, cognitive—including the social context of the crisis. For many situational and developmental crises, the first step will be to categorize existing

TABLE 18.1 (Continued)

Modality	Variables[b]
	Feeling unsafe in the residential area (3)
	Sex-related anxieties (4)
	Fear of men (42%, 9)
	Hostility towards men (17%, 9)
	Decreased satisfaction from sexual activities (7)
	Sadness (5)
Somatic	Decreased libido (31%, 17), (61%, 2)
	Difficulties either experiencing any sexual feelings or being orgasmic during sex (41%, 6), (23%, 2, 33%, 1)
	Pain and discomfort during intercourse (25%, 6) (15%, 2)
	Fatigue and exhaustion, low energy level (5)
Interpersonal	Visits to parents (48%, 4)
	Requests for emotional support from friends (20%, 4)
	Mistrust in heterosexual relationships (23%, 9)
	Decrease in initiating intercourse (6)
Cognitive	Nightmares (32%, 3), (49%, 11)
	Preoccupation with negative opinion of significant others (6)
	Flashbacks during intercourse (6)
	Sexual aversions (13)
	Low self-esteem (12)
	Self-perceptions of being alienated, isolated (13)
	Shame (13)
	Guilt (13)

(4) Burgess and Holmstrom 1974a
(5) Burgess and Holmstrom 1974b
(6) Burgess and Holmstrom 1979
(7) Feldman-Summers, Gordon and Meagher 1979
(8) Kilpatrick, Veronen and Resik 1979b
(9) Medea and Thompson 1974
(10) Peters 1973
(11) Peters 1975
(12) Veronen and Kilpatrick 1980
(13) Symptoms that have been assigned this number have been described by several investigators; quantitative data were not mentioned, however. For a summarized description the reader is referred to Katz and Mazur 1979.

knowledge using the multimodal framework. For example, Table 18.1 summarizes existing literature on the long-term effects of rape according to our five BASIC person subsystems (from Striegel-Moore and Slaikeu 1982). As crisis theory predicts, a review of recent studies indicates that rape can have noticeable negative effects on a woman's daily routine, her feelings, physical well-being, interpersonal relationships, and cognitive functioning. Unfortunately, it is not possible to draw clear conclusions on factors contributing to positive and negative outcome since none of the studies reviewed collected data on all five modalities, follow up was conducted at different times, and data are not available on the extent to which the rape victims did or did not accomplish the four tasks of crisis resolution described in this book.

One direction for future research might be to re-code data from previous studies on short- and long-term effects of rape using multimodal categories. The same procedure could be applied to available data on other disorders such as post-traumatic stress disorder (PTSD) (Williams 1980). For example, content analysis of interview data with rape victims or veterans suffering from PTSD could measure disruptions (or lack thereof) in subjects' BASIC functioning (months or years after the rape or combat experience) and correlate this with subjects' reports on the extent to which they did or did not accomplish the four tasks of crisis resolution described in Chapter 8. One would hypothesize an inverse relationship between progress on the four tasks and the existence of psychiatric symptoms in the months and years following the original event(s), whether rape or combat trauma.

Inventories will need to be developed which

TABLE 18.2   PROCESS/OUTCOME RESEARCH PARADIGM FOR CRISIS INTERVENTION

	Process 1	Outcome 1a	Outcome 1b
Intervention	Psychological first aid (PFA)		
Time frame	During PFA contact	End of PFA	Several days after PFA contact
Data sources	Audio/videotapes of PFA contact, verbatim transcripts of interviews, observation of live interviews	Audio/videotapes of PFA contact	Telephone follow up with client
Variables measured	State of client's crisis: precipitating event BASIC profile context (family/social group) Helper performance on 5 components of Psychological first aid	State of client's crisis: BASIC profile Helper performance on 3 objectives of PFA: (1) providing support (2) reducing lethality (3) linking to helping resource	Client coping (R. Lazarus 1980): (a) managing subjective reactions; (b) problem solving

reliably measure BASIC functioning, and also track client progress in negotiating specific aspects of the four tasks of crisis resolution. (See Appendices A and B.) As a start, some readily available clinical questionnaires such as the SCL-90R (Derogatis 1976) can be scored according to the five BASIC subsystems, even though they were not specifically designed for this purpose. Whichever instruments are used, our view is that collecting multimodal data on the course of life crises has the potential for lending considerably more rigor to the selection of treatment strategies than presently exists. If we can generate more knowledge on how specific precipitating events affect individual functioning in all five modalities, as well as how individuals work through specific crises—whether situational crises such as rape, or developmental crises such as an unwelcome retirement—then we can refine guidelines for treatment of those who need outside assistance.

PROCESS AND OUTCOME STUDIES

A true test of the efficacy of various intervention strategies can come only through studies which link both process and outcome in the same investigation (Auerbach and Kilmann 1977; Slaikeu, Tulkin and Speer 1975). Table 18.2 summarizes the stages at which we can measure both helper performance and client progress through the course of a client's life crisis. Congruent with the distinction between psychological first aid and crisis therapy, we can measure process variables at two points: during psychological first aid (Process 1), and during crisis therapy (Process 2). Similarly, each intervention presents at least two opportunities to measure outcome. The first is at

TABLE 18.2 PROCESS/OUTCOME RESEARCH PARADIGM FOR CRISIS INTERVENTION (Continued)

Process 2	Outcome 2a	Outcome 2b	Outcome 2n
Crisis therapy			
During therapy sessions (weeks months)	End of crisis therapy, e.g., 6 to 8 weeks	Six months later	Several years later
Audio/videotapes of therapy sessions; questionnaires	Audio/videotapes of therapy sessions; structured interview with client and family; questionnaire for therapist and client	Structured interview with client and family; questionnaires	Structured interview with client and family; questionnaires
(a) Client's BASIC functioning (from Table 8.1) (b) Therapist's selection and implementation of treatment strategies; client progress on four tasks of crisis resolution (physical survival, expression of feelings, cognitive mastery, behavioral/interpersonal adjustments)	Client's BASIC functioning, post-crisis (a) equilibrium (b) integration (c) readiness to face the future (d) growth	See Outcome 2a	See Outcome 2a

the very end of a psychological first aid interview/phone contact/conversation (Outcome 1a), while the second comes several days later (Outcome 1b). The outcome of crisis therapy is measured first at the termination of formal therapy sessions (Outcome 2a), and can be measured again in subsequent weeks, months, years (Outcome 2b, 2c, . . . , 2n). The variables listed in Table 18.1 are based on theoretical constructs and intervention strategies used in our earlier description of the comprehensive crisis intervention model. The various strategies outlined in Chapters 6 and 8 for psychological first aid and crisis therapy, respectively, become process variables in a research framework. Similarly, the objectives of psychological first aid—providing support, reducing lethality, linking to a helping resource—are actually outcome variables for this aspect of crisis intervention. The desired goal of crisis therapy—resolution of the crisis, defined as integration of the crisis event into the fabric of life and a client's openness/readiness to face the future—becomes the chief outcome criterion for crisis therapy research. The chief process variables for crisis therapy involve client behavior oriented around the four tasks of crisis resolution: physical survival, expression of feelings, cognitive mastery, behavioral/interpersonal adjustments; and therapist activity aimed at facilitating these working-through activities. It is reasonable that some investigations will examine only one portion of the overall picture, for example, process variables in psychological first aid (Process 1) while others will look at the relationship between process and outcome variables, such as client coping (Outcome 1a) as a function of helper performance on the five components of psychological first aid (Process 1).

Process 1: Psychological First Aid

The initial contact between the crisis client and the helper provides the first opportunity to study how the client asks for help, and also the kind of assistance given by counselors. Process 1 variables can be measured from taped interactions of psychological first aid (PFA) contact, or through observations of live interviews. Two sets of variables are measured. The first is the nature of the client's crisis. Whether or not the client is in crisis is determined by whether (a) a precipitating event can be identified, and (b) there is sufficient disorganization/disequilibrium in BASIC functioning to lead to a breakdown in coping. According to R. Lazarus (1980), the latter is defined by a client's reported inability to manage the "subjective components" of the crisis, which means disruption in any of the five BASIC subsystems, and/or an inability to engage in problem solving (measured primarily in terms of cognitive functioning). A number of studies have investigated the crisis state (Halpern 1973; Viney 1976; and others listed in Chapter 2) though none (with the exception of Sank 1979) have organized the data according to a multimodal assessment framework. It is possible to create symptom checklists, based on the BASIC personality variables, to determine the precise impact of the precipitating event on each of the modalities. Even though crisis assessment during PFA is much more limited than during crisis therapy (discussed next), there is still a need to refine assessment questions that can be made over the telephone, in a hospital waiting room, or in an office.

The primary research strategies during Process 1 involve coding both client and helper behavior during the PFA interview. How does the client present him/herself and the crisis? What does the helper do in response? How do helper comments change over the course of the interview? To what extent does the helper accomplish the five components of PFA outlined in Chapter 6?

Table 18.3 lists preliminary coding categories which have been developed for helper and client behavior using the PFA model.[1] Each

---

[1] A coding manual is available from the author. See address listed in Appendix A.

TABLE 18.3 PSYCHOLOGICAL FIRST AID CODING CATEGORIES

Component	Helper Behavior	Client Behavior
I. Psychological contact	Invites client to talk Expresses concern/caring Makes empathic statement	Asks for help Expresses appreciation for help offered. Other comment about helper/client relationship (positive or negative).

II. Dimensions of the problem	Makes statement about:
	  Precipitating event
	  Background information:
	    Age
	    Address (neighborhood,
	      community, culture)
	    Marital history
	    Friendships
	    Work status
	  Precrisis BASIC functioning
	    Behavioral
	    Affective
	    Somatic
	    Interpersonal
	    Cognitive
	  Crisis BASIC functioning
	    Behavioral
	    Affective
	    Somatic
	    Interpersonal
	    Cognitive
	  Lethality:
	    Response to cue
	    Inquiry about plan
	    Previous attempts
	    Significant others
	  Possible impact of crisis on others,
	    e.g. family, neighbors, friends,
	  Future concerns (e.g., impending
	    decisions)
	  Personal resources/strengths
	  Social resources/strengths
	  Most immediate concerns
		See *Helper Behavior*.

III. Possible solutions	Asks about solutions attempted in the
	  past
	Makes further inquiry about previously
	  attempted solutions
	Refines previously attempted solutions
	Proposes new solution:
	  New behavior for client
		Discusses solutions attempted in the
		  past
		Introduces new solutions:
		  New client behavior
		  New client attitude
		  Third party intervention
		  Environmental change
		Responds to helper's suggested solutions:
		  Positive

TABLE 18.3 (Continued)

Component	Helper Behavior	Client Behavior
	New attitude for client (redefinition of problem)	New client behavior
	Outside (third party) help:	New client behavior
	Helper	New client attitude
	Other	Third party intervention
	Environmental change (e.g., temporary change of residence, hospitalization)	Environmental change
		Responds to helper's proposed ideas: Negative
		New client behavior
		New client attitude
		Third party intervention
		Environmental change
IV. Concrete action	Reassures client re: action to be taken (including possibility of client taking no action)	Commitment/agreement re: Client action:
		Physical survival
		Managing feelings
	Gives advice (opinion) on what to do, how to feel, what to think, how to manage somatic complaints, etc.	Change in thinking
		Behavior/interpersonal adjustment
	Initiates involvement of third party	Helper action
	Initiates controlling intervention:	Third party action
	Physical holding, calling police, hospitalization, calling department of social services to take child from home, etc.	
V. Follow up	Suggests follow up contact	Discusses possibility of follow up
	Discusses concrete details for follow up (e.g., time place, etc.)	Discusses concrete details of follow up
	Makes contract for follow up	Contract for follow up

helper and caller speech unit is assigned to one of the content categories.

The model assumes that a PFA interview involves five distinct components—contact between the helper and client, definition of the problem, exploration of possible solutions, commitment to a concrete action plan, and planning for followup—and that both helper and client play a role in each. The PFA training guidelines (Chapter 6) put the primary burden for each component on the helper's shoulders—"making" psychological contact, "examining" dimensions of the problem, etc.—though in reality some clients are more cooperative, or able to assist in this endeavor, than others. Therefore, a comprehensive research analysis of the PFA process must examine the extent to which helpers have to probe or to which clients volunteer information. A glance at the list in Table 18.3 indicates that coding these behaviors allows measurement of the extent to which the helper covers all five components of PFA (including specific behaviors such as assessment of lethality), and measures also the level of "directiveness" taken (Component IV, concrete action). Analysis of caller data yields, in similar fashion, the caller preoccupations during the interview and the relative spread of comments over the five components during the interview. Analysis of the sequencing of remarks (and whether each is a question or a statement) these content categories with temporal variables (helper and client talk-time, silence patterns, and the like [Blumenthal, Tulkin, and Slaikeu 1976; Slaikeu 1979]) will facilitate testing the most important hypotheses on the process of first-order crisis intervention. These data can then be analyzed in conjunction with various outcome measures.

Outcome 1a:
End of Psychological First Aid Contact

The first opportunity for measuring crisis intervention outcome occurs at the end of the psychological first aid conversation. When the helper and client have finished talking, we can determine whether the three objectives of PFA—support, reduction of lethality, and linkage to a helping resource—have been achieved. By drawing on the process data for PFA (Table 18.3) each of these outcome variables can be coded as follows:

(a) Support provided:
    Coded from number and quality of psychological contact statements offered by helper (Component I of PFA);
(b) Lethality reduced:
    Coded from assessment of lethality (II), solutions explored (III), and action taken (IV);
(c) Linkage to helping resource accomplished:
    Coded from discussion of follow up (V).

These three outcome variables are actually created by summing a number of Process 1 variables taken from audio/video tapes or live interviews, and can be thought of as the "bottom line" of a PFA contact. As an adjunct to objective coding by independent observers, it is also possible to have clients rate the sessions on whether they believe these three objectives have been achieved. In any case, the objectives of PFA which clinicians use to guide their work can be readily translated into codable outcome categories for PFA.

Outcome 1b:
Client Coping

Since crisis theory rests on the assumption that individual crises stem from a breakdown in coping (Caplan 1964), it follows that one of the earliest outcome measures should be the extent to which a client has regained his/her ability to cope with the situation. Our crisis model assumes that the counselor's ability to perform the five components of psychological first aid (with its three objectives of support, reduction of lethality, and linkage to help) will lead to an improvement in the client's ability to cope. This hypothesis can be tested at Outcome 1b. Following the theoretical coping framework outlined earlier (Lazarus 1980), the chief questions about client coping are: (a) can the client manage the subjective components of the problem (disruptive feelings, cognitive disorganization/confusion, somatic complaints, behavioral/interpersonal difficulties), and (b) can the client engage in problem solving (primarily a cognitive process but with correlates in the other four personality subsystems) sufficient to begin working through the crisis? While we might expect clients to show some change along these dimensions at the immediate end of a PFA contact, one would predict more changes in the several days after the contact when the client has had a chance to implement strategies set in motion during the initial discussion. Data can be collected from a structured telephone or face-to-face interview. Slaikeu et al. (1975) have established that telephone follow up is possible even with callers to a suicide prevention service. In other settings, where anonymity is not as great an issue (outpatient counseling services, emergency rooms, and the like), it would be possible to design a telephone follow up questionnaire that would directly assess the client's ability to cope according to the dimensions listed. Research designs can be developed that investigate the association between high and low levels of counselor performance according to the five components of PFA (Process 1) and changes in client coping (Outcome 1b). Further investigations of Outcome 1b should look at other influences on client coping, for example, discussions with family and friends, since crisis clients often receive advice/help from a number of people at the same time. Slaikeu et al. (1975), for example, found that many callers to a crisis center who did not subsequently "show" for scheduled face-to-face appointments had received help from other resources, therby reducing their need for further counseling.

Process 2: Crisis Therapy

The distinguishing features of the crisis therapy model described in Chapter 8 are (a) its use of a multimodal personality framework to assess pre-crisis, crisis, and post-crisis functioning, and (b) its targeting of therapeutic techniques to the four tasks of crisis resolution—physical survival, expression of feelings, cognitive mastery, and behavioral/interpersonal adjustments. Each of these features of the therapy model opens the door for systematic research on how clients resolve crises and which therapeutic strategies are most useful in facilitating crisis resolution. Instruments such as the Crisis Questionnaire (CQ) can be used to collect data on the state of client's crisis as therapy begins. The CQ yields client self-report data on the nature of the precipitating event and its impact on behavior, feelings, physical functioning, interpersonal relationships, and thought/images. As mentioned above, the SCL-90 (Derogatis 1975) is a brief symptom checklist which can be analyzed according to the five BASIC subsystems for crisis therapy.

The Crisis Assessment Summary (Table 8.2) can be used to summarize data for each client's crisis based on information from several data sources. By comparing this profile with follow-up data it is possible to track changes in each of the five subsystems from precrisis to crisis to postcrisis functioning. As we shall discuss, these instruments can thereby give an empirical basis for judgments about crisis resolution and growth (as opposed to debilitation or psychological impairment).

The heart of crisis therapy process research, however, lies in an analysis of therapists' selection and implementation of treatment strategies. Our model suggests that all treatment strategies be aimed at helping the client to achieve the four tasks of crisis resolution. Process analysis, then, must capture both client activity and therapist activity under each of the four headings: physical survival, expression of feelings, cognitive mastery, and behavioral/interpersonal adjustments. These variables can be coded from either taped or live sessions. It is important to record both what clients do and say (including reports of activities outside the therapy hour—discussions with spouse, employer, etc.) as well as the therapeutic techniques used by counselors. Tallies of these process data can then be compared with various outcome categories (discussed next) to determine which combinations of techniques are most effective in which circumstances. Behavioral checklists can be developed that code feelings expressed during the therapy hour, client's cognitive understanding of the crisis event and its implications, somatic complaints and remedies attempted, and changes in behavioral/interpersonal functioning through the course of crisis therapy. However the coding system is developed, it should record information on each of the following for any therapy session:

1. Client activity on each of the four tasks;
2. Therapist comments/strategies that facilitate/inhibit accomplishment of these tasks; and,
3. An independent coder's ratings on clients' movement through each of the four tasks.

Only by recording what strategies therapists implement and what activities clients undertake will we be able to further our understanding of the therapeutic factors that facilitate crisis resolution. Though the techniques are available (see Glossary) and are currently in use by practitioners, process analysis such as this has the potential for bringing even greater precision to therapeutic planning.

Outcome 2a:
End of Crisis Therapy

In Chapter 2 we described crisis resolution as a process of working through the crisis experience (negotiating the four tasks just described) with a clearly defined outcome–a state wherein equilibrium is restored, the crisis event is functionally integrated into the fabric of life, and the individual is open/ready to face the future. The termination of crisis therapy provides the first opportunity to measure these outcome variables.

Each of the three outcome variables—restoration of equilibrium, integration of the crisis event into the fabric of life, and readiness to face the future—can be operationalized according to the multimodal personality framework and measured at the end of crisis therapy. Each variable has behavioral, affective, somatic, interpersonal, and cognitive components. *Equilibrium*, for example, can be defined as reduction of unwanted symptoms (headaches, anxiety) in the five subsystems. *Integration* of the crisis event into the fabric of life is measured primarily by assessing the client's cognitive mastery of the situation, whether it be the death of a loved one, loss of a limb, reaction to physical assault, unemployment, or whatever. Indications of integration include a reality-based understanding of the precipitating event, (including possibly the client's role in causing it), the implications for the person and his/her family, and a realistic appraisal of future possibilities (an appreciation of how life will be changed, without over generalizing from the event to other aspects of the individual's life). Poor cognitive mastery, indicating that the crisis event has not been integrated into the fabric of life, would include an unrealistic appraisal of the event and its implications (after a divorce, "I will never trust another woman/man again"), denial of the event and/or its implications, over generalizing, catastrophizing, and the like. The integration outcome variable also has behavioral, interpersonal, somatic, and affective components. The phobias that can result from life crises are perhaps the most dramatic examples of behavioral manifestations when the crisis event has not been integrated into the fabric of life. Similarly, some individuals seem to "wall off" the crisis event and anything related to it so that functioning in particular areas of life is severely limited.

In a similar manner, the outcome variable *"openness/readiness"* to face the future can be operationalized in terms of the five personality subsystems. At the end of crisis therapy, an assessment is made about the extent to which an individual feels (affective subsystem) ready to return to work, relate to other people, continue with other life routines; believes he/she can carry on (cognitive); and engages in behavior appropriate to a return to such commitments (behavior).

Finally, it is possible to assess whether or not the crisis experience has led to *growth* by examining any of the following: increased coping skills (behavioral and cognitive subsystems), a broadened world view or improved self-image (cognitive), improved interpersonal relationships and sensitivities (interpersonal), and the like.

Measurement of these variables can take place through structured interviews with clients, interviews of immediate family members, and/or therapist observations/ratings. Follow-up instruments modeled after items from the Crisis Assessment Summary (see Table 8.2), comparing BASIC functioning at pre-crisis, crisis, and post-crisis stages, can lend precision to the measurement of outcome variables such as growth through the three time periods.

Outcome 2b,..., 2n   Follow up of crisis cli-
Crisis Resolution   ents in the months and
                              years after the crisis
event (and therapy) allows for an even richer
assessment of crisis resolution than at the
time closer (several weeks) to the precipitating event. Six months to one year later the
client's reorganized life will have stabilized
somewhat allowing for clearer descriptions of
behavioral, affective, somatic, interpersonal,
and cognitive functioning. The outcome variables—equilibrium, integration, readiness to
face the future, and growth—are the same as
for Outcome 2a, as are the assessment possibilities. Each client's BASIC functioning can
be compared with earlier profiles.

SUMMARY   As this sketch of a
                    research paradigm sug-
gests, studies linking both process and outcome
variables are clearly possible. By virtue of the
increased precision we can bring to each set of
variables just described, we should soon be able
to take great strides toward increasing our
knowledge of effective intervention strategies.
No less than three decades of work by practitioners—social workers, psychiatrists, psychologists, pastoral counselors, paraprofessionals,
volunteer telephone workers, and others—
attest to the staying power of the crisis concept, though considerably more attention from
behavioral scientists will be needed if the
model is to become a true "theory." Hopefully, the model and research paradigm presented
will stimulate other behavioral scientists to
turn their research skills to the life events
which mark dramatic turning points for us all.

Crisis Intervention Research Instruments

Researchers associated with the author's consulting practice (Austin, Texas) are in the process of developing several instruments that can be used for both clinical assessment and research in crisis intervention. *The Psychological First Aid Coding Manual* gives instructions for coding helper and client interactions during a PFA Session. Data can be coded from audio or video tapes and scored to give information on helper performance on the five components of psychological first aid. The manual can also be used as an aid to training workers in psychological first aid procedures.

The BASIC Crisis Inventory (BCI) is a checklist that assesses strengths and weaknesses in the five BASIC person subsystems (behavioral, affective, somatic, interpersonal, and cognitive). It also assesses progress on the four tasks of crisis resolution (physical survival, expression of feelings, cognitive mastery, and behavioral/interpersonal adjustments). The BCI can be used to record changes in a client's BASIC profile from crisis to follow-up.

The Crisis Follow-up Questionnaire lists items which can be tailored for use in individual client follow-up (via written questionnaires or telephone calls) as well as in research designs.

We invite other researchers and clinicians to join in the process of pilot testing these instruments, and to share their ideas and experiences with us as these and other instruments are developed. Address correspondence to: Karl A. Slaikeu, Ph.D., 1104 West Avenue, Suite 103, Austin, Texas 78701.

appendix B

Crisis Questionnaire[1]

Name:_____   Age: _____

Marital Status: _____   Occupation: _____

                                             Date: _____

Directions

You have recently experienced a very stressful event. This questionnaire provides your counselor with valuable information about what happened and the effect on various aspects of your life. Please fill out this form as completely as possible. If you have any questions, feel free to ask your counselor for clarification.

     Your answers are kept confidential and are accessible only to your counselor and his/her therapeutic team.

The first set of questions is about the *event* that caused you to seek counseling. Please describe briefly what happened:

_____

_____

_____

Were there other people involved?
No (   )
Yes (   )
When did it happen?

_____

_____

---

[1]Prepared by Karl A. Slaikeu and Ruth Striegel-Moore (1982).

1. Since *the crisis event* happened, I have noticed changes in:
   - ( )   my sleeping habits
     - ( ) sleep more   ( ) sleep less
   - ( )   my eating habits
     - ( ) eat more   ( ) eat less   ( ) changed my diet
   - ( )   my smoking
     - ( ) smoke more   ( ) smoke less
   - ( )   my alcohol consumption
     - ( ) drink more   ( ) drink less
   - ( )   my use of drugs and medicine
     - ( ) take more   ( ) take less
   - ( )   my work habits
     - ( ) work more   ( ) work less
   - ( )   my leisure activities
     - ( ) spend more time having fun   ( ) spend less time having fun
   - ( )   my exercise routine
     - ( ) exercise more   ( ) exercise less.

Please check the following about your behavior before the crisis event.

No   Yes   I was satisfied with:
( )   ( )   my work habits
( )   ( )   my eating habits
( )   ( )   my exercise habits
( )   ( )   my leisure time activities
( )   ( )   my consumption of drugs/alcohol
( )   ( )   my sleeping habits.

Taking everything into consideration, before the crisis event happened, overall I was:
( )   very satisfied with my life
( )   moderately satisfied with my life
( )   fairly satisfied with my life
( )   somewhat dissatisfied with my life
( )   dissatisfied with my life.

2. Please list 3 of your favorite activities during the last year.

   1 _____

   2 _____

   3 _____

3. Compared to one year ago, the time now spent on these activities is:

   much less   less   the same   more   much more

   Activity 1
   Activity 2
   Activity 3

The following questions give your counselor an understanding of the feelings that are most characteristic for you at this time in your life.

1. Read over the list of feelings and check those which describe how you have been feeling lately.
   - ( ) excited   ( ) overwhelmed   ( ) energetic
   - ( ) angry   ( ) tense   ( ) guilty
   - ( ) lonely   ( ) cheerful   ( ) delighted

( ) happy   ( ) optimistic   ( ) comfortable
( ) sad   ( ) restless   ( ) bored
( ) "numbed"   ( ) afraid   ( ) exhausted
( ) relaxed   ( ) jealous   ( ) other
( ) contented

Read over the list of feelings again and select as many as five that were characteristic for you *before* the crisis event.

1 _____   4 _____

2 _____   5 _____

3 _____

2. List up to 3 feelings that you want to experience *less often*:

1 _____

2 _____

3 _____

List up to 3 feelings that you want to experience *more often*:

1 _____

2 _____

3 _____

Please complete these sentences:

I feel at my best when _____

_____

_____

I feel worst when _____

_____

_____

The next questions concern your bodily well-being.
Since the crisis event, I have had:

( ) headaches   ( ) weight loss
( ) heart tremors   ( ) bowel difficulties
( ) stomach aches   ( ) painful menstruation
( ) abdominal pain   ( ) dizzy spells
( ) decreased interest in sex   ( ) asthma
( ) high/low blood pressure   ( ) arthritis
( ) allergies   ( ) decreased energy
( ) tics   ( ) other

Please read over this list again and circle those problems that have troubled you at some point earlier in your life, i.e., before this current crisis. Are you currently undergoing medical treatment as a result of the crisis event?

( ) No
( ) Yes Name of Physician: _____

Do you take medicine for any of your current health problems?
( ) No
( ) Yes, please specify _____

_____

Please estimate how physically tense you feel currently.
              1   2   3   4   5   6   7
Comfortably relaxed ( ) ( ) ( ) ( ) ( ) ( ) ( ) Extremely tense

What part of your body feels most tense? _____

_____

Do you feel close to your family?
Yes, very close ( ) moderately close ( ) neutral ( ) distant ( ) very distant ( )
List your best friends, using their first names:

1 _____

2 _____

3 _____

Who is currently the most important person in your life?

_____

Are you a member of a social club, church, fraternity, etc?
( ) No
( ) Yes, specify: _____

When you need help or when you want to talk with someone, do you contact other people?
( ) No, I don't like asking for help.
( ) Yes, I contact 1 _____ and/or

                  2 _____ and/or

                  3 _____ and/or

                  4 _____

Check which of the following statements apply to you:
False   True   The crisis event prevents me from reaching a very important goal.
( )   ( )
              (specify) _____

_____

( )   ( )   I think about this event over and over again.
( )   ( )   Somehow I feel responsible for what has happened.

(specify) _____

_____

( )   ( )   I suffer from nightmares about the event.

When I picture myself right now _____

_____

When I think now of what happened, I realize that I should _____

_____

Now that this (crisis event) has happened, I _____

_____

I consider killing myself   ( ) never   ( ) sometimes   ( ) very often
I feel like hurting someone else   ( ) never   ( ) sometimes   ( ) very often
Please give a brief description of yourself.

_____

_____

_____

Taking everything into consideration, currently I am:
( )   very satisfied with my life
( )   moderately satisfied with my life
( )   fairly satisfied with my life
( )   somewhat dissatisfied with my life
( )   dissatisfied with my life

My best characteristics are _____

_____

I hope counseling can help me to _____

_____

_____

I would like my counselor to be _____

_____

_____

Glossary of Crisis
Therapy Techniques

Ruth H. Striegel-Moore
Karl A. Slaikeu

Stimulated by the glossary in A. Lazarus's (1981) book on multimodal therapy, this glossary contains a selection of therapeutic techniques that have been effective in crisis therapy and psychotherapy in general. The glossary provides a brief description of each technique and offers references for the clinician to broaden his/her knowledge and to facilitate acquisition of these skills. Terms used in definitions that appear as separate items in the glossary are italicized. Furthermore, whenever possible, special reference is made to literature that can be recommended for the client. Books or articles intended for client use are marked with an asterix (*).

While this glossary may be of help in enhancing clinical skills by providing information, it is by no means a substitute for professional training. When used without an adequate understanding of human behavior, knowledge of psychopathology, and basic clinical skills, these techniques are reduced to gimmicks that may, with some luck, produce change, but that may also lead to further deterioration of the client's physical and psychological well-being. No matter what technique is selected and applied, it is the clinician's responsibility to make choices on the basis of a sound clinical diagnosis and evaluation of all possible outcomes.

ACTIVE LISTENING In active listening, the therapist attends carefully, both physically and psychologically, to the messages transmitted by the client. The therapist communicates understanding and empathy by reformulating and summarizing the client's explicit statements, by attending to and commenting on the client's nonverbal or paraverbal signals, and by guiding the client toward clarification and expansion of the issues addressed. It is important to allow the client to direct the flow of the conversation and to avoid critical or judgmental statements.

References

Carkhuff, R.F. *Helping and human relations*. New York: Holt, Rinehart & Winston, 1969.

Egan, G. *The skilled helper*. Monterey, California: Brooks/Cole Publishing Co., 1975.

Gordon, T. *Parent effectiveness training*. New York: McKay, 1970.

ANGER-CONTROL Anger management, as practiced by Novaco (1979), is an off-shoot of *stress-inoculation training*. Novaco considers anger as having positive functions and therefore does not teach its suppression. Rather, the goal of the training is to learn to recognize anger and to express it adaptively. The first phase, preparation, consists of education about anger arousal and its determinants, identification of the situations that trigger anger, discrimination of adaptive versus maladaptive occurrences of anger, and introduction of anger-management techniques as coping strategies to handle conflict and stress. The second phase, skill acquisition, involves learning cognitive and behavioral coping skills. On the cognitive level, the client is taught to modify the appraisal of the situation in which anger arises. The client learns self-instructional statements which serve as an internal guide to behavior. Furthermore, *problem solving* is emphasized. The behavioral component includes *relaxation training*, impulse delay, and training in verbal communication. The various coping techniques are taught by instruction, *modeling*, and *behavioral rehearsal*. In the third phase, application, the therapist induces anger and these simulated provocations are used for training the newly acquired skills.

References

Novaco, R.W. The cognitive regulation of anger and stress. In P.C. Kendall & S. Hollon (Eds.), *Cognitive-behavioral interventions*. New York: Academic Press, 1979, Chapter 8.

ANGER EXPRESSION   Anger is a commonly experienced emotion during a crisis state. However, overt expression of anger is often socially reprimanded and many clients find it difficult to acknowledge or recognize their anger. The goal of anger expression is to help the client understand and accept feelings of anger, because only when anger is "owned" can it be eliminated through rational argument or expressed adequately using assertive statements.

The therapist can facilitate anger expression by self-disclosing statements ("If this had happened to me, I would be very angry"), by probing statements ("Didn't that make you angry?"), or by role reversal with the therapist playing the client and openly expressing anger.

In a group setting, participants who are more free in their expression of anger can serve as models for more inhibited clients and the group facilitator should encourage open sharing of feelings.

References

Lazarus, A. *The practice of multimodal therapy*. New York: McGraw-Hill Book Co., 1981.

Wheeler, H. Silent victims of incest—peer group project. In A.W. Burgess & B.A. Baldwin (Eds.), *Crisis intervention: Theory and practice*, 1981, 258–274.

ANGER PROVOCATION   This technique encourages clients to express their repressed anger toward the therapist, who makes himself/herself a target for the anger. The rationale for such an approach is that anger can motivate the client and thus help overcome pathological passivity. Anger provocation involves an aggressive-abrasive attitude on the part of the therapist. Examples include being deliberately late for appointments, ignoring the client during the session (e.g., reading a journal instead of talking with the client), and responding supportively as soon as the client expresses anger about such treatment.

In the literature, anger provocation is mainly reported in dealing with severely depressed clients. Anger provocation should only be used in exceptional cases when other efforts to mobilize the client have failed.

References

Brodsky, L. *Anger provocation as a crisis intervention technique*. Hospital & Community Psychology, 1977, *28*, 533–536.

Liberman, R. A behavioral approach to group dynamics II. Reinforcing and prompting hostility to the therapist in group therapy. *Behavior Therapy*, 1970, *1*, 312–327.

ANTICIPATORY GUIDANCE

In anticipatory guidance, the therapist helps the client to anticipate certain external or internal events and to prepare the individual in crisis for these events. Knowing what long-term consequences a certain crisis event may have helps the client to plan and mobilize effective coping strategies in advance, which increases the likelihood of adaptive emotional adjustment to inevitable changes or transitions. Anticipatory guidance can be used both prior to a crisis-precipitating event and during crisis therapy.

References

Caplan, G. *Principles of preventive psychiatry*. New York: Basic Books, Inc., 1964.

Sutherland, S. & Scherl, D.J. Patterns of response among victims of rape. *American Journal of Orthopsychiatry*, 1970, *40*, 503–511.

ANXIETY MANAGEMENT TRAINING

See *stress inoculation training*.

ASSERTIVENESS TRAINING

A variety of techniques have been used to help clients to behave more assertively in interpersonal relationships. Alberti and Emmons (1970) define assertive behavior as that which "enables a person to act in his/her best interest, to stand up for himself/herself without feeling undue anxiety, to express his/her honest feelings comfortably or to exercise his/her rights without denying the rights of others" (p. 27). Treatment packages usually include skills training, development of anxiety—antagonistic responses, and attitude change. The components of skill training are *modeling, role playing, behavioral rehearsal, feedback,* and *reinforcement*. To acquire anxiety—antagonistic responses, *relaxation training* and exposure (imaginative or *in vivo*) are used. When the client's cognitions, values, or attitudes inhibit assertive responses, *cognitive restructuring*, challenging of irrational beliefs and discussion of expectations about the effects of new assertive behavior on others is helpful.

Most training programs include *homework assignments* to provide further practice and to increase generalization. Assertiveness can be taught individually or in groups.

References

*Alberti, R. & Emmons, M.L. *Your perfect right; a guide to assertive behavior*. San Luis Obispo, Calif.: Impact, 1970.

Lange, A.F. & Jakubowski, P. *Responsible assertive behavior*. Champaign, Ill.: Research, 1976.

*Phelps, S. & Austin, N. The assertive woman. San Luis Obispo, Calif.: Impact, 1975.

Whiteley, J. & Flowers, J., (Eds.) *Approach to assertion training*. Monterey, Calif.: Brooks/Cole, 1978.

AUTOGENIC TRAINING

This relaxation technique was first developed by Schultz and Luthe (1959) and involves control of bodily and imaginal functions through auto suggestion. Under the close guidance of an instructor, the client first learns to relax various muscle groups. Lying on the floor or on a firm bed, the exercises start with regular deep breathing, after which the clients are instructed to subvocally tell themselves "my feet feel heavy and warm," and to concentrate on this feeling. These "heavy and warm" instructions are repeated for all major muscle parts. In advanced autogenic training, suggestions for controlling different organ systems are learned and finally the production of suggested fantasies is added.

References

Schultz, J.H., & Luthe, W. *Autogenic training*. New York: Grune & Stratton, 1959.

BEHAVIOR REHEARSAL

The client is taught new behaviors by practicing them during the therapy session. Behavior rehearsal provides an intermediate step in changing behavior, with the eventual behavior change occurring as the client tries out the new behavior pattern. Rehearsal procedures are appropriate for dealing with behavioral deficits and in preparing the client for novel situations (e.g., a rape victim for the court trial). Usually behavior rehearsal involves four stages: preparing the client (explaining the need for learning a new behavior pattern, getting the client's consent to use behavioral rehearsal as a method, and helping the client overcome initial uneasiness); selecting target situations; behavior rehearsal; and transfer to everyday situations. Behavior rehearsal usually is construed as a gradual shaping process and can be combined with other techniques, such as *modeling* and *feedback*.

References

Goldfried, M.R. & Davison, G.C. *Clinical Behavior*

Therapy. New York: Holt, Rinehart & Winston, 1976, Chapter 7.

Eisler, M. & Hersen, M. Behavioral techniques in family-oriented crisis intervention. *Archives of General Psychiatry*. 1973, *28*: 111-116.

BIBLIOTHERAPY

In its broadest meaning, bibliotherapy refers to the use of literary works, including fiction, in the treatment of physical or psychological problems. A special subcategory is self-help treatment programs, describing specific sets of therapeutic procedures that can be acquired without a therapist. Self-help books are found on a variety of techniques including behavioral, Gestalt, rational-emotive, transactional, and hypnotic procedures. In the 1970s, the "do-it-yourself" trend found its way into psychotherapy, resulting in numerous publications. References for books or pamphlets which address psychological problems and behavior change in general are listed under "self-help" in this glossary. Publications that address more specific problems are found under that glossary listing.

References

Glasgow, R.W. & Rosen, G.M. Behavioral bibliotherapy: A review of self-help behavior therapy manuals. *Psychological Bulletin*; 1978, *85*, 1-23.

BIOFEEDBACK

In biofeedback training, the client is provided with continuous information regarding the activity of a particular physiological parameter. Most often used are the electromyographic activity (electromyogram: EMG), the electroencephalographic rhythms (electroencephalogram: EEG), and the heart rate (electrocardiogram: EKG). In clinical biofeedback, the client characteristically attempts to change some physiological response in a direction thought to be beneficial. When used to teach muscle relaxation, EMG feedback is chosen. After carefully explaining the procedure, the therapist or technician, trains the client in 20-minute intervals either in a laboratory or, given the availability of portable equipment, in the practitioner's office. To facilitate transfer of training, clients are also often taught relaxation techniques that do not require electronic equipment. (See *Deep Muscle Relaxation*.)

References

Budzyniski, T.H., Stoyva, J.M., & Peffer, K.E. Biofeedback techniques in psychosomatic disorders. In Goldstein, A. & Foa, E.B. (Eds.), *Handbook of behavioral interventions*. New York: John Wiley & Sons, 1980.

Gardner, K.R. & Montgomery, S. *Clinical biofeedback: A procedural manual*, Baltimore: Williams & Wilkins, 1977.

BREATH CONTROL

The client is instructed in deep, diaphragmatic breathing. After exhaling, the next step is to inhale air while at the same time pushing the diaphragm down and out (making a big belly), thus providing enough space for the air to stream into the lungs. Then the air is released slowly while, at the same time, the abdomen is gradually pulled in. The client is instructed to count rhythmically during the exercise, and to spend an equal amount of time for inhalation and exhalation. Breath control is often used as an adjunct to or in place of other *relaxation techniques*. It is also a valuable part of *anxiety management* or *stress inoculation*.

References

Rawls, E.S. *A handbook of yoga*. New York: Pyramid Books, 1974.

COGNITIVE RESTRUCTURING

Cognitive or systematic rational restructuring is aimed at clarifying and changing client's thought patterns. Developed from Ellis's (1974) Rational Emotive Therapy, the goal is to help clients develop the ability to evaluate potentially upsetting events more realistically. There are several approaches to cognitive restructuring, all of which are very similar (Meichenbaum 1977). Goldfried and Goldfried (1980) use a four-step procedure to implement rational restructuring. First, the client learns to realize that cognitions mediate emotional arousal. Second, the client is taught to recognize the irrationality of certain beliefs. Examples of common distortions in self definition, self-defeating life goals/ideals, and irrational beliefs about other people and life in general are listed in Hammond and Stanfield (1981). Third, the client is helped to see how these unrealistic cognitions mediate maladaptive emotions. Finally, the client is taught to change these unrealistic cognitions. The client consciously and deliberately engages in doing something differently when feeling upset. The emotional response is taken as a cue to stop action and reappraise the situation. The intention is for a more realistic appraisal to lead to more adaptive emotional and behavioral responses.

References

Ellis, A. *Growth through reason* (2nd. ed.). Hollywood, Calif.: Wilshire Books, 1974.

Goldfried, M.R., & Goldfried, A.P. Cognitive
change methods. In F.H. Kanfer & A.P. Goldstein (Eds.), *Helping People Change* (2nd ed.).
New York: Pergamon Press, 1980.

Hammond, D.C., & Stanfield, K. *Multidimensional
psychotherapy: A counselors' guide for the
map form*. Champaign, Ill.: Institute for Personality and Ability Testing, 1977.

Meichenbaum, D.H. *Cognitive behavior modification*. New York: Plenum Press, 1977.

Tosi, D., & Moleski, R.L. Rational-emotive crisis
intervention therapy. *Rational Living*, 1975,
10, 32-37.

DECISION MAKING

Decision making is an important part in *prob-lem-solving training*, but can also be taught separately. Decision-making training teaches the client to evaluate various alternatives and to make a wise choice among them. The evaluation focuses on four types of consequences: (1) personal; (2) social; (3) overall short-term; (4) overall long-term. In addition, the client needs to evaluate the usefulness of the expected consequences. It is important to communicate to the client that it is impossible to forecast the future; consequently, the likelihood of any particular outcome can only be stated in general terms. Equally important is to help the client come to terms with the fact that for some problem situations there are no really "good" solutions, but that nevertheless one can choose a best option.

References

Goldfried, M.R., & Davison, G.C. *Clinical behavior
therapy*. New York: Holt, Rinehart & Winston,
1976, Chap. 9.

Simon, H.A. A behavioral model of rational choice.
Quarterly Journal of Economics, 1955, *69*,
99-118.

DEEP MUSCLE RELAXATION

This relaxation technique was developed by Jacobson (1974) and involves tension-relaxation contrast training. The client is instructed to alternate tensing and letting go of each major muscle area— hands, arms, chest, shoulders, upper back, lower back, abdomen, buttocks, thighs, calf muscles, feet, neck, throat, jaws, eyes, and forehead. *Total relaxation* usually is performed sitting in a reclining chair and including all muscle areas in a training session.

Differential relaxation can be practiced while performing other activities at the same time. Here the client deliberately relaxes those muscles which are not in use during an ongoing activity. For example, while typing a letter, a secretary can learn to deliberately let go of tension in her forehead. Usually, differential relaxation is taught after the client has mastered total muscle relaxation.

References

Bernstein, D.A., & Borkovec, T.D. *Progressive
relaxation training*. Champaign, Ill.: Research
Press, 1973.

Jacobson, E. *Progressive relaxation*. Chicago: University of Chicago Press, Midway Reprint, 1974.

DIET AND NUTRITION

The importance of a well-balanced diet for physical health and for psychological well-being has become a popular topic among professionals and their patients/ clients. This popularity is reflected in the increasing number of books on nutrition and the frequency with which diets are discussed in magazines and journals. The nutrients needed do not only depend on a person's anatomical and physiological characteristics, but also on psychological variables, such as the amount of stress experienced. Stress, for example, increases the amount of vitamins required (Davis 1970). Nutritional deficiencies can cause a vast array of psychological side effects, such as headaches, nausea, moodiness, and irritability (Thorn, Quinby, & Clinton 1943). There is a wide variety of books that are well written and valuable to use as an adjunct to individual counseling. Casale's (1975) diet food finder provides a review of more than 200 books on nutrition in general and on special diets and is a helpful guide to references for specific nutritional questions.

References

Casale, F.T. *The diet food finder*. New York: R.R. Bowker Company, 1975.

*Davis, A. *Let's eat right to keep fit*. (2nd ed.). New York: Signet, 1970.

Thorn, G.W., Quinby, J.T., & Clinton, M. A comparison of the metabolic effects of isocaloric meals of varying compositions with special reference to the prevention of postprandial hypoglycemic symptoms. *Annals of Internal Medicine*, XVIII, 1943, 913.

Williams, R.J. *Nutrition in a nutshell*. Garden City, N.Y.: Doubleday in Garden City, 1962.

EMPTY CHAIR

The empty chair, one of Fritz Perls (1969) Gestalt therapy techniques, is used to help clients clarify feelings, attitudes, and beliefs, and to reconcile (achieve closure) on conflicting polarities. The client is seated in a chair that is facing an empty chair. The client is encouraged to start a dialogue between the conflicting thoughts, feelings, etc., switching chairs for each side taken. The empty-chair technique can also be used to clarify relationships with other people. To do this, the client imagines another person in the empty chair and engages in a dialogue with this person, first speaking for himself/herself, then switching chairs and responding for the imaginal person.

References

*James, M., & Jongeward, D. *Born to win*. New York: Signet, 1978.

*Perls, F. *Gestalt therapy verbatim*. Lafayette, Calif.: Real People Press. 1969.

Perls, F., Hefferline, R.F., & Goodman, D. *Gestalt therapy*. New York: Dell Publishing Co., 1951.

ESTABLISHING A THERAPEUTIC RELATIONSHIP

Almost every approach to psychotherapy emphasizes the importance of the therapist-client relationship for client improvement. The better the relationship, the more likely it is that clients will be open and expressive about their feelings and the more likely they will listen to and accept the therapist's suggestions. In the literature, several variables have been discussed as enhancing the helping relationship. On the therapist's part, empathy, warmth, self-confidence, expertness, active participation, and the ability to convey hope are considered crucial (Frank 1961). Further, the client's expectations about the process and outcome of therapy need to be explored and incorporated into the treatment plan whenever possible. While it is impossible to design a "cookbook" on how to establish and maintain a good relationship with a client, several textbooks contain valuable suggestions regarding the components of desirable therapist behavior (e.g., Goldstein 1975).

Wolberg's (1967) list of behaviors to be avoided is important in crisis therapy: exclamations of surprise or over-concern; threats or criticisms; moralistic judgments; and ridiculing, belittling, or blaming the client for an experience.

References

Frank, J.D. *Persuasion and healing*. Baltimore: Johns Hopkins Press, 1961.

Goldstein, A.P. Relationship-enhancement methods. In F.H. Kanfer & A.P. Goldstein (Eds.), *Helping people change*. New York: Pergamon Press, 1975.

Wolberg, L.R. *The technique of psychotherapy*, (2nd. ed.), New York: Grune & Stratton, 1967.

FAMILY THERAPY

In its broadest sense, family therapy includes all therapeutic efforts aimed at changing the family as a group, rather than working with one family member only.[1] Historically, family therapy was developed primarily through work with severely disturbed individuals. There have been several charismatic leaders who each developed their own schools with specific intervention techniques and an effort toward theoretical integration [Jackson and Weakland (1961), Satir (1967), Haley (1971), Minuchin (1974), Whitaker (1975)]. A fairly recent development is the advent of behavioral family interventions, mostly rather specific skill-training programs [Patterson & Guilliom (1968), Becker (1971)]. With regard to crisis intervention with families, Kinney (1978) uses the homebuilders programs, Rueveni (1981) suggests *networking*, Eisler & Hersen (1973) recommend family *probelm-solving* training, and Langsley (1978) describes a multicomponent therapy approach including *problem solving*, negotiation, individual therapy, medication, and rehabilitation.

---

[1]*Marital therapy*, though a form of family therapy, is described in a separate paragraph below.

References

Becker, W.C. *Parents are teachers*. Champaign, Ill.: Research Press, 1971.

Eisler, M., & Hersen, M. Behavioral techniques in family oriented crisis intervention. *Archive of General Psychiatry*, 1973, *28*, 111-116.

Haley, F. *Changing families*. New York: Grune & Stratton, 1971.

Jackson, D., & Weakland, J. Conjoint family therapy: Some considerations on theory, technique and results. *Psychiatry*, 1961, *24*, 30-45.

Kinney, F. Homebuilders: An in-home crisis intervention program. *Children Today*, 1978, January-February, 15-35.

Langsley, D.G. Three models of family therapy: prevention, crisis treatment or rehabilitation. *The Journal of Clinical Psychiatry*, 1978, *39*, 792-796.

Minuchin, S. *Families and family therapy*. Cambridge, Mass.: Harvard University Press, 1974.

Patterson, G.R., & Guilliom, M.E. *Living with children: New methods for parents and teachers*. Champaign, Ill.: Research Press, 1968.

Rueveni, U. *Networking families in crisis: Intervention strategies with families and social networks*. New York: Human Sciences Press, 1979.

Satir, V. *Conjoint family therapy: A guide to theory and technique*. (Rev. Ed.). Palo Alto, Calif.: Science and Behavior Books, 1967.

Whitaker, C. A family therapist looks at marital therapy. In A. Gurman & D. Rice (Eds.), *Couples in conflicts: New directions in marital therapy*. New York: Axronson, 1975.

FEEDBACK

This term originated in cybernetics and when used in psychotherapy refers to providing the client with information about himself/herself on certain aspects of behavior.

Feedback can take many forms, such as praise, reward, verbal instructions, or video recording. Feedback enhances the effectiveness of and is used in various skills-training programs.

References

Edelstein, B.A., & Eisler, R.M. Effects of modeling and modeling with instructions and feedback on the behavioral components of social skills. *Behavior Therapy*, 1976, *7*, 382–389.

Hanson, P. The Johari window: A model for soliciting and giving feedback. In J.E. Jones and J.W. Pheiffer (Eds.), *The 1923 annual handbook for group facilitators*. La Jolla, CA.: University Associates Publishers, Inc., 1973.

References

Meichenbaum, D.H. *Cognitive behavior modification: An interpretive approach*. New York: Plenum Press, 1977.

Veronen, L.F., Kilpatrick, D.G., & Resick, P.A. Stress inoculation training for victims of rape. Paper presented at the workshop *The rape victim: Current issues in research and treatment*. Twelfth Annual Convention of the Association for Advancement of Behavior Therapy, Chicago, Ill., November 18, 1978.

GUIDED SELF-DIALOGUE

This technique builds cognitive coping skills. It was developed by Meichenbaum (1974) in conjunction with his *stress inoculation training*. When teaching guided self-dialogue as a coping strategy, the therapist first helps the client to focus on internal dialogue, or on self-statements the client thinks in problem situations. Client and therapist identify irrational, faulty, and self-defeating self-statements (I can never solve this problem) and task-enhancing statements are generated to replace the negative self-dialogue. When preparing for a problem situation, the client asks and answers questions that help to analyze the situation more rationally (What do I have to do here?). When dealing with the problem, the client covertly generates coping self-statements such as "take one step at a time"; "you can do it, you have managed similar problems before."

Another important group of self-statements involves the covert verbalization of self-praise [You had a plan and it worked, You did a pretty good job, (Veronen, Kilpatrick, & Resick 1978)]. Usually, the client first learns to rehearse the utilization of self-statements in the therapy session. As he/she acquires these skills, *homework assignments* are given using situations of gradually increasing difficulty.

HOMEWORK ASSIGNMENTS

Assigning particular tasks to be completed by the client between therapy sessions has long been used in psychotherapy (Herzberg 1945), but is especially popular in behavior-modification approaches. Homework is given to assist in *relaxation training, desensitization*, and *skill training*. It is hoped that such assignments contribute to an active role of the client in therapy, increased practice of behavior that is difficult for the client, and a better generalization from the success in the therapeutic setting to the client's natural environment. Homework assignments range from filling out behavioral observation charts (self and other) or questionnaires, monitoring thoughts, practicing new behaviors, to reading suggested literature (see also *bibliotherapy*). When giving homework, it is important to discuss the rationale with the client and to carefully plan the assignments in order to avoid resistance or failure experiences.

References

Herzberg, A. *Archive psychotherapy*. New York: Grune & Stratton, 1945.

Shelton, J.L., & Acherman, J.M. *Homework in counseling & psychotherapy*. Springfield, Ill.: Charles C. Thomas, 1974.

HOT SEAT   The hot seat is one of the two chair techniques (the other one is called *empty chair*) developed by Perls (1969). Perls uses the hot seat to perform individual therapy in a group setting, the hot seat being assigned to that client who is ready to work on a problem. Perls assumes that the presence of others increases the effectiveness of the client's self-revelations and induces social pressure to follow through with commitments to change. Oftentimes the hot seat is combined with the *empty chair*.

References

Fagan, F., & Shepherd, I.L. (Eds.), *Gestalt therapy now*. New York: Harper & Row, 1970.

Perls, F. *Gestalt therapy verbatim*. Lafayette, Calif.: Real People Press, 1969.

HYPNOSIS   While Eastern cultures have a long tradition in hypnotic techniques, especially those involving auto-suggestions (like meditation), hypnosis became accepted in Western countries only around 1800, when scientists in France (Mesmer) and Great Britain (Eisdale and Braid) began to study hypnotic phenomena. The usual hypnotic procedure begins with an induction, instructions designed to lead the client from a waking state into a trance state, in which the client is more receptive and has heightened suggestibility. The trance state is usually attained by instructing the client to gaze at an object, while the therapist repeats various suggestions (relaxation, tiring of the eyes, heightened awareness of sensations). The hypnotic state is deepened with further suggestions, and the client's awareness focuses more and more exclusively on the therapist's voice. Various strategies of inducing hypnosis have been developed (Kroger 1976). Examples for the clinical use of hypnosis include symptom removal and symptom substitution (Karlin & McKeon 1976), facilitation of awareness of unconcious material (Gill & Brenman 1959), and the control of pain (Hilgard & Hilgard 1975). As an adjunct in crisis therapy, Baldwin (1978) claims that hypnosis enhances the effect of nonhypnotic techniques because of a redistribution of attention, an increased availability of memories, a heightened ability for fantasy production and creativity, and an increase in suggestibility.

References

Baldwin, B.A. Crisis intervention and enhancement of adaptive coping using hypnosis. *The American Journal of Clinical Hypnosis*, 1978, *21*, 38-44.

Frankel, F.H., & Zamansky, H.S. (Eds.), *Hypnosis at its bicentennial: Selected papers*. New York: Plenum Press, 1978.

Gill, M.M., & Brenman, M. *Hypnosis and related states: Psychoanalytic studies in regression*. New York: International University Press, 1959.

Hilgard, E.R., & Hilgard, J.R. *Hypnosis in the relief of pain*. Los Altos, Ca.: William Kaufman, 1975.

Karlin, R.A., & McKeon, P. The use of hynposis in multimodal therapy. In A.A. Lazarus, *Multimodal behavior therapy*. New York: Springer, 1976.

Kroger, W.S. *Clinical and experimental hypnosis* (2nd. ed.). Philadelphia: J.B. Lippencott, 1976.

IMAGERY: COPING AND POSITIVE   Imagery in general refers to the mental picture or cognitive representation of personal experiences or situations. It can be utilized in therapy as a substitute for reproducing a real-life situation (e.g., fantasizing giving a speech to a large audience), as in *systematic desensization*. Homme (1965) and later Cautela (1971) and Kazdin (1976) are among the proponents who use the client's mental pictures in conjunction with other behavioral techniques.

When coping imagery is induced, the client is instructed to fantasize about being able to cope with a specific difficult situation. In other words, the client pictures himself/herself performing an activity that is very difficult or highly anxiety-producing.

Closely related to coping imagery is positive imagery, where the client fantasizes a positive self-image. In Suskind's (1970) idealized self-image technique, the client is asked to imagine some desirable change in her/his behavior and then is encouraged to actively superimpose this idealized self-image on the current self-image. The rationale for this procedure is the assumption that the new positive self-image serves as a basis for initiating new behaviors which are congruent with this new self-image.

References

Cautela, F.R. Covert extinction. *Behavior Therapy*, 1971, *2*, 192-200.

Ellis, A., & Abrahms, E. *Brief psychotherapy in medical and health practice*. New York: Springer, 1978.

Homme, L.E. Perspectives in psychology—XXIV control of coverants: the operants of the mind. *Psychological Record*, 1965, *15*, 501–511.

Kazdin, A.E. Assessment of imagery during covert modeling of assertive behavior. *Journal of Behavior Therapy and Experimental Psychiatry*, 1976, *7*, 213-219.

Singer, J.L. *Imagery and daydream methods in psychotherapy and behavior modification*. New York: Academic Press, 1974.

Susskind, D.F. The idealized self-image (ISI): A new technique in confidence training. *Behavior Therapy*, 1970, *1*, 538-541.

IMPLOSION (FLOODING)

Implosion was first developed by Stampfel (1966) and belongs to the category of anxiety-reduction techniques. It is based on the assumption that any fear can be extinguished by providing the client with the experience that an expected and highly feared outcome does not occur. Therefore, the fundamental task of the therapist is to repeatedly re-present, reinstate, or symbolically reproduce those situations to which the anxiety response has been conditioned. When creating an anxiety-producing situation, either in vivo or in the client's imagination, the therapist attempts to attain a maximal level of anxiety. When a high level of anxiety is experienced, the client is held at this level until a diminuation of the anxiety-eliciting value of the situation occurs. The same situation is presented again and again until it ceases to elicit anxiety. Variations of the situation are introduced to further generalization. Usually the client is given *homework assignments* to provide additional repetitions.

References

Levis, D.J. Implementing the technique of implosive therapy. In A. Goldstein, & E. Foa (Eds.), *Handbook of behavioral intervention*, New York: John Wiley & Sons, 1980.

Levis, D.J., & Hare, N.A. A review of the theoretical and rationale and empirical support for the extinction approach of implosive (flooding) therapy. In M. Hersen, M. Eisler, & P.M. Miller (Eds.). *Progress in behavior modification*. New York: Academic Press, 1977.

Stampfel, T.G. Implosive therapy. Part I: The Theory. In S.G. Armitage (Ed.), *Behavior modification techniques in the treatment of emotional disorders*. Battle Creek, Mich.: U.S. Veteran Administration, 1966.

INDUCED AFFECT   This technique aims at a release of emotions and is used with clients who have been victims in a traumatic event, such as assault or rape. After first being instructed to relax, the client is queried about the traumatic event and is asked to describe every detail about it. The therapist encourages the free expression of emotions and supports the client in clarifying the feelings associated with the event. This procedure helps the client to get in touch with the various emotions present at the time of the event, including those which have been forgotten or blocked out, and to accept and work through the feelings. (Kilpatrick & Veronen 1983).

References

Kilpatrick, D.G., & Veronen, L.J. Treatment for rape-related problems: Crisis intervention is not enough. In L.H. Cohen, W. Claiborn & G. Specter (Eds.), *Crisis intervention*. New York: Human Sciences Press, 1983.

INTERPERSONAL   Interpersonal (social)
SKILLS TRAINING   skills include a wide range of behaviors that are important whenever an individual interacts with other people. Examples of programs for enhancing social skills include training in *assertiveness*, communication, conversation (Galassi and Gallassi 1977), dating (Melmick 1973), job interviewing (Prazak 1969), fighting fair (Bach and Wyden 1970), self-disclosure, and others. The major techniques used are *modeling, role playing, role reversal, feedback, coaching, and homework exercises.*

References

Flowers, J.V., & Booraem, C.D. Simulation and role playing methods. In F.H. Kanfer & A.P.

Goldstein (Eds.), *Helping people change*. (2nd ed.). New York: Pergamon Press, 1980.

*Galassi, M.D., & Gallassi, J.P. *Assert yourself: How to be your own person* New York: Human Sciences Press, 1977.

Melmick, F.A. A comparison of replication techniques in the modification of minimal dating behavior. *Journal of Abnormal Psychology*, 1973, *81*, 51-59.

Prazak, J.A. Learning job-seeking interview skills. In J.D. Krumboltz & C.E. Thorsen (Eds.), *Behavioral counseling: Cases and techniques*. New York: Holt, Rinehart & Winston, 1969.

Quinsley, V.L., & Varney, G.W. Social skills game: A general method for the modeling and practice of adaptive behavior. *Behavior therapy*, 1977, *8*, 279-281.

MARITAL (COUPLE)   As in *family therapy*,
THERAPY   the field of marital or couple therapy is characterized by a wide range of theoretical orientations. Stahmann (1977) provides an overview of the major current forms of marital interventions. (1) In conjoint therapy, both partners are seen together by one therapist. (2) In tandem counseling, individual sessions are alternated, an approach that includes the treatment of individual problems. (3) A collaborative approach is used when both partners are seen individually and within the same time span, but have different therapists. (4) Concurrent therapy refers to an approach where both partners are seen by the same therapist, but in individual sessions. (5) In individual therapy, only one partner is in therapy, an approach that has been shown considerably less effective than the conjoint forms (Cookerly 1976). Influenced by social learning theory and sociological concepts, there has been a trend towards systematic and structured approaches in marital interventions, especially in behavioral marriage therapy. The general

goals are an increase in the rate of rewarding interactions, with a decrease of aversive exchanges; an improvement in concrete conflict resolution strategies and problem-solving skills; and better communication. Techniques involve training in communication (Gottman, Notarius, Gonso, & Markman 1979), contracting and negotiation (Weiss 1975) fighting fair (Bach & Wyden 1970), problem solving (Jacobson 1977), and conflict resolution (Harrell & Guerney 1976).

References

Bach, G.R., & Wyden, P. *The intimate enemy*. (20th ed.). New York: Hearst Publishing, 1970.

Cookerly, J.R. Evaluating different approaches to marriage counseling. In D.H.L. Olson (Ed.), *Treating Relationships*. Lake Mills, Ia.: Graphic, 1976.

Gottman, J., Notarius, C., Gonso, J., & Markman, H. *The couple's guide to communication* (4th ed.). Champaign, Ill.: Research Press, 1979.

Harrell, F., & Guerney, B. Training married couples in conflict negotiation skills. In D.H.L. Olson (Ed.), *Treating relationships*. Lake Mills, Ia.: Graphic, 1976.

Jacobson, N.S. Problem solving and contingency contracting in the treatment of marital discord. *Journal of Consulting and Clinical Psychology*, 1977, *45*, 92-100.

*Lederer, W.J., & Jackson, D.D. *Mirages of marriage*. New York: Norton, 1968.

Stahmann, R.F. Treatment forms for marital counseling. In R.F. Stahmann & W.J. Hiebert, *Counseling in marital and sexual problems*, Baltimore, Md.: Williams & Williams Co., 1977.

Weiss, R.L. Contracts, cognition, and change: A behavioral approach to marriage therapy. *Counseling Psychologist*, 1975, *5*, 15-26.

MASSAGE

Massage techniques are used to ease muscular tension. When performed skillfully, massage increases the blood circulation locally, releases muscle tension and reduces pain. The beneficial effects of massage can be augmented by *relaxation training* and *physical exercises* such as gymnastics or other sports.

References

Benjamin, B.E. *Are you tense? The Benjamin system of muscular therapy*. New York: Pantheon Books, 1978.

Downing, G. *The massage book*. New York: Bookworks/Random House, 1972.

MEDITATION (YOGA)

Various meditative techniques have been recommended for therapeutic purposes. They all have in common that the client is instructed to sit quietly and maintain concentration on a particular thought, word, or object. Meditation can be used as a relaxation technique, but often is included in yoga with a primarily religious focus, namely progressing toward a union with God. Meditation techniques are very similar to self-hypnosis techniques (in which the clients give suggestions to themselves).

An example of a meditation exercise is the candle concentration in which a burning candle is used as a fixation point. The client is instructed to look at the flame and to breathe rhythmically, then to close the eyes and try to retain the image of the candle. If the image fades, the client can reopen the eyes briefly and then close them again and continue imagining the flame. As the meditation progresses, the client contemplates the positive aspects of the light and imagines having the light within him/herself. The goal of meditation is to reach a state of relaxation, new harmony and peace with oneself through positive self-suggestions.

References

Coe, W. Expectations, hypnosis and suggestion in behavior change. In F.H. Kanfer & A.P. Goldstein, (Eds.), *Helping people change* (2nd ed.). New York: Pergamon Press, 1980.

Eliade, M. Yoga: Immortality and freedom. (2nd. ed.). New York: Bollingen, 1970.

*Rawls, E.S. *A handbook of yoga*. New York: Pyramid Book, 1974.

MODELING This technique is used to teach new behaviors, to increase the frequency of desirable behaviors, and to decrease fears. In the most simple form of modeling, the client is exposed to one or more individuals who demonstrate the target behavior. The model can be presented live, symbolically (video), or imagined (covert modeling).

Variations of this basic procedure are participant modeling (the client enacts the target behavior during the modeling sequence), guided modeling (during which the therapist provides direct help), and the combination of modeling with reinforcement of successful efforts. Practicing the target behavior is an important aspect in successful modeling. Consequently, apart from *behavior rehearsal* during the sessions, *homework assignments* are common.

References

Eisler, M., & Hersen, M. Behavioral techniques in family-oriented crisis intervention. *Archive of General Psychiatry*, 1973, *28*, 111-116.

Rimm, D.C., & Masters, F.C. *Behavior therapy* (2nd ed.). New York: Academic Press, 1979, Chap. 4.

NETWORKING Networking is a therapeutic approach which aims at mobilization of family and friendship support systems. The client's social network is brought together to join in a collaborative effort to solve a crisis. General goals for network intervention are to facilitate participation; to develop and encourage sharing of the problems and the exchange of opinions; to facilitate problem solving, especially when the efforts toward crisis resolution are at an impasse; and to assist in the development of temporary support groups.

References

Rueveni, U. *Networking families in crisis: Intervention strategies with families and social networks*. New York: Human Sciences Press, 1979.

PAIN CONTROL Similar to *stress inoculation* for *anxiety* or *anger*, pain control programs have been developed to teach the client to cope with expected, acute, or chronic pain. Most procedures are rather complex, containing informational aspects to influence the cognitive appraisal, *relaxation training* (*biofeedback*) to decrease tension associated with pain, and *cognitive restructuring* to foster coping with the discomfort.

References

Turk, D.C. Coping with pain: A review of cognitive control techniques. In M. Fenestein, L.B. Sacks, & I.D. Turkat (Eds.), *Psychological approaches to pain control*. New York: Wiley-Interscience, in press.

Turk, D.C., & Genest, M. Regulation of pain: The application of cognitive and behavioral techniques for prevention and remediation. In P.C. Kendall & S.D. Hollon (Eds.), *Cognitive behavioral interventions*. New York: Academic Press, 1979.

Turk, D.C., Meichenbaum, D., & Berman, W.H. Application of biofeedback in the regulation of pain: A critical review. *Psychological Bulletin*, 1979, *86*, 1322-1338.

PARADOXICAL TECHNIQUES

Paradoxical techniques were developed to overcome clients' resistance to change. Clinicians sometimes have to deal with clients who experience a basic conflict: on one hand they want to change, and on the other hand, they want to maintain their symptoms. While various theoretical explanations have been suggested, the most prominent theoretical statements have been made by family therapists working within a structural or systems theory framework (Watzlawick, Weakland, Fisch 1974; Haley 1975). The assumption is that the symptom serves the function of keeping the system in homeostasis. The main paradoxical techniques are redefinition, escalation or crisis induction by prescribing the symptom, and redirection. In redefinition, the problem is given a new meaning, usually a positive one. In symptom escalation (or massed practice), the client is encouraged to perform the undesired behavior frequently and on purpose. A related technique is crisis induction. Here the therapist agrees with the client's overdramatization of a problem, tells the client that he/she will never be completely well again, and that the only help a therapist can offer is to learn how to live with the problem. Finally, redirection is similar to symptom escalation except that the behavior is prescribed for a certain amount of time during the day or under certain circumstances only.

There is very little research on the effectiveness of paradoxical interventions or on circumstances under which they are appropriate. Generally, it is recommended to only use them when therapy is at an impasse, and to carefully plan them with regard to both timing and the way they are presented. Inexperienced therapists are usually discouraged from using these techniques.

References

Haley, J. Paradoxes in play, fantasy and psychotherapy. *Psychiatric Research Reports*, 1975, *2*, 52-58.

L'Abale, L., & Weeks, G. A bibliography of paradoxical methods in psychotherapy of family systems. In *Family Process*, 1978, *17*, 95-83.

Watzlawick, P., Weakland, F., & Fisch, R. *Change: Principles of problem formation and problem resolution*. New York: W.W. Norton, 1974.

PHYSICAL EXERCISE

The importance of physical fitness to mental health has been emphasized by clinicians of highly diverse theoretical backgrounds. Lazarus (1975) considers fitness training as a coping response, Solomon and Bumpus (1978) focus on the sense of mastery which is associated with physical performance, while Selye (1976) postulates that exercise provides a diversion from anxiety-producing cognitions. In a review of the impact of fitness training on mental health, Folkins and Sime (1981) concluded that fitness training leads to improvements in mood, self-concept, and work performance. Cooper (1968, 1970) offers concrete guidance on developing exercise programs around a wide range of activities, e.g., walking, jogging, cycling, swimming, handball, and many others.

References

*Cooper, K.H. *Aerobics*. New York: Bantam, 1968.

*Cooper, K.H. *The new aerobics*. New York: Bantam, 1970.

Folkins, C.H., & Sime, W.E. Physical fitness training and mental health. *American Psychologist*, 1981, *36*, 373-389.

Gomez, J. *How not to die young*. New York: Pocket Books, 1973.

Lazarus, R.S. A cognitively oriented psychologist looks at biofeedback. *American Psychologist*, 1975, *30*, 553-561.

Seyle, H. Stress and physical activity. *McGill Journal of Education*, 1976, *11*, 3-14.

Solomon, E.G., & Bumpus, A.K. The running meditation response: An adjunct to psychotherapy. *American Journal of Psychotherapy*, 1978, *32*, 583-592.

PROBLEM-SOLVING Problem-solving techniques have been developed within a skill building approach in psychotherapy. Rather than focusing solely on the presenting problem, the therapist teaches a set of more general coping skills which enable the client to deal with future problems more effectively. Problem-solving training is an important part of any crisis therapy since crisis presents a breakdown in coping, an impasse in problem solving. Problem-solving training expands the client's coping repertoire and thus contributes to growth. It also gives the client an active role in therapy which helps to counteract dependency tendencies. In general, problem-solving therapy encompasses five basic components: (1) During the general orientation, attitudes toward problems are explored and the client is helped to recognize that problematic situations are a normal aspect of living, that there are many ways to cope with problems, and that it is important to refrain from responding impulsively when faced with a problem. (2) During problem definition, the various aspects of a given problem situation are delineated in concrete and specific terms. (3) Once the problem is clearly defined, alternative solutions are generated using brainstorming. (4) The generated alternative solutions are then evaluated regarding their utility, weighing the positive aspects (gains) against the nega-

tive aspects (costs). (5) Finally, the client is encouraged to act on his/her decision and to evaluate the extent to which the problem situation was resolved. In case the problem has not been settled satisfactorily, the client is advised to go back to the problem definition stage and work through all the steps again. (D'Zurilla and Goldfried 1971).

References

D'Zurilla, T.J., & Goldfried, M.R. Problem solving and behavior modification. *Journal of Abnormal Psychology*, 1971, *78*, 197-226.

Goldfried, M.R. Psychotherapy as coping skill training. In M.J. Mahoney (Ed.), *Psychotherapy process: Current issues and future directions*. New York: Plenum Press, 1979.

Strickler, M., & Bonnefil, M. Crisis intervention and social casework: Similarities and differences in problem solving. In S. Nass, *Crisis intervention*. Dubuque, Ia.: Kendall/Hunt, 1977.

RATIONAL EMOTIVE THERAPY (RET) RET was developed by A. Ellis (1962) whose basic theory is that emotional arousal and maladaptive behavior are mediated by one's interpretation of situations. He states that there are several irrational beliefs, expectations, or assumptions with which many people in our culture tend to approach situations. Examples include that one needs to be loved and accepted by virtually everybody, that one should be thoroughly competent, adequate, and achieving in all possible respects, and many more. The more irrational beliefs a person holds, the more one can expect a mislabeling of situations, with subsequent emotional arousal and/or maladaptive behavior. RET can be summarized with the A - B - C - D - E paradigm (Ellis and Grieger 1977): The person is faced with an activating experience—A, triggering certain beliefs—B (a chain of thoughts), which are conceptualized as internal self-statements. Some of these beliefs are irrational. The consequences—C—are negative emotions and related behaviors. The rational emotive therapist disputes the irrational beliefs—D—by helping the client to critically examine the validity or rationality of the self-statements. Emphasis is placed on learning to discriminate between rational and irrational statements. Successful therapy results in elimination of irrational thoughts—E—with subsequent symptom relief.

Homework assignments are an important part of RET, including *bibliotherapy*, in vivo desensitization tasks, *cognitive restructuring* exercises and *coping imagery*.

References

Ellis, A. *Reason and emotion in psychotherapy.* New York: Lyle Stuart, 1962.

*Ellis, A. *How to master your fear of flying.* New York: Curtis Books, 1972.

*Ellis, A. *How to live with a neurotic* (Rev. ed.). New York: Crow Publishers, 1975.

*Ellis, A., & Harper, R.A. *A new guide to rational living.* Englewood/Cliffs, New York: Prentice-Hall, 1975.

Ellis, A., & Grieger, R. *Handbook of rational emotive therapy.* Berlin & New York: Springer-Verlag, 1977.

Tosi, D.J., & Moleski, R.L. Rational-emotive crisis intervention therapy. *Rational Living,* 1975, *10,* 32–37.

Trexler, L.D. A review of rational-emotive psychotherapy outcome studies. In J. Wolfe & E. Brand (Eds.), *Twenty Years of Rational Therapy.* New York: Institute for Rational Living, 1977.

ROLE PLAYING

Role playing has two meanings in psychotherapy: one, enacting the replication of a situation in the client's past; two, enacting a set of behaviors that are different from the client's usual behavior. However, these two variations of role playing are related. Often the enactment of a problematic situation serves as a starting point to teach the client new ways of dealing with this situation. Role playing can be used as an assessment technique to gain information beyond the client's verbal description (such as evaluating the client's social skills) and to teach new behavior. Role playing is a main ingredient in the various skill building programs.

References

Eisler, M., & Hersen, M. Behavioral techniques in family-oriented crisis intervention. *Archive of General Psychiatry,* 1973, *28,* 111–116.

Flowers, J.V., & Booraem, C.D. Simulation and role playing methods. In F.H. Kanfer & A.P. Goldstein: *Helping people change* (2nd. ed.). New York: Pergamon Press, 1980.

SELF-HELP

Efforts to promote behavior change that involve only minimal or no therapist contact are called self-help. Self-help programs can be followed by the individual client only, or they may involve participation in a group, where all group members suffer from the same problem and try to facilitate change by providing each other support.

Individual self-help (self-modification) programs have emerged predominantly from the behavior modification tradition (Tenor 1978) with Karen Horney's (1942) book on self-analysis representing an exception to this trend. Many self-help programs have been developed by clinicians or academicians, who disseminate their knowledge with self-help books. (See also *bibliotherapy*.) Self-help groups, on the other hand, have been developed when several individuals with similar problems decide to form a group where everybody can share their problems and where all participants work together toward solutions. The list of self-help groups is endless, including "Alcoholics Anonymous (AA)," "Take Pounds off Sensibly (TOPS)," "Parents without Partners," and many others. Several books have been published to provide guidelines for self-help groups (such as Orbach 1976).

References

Horney, K. *Self-analysis*. New York: Norton, 1942.

Orbach, S. *Fat is a feminist issue* (2nd. ed.). New York: Paddington Press, 1978.

Tenor, D. *Super self: A woman's guide to self-management*. New York: Jovel HBJ, 1978.

*Watson, D.L., & Tharp, R.G. Self-directed behavior: Self-modification for personal adjustment. Monterey, Calif.: Brooks/Cole, 1972.

Self-Help Books: Individual Approaches:

Atkin, E., & Rubin, E. *Part-time father*, New York: Signet Edition, 1977.

Baer, F. *The second wife: How to live happily with a man who has been married before*. New York: Doubleday, 1972.

Barnes, E. *What do you say after you say hello?* New York: Grove Press, 1972.

Colgrove, M., Bloomfield, K.K., & McWilliams, P. *How to survive the loss of love*. New York: Bantam Books, 1976.

Ellis, A. *How to live with and without anger*. New York: Readers Digest Press, 1977.

Gardner, R. *The boys and girls book about divorce, with an introduction for parents*. New York: Bantam. 1971.

Lazarus, A.A., & Fay, A. *I can do it if I want to*. New York: William Morrow & Co., 1975.

Roosevelt, R., & Lofas F. *Living in step*. New York: Stein and Day, 1976.

Satir, V. *People making*. Palo Alto, Calif.: Science and Behavior Books, 1972.

Selye, H. *Stress without distress*. New York: Signet, 1974.

Tay, A. *Making things better by making them worse*. New York: Hawthorne, 1978.

Wolfolk, R., & Richardson, F. *Stress, sanity and survival*. New York: Simon & Schuster, 1978.

STRESS INOCULATION TRAINING

Originally, stress inoculation was proposed for the treatment of anxiety (Meichenbaum 1975) though later was expanded to *anger* and *pain*. It is a coping-skills approach enhancing the client's ability to respond to stressful situations with less disturbing emotions and a higher level of behavioral adaptation. Treatment incorporates three phases: cognitive preparation, skill acquisition, and application training. The underlying rationale for a coping approach to such stressors as fears, pain, or anger is that they are unavoidable aspects of life which must be managed and, as a result of the training, these stressors become ones that trigger the newly acquired coping responses.

References

Meichenbaum, D. A self-instructional approach to stress management: A proposal for stress inoculation training. In C. Spielberger & I. Sarason (Eds.), *Stress & anxiety*, Vol. 2, New York: Wiley, 1975.

Veronen, L.F., Kilpatrick, D.G., & Resick, P.A. *Stress inoculation training for victims of rape*. Paper presented at the workshop "The rape victim: Current issues in research and treatment." 12th Annual Convention of the Association for Advancement of Behavior Therapy, Chicago, Ill., November 18, 1978.

SYSTEMATIC DESENSITIZATION

This anxiety reduction technique was first developed by Salter (1949) and Wolpe (1958). It is based on the assumption that a fear response can be inhibited by substituting an activity which is antagonistic to the fear response. Desensitization entails exposing the client to a hierarchy of aversive situations while the client is performing an activity that is incompatible with anxiety. To counter-condition the fear response, most often relaxation is used in which case *relaxation training* prior to the desensitization program is implemented. The gradual exposure to the feared situation can be performed in the person's fantasy—using imagination, or in real life—in vivo. Usually, the procedure is started with a fairly nonthreatening situation and when this has been mastered and does not evoke anxiety any more, training progresses to a more threatening level. The client is encouraged to practice the newly learned response in his/her natural environment to provide further exposure and to ensure generalization from the therapist's office to everyday life.

In *contact desensitization* (Bandura 1969), the client can observe a model, not necessarily the therapist, approaching and mastering the feared situation. *Emotive imagery* (Lazarus and Abramovitz 1962) is an attempt to adapt desensitization proper to children. Here anxiety inhibiting images, such as being a hero or being together in an adventure with a hero, are elicited by telling the child an anxiety story. Gradually, the feared situations or events are woven into the story until the child has mastered all items of the hierarchy. Systematic desensitization can be combined with *positive imagery, coping imagery,* and *self-statements.*

References

Bandura, A. *Principles of behavior modification.* New York: Holt, Rinehart & Winston, 1969.
Lazarus, A.A., & Abramovitz, A. *Learn to relax.*

A recorded course in muscular relaxation. Johannesburg: Troubadour Records, 1962.
Salter, A. *Conditioned reflex therapy.* New York: Creative Age, 1949.
Wilkins, W. Desensitization: Social & cognitive factors underlying the effectiveness of Wolpe's procedure. *Psychological Bulletin,* 1971, *76,* 311–317.
Wolpe, F. *Psychotherapy by reciprocal inhibition.* Stanford: Stanford University Press, 1958.

THOUGHT STOPPING

As its name implies, this technique aims at terminating unwanted cognitions, such as ruminations, self-defeating thoughts, fear-evoking thoughts (Wolpe 1958). The client is asked to intentionally think about the undesired cognition. When the client indicates being deeply immersed in the cognition, the therapist shouts "stop." Often this produces a startle response which may interrupt the undesired thought. Using this experience as a rationale, the client then is instructed to practice thought-stopping as a rationale, and the client then is instructed to practice thought-stopping himself/herself. Initially, the client is told to exclaim the "stop" command, but eventually the self-presented signal is to be given covertly.

References

Mahoney, M.J. *Cognition and behavior modification.* Cambridge, Mass.: Ballinger, 1974.
Rimm, D.C. Thought stopping and covert assertion in the treatment of phobias. *Journal of Consulting and Clinical Psychology,* 1973, *41,* 466–467.
Wolpe, J. *Psychotherapy by reciprocal inhibition,* Stanford, Calif.: Stanford University Press, 1958.

YOGA For some, yoga is a belief system with the purpose of achieving a final trance state to obtain union with a universal self, or God (Devi 1963), while others use its auto suggestive exercises for relaxation. Hatha Yoga emphasizes relaxation postures and breathing and can be practiced daily.

References

Devi, I. *Renew your life through yoga*, Englewood Cliffs, N.J.: Prentice-Hall, 1963.

Eliade, M. Yoga. *Immortality and freedom*, Princeton, N.J.: Princeton University Press, 1969.

*Rawls, E.S. *A handbook of yoga*. New York: Pyramid Books, 1964.

*Yesudian, S. *Yoga week by week*. New York: Harper and Row, 1975.

References

Abarbanel, G. Helping victims of rape. *Social Work*, 1976, *21*, 478–482.

Abram, H.C. Survival by machine: The psychological stress of chronic hemodialysis. *International Journal of Psychiatry in Medicine*, 1970, *1*, 37–51.

ACOG: Technical bulletin number 14. The American College of Obstetricians and Gynecologists, July, 1970.

Adelman, C.S. Psychological intervention into the crisis of rape. In Viano, E.C., *Victims and society*, Washington, D.C.: Visage, 1976.

Aguilera, D.C., Messick, J.M., & Farrell, M.S. *Crisis intervention: Theory and methodology*. St. Louis, Missouri: C.V. Mosby, 1974.

Alberti, R. & Emmons, M.L. *Your perfect right; a guide to assertive behavior*. San Luis Obispo, Calif.: Impact, 1970.

Albrecht, G.L., & Higgins, P.C. Rehabilitation success: The interrelationships of multiple criteria. *Journal of Health and Social Behavior*, 1977, *18*, 36–45.

Alger, I. Family therapeutic approaches to the medically ill patient. In T.B. Karasu & R.I. Steinmuller (Eds.), *Psychotherapeutics in medicine*. New York: Grune and Stratton, 1978.

Amdur, M.A. (Ed.), & Tuder, E.N. Observations of psychiatric consultation in emergency room settings. *Psychosomatics*, 1975, *16*, 73–76.

Andrew, J.M. Recovery from surgery, with and without preparatory instruction, for three coping styles. *Journal of Personality and Social Psychology*, 1970, *15*, 223–226.

Argyle, M. *The social psychology of work*. New York: Taplinger, 1972.

Armstrong, B. Court sets standard of imminent danger. *APA Monitor*, July/August, 1980, 16.

Atkin, E., & Rubin, E. *Part-time father*. New York: Signet Edition, 1977.

Auerbach, S.M., & Kilmann, P.R. Crisis intervention: A review of outcome research. *Psychological Bulletin*, 1977, *84*, 1189–1217.

Bach, G.R., & Wyden, P. *The intimate enemy* (20th ed.). New York: Hearst Corp., 1970.

Baer, F. *The second wife: How to live happily with a man who has been married before*. New York: Doubleday, 1972.

Bahnson, C.B. Psychologic and emotional issues in cancer: The psychotherapeutic care of the cancer patient. *Seminars in Oncology*, 1975, *4*, 293–308.

Bahr, L.F. *Family crisis: The effect of the diagnosis of a defective child upon the family unit*. Unpublished manuscript, University of South Carolina, 1980.

Baker, G.W., & Chapman, C.W. (Eds.). *Man and society in disaster*. New York: Basic Books, 1962.

Baldwin, B.A. Crisis intervention: An overview of theory and practice. *The Counseling Psychologist*, 1979, *8*, 43–52.

Baldwin, B.A. Crisis intervention and enhancement of adaptive coping using hypnosis. *The American Journal of Clinical Hypnosis*, 1978, *21*, 38–44.

Bandura, A. *Principles of behavior modification*. New York: Holt, Rinehart, and Winston, Inc., 1969.

Bard, M. *Training police as specialists in family crisis intervention*. Washington, D.C.: National Institute of Law Enforcement and Criminal Justice, 1970.

Bard, M., & Berkowitz, B. A community psychology consultation program in police family crisis intervention: Preliminary impressions. *International Journal of Social Psychiatry*, 1969, *15*, 209–215.

Barnes, E. *What do you say after you say hello*? New York: Grove Press, 1972.

Bart, P.B. Rape doesn't end with a kiss. *Viva*, 1975, June 41–42.

Bartolucci, G., & Drayer, C.S. An overview of crisis intervention in the emergency rooms of general hospitals. *American Journal of Psychiatry*, 1973, *130*, 953–960.

Barton, D. The need for including instruction on death and dying in the medical curriculum. *Journal of Medical Education*, 1972, *47*, 169–175.

Barton, D., Flexner, J., Van Eys, J., & Scott, C.E. Death and dying: A course for medical students. *Journal of Medical Education*, 1972, *47*, 495–951.

Bassuk, E.L., & Gerson, S. Into the breach: Emergency psychiatry in the general hospital. *General Hospital Psychiatry*, 1979, *1*, 31–45.

Bauer, S., & Balter, L. Emergency psychiatric patients in a municipal hospital: *Psychiatric Quarterly*, 1971, *45*, 382–393.

Baum, A., Lake, C.R., Gatchel, R.J., Baum, C.S., & Streufert, S. *Chronic stress at Three Mile Island: Self report, behavioral, and biochemical evidence*. Unpublished manuscript, Uniformed Services University of the Health Sciences, Bethesda, Maryland, 1982.

Bazeley, P., & Viney, L.L. Women coping with crisis: A preliminary community study. *Journal of Community Psychology*, 1974, *2*, 321–329.

Beahan, L. Emergency mental health services in a general hospital. *Hospital and Community Psychiatry*, 1970, *21*, 81–84.

Beck, A.T. Cognition, affect, and psychopathology. *Archives of General Psychiatry*, 1971, *24*, 495–500.

Beck, A.T. *Cognitive therapy and the emotional disorders*. New York: International University Press, 1976.

Beck, A.T. *Depression: Clinical, experimental, and theoretical aspects*. New York: Harper & Row, 1967.

Beck, A.T. Role of fantasies in psychotherapy and psychopathology. *Journal of Nervous and Mental Disease*, 1970, *150*, 3–17.

Beck, A.T., Resnik, H.L.P., & Lettieri, D.J. *The prediction of suicide*. Bowie, Md.: The Charles Press Publishers, Inc. 1974.

Becker, W.C. *Parents are teachers*. Champaign, Ill.: Research Press, 1971.

Becker, J.V., Abel, G.G., & Skinner, L.J. The impact of a sexual assault on the victim's sexual life. *Victimology*, 1979, *4*, 229–235.

Beigel, A., & Russell, H.E. Suicidal behavior in jail-prognostic considerations. *Hospital and Community Psychiatry*, 1972, *23*, 361–363.

Beisser, A.R. Denial and affirmation in illness and health. *American Journal of Psychiatry*, 1979, *136*, 1020–1030.

Belfer, M.L., Mulliken, J.B., & Cochran, T.C. Cosmetic surgery as an antecedent of life change. *American Journal of Psychiatry*, 1979, *136*, 199–201.

Bell, L.H. *Community mental health: A black perspective*. Unpublished manuscript, 1977.

Belsky, J. Child maltreatment: An ecological integration. *American Psychologist*, 1980, *35*(4), 320–335.

Benjamin, A. *The helping interview* (3rd ed.). Boston: Houghton Mifflin, 1981.

Benjamin, B.E. *Are you tense? The Benjamin system of muscular therapy*. New York: Pantheon Books, 1978.

Berg, D. Crisis intervention concepts for emergency telephone services. *Crisis Intervention*, 1970, *4*, 11–19.

von Bertalanffy, L. *General system theory: Foundations, development, applications*. New York: George Braziller, 1968.

Bernstein, B.E. Lawyer and counselor as an interdisciplinary team: Interfacing for the terminally ill. *Death Education*, 1977a, *1*, 277–291.

Bernstein, B.E. Lawyer and counselor as an interdisciplinary team: Premarital counseling. *Family Coordinator*, 1977b, *26*, 415–420.

Bernstein, D.A., & Borkovec, T.D. *Progressive relaxation training*. Champaign, Ill.: Research Press, 1973.

Berrien, F.K. *General and social systems*. New Brunswick, N.J.: Rutgers University Press, 1968.

Bersoff, D.N. Therapists as protectors and policemen: New roles as a result of Tarasoff. *Professional Psychology*, 1976, *7*, 267–273.

Bessel, H., & Palomares, U.H. *Human development program*. Los Angeles: Vulcan Binders, 1969.

Binder, D.A., & Price, S.C. *Legal interviewing and counseling*. St. Paul: West Publishing Co., 1977.

Birnbaum, F., Coplon, J., & Scharff, I. Crisis intervention after a natural disaster. In R.H. Moos (Ed.), *Human adaptation: Coping with life crises*. Lexington, Mass.: D.C. Heath, 1976.

Blackburn, H. The potential for preventing reinfarction. In W.K. Wenger & H.K. Hellerstein (Eds.), *Rehabilitation of the coronary patient*. New York: John Wiley & Sons, 1978.

Blakesley, J. Personal communication. *South Carolina Educational Television:* 1980.

Blane, H., Muller, J., and Chafetz, M. Acute psychiatric services in the general hospital, II. Current states of emergency psychiatric services. *American Journal of Psychiatry*, 1967, *124*, 37–45.

Blanton, J. Self-study of family crisis intervention in a police unit. *Professional Psychology*, 1976, *7*(1), 61–67.

Bleach, G., & Claiborne, W.L. Initial evaluation of hotline telephone crisis centers. *Community Mental Health Journal*, 1974, *10*, 387–394.

Blizzard, S. The minister's dilemma. *The Christian Century*, April 25, 1956.

Bloch, A.M. Combat neurosis in inner-city schools. *American Journal of Psychiatry*, 1978, *135*, 1189–1192.

Bloom, B.L. *Community mental health: A general introduction.* Monterey, Calif: Brooks/Cole Publishing Company, 1977.

Bloom, N.D., & Lynch, J.G. Group work in a hospital waiting room. *Health and Social Work*, 1979, *4*, 48–63.

Blumberg, B.D. Psychological sequelae of elective abortion. *Western Journal of Medicine*, 1975, *123*, 188–193.

Blumenthal, D., Tulkin, S.R., & Slaikeu, K.A. Analysis of temporal variables in telephone calls to a suicide and crisis service: A comparison of clients who show for appointments and those who do not show. *Psychotherapy: Therapy, Research and Practice*, 1976, *13*, 177–182.

Boekelheide, P.D. The diagnostic therapeutic preabortion interview. *Journal of the American College Health Association*, 1978, *27*, 157–160.

Bohannan, P. (Ed.). *Divorce and after.* New York: Doubleday, 1970.

Boisen, A. *The exploration of the inner world.* New York: Harper and Brothers, 1936.

Borgman, R., Edmunds, M., & MacDicken, R.A. *Crisis intervention: A manual for child protective workers.* United States Department of Health, Education and Welfare, DHEW Publication No. (OHDS) 79–30196. 1979.

Bosch, A. *AFL-CIO*, Washington D.C., Personal communication. 1979.

Bower, E.M. The modification, mediation, and utilization of stress during the school years. *American Journal of Orthopsychiatry*, 1964, *34*, 667–674.

Bower, E.M. Primary prevention of mental and emotional disorders: A frame of reference. In N. Lambert (Ed.), *The protection and promotion of mental health in schools.* (Mental Health Monograph #5). Washington, D.C.: United States Government Printing Office, 1965.

Bozzetti, L.P., & Kane, T.J. Drug over-use and the emergency room, some methodological considerations relating to follow-up care. *Drug Forum*, 1977–78, *6*, 349–360.

Brekke, M.L., Strommen, M.P., & Williams, D.L. *Ten faces of ministry.* Minneapolis: Augesburge Publishing House, 1979.

Brim, O.G. Theories of the male mid-life crisis. In K. Schlossberg and D. Entine (Eds.), *Counseling Adults*. Monterey, Calif.: Brooks/Cole, 1977.

Brodsky, C.M. Clergyman as psychotherapists: Problems in interrole communication. *Community Mental Health Journal*, 1968, *4*, 482–491.

Brodsky, L. Anger provocation as a crisis intervention technique. *Hospital & Community Psychology*, 1977, *28*, 533–536.

Bronfenbrenner, U. *The ecology of human development: Experiments by nature and design*. Cambridge, Massachusetts: Harvard University Press, 1979.

Brophy, J.E. *Child development and socialization*. Chicago: Science Research Associates, Inc., 1977.

Broussard, W.J., & DeLargey, R.J. The dynamics of the group outplacement workshop. *Personnel Journal*, 1979, *58*, 855–857.

Brown, A., & Stickgold, A. Marijuana flashback phenomena. *Journal of Psychedelic Drugs*, 1976, *8*, 275–283.

Brown, H.F., Crisis intervention treatment in child abuse programs. *Social Casework*, 1979, *60*(7), 430–433.

Brown, H.F., Burditt, V.B., & Liddell C.W. The crisis of relocation. In H.J. Parad (Ed.), *Crisis intervention: Selected readings*. New York: Family Service Association of America, 1965.

Bryant, E.H. Teacher in crisis: A classmate is dying. *Elementary School Journal*, 1978, *78*, 233–241.

Bryant, E.H., & Caplan, G. Opportunities for school psychologists in the primary prevention of mental disorders in children. In N. Lambert (Ed.), *The protection and promotion of mental health in schools*. (Mental Health Monograph #5). Washington D.C.: United States Government Printing Office, 1965.

Buckley, W. (Ed.). *Modern systems research for the behavioral scientist*. Chicago: Aldine Publishing Co., 1968.

Budzyniski, T.H., Stoyva, J.M., & Peffer, K.E. Biofeedback Techniques in Psychosomatic Disorders. In A. Goldstein & E.B. Foa (Eds.), *Handbook of behavioral interventions*, New York: John Wiley & Sons, 1980.

Buhler, C. Genetic aspects of the self. *Annals of New York Academy of Sciences*, 1962, *96*, 730–764.

Bunn, T.A., & Clarke, A.M. Crisis intervention: An experimental study of the effects of a brief period of counseling on the anxiety of relatives of seriously injured or ill hospital patients. *British Journal of Medical Psychology*, 1979, *52*, 191–195.

Burchfield, S.R. The stress response: A new perspective. *Psychosomatic Medicine*, 1979, *41*, 661–672.

Burgess, A.W. & Baldwin, B.A. *Crisis intervention theory and practice, a clinical handbook*. Englewood Cliffs, New Jersey: Prentice-Hall, Inc., 1981.

Burgess, A.W., & Holmstrom, L.L. Rape: Sexual disruption and recovery. *American Journal of Orthopsychiatry*, 1979, *49*, 648–657.

Burgess, A.W., & Holmstrom, L.L. Crisis and counseling requests of rape victims. *Nursing Research*, 1974a, *23*, 196–202.

Burgess, A.W., & Holmstrom, L.L. *Rape: Victims of crisis.* Bowie, Md.: R.J. Brady Co., 1974b.

Burgess, A.W., & Holmstrom, L.L. The rape victim in the emergency ward: *American Journal of Nursing*, 1973, *73*, 1740–1745.

Burgess, A.W., & Johansen, P.N. Assault: Patterns of emergency visits: *Journal of Psychiatric Nursing and Mental Health Services*, 1976, *14*, 32–36.

Burnett, B.B., Carr, J.J., Sinapi, J., & Taylor, R. Police and social workers in a community outreach program. *Social Casework*, 1976, *57*(1), 41–49.

Burnside, I.M. Crisis intervention with geriatric hospitalized patients. *Journal of Psychiatric Nursing and Mental Health Services*, 1970, *8*, 17–20.

Butcher, J.N. The role of crisis intervention in an airport disaster. *Aviation, Space, and Environmental Medicine*, November, 1980, 1260–1262.

Butcher, J.N., & Koss, M.P. Research on brief and crisis oriented psychotherapies. In S.L. Garfield & A. Bergin (Eds.), *Handbook of psychotherapy and behavior change: An empirical analysis* (2nd ed.). New York: John Wiley & Sons, 1978, 725–768.

Butcher, J.N., & Maudal, G.R. Crisis intervention. In I. Weiner (Ed.), *Clinical methods in psychology*. New York: Wiley Interscience, 1976.

Byrne, D.G., & Whyte, H.M. Dimensions of illness behavior in survivors of myocardial infarction. *Journal of Psychosomatic Research*, 1978, *22*, 485–491.

Byrne, D.G., & Whyte, H.M. Severity of illness and illness behavior: A comparative study of coronary care patients. *Journal of Psychosomatic Research*, 1979, *23*, 57–61.

Cairnes, N.U., Lansky, S.B., & Klopovich, P. Meeting the educational needs of children with cancer. *The National Cancer Institute*, United States Department of Health, Education and Welfare.

Campbell, T.J., & Alander, R.P. An evaluative study of an alcohol and drug recovery program. *Human Resource Management*, 1975, *14*, 16–18.

Cantor, D.W. School-based groups for children of divorce. *Journal of Divorce*, 1977, *1*, 183–187.

Caplan, F. (Ed.). *The first twelve months of life: Your baby's growth month by month*. New York: Grosset & Dunlap, 1973.

Caplan, G. Patterns of parental response to the crisis of premature birth. *Psychiatry*, 1960, *23*, 365–374.

Caplan, G. *An approach to community mental health*. New York: Grune & Stratton, 1961.

Caplan, G. *Principles of preventive psychiatry*. New York: Basic Books, Inc., 1964.

Caplan, G. (Ed.). *Prevention of mental disorders in children*. New York: Basic Books, 1967.

Caplan, G. *Support systems and community mental health*. New York: Behavioral Publications, Inc., 1976.

Capone, M.A., Westie, K.S., Chitwood, J.S., Feigenbaum, D., & Good, R.S. Crisis intervention: A functional model for hospitalized cancer patients. *American Journal of Orthopsychiatry*, 1979, *49*, 598–607.

Carey, A. Helping the child and the family cope with death. *International Journal of Family Counseling*, 1977, *5*, 58–63.

Carkhuff, R.F. *Helping and human relations*. New York: Holt, Rinehart & Winston, 1969.

Casale, F.T. *The diet food finder*. New York: R.R. Bowker Company, 1975.

Cath, S.H. Some dynamics of the middle and later years. In H.J. Parad (Ed.), *Crisis intervention: Selected readings*. New York: Family Service Association of America, 1965.

Cautela, F.R. Covert extinction. *Behavior Therapy*, 1971, *2*, 192–200.

Cesnik, B.I., Pierce, N., & Puls, M. Law enforcement and crisis intervention services: A critical relationship. *Suicide and Life-Threatening Behavior*, 1977, *7*(4), 211–215.

Chafetz, M. Research in the alcohol clinic and around-the-clock psychiatric service at the Massachusetts General Hospital. *American Journal of Psychiatry*, 1968, *124*, 1974–1979.

Clinebell, H.J. *Basic types of pastoral counseling*. Nashville: Abington, 1966.

Cochrane, C.T., & Myers, D.V. *Children in crisis: A time for caring, a time for change*. Beverly Hills: Sage Publications, 1980.

Coe, W. Expectations, hypnosis and suggestion in behavior change. In F.H. Kanfer, A.P. Goldstein, *Helping people change* (2nd ed.). Elmsford, N.Y.: Pergamon Press, 1980.

Cohen, M.M., & Wellisch, D.K. Living in limbo: Psychosocial intervention in families with a cancer patient. *American Journal of Psychotherapy*, 1978, *32*, 561–571.

Cohen, R.E. & Ahearn, F.L. *Handbook for mental health care of disaster victims*. Baltimore, Md.: The Johns Hopkins University Press, 1980.

Cohen, R.N. Tarasoff vs. Regents of the University of California. The duty to warn: Common law and statutory problems for California psychotherapists. *California Western Law Review*, 1978, *14*, 153–182.

Cohen, S. Flashbacks. *Drug Abuse and Alcoholism Newsletter*, 1977, *6*, 1–4.

Cohen S., & Lazarus, R.S. Active coping processes, coping dispositions, and recovery from surgery. *Psychosomatic Medicine*, 1973, *35*, 375–389.

Colgrove, M., Bloomfield, K.K., & McWilliams, P. *How to survive the loss of love*. New York: Bantam Books, 1976.

Company Help for the Laid-off. *Business Week*, February 4, 1980, 88–89.

Conger, J. *Adolescence: Generation under pressure*. New York: Harper & Row, 1979.

Conroe, R.M., Cassata, D.M. & Racer, H.J. A systematic approach and brief psychological intervention in the primary care setting. *The Journal of Family Practice*, 1978, *7*, 1137–1142.

Coogler, O.J. *Structured mediation in divorce settlement: A handbook for marital mediators*. Lexington, Mass.: D.C. Heath, 1978.

Cookerly, J.R. Evaluating different approaches to marriage counseling. In D.H.L. Olson (Ed.), *Treating relationships*. Lake Mills, Ia.: Graphic, 1976.

Cooper, K.H. *Aerobics*. New York: Bantam, 1968.

Cooper, K.H. *The new aerobics*. New York: Bantam, 1970.

Cousins, N. *Anatomy of an illness as perceived by the patient: Reflections on healing and regeneration*. New York: W.W. Norton, Inc., 1979.

Cowen, E.L., Trost, M.A., Lorion, R.P., & Dorr, D. *New ways in school mental health*. New York: Human Sciences Press, 1975.

Craig, T., Huffine, C., & Brooks, M. Completion of referral to psychiatric services by inner-city residents. *Archives of General Psychiatry*, 1974, *31*, 353–357.

Crime in the United States, 1979: FBI Uniform Crime Reports. Superintendent of Documents, United States Government Printing Office, Washington, D.C., 20402.

Croog, S.H. Social aspects of rehabilitation after myocardial infarction: A selective review. In N.K. Wenger & H.K. Hellerstein (Eds.), *Rehabilitation of the coronary patient*. New York: Wiley, 1978.

Croog, S.H., & Levin, S. *The heart patient recovers: Social and psychological factors*. New York: Human Sciences Press, 1977.

Crow, G.A. *Crisis intervention: A social interaction approach*. New York: Association Press, 1977.

Crowder, J.E., Yamamoto, J., & Simonowitz, J. Training registered nurses as bereavement counselors in an occupational health service. *Hospital and Community Psychiatry*, 1976, *27*, 851–852.

Crupie, J.E. Psychiatric syndromes and other problems in critical care units. *Journal of the Tennessee Medical Association*, 1976, *69*, 851–854.

Cummings, N.A. Prolonged (ideal) versus short term (realistic) psychotherapy. *Professional Psychology*, 1977, *8*, 491–501.

Danish, S.J. Human development and human services: A marriage proposal. In I. Iscoe, B.L. Bloom & C.C. Spielberger (Eds.), *Community psychology in transition*. New York: Halstead, 1977.

Danish, S.J., & D'Augelli, A.R. Promoting competence and enhancing development through life development intervention. In L.A. Bond & J.C. Rosen (Eds.), *Competence and coping during adulthood*. Hanover, New Hampshire: University Press of New England, 1980.

Danish, S.J., Smyer, M.A., & Nowak, C.A. Developmental intervention: Enhancing life-event processes. In P.B. Baltes & O.G. Brim, Jr. (Eds.), *Life span development and behavior* (Vol. 3). New York: Academic Press, 1980.

Danto, B.L. Crisis intervention in a classroom regarding the homicide of a teacher. *The School Counselor*, 1978, *26*.

Datan, N., & Ginsberg, L.H. (Eds.). *Life-span developmental psychology: Normative life crises.* New York: Academic Press, 1975.

D'Augelli, A.R., Handis, M.H., Brumbaugh, L., Illig, V., Searer, R., Turner, D.W., & D'Augelli, J.F. The verbal helping behavior of experienced and novice telephone counselors. *Journal of Community Psychology*, 1978, *6*, 222–228.

David, D.J., & Barrit, J.A. Psychosocial aspects of head and neck cancer surgery. *Australian and New Zealand Journal of Surgery*, 1977, *47*, 584–589.

Davidson, S. The clinical effects of massive psychic trauma in families of holocaust survivors. *Journal of Marital and Family Therapy*, 1980, *6*, 11–21.

*Davis, A. *Let's eat right to keep fit* (2nd ed.). New York: Signet, 1970.

Defrain, J.D., & Ernst, L. The psychological effects of sudden infant death syndrome on surviving family members. *Journal of Family Practice.* 1978, *6*, 985–989.

DeLong, R.D. Individual differences in patterns of anxiety arousal, stress-relevant information, and recovery from surgery (Doctoral Dissertation, University of California, Los Angeles, 1970). *Dissertation Abstracts International*, 1971, *32*, 554b.

Delworth, V., Rudow, E.H., & Taub, J. *Crisis Center/Hotline: A guidebook to beginning and operating*. Springfield Ill.: Charles C. Thomas, 1972.

Derogatis, L.R. The SCL–90 and MMPI: A step in the validation of a new self-report scale. *British Journal of Psychiatry*, 1976, *128*, 280–289.

Deutsch, M. *The resolution of conflict: Constructive and destructive processes.* New Haven: Yale University Press, 1973.

Devi, I. *Renew your life through yoga.* Englewood Cliffs, N.J.: Prentice-Hall, 1963.

Diagnostic and Statistical Manual of Mental Disorders (3rd ed.). (DSM–III). Washington, D.C.: American Psychiatric Association, 1980.

Dinkmeyer, D. Top priority: Understanding self and others. *The Elementary School Journal*, 1971, *72*, 62–71.

Dinkmeyer, D., & Caldwell, E. *Developmental counseling and guidance: A comprehensive school approach*. New York: McGraw-Hill, 1980.

Dixon, M.C., & Burns, J.L. Crisis theory, active learning and the training of telephone crisis volunteers. *Journal of Community Psychology*, 1974, *2*, 120–125.

Dohrenwend, B.S., & Dohrenwend, B.P. (Eds.). *Conference on stressful life events: Their nature and effects*. New York: John Wiley & Sons, 1974.

Downing, G. *The massage book*. New York: Bookworks/Random House, 1972.

Dressler, D.M. The management of emotional crises by medical practitioners. *Journal of the American Medical Women's Association*, 1973, *28*, 654–659.

Driscoll, J., Meyer, R., & Schanie, C. Training police in family crisis intervention. *Journal of Applied Behavioral Sciences*, 1973, *9*, 62–82.

Drotar, D., & Granofsky, M.A. Mental health intervention with children and adolescents with end-stage renal disease. *International Journal of Psychiatry in Medicine*, 1977, *7*, 179–192.

Duncan, D.S. Negative reaction to drug users by emergency room personnel. *Journal of Psychodelic Drugs*, 1977, *9*, 103–105.

Dynes, R.D., & Quarantelli, E.L. The family and community context of individual reactions to disaster. In H.J. Parad, H.L.P. Resnik, & L.G. Parad (Eds.), *Emergency and disaster management: A mental health sourcebook*. Bowie, Md.: The Charles Press Publishers, Inc., 1976.

D'Zurilla, T.J., & Goldfried, M.R. Problem solving and behavior modification. *Journal of Abnormal Psychology*, 1971, *78*, 197–226.

Edelstein, B.A., & Eisler, R.M. Effects of modeling and modeling with instructions and feedback on the behavioral components of social skills. *Behavior Therapy*, 1976, *7*, 382–389.

Egan, G. *The skilled helper*. Monterey, Calif.: Brooks/Cole Publishing Co., 1975.

Eiser, C. Psychological development of the child with leukemia: A review. *Journal of Behavioral Medicine*, 1979, *2*, 141–157.

Eisler, M., & Hersen, M. Behavioral techniques in family-oriented crisis intervention. *Archive of General Psychiatry*, 1973, *28*, 111–116.

Eliade, M. Yoga. *Immortality and freedom*. Princeton, N.J.: Princeton University Press, 1969.

Eliade, M. Yoga. *Immortality and freedom* (2nd ed.). New York: Bollingen, 1970.

Ellis, A. *Growth through reason* (2nd ed.). Hollywood, Calif.: Wilshire Books, 1974.

Ellis, A. *How to live with a neurotic* (Rev. ed.). New York: Crow Publishers, 1975.

Ellis A. *How to live with and without anger*. New York: Readers Digest Press, 1977.

Ellis, A. *How to master your fear of flying*. New York: Curtis Books, 1972.

Ellis, A. *Humanistic psychotherapy*. New York: McGraw-Hill, 1974.

Ellis, A. *Reason and emotion in psychotherapy*. New York: Lyle Stuart, 1962.

Ellis, A., & Abrahms, E. *Brief psychotherapy in medical and health practice.* New York: Springer, 1978.

Ellis, A., & Grieger, R. *Handbook of rational emotive therapy.* Berlin & New York: Springer-Verlag, 1977.

Ellis, A., & Harper, R.A. *A new guide to rational living.* North Hollywood, Calif.: Wilshire Book Co., 1961.

Emerson, R.M., & Messinger, S.L. The micro-politics of trouble. *Social Problems,* 1977, *25,* 121–134.

Employee Benefit Plan Review. Alcoholism programs in the workplace, December 1979, 106–107.

Epperson, M.M. Families in sudden crisis: Process and intervention in a critical care center. *Social Work in Health Care,* 1977, *2,* 265–273.

Epstein, H. *Children of the holocaust: Conversations with sons and daughters of survivors.* New York: Putnam, 1980.

Erikson, E.H. *Childhood and society.* New York: W.W. Norton, 1963.

Erikson, E.H. *Adulthood: Essays.* New York: W.W. Norton, 1978.

Estimating the social costs of national economic policy: Implications for mental and physical health, and criminal aggression. A study prepared for the use of the Joint Economic Committee, Congress of the United States. United States Government Printing Office, Washington, D.C., 1976.

Evans, D.R. Use of the MMPI to predict effective hotline workers. *Journal of Clinical Psychology,* 1977, *33,* 1113–1114.

Evans, D.R., Uhlemann, M.R., & Hearn, M.T. Microcounseling and sensitivity training with hotline workers. *Journal of Community Psychology,* 1978, *6,* 139–146.

Fagan, F., Shepherd, I.L. (Eds.), *Gestalt therapy now.* New York: Harper & Row, 1970.

Fagin, L.H. The experience of unemployment: The impact of unemployment. *NU Quarterly,* Winter, 1979, 48–74.

Farberow, N. Clinical developments in suicide prevention in the USA. *Crisis,* 1980, *1,* 16–26.

Farberow, N.L. (Ed.). *The many faces of suicide.* New York: McGraw-Hill, 1980.

Farberow, N., & Litman, R.E. Suicide prevention. In H.L.P. Resnik, H.L. Ruben, & D.D. Ruben (Eds.), *Emergency psychiatric care: The management of mental health crises.* Bowie, Maryland: The Charles Press Publishers, Inc., 1975.

Farberow, N.L., & Shneidman, E.S. (Eds.). *The cry for help.* New York: McGraw-Hill, 1961.

Farrell, H.M. Crisis intervention following the birth of a handicapped child. *Journal of Psychiatric Nursing and Mental Health Services,* 1977, *15,* 32–36.

Faust, D.S., & Caldwell, H.S. *Community attitudes toward the child with a life threatening illness*. Paper presented at the annual meeting of the American Psychological Association, New York, 1979.

FBI Uniform Crime Reports, *Crime in the United States*. Washington, D.C.: U.S. Department of Justice, 1979, 302–313.

Feldman, E. Teachers need counseling too. *Innovations*, 1979, *6*, 39–40.

Feldman-Summers, S., Gordon E.P., & Meagher, J.R. The impact of rape on sexual satisfaction. *Journal of Abnormal Psychology*, 1979, *88*, 101–105.

Figley, C.R., & Sprenkle, D.H. Delayed stress response syndrome: Family therapy implications. *Journal of Marriage and Family Counseling*, 1978, *4*, 53–60.

Filipowicz, C.A. The troubled employee: Whose responsibility? *The Personnel Administrator*, 1979, *24*, 17–22.

Fink, S.L., Beak, J., & Taddeo, K. Organizational crisis and change. *Journal of Applied Behavioral Science*, 1971, *7*, 15–37.

Finkel, N.J. Stress and traumas: An attempt at categorization. *American Journal of Community Psychology*, 1974, *2*, 265–273.

Finlayson, M.A.J., & Rourke, B.P. Locus of control as a predictor variable in rehabilitation medicine. *Journal of Clinical Psychology*, 1978, *34*, 367–368.

Fiske, M. *Middle-age: The prime of life?* New York: Harper & Row, 1979.

Flowers, J.V., & Booraem, C.D. Simulation and role playing methods. In F.H. Kanfer & A.P. Goldstein, *Helping people change* (2nd ed.). Elmsford, N.Y.: Pergamon Press, 1980.

Floyd, J., & Viney, L.L. Ego identity and ego ideal in the unwed mother. *British Journal of Medical Psychology*, 1974, *47*, 273–281.

Folkins, C.H., & Sime, W.E. Physical fitness training and mental health, *American Psychologist*, 1981, *36*, 373–389.

Follingstad, D.R. *A reconceptualization of issues in the treatment of a battered woman*. Presented at the semiannual meeting of the South Carolina Psychological Association, Fall, 1977.

Fordyce, W.E. *Behavioral methods for chronic pain and illness*. St. Louis: C.V. Mosby, 1976.

Fowler, D.E., & McGee, R.K. Assessing the performance of telephone crisis workers: The development of a technical effectiveness scale. In D. Lester & G.W. Brockopp (Eds.), *Crisis intervention and counseling by telephone*. Springfield, Ill.: Charles C. Thomas, 1973.

France, K. Evaluation of late volunteer crisis counseling workers. *American Journal of Community Psychology*, 1975, *3*, 197–219.

Franciosi, R.A., & Friedman, G.R. Sudden infant death syndrome: A medical and psychological crisis. *Archives of the Foundation of Thanatology*, 1977, *6*, 18–19.

Frank, J.D. *Persuasion and healing*. Baltimore, Md.: Johns Hopkins Press, 1961.

Frankel, F.H., & Zamansky, H.S. (Eds.), *Hypnosis at its bicentennial: Selected papers*. New York: Plenum Press, 1978.

Frazier, W.H., & Moynihan, B. The emergency service based rape counseling team. *Connecticut Medicine*, 1978, *42*, 91–96.

Frederick, C.J. Current thinking about crisis or psychological intervention in United States disasters. *Mass Emergencies*, 1977a, *2*, 43–50.

Frederick, C.J. Suicide in the United States. *Health Education*, 1977b, *8*, 17–22.

Freeman, H.A. *Counseling in the United States*. Dobbs Ferry, N.Y.: Oceana Publications, 1967.

Freeman, H.A. *Legal interviewing and counseling*. St. Paul: West Publishing, 1964.

Freeman, H.A., & Weinhofen, H. *Clinical law training; Interviewing and counseling*. St. Paul: West Publishing, 1972.

Fried, M. Grieving for a lost home. In R.H. Moos (Ed.), *Human adaptation: Coping with life crises*. Lexington, Massachusetts: D.C. Heath & Company, 1976.

Galassi, M.D., & Galassi, J.P. *Assert yourself: How to be your own person*. New York: Human Sciences Press, 1977.

Gardner, K.R., & Montgomery S. *Clinical biofeedback: A procedural manual*. Baltimore: Williams & Wilkins, 1977.

Gardner, R. *The boys and girls book about divorce, with an introduction for parents*. New York: Bantam edition, 1971.

Garrity, T.F. Morbidity, mortality, and rehabilitation. In W.D. Gentry & R.B. Williams (Eds.). *Psychological aspects of myocardial infarction and coronary care*. St. Louis: Mosby, 1975.

Gedan, S. Abortion counseling with adolescents. *American Journal of Nursing*, 1974, *74*, 1856–1858.

Gelles, R.J. Abused wives: Why do they stay? *Journal of Marriage and the Family*, 1976, *38*, 659–668.

Gelles, R.J. *The violent home: A study of physical aggression between husbands and wives*. Beverly Hills: Sage Publications, Inc., 1972.

Genthner, R. Evaluating the functioning of community based hotlines. *Professional Psychology*, 1974, *5*, 409–414.

Getz, W.L., Altman, D.C., Berleman, W.C., & Allen, W.D. Paraprofessional crisis counseling in the emergency room. *Health and Social Work*, 1977, *2*, 57–63.

Getz, W., Wiesen, A.E., Sue, S., & Ayers, A. *Fundamentals of crisis counseling*. Lexington, Ma.: D.C. Heath and Co., 1974.

Getz, W.L., Fujita, B.N., & Allen, D. The use of paraprofessionals in crisis intervention. *American Journal of Community Psychology*, 1975, *3*, 135–144.

Giacquinta, B. Helping families face the crisis of cancer. *American Journal of Nursing*, 1977, *77*, 1585–1588.

Gill, M.M., & Brenman, M. *Hypnosis and related states: Psychoanalytic studies in regression*. New York: International University Press, 1959.

Gilligan, C. *Adulthood: Developmental rites of passage*. Symposium at the Annual ·
Meeting of the New England Psychological Association, 1978.

Gilligan, C. *In a different voice: Psychological theory and women's development*.
Cambridge, Massachusetts: Harvard University Press, 1983.

Gilligan, C. Woman's place in man's life cycle. *Harvard Educational Review*, 1979,
49, 431–446.

Ginott, H. *Between parent and child: New solutions to old problems*. New York:
MacMillian, 1965.

Glasgow, R.W., & Rosen, G.M. Behavioral bibliotherapy: A review of self-help behavior therapy manuals. *Psychological Bulletin*, 1978, *85*, 1–23.

Glass, A.J. Psychological aspects of disaster. *Journal of the American Medical
Association*. 1959, *171*, 188–191.

Glasser, W. *Reality therapy*. New York: McGraw-Hill, 1980.

Gleser, G.C., Green, B.L., & Winget, C. *Prolonged psychosocial effects of disaster:
A study of Buffalo Creek*. New York: Academic Press, 1981.

Goldfried, M.R. Psychotherapy as coping skill training. In M.J. Mahoney (Ed.),
Psychotherapy process: Current issues and future directions. New York:
Plenum, 1979.

Goldfried, M.R., & Davidson, G.C. *Clinical behavior therapy*. New York: Holt,
Rinehart, & Winston, 1976.

Goldfried, M.R., & Goldfried, A.P. Cognitive change methods. In F.H. Kanfer &
A.P. Goldstein (Eds.), *Helping people change* (2nd ed.). New York:
Pergamon Press, 1980.

Goldstein, A.P. Relationship-enhancement methods. In F.H. Kanfer & A.P. Goldstein (Eds.), *Helping people change*. Elmsford, N.Y.: Pergamon Press,
1975.

Goldstein, A.P., Monti, P.J., Sardino, T.J., & Green, D.J. *Police crisis intervention*. Elmsford, N.Y.: Pergamon Press, 1979.

Goldstein, A.P., Sprafkin, R., & Gershaw, N.J. *Skill training for community living:
Applying structural learning therapy*. Elmsford, N.Y.: Pergamon Press, 1976.

Goldstein, T. Bar panel bids law schools stress practical training. *The New York
Times*, August 16, 1979a.

Goldstein, T. Legal education debate focuses on theoretical versus practical.
The New York Times, January 8, 1979b.

Gomez, J. *How not to die young*. New York: Pocket Books, 1973.

Goode, W.J. *After divorce*. Glencoe, Ill.: Free Press, 1956.

Gordon, R.H. Efficacy of a group crisis counseling program for men who accompany women seeking abortions. *American Journal of Community Psychology*, 1978, *6*, 239–246.

Gordon, T. *Parent effectiveness training: The no lose program for raising responsible children*. New York: P.H. Wyden, 1970.

Gottman, J. Marital interaction: *Experimental investigations*. New York: Academic Press, Inc., 1979.

Gottman, J., Notarius, C., Gonso, J., & Markman, H. *The couple's guide to communication* (4th ed.). Champaign, Ill.: Research Press, 1979.

Gottschalk, L.A., & Gleser, G.C. *The measurement of psychological states through the content analysis of verbal behavior*. Berkeley: University of California Press, 1969.

Gould, R. *Transformations: Growth and change in adult life*. New York: Simon & Schuster, 1978.

Grady, M. An assessment of the behavioral scientist's role with the dying patient and the family. *Military Medicine*, 1975, *140*, 789–792.

Grauer, H., & Frank, D. Psychiatric aspects of geriatric crisis intervention. *Canadian Psychiatric Association Journal*, 1978, *23*, 201–207.

Gray, B., Nida, R.A., & Coonfield, T.J. Empathic listening test: An instrument for the selection and training of telephone crisis workers. *Journal of Community Psychology*, 1976, *4*, 199–205.

Greenbaum, C.W., Rogosky, I., & Shalit, B. The military psychologist during wartime: A model based on action research and crisis intervention. *Journal of Applied Behavioral Sciences*, 1977, *13*, 7–21.

Greer, F.L., & Weinstein, R.S. Suicide prevention center outreach: Callers and noncallers compared. *Psychological Reports*, 1979, *44*, 387–393.

Griffin, J.J. The pastoral counselor has no clothes on! *The Journal of Pastoral Care*, 1980, *34*, 168–176.

Groner, F. Delivery of clinical social work services in the emergency room: A description of an existing program. *Social Work in Health Care*, 1978, *4*, 19–29.

Grumet, G.W., & Trachtman, D.L. Psychiatric social workers in the emergency room. *Health and Social Work*, 1976, *1*(3), 113–131.

Gurin, G., Veroff, J., & Feld, S. *Americans view their mental health*. New York: Basic Books, 1960.

Gutmann, D.G. Parenthood: A key to the comparative study of the life cycle. In N. Datan & L.H. Ginsberg (Eds.), *Life-span developmental psychology: Normative life crises*. New York: Academic Press, 1975.

Hackett, T.P., & Cassem, N.H. Psychological aspects of rehabilitation after myocardial infarction. In N.K. Wenger & H.K. Hellerstein (Eds.), *Rehabilitation of the coronary patient*. New York: John Wiley & Sons, 1978.

Haley, F. *Changing families*. New York: Grune & Stratton, 1971.

Haley, J. Paradoxes in play, fantasy and psychotherapy. *Psychiatric Research Reports*, 1975, *2*, 52–58.

Haley, J. *Problem-solving therapy*, San Francisco: Jossey-Bass, 1976.

Halpern, H.A. Crisis theory: A definitional study. *Community Mental Health Journal*, 1973, *9*, 342–349.

Halpern, H.A., Canale, J.R., Grant, B.L., & Bellamy, C. A systems crisis approach to family treatment. *Journal of Marital and Family Therapy*, 1979, *5*, 87–94.

Hamera, E.K., & Shontz, F.C. Perceived positive and negative effects of life-threatening illness. *Journal of Psychosomatic Research*, 1978, *22*, 419–424.

Hamilton, D. When the police enter a family fight. *Boulder Daily Camera*: Focus Section 3–6, February 11, 1973.

Hammond, D.C., & Stanfield, K. *Multidimensional psychotherapy, A counselor's guide for the map form*. Champaign, Illinois: Institute for Personality and Ability Testing, 1977.

Hancock, E. Crisis intervention in a newborn nursery intensive care unit. *Social Work in Health Care*, 1976, *1*, 421–432.

Hankoff, L.D., Mischorr, M.T., Tomlinson, K.E., & Joyce, S.A. A program of crisis intervention in the emergency medical setting. *American Journal of Psychiatry*, 1974, *131*, 47–50.

Hansel, N. Reception service in emergency contents. In H.J. Parad, H.L.P. Resnik, & L.G. Parad (Eds.), *Emergency and disaster management: A mental health sourcebook*. Bowie, Md.: The Charles Press Publishers, 1976.

Hanson, P. The Johari Window: A model for soliciting and giving feedback. In J.E. Jones & J.W. Pheiffer (Eds.), *The 1923 annual handbook for group facilitators*. La Jolla, Calif.: University Associates Publishers, Inc., 1973.

Harrell, F., Guerney, B. Training married couples in conflict negotiation skills. In D.H.L. Olson (Ed.), *Treating relationships*. Lake Mills, Ia.: Graphic, 1976.

Harshbarger, D. An ecological perspective on disaster intervention. In H.J. Parad, H.L.P. Resnik, & L.G. Parad (Eds.), *Emergency and disaster management: A mental health sourcebook*. Bowie, Md.: The Charles Press Publishers, 1976.

Hart, L.E. & King, G.D. Selection vs. training in the development of paraprofessionals. *Journal of Counseling Psychological*, 1979, *26*, 235–241.

Haugk, K.C., & Dorr, D. The development and evaluation of a community mental health education program for seminarians. *American Journal of Community Psychology*, 1976, *4*, 283–292.

Havighurst, R.J. *Developmental tasks and education*. New York: Longmans, Green, & Co., 1952.

Hay, D., & Oken, D. The psychological stresses of intensive care unit nursing. *Psychosomatic Medicine*, 1972, *34*, 109–118.

Haywood, C., & Leuthe, J. *Crisis intervention in the 1980's: From networking to social influence*. Paper presented at the annual meeting of the American Psychological Association, September 4, 1980, Montreal, Canada.

Haywood, C. The future role of crisis intervention centers: Theoretical base and principles of intervention: I. An overview of the ark model for stress modulation and crisis intervention. *Crisis Intervention*, 1977, *8*, 56–73.

Hearst, P. *Every secret thing*. Garden City, New York: Doubleday, 1982.

Heaton, M.E., Ashton, P.T., & Powell, E.R. *Coding the "cry for help."* Paper presented at the annual meeting of the American Association of Suicidology, Detroit, 1972.

Helfer, R.E., & Kempe, C.H. (Eds.). *Child abuse and neglect: The family and the community*. Cambridge, Mass.: Ballinger Publishing Co., 1976.

Heller, D.B., & Schneider, C.D. Interpersonal methods for coping with stress: Helping families of dying children. *Omega*, 1978, *8*, 319–329.

Henderson, H.E. Helping families in crisis: Police and social work intervention. *Social Work*, 1976, *21*(4), 314–315.

Herzberg, A. *Active psychotherapy*. New York: Grune & Stratton, 1945.

Hilgard, E.R., & Hilgard, J.R. *Hypnosis in the relief of pain*. Los Altos, Calif.: Wm. Kaufmann, 1975.

Hill, G.E. Guidance in the elementary schools. Position paper for the APGA Committee on Dimensions in Elemental School Guidance, 1964.

Hill, R. Generic features of families under stress. *Social Case Work*, 1958, *39*, 139–150.

Hiltner, S. *Pastoral counseling*. Nashville: Abingdon Press, 1949.

Hiltner, S. *Preface to pastoral theology*. Nashville: Abingdon Press, 1958.

Hiltner, S., & Colston, L.G. *The conduct of pastoral counseling*. Nashville: Abingdon Press, 1961.

Hirchowitz, R.G. The human aspects of managing transition. *Personnel*, 1974, *51*, 8–17.

Hoehn-Saric, R. Evaluation of psychiatric training in the emergency room. *Comprehensive Psychiatry*, 1977, *18*, 585–589.

Hoff, L.A. *People in crisis: Understanding and helping*. Menlow Park, California: Addison-Wesley Publishing Company, 1978.

Hoffman, I., & Futterman, E.H. Coping with waiting: Psychiatric intervention and study in the waiting room of a pediatric oncology clinic. *Comprehensive Psychiatry*, 1971, *12*, 36–47.

Holahan, S.J., & Spearly, J.L. Coping and ecology: An integrative model for community psychology. *American Journal of Community Psychology*, 1980, *8*, 671–685.

Holloman, C.R. Mental health on the job: Whose responsibility? *Business Horizons*, 1973, *16*, 73–80.

Holmes, T.H., & Masuda, M. Life change and illness susceptibility. In B.S. Dohrenwend & B.P. Dohrenwend (Eds.), *Stressful life events: Their nature and effects*. New York: John Wiley & Sons, 1973.

Holmes, T.H., & Rahe, R.H. The social readjustment rating scale. *Journal of Psychosomatic Research*, 1967, *11*, 213–218.

Homme, L.E. Perspectives in psychology—XXIV control of covenants: The operants of the mind. *Psychological Record*, 1965, *15*, 501–511.

Horney, K. *Self-analysis*. New York: W.W. Norton, 1942.

Horowitz, M.J. Diagnosis and treatment of stress response syndromes: General principles. In H.J. Parad, H.L.P. Resnik & L.G. Parad (Eds.), *Emergency and disaster management: A mental health sourcebook*, Bowie, Md.: The Charles Press Publishers, 1976.

Horowitz, M.J., & Solomon, G.F. A prediction of delayed stress response syndromes in Vietnam veterans. *Journal of Social Issues*, 1975, *31*, 67–80.

Horstman, P.L. Assaults on police officers: How safe are you? In R.W. Kobetz (Eds.), *Crisis intervention and the police: Selected readings*, Gaithersburg, Md.: International Association of Chiefs of Police, 1974.

Hunt, R.A. *The Christian as minister.* Printed by the Board of Higher Education and ministry, The United Methodist Church, Nashville, Tn., 1977.

Ianzito, B.M., Fine, J., Sprague, B., & Pestana, J. Over-night admission for psychiatric emergencies. *Hospital and Community Psychiatry*, 1978, *29*, 728–730.

Iscoe, I. Community Psychology and the competent community. *American Psychologist*, 1974, *29*, 607–613.

Iscoe, I. Realities and trade offs in a viable community psychology. *American Journal of Community Psychology*, 1977, *5*, 131–154.

Iscoe, I., Hill, F., Harmon, M., & Coffmann, D. Telephone counseling via cassette tapes. *Journal of Counseling Psychology*, 1979, *26*, 166–168.

Ishikawa, E., & Swain, D.L. (Tr.) *Hiroshima and Nagasaki: The physical, medical, and social effects of the atomic bombings*. New York: Basic Books, Inc., 1981.

Izzo, L.D., & Isaacson, R.V. *New ways in school mental health: Early detection and prevention of school maladaptation*. New York: Human Sciences Press, 1975.

Jackson, D., & Weakland, J. Conjoint family therapy: Some considerations on theory, technique and results. *Psychiatry*, 1961, *24*, 30–45.

Jaco, E.G. Ecological aspects of patient care and hospital organization. In B.S. Georgopoulos (Ed.), *Organization research on health institutions*. Ann Arbor: The University of Michigan, 1972.

Jacobs, P. The consulting psychologists' emerging role in law enforcement. *Professional Psychology*, August, 1976, 256–266.

Jacobsen, P.H., & Howell, R.J. Psychiatric problems in emergency rooms. *Health and Social Work*, 1978, *3*, 88–107.

Jacobson, E. *Progressive relaxation*. Chicago: University of Chicago Press, Midway Reprint, 1974.

Jacobson, G.F., Strickler, M., & Morley, W.E. Generic and individual approaches to crisis intervention. *American Journal of Public Health*, 1968, *58*, 339–343.

Jacobson, N.S. Problem solving and contingency contracting in the treatment of marital discord. *Journal of Consulting and Clinical Psychology*, 1977, *45*, 92–100.

James, M., & Jongeward, D. *Born to win*. New York: Signet, 1978.

Jamison, R., & Johnson, J.E. Empathy and therapeutic orientation in paid and volunteer crisis phone workers, professional therapist and undergraduate college students. *Journal of Community Psychology*, 1975, *3*, 269–274.

Janis, I. *Psychological stress*. New York: John Wiley & Sons, 1958.

Jellinek, M. Referrals from a psychiatric emergency room: Relationship of complaints to demographic and interview variables. *American Journal of Psychiatry*, 1978, *135*, 209–213.

Johnston, M. Anxiety in surgical patients. *Psychological Medicine*, 1980, *10*, 145–152.

Joint Commission on Accreditation of Hospitals: Principles for accreditation of community mental health services program, 1979. (Available from 875 North Michigan Avenue, Chicago, Ill., 60611.)

Joint Economic Committee Report of the 94th United States Congress, Revised December 27, 1976. Washington, D.C.: United States Government Printing Office, 1976.

Jones, N.H. Grief and involuntary career change: Its implications for counseling. *Vocational Guidance Quarterly*, 1979, *27*, 196–201.

Jones, S.L., Jones, P.K., & Meisner, B.S. Identification of patients in need of psychiatric intervention. Visiting and emergency facility. *Medical Care*, 1978, *16*, 372–382.

Jones, W.A. The A-B-C method of crisis management. *Mental Hygiene*, 1968, *52*, 87.

Kadel, T.E. *Growth in ministry*. Philadelphia: Fortress Press, 1980.

Kahn, R.L., & Cannell, C.F. *The dynamics of interviewing, techniques and cases*. New York: John Wiley & Sons, 1965.

Kales, J.D., & Kales, A. Managing the individual and family in crisis. *American Family Physician*, 1975, *12*, 109–115.

Kalis, B. Crisis theory: Its relevance for community psychology and directions for development. In *Community psychology and mental health: Perspectives and challenges*. San Francisco: Chandler, 1970.

Kaminsky, B.A., & Sheckter, L.A. Abortion counseling in a general hospital. *Health and Social Work*, 1979, *4*, 93–103.

Kantor, S.E., & Caron, H.S. *Intensive crisis intervention with ex-convicts: A controlled field experiment*. Paper presented at the annual meeting of the American Psychological Association, Toronto, 1978.

Kaplan, L.S. A matter of loss: Living on, surviving sadness. *The School Counselor*. March, 1979, pp. 229–235.

Karlin, R.A., & McKeon, P. The use of hypnosis in multimodal therapy. In A.A. Lazarus, *Multimodal behavior therapy*. New York: Springer, 1976.

Kastenbaum, R. *Growing old: Years of fulfillment*. New York: Harper & Row, 1979.

Katz, S., & Mazur, M.A. Understanding the rape victim: A synthesis of research findings. New York: John Wiley & Sons, 1979.

Kazdin, A.E. Assessment of imagery during covert modeling of assertive behavior. *Journal of Behavior Therapy and Experimental Psychiatry*, 1976, *7*, 213–219.

Keily, W.F. Psychiatric syndromes in critically ill patients. *Journal of the American Medical Association*, 1976, *235*, 2759–2761.

Keith, C.R., & Ellis, D. Reactions of pupils and teachers to death in a classroom. *School Counselor*. 1978, *25*, 228–234.

Kemeny, J.G. *Report of the President's Commission on the Accident at Three Mile Island*. Washington, D.C., 1979.

Kennedy, C.E. *Human development: The adult years and aging*. New York: Macmillan, 1978.

Kessler, S. *Creative conflict resolution: Mediation*. Atlanta, Georgia: National Institute for Professional Training, 1978.

Kilpatrick, D.G., & Veronen, L.J. Treatment for rape-related problems: Crisis intervention is not enough. In L.H. Cohen, W. Claiborn & G. Specter (Eds.), *Crisis intervention*. New York: Human Sciences Press, 1983.

Kilpatrick, D.G., Veronen, L.J., & Resick, P.A. Assessment of the aftermath of rape: Changing patterns of fear. *Journal of Behavioral Assessment*, 1979b, *1*, 133–148.

Kimbrell, G.M., & Slaikeu, K.A. *The role of crisis theory in chronic illness*. Unpublished manuscript, University of South Carolina, 1981.

Kimmel, D.C. *Adulthood and aging*. New York: John Wiley & Sons, 1980.

Kinney, F. Homebuilders: An in-home crisis intervention program. *Children Today*, January-February, 1978, 15–35.

Kinsella, J.K., & Africano, A. Emergency care and evaluation of the alcohol patient. *Connecticut Medicine*, 1977, *41*, 655–661.

Kinzel, R. Resolving executives' early retirement problems. *Personnel*, 1974, *51*, 55–64.

Klein, D.C., & Lindemann, E. Preventive intervention in individual and family crisis situations. In G. Caplan (Ed.), *Prevention of mental disorders in children*. New York: Basic Books, 1961.

Klein, D.C., & Ross, A. Kindergarten entry: A study of role transition. In M. Krugman (Ed.), *Orthopsychiatry and the school*. New York: American Orthopsychiatry Association, 1958.

Klein, R. A crisis to grow on. *Cancer*, 1971, *28*, 1660–1665.

Kling, R. Chronicity at what price? Overview of the interrelationship between pediatric cancer centers and the community. In J.L. Schuman & M.J. Kupst (Eds.), *The child with cancer: Clinical approaches to psychosocial care—Research in psychosocial aspects*. Springfield, Ill.: Charles C. Thomas, 1980.

Klingman, A. Children in stress: Anticipatory guidance in the framework of the educational system. *Personnel and Guidance Journal*, 1978, *57*, 22–26.

Knesper, D.J., Landau, S.G., & Looney, J.G. Psychiatric Education in the emergency room: Must teaching stop at 5 p.m.? *Hospital and community psychiatry*, 1978, *29*, 723–797.

Knickerbocker, D.A., & McGee, R.K. Clinical effectiveness of non-professional and professional telephone workers in a crisis intervention center. In D. Lester & G. Brockopp (Eds.), *Crisis intervention and counseling by telephone*. Springfield, Ill.: Charles C. Thomas, 1972.

Knickerbocker, D.A., & McGee, R.K. Clinical effectiveness of volunteer crisis workers on the telephone. In D. Lester and G. Brockopp (Eds.), *Crisis intervention and counseling by telephone*. Springfield, Illinois: Charles C. Thomas, 1973.

Kopel, K., & Mock. L.A. The use of group sessions for emotional support of families of terminal patients. *Death Education*, 1978, *1*, 409–422.

Korchin, S.J. *Modern clinical psychology*. New York: Basic Books, Inc., 1976.

Kraus, S. The crisis of divorce: Growth promoting or pathogenic? *Journal of Divorce*, 1979, *3*, 107–119.

Kroger, W.S. *Clinical and experimental hypnosis* (2nd ed.). Philadelphia: J.B. Lippencott, 1976.

Kubler-Ross, E. *On death and dying*, New York: Macmillan, 1969.

Kuenzi, S.H., & Fenton, M.V. Crisis intervention in acute care areas. *American Journal of Nursing*, 1975, *75*, 830–834.

Kupst, M.J., & Schulman, J.L. Family coping with leukemia in a child: Initial reactions. In J.L. Shulman & M.J. Kupst, (Eds.), *The child with cancer*. Springfield, Ill.: Charles C. Thomas, 1980.

L'Abale, L., & Weeks, G. A bibliography of paradoxical methods in psychotherapy of family systems. In *Family Process*, 1978, *17*, 83–95.

Lamberson, T.O. Realities of retirement counseling point of the need for corporate counseling programs. *Risk Management*, 1978, *25*, 28–31.

Lane, D.J. Family adjustment to the crisis of child disability. *Dissertation Abstracts International*, 1976, *37*, 441–B.

Lange, A.F., & Jakubowski, P. *Responsible assertive behavior*. Champaign, Ill.: Research, 1976.

Langer, E.J., Janis, I.L., & Wolfer, J. Reduction of psychological stress in surgical patients. *Journal of Experimental Social Psychology*, 1975, *11*, 155–165.

Langsley, D.G. Crisis intervention: Managing stress-induced personal and family emergencies. *Behavioral Medicine*, 1978, *5*, 31–33; 36–37.

Langsley, D.G. Three models of family therapy: prevention, crisis treatment or rehabilitation. *The Journal of Clinical Psychiatry*, 1978, *39*, 792–796.

Lascari, A.D. The dying child and the family. *The Journal of Family Practice*, 1978, *6*, 1279–1286.

Lavey, E.B., & Winkle, R.A. Continuing disability of patients with chest pains and normal coronary arteriograms. *Journal of Chronic Disease*, 1979, *32*, 191–196.

Lawrence, D.B., & Steinbrecher, D.D. Occupational alcoholism programs-wave of the future. *Personnel*, 1979, *56*, 43–45.

Lazare, A., Cohen, F., Jacobson, A., Williams, M., Mignone, R., & Zisook, S. The walk-in patient as a "customer": A key dimension in evaluation and treatment. *American Journal of Orthopsychiatry*, 1972, *42*, 872–883.

Lazare, A., Eisenthal, S., & Wasserman, L. The customer approach to patienthood. *Achives of General Psychiatry*, 1976, *32*, 553–558.

Lazarus, A.A. *The practice of multimodal therapy*. New York: McGraw-Hill Book Co., 1981.

Lazarus, A.A. (Ed.). *Multimodal behavior therapy*. New York: Springer Publishing Co., 1976.

Lazarus, A.A., & Abramovitz, A. *Learn to relax*. A recorded course in muscular relaxation. Johannesburg: Troubadour Records, 1962.

Lazarus, A.A., & Fay, A. *I can if I want to*. New York: William Morrow & Co., 1975.

Lazarus, R.S. A cognitively oriented psychologist looks at biofeedback. *American Psychologist*, 1975, *30*, 553–561.

Lazarus, R.S. The stress and coping paradigm. In L.A. Bond & R.C. Rosen (Eds.), *Competence and coping during adulthood*. New Hampshire: University Press of New England, 1980.

Lederer, W.J., & Jackson, D.D. *Mirages of marriage*. New York: W.W. Norton, 1968.

Leeman, C.C. Diagnostic errors in emergency room and medicine: Physical illness in patient label "psychiatric" and vice-versa. *International Journal of Psychiatry in Medicine*, 1975, *6*, 553–540.

Lefort, S. Care of the rape victim in emergency. *Canadian Nurse*, 1977, *73*, 42–45.

Lester, D. Demographic vs. clinical prediction of suicide behaviors: A look at some of the issues. In A.T. Beck, H.L.P. Resnik, & D.J. Lettieri (Eds.), *The prediction of suicide*. Bowie, Md.: The Charles Press Publishers, 1974.

Lester, D. Steps toward the evaluation of a suicide prevention center: Part I. *Crisis Intervention*, 1970, *2*, 42–45.

Lester, D. The use of the telephone in counseling and crisis intervention: In Ithiel DeSola Pool (Ed.), *The Social Impact of the Telephone*. Boston: MIT Press, 1977.

Lester, D., & Brockopp, G. *Crisis intervention and counseling by telephone.* Springfield, Ill.: Charles C. Thomas, 1973.

Leupnitz, D.A. Children of divorce: A review of the psychological literature. *Law and Human Behavior*, 1978, *2*, 167–179.

Leupnitz, D.A. Which aspects of divorce affect children? *The Family Coordinator*, 1979, January, 79–85.

Levav, I., Greenfield, H., & Baruch, E. Psychiatric combat reactions during the Yom Kippur War. *American Journal of Psychiatry*, 1979, *136*, 637–641.

Levenberg, S.B. Building consultive relationships with rural fundamentalist clergy. *Professional Psychology*, 1976, 553–558.

Levenberg, S.B., Jenkens, C., & Wendorf, D.J. Studies in family oriented crisis intervention with hemodialysis patients. *International Journal of Psychiatry in Medicine*, 1978, *9*, 83–92.

Levine, A. *Love Canal: Science, politics, people.* Lexington, Mass.: Lexington Books, 1982.

Levine, M. Residential change and school adjustment. In R.H. Moos (Ed.). *Human adaptation: Coping with life crises.* Lexington, Mass.: D.C. Heath & Co., 1976.

Levine, M., and Levine, A. *A social history of helping services: Clinic, court, school, and community.* New York: Appleton-Century-Crofts, 1970.

Levine, S.V. Draft dodgers: Coping with stress, adapting to exile. In R.H. Moos (Ed.), *Human adaptation: Coping with life crisis.* Lexington, Mass.: D.C. Heath & Co., 1976.

Levinson, D.J. *The seasons of a man's life.* New York: Alfred A. Knopf, 1978.

Levinson, D.J., Darrow, C.M., Klein, E.B., Levinson, M.H., & McKee, B. Periods in the adult development of men: Ages 18 to 45. *The Counseling Psychologist*, 1976, *6*, 21–25.

Levinson, R.M. Family crisis and adaptation: Coping with a mentally retarded child. *Dissertation Abstracts International*, 1976, *36*, 8336–A.

Levis, D.J. Implementing the technique of implosive therapy. In A. Goldstein, & E. Foa, (Eds.), *Handbook of behavioral intervention.* New York: John Wiley & Sons, 1980.

Levis, D.J., & Hare, N.A. A review of the theoretical and rationale and empirical support for the extinction approach of implosive (flooding) therapy. In M. Hersen, M. Eisler, & P.M. Miller (Eds.), *Progress in behavior modification.* New York: Academic Press, 1977.

Levy, L. The role of a natural mental health service delivery system in dealing with basic human problems. In G.A. Specter & W.L. Clairborn (Eds.), *Crisis Intervention.* New York, N.Y.: Behavioral Publication, 1973.

Levy, J.M., & McGee, R.J. Childbirth as a crisis: A test of Janis' theory of communication and stress resolution. *Journal of Personality and Social Psychology*, 1975, *31*, 171–179.

Lewis, M.S., Gottesman, D., & Gutstein, S. The course and duration of crisis. *Journal of Consulting and Clinical Psychology*, 1979, *47*, 128–134.

Liberman, R. Police as a community mental health resource. *Community Mental Health Journal*, 1969, *5*, 111–120.

Liberman, R. A behavioral approach to group dynamics II. Reinforcing and prompting hostility to the therapist in group therapy. *Behavior Therapy*, 1970, *1*, 312–327.

Lidell, H.G., & Scott, R. *The Greek–English Lexicon*. Oxford: The Clarendon Press, 1968.

Lieberman, G.L. Children of the elderly as natural helpers: Some demographic considerations. *American Journal of Community Psychology*, 1978, *6*, 489–498.

Lieberman, M.A. *Adaptive processes in later life*. Paper presented at the W. Virginia Life Span Conference, May, 1974.

Lifton, R.J., & Olson, E. Death imprint in Buffalo Creek. In H.J. Parad, H.L.P. Resnik, & L.G. Parad (Eds.), *Emergency and disaster management: A mental health sourcebook*. Bowie, Maryland: The Charles Press Publishers, Inc., 1976.

Lindeman, B. Widower, Heal thyself. In R.H. Moos (Ed.), *Human adaptations: Coping with life crises*. Lexington, Massachusetts: D.C. Heath & Company, 1976.

Lindemann, E. Symptomology and management of acute grief. *American Journal of Psychiatry*, 1944, *101*, 141–148.

Lindenburg, E. The need for crisis intervention in hospitals. *Hospitals*, 1972, *46*, 52–55.

Linn, L. Emergency room psychiatry: A gateway to community medicine: *Mount Sinai Journal of Medicine*, 1971, *38*, 110–120.

Lister, T.M. A study of the effectiveness of the Vermillim Hotline training program in increasing the skills of communicating empathy and discrimination. *Dissertation Abstracts International*, 1976, *36*, 4136.

Lister, T.M. *To care is not enough: A crisis intervention training manual*. Brumilliun, South Dakota: Education Research Service Center, University of South Dakota, 1976.

Liston, E.H. Psychiatric aspects of life threatening illness: A course for medical students. *Psychiatry in Medicine*, 1974, *5*, 51–56.

Llinas, J.J. Crisis intervention: A technique physicians should master. *Michigan Medicine*, 1976, *75*, 446–447.

Loving, N. *Responding to spouse abuse and wife beating: A guide for police*. Washington, D.C.: Police Executive Research Forum, 1981a.

Loving, N. *Spouse abuse: A curriculum guide for police trainers*. Washington, D.C.: Police Executive Research Forum, 1981b.

Lowenthal, M.F., Thurnher, M., Chiriboga, D. *Four stages of life* (1st ed.). San Francisco: Jossey-Bass Publishers, 1975.

Maas, H.S., & Kuypers, J.A. *From thirty to seventy*. San Francisco: Jossey-Bass Publishers, 1974.

Mahoney, M.J. *Cognition and behavior modification*. Cambridge, Mass.: Ballinger Publishing Co., 1974.

Mann, P. *Psychological consultation with a police department*. Springfield, Ill.: Bannerstone House, 1973.

Maris, R.W. *Pathways to suicide: A survey of self-destructive behaviors*. Baltimore, Maryland: Johns Hopkins University Press, 1981.

Martindale, D. Psychological stress among air traffic controllers. *Psychology Today*, 1977, *10*, 70–72.

Maslow, A. *Motivation and personality*. New York: Harper, 1954.

Mayer, N. *The male mid-life crisis: Fresh starts after forty*. New York: Doubleday, 1978.

Mayou, R., Foster, A., & Williamson, B. Psychosocial adjustment in patients one year after myocardial infarction. *Journal of Psychosomatic Research*, 1978, *22*, 447–453.

McCarroll, J.R., and Skudder, P.A. Conflicting concepts of function: Shown in a national survey. *Hospitals*, 1960, *34*, 35–38.

McCarthy, B.W. and Berman, A.L. A student operated crisis center. *Personnel and Guidance Journal*, 1971, *49*, 523–528.

McCombie, S.L., Bassuk, E., Savitz, R., and Pell, S., Development of a medical center rape crisis intervention program. *American Journal of Psychiatry*, 1976, *133*, 418–421.

McCombie. S.L. *The rape crisis intervention handbook: A guide for victim care*. New York: Plenum Press, 1980.

McCord, J.B., & Packwood, W.T. Crisis centers and hotlines: A survey. *Personnel and Guidance Journal*, 1973, *51*, 723–728.

McFarlane, A.H., Norman, G.R., Streiner, D.C., Roy, R., & Scott, D.J. A longitudinal study of the influence of the psychosocial environment on health status: A preliminary report. *Journal of Health and Social Behavior*, 1980, *21*, 124–133.

McGee, R.K. *Crisis intervention in the community*. Baltimore: University Park Press, 1974.

McGee, R.K. Perspectives on suicide. Speech delivered at National Conference on Preventing the Youthful Suicide. Southern Methodist University, Dallas, Texas, October, 1976.

McGee, R.K., & Heffron, E.F. The role of crisis intervention services in disaster recovery. In H.J. Parad, H.L.P. Resnik, & L.G. Parad (Eds.), *Emergency and disaster management: A mental health sourcebook*. Bowie, Md.: The Charles Press Publishers, 1976.

McLean, A.A. Job stress and the psychosocial pressures of change. *Personnel*, 1967, *53*, 404–409.

McMurrain, T. *Intervention in human crises: A guide for helping families in crisis*. Atlanta, Ga.: Humanics Press, 1975.

McNeil, John D. *Curriculum administration: Principals & techniques of curriculum development*. New York: Macmillan, 1964.

Medea, A., and Thompson, K. *Against rape: A survival manual for women: How to cope with rape physically and emotionally*. New York: Farrar, Straus and Giraux, 1974.

Meichenbaum, D. A self-instructional approach to stress management: A proposal for stress inoculation training. In: C. Spielberger & I. Sarason (Eds.), *Stress & anxiety*, Vol. 2, New York: John Wiley & Sons, 1975.

Meichenbaum, D.H. *Cognitive-behavior modification: An interpretive approach*. New York: Plenum Press, 1977.

Melamed, B.G., & Siegel, L.T. Reduction in anxiety in children facing hospitalization and surgery by use of filmed modeling. *Journal of Consulting and Clinical Psychology*, 1975, *43*, 511–521.

Melmick, F.A. A comparison of replication techniques in the modification of minimal dating behavior. *Journal of Abnormal Psychology*, 1973, *81*, 51–59.

Mendel, W., & Rapport, S. Determinants of the decision for psychiatric hospitalization. *Archives of General Psychiatry*, 1969, *20*, 321–328.

Miles, A. Some psycho-social consequences of multiple sclerosis: Problems of social interaction and group identity. *British Journal of Medical Psychology*, 1979, *52*, 321–331.

Miller, K., & Iscoe, I. The concept of crisis: Current status and mental health implications. *Human Organization*, 1963, *22*, 195–201.

Miller, M. The physician and the older suicidal patient. *The Journal of Family Practice*, 1977, *5*, 1028–1029.

Miller, W. The telephone in out-patient psychotherapy. *American Journal of Psychotherapy*, 1973, *27*, 15–26.

Million, T., Green, C.J., & Meager, R.B. The MBHI: A new inventory for the psychodiagnostician in medical settings. *Professional Psychology*, 1979, *10*, 529–547.

Minuchin, S. *Families and family therapy*. Cambridge, Mass.: Harvard University Press, 1974.

Moos, R.H. (Ed.). *Human adaptation: Coping with life crises*. Lexington, Mass.: D.C. Heath & Co., 1976.

More help for emotionally troubled employees. *Business Week*, March 12, 1979, 97–102.

Morgan, J.P., & King, G.D. Calls to a telephone counseling service. *Journal of Community Psychology*, 1977, *5*, 112–115.

Morse, W.C. The helping teacher/crisis teacher concept. *Focus on Exceptional Children*. Vol. *8*, Denver, Colorado: Love Publishing Company, 1976.

Morse, W.C. Mental Health in the classroom: The crisis teacher. *Today's Education*, 1972, *61*, 52–54.

Motto, J.A. New approaches to crisis intervention. *Suicide and Life-threatening Behavior*, 1979, *9*, 173–184.

Mumford, E., & Skipper, J.K. *Sociology in Hospital Care*. New York: Harper and Row, 1967.

Murphy, G.E., Wetzel, R.D., Swallow, C.S., and McClure, J.N. Who calls the suicide prevention center: A study of fifty-five persons calling on their own behalf. *American Journal of Psychiatry*, 1969, *126*, 314–324.

Neff, W.S. *Work and Human Behavior*. Chicago, Ill.: Oldine, 1977.

Neill, S.B. Crisis counseling. *American Education*, 1977, *13*, 17–22.

Nelson, D. *Personal Communication*, 1980.

Neugarten, B.L., & Assoc. *Personality in middle and late life*. New York: Atherton Press, 1964.

Neugarten, B.L. (Ed.). *Middle age and aging: A reader in social psychology*. Chicago: University of Chicago Press, 1968.

Neugarten, B.L. Adaptation and the life cycle. *The Counseling Psychologist*, 1976, *6*, 16–20.

Neugarten, B.L. Time, age, and the life cycle. *The American Journal of Psychiatry*, 1979, *136*, 887–893.

Newman, R.G. *Psychological consultation in the schools*. New York: Basic Books, 1967.

Novaco, R.W. The cognitive regulation of anger and stress. In P.C. Kendall & S. Hollon (Eds.), *Cognitive-behavioral interventions*. New York: Academic Press, 1979, Chapter 8.

Nowak, C. *Research in life events: Conceptual considerations*. Paper presented at the 31st annual scientific meeting of the Gerontological Society, Dallas, November, 1978.

Ojemann, R.H. Incorporating psychological concepts in the school curriculum. In H.F. Clarizio (Ed.), *Mental Health and the Educative Process*. Chicago: Rand-McNally, 1969.

O'Malley, J., Foster, D., Koocher, G., & Slavin, L. Psychiatric sequelae of surviving childhood cancer. *American Journal of Orthopsychiatry*, 1979, *49*, 608–616.

O'Malley, J., Foster, D., Koocher, G., & Slavin, L. Visible physical impairment and psychological adjustment among pediatric cancer survivors. *American Journal of Psychiatry*, 1980, *137*, 94–96.

Oradei, D.M., & Waite, N.S. Group psychotherapy with strike patients during the immediate recovery phase. *American Journal of Orthopsychiatry*, 1974, *44*, 386–395.

Orbach, S. *Fat is a feminist issue* (2nd ed.). New York: Paddington Press, 1978.

Otten, M.W. and Kahn, M. Effectiveness of crisis center volunteers and the POI. *Psychological Reports*, 1975, *37*, 1107–1111.

Palarea, E., Medical evaluation of the psychiatric patient. *Journal of American Geriatric Society*, 1965, *13*, 14.

Palmore, E.B. (Ed.). *Normal aging*. Durham: Duke University Press, 1974.

Parad, H.J., Resnik, H.L.P., & Parad, L.G. *Emergency and disaster management: A mental health sourcebook*. Bowie, Md.: The Charles Press Publishers, 1976.

Parke, R.D. Socialization into child abuse: A social interactional perspective. In J.L. Tapp & F.J. Levine (Eds.), *Law, justice, and the individual in society: Psychological and legal issues*. New York: Holt, Rinehart & Winston, 1977.

Parkes, C.M. The first year of bereavement: A longitudinal study of the reaction of London widows to the death of their husbands. *Psychiatry*, 1970, *33*, 444–467.

Parkes, C.M. *Bereavement: Studies of grief in adult life*. London: Tavistock, 1972.

Parkes, C.M., & Brown, J.R. Health after bereavement. *Psychosomatic Medicine*, 1972, *34*, 449–461.

Parks, R.M. Parental reactions to the birth of a handicapped child. *Health and Social Work*, 1977, *2*, 51–66.

Pasewark, R.A. and Albers, D.A. Crisis intervention: Theory in search of a program. *Social Work*, 1972, *17*, 70–77.

Patterson, G.R., & Gulliom, M.E. *Living with children: New methods for parents and teachers*. Champaign, Ill. Research Press, 1968.

Patterson, D.Y. Psychiatric practice in an HMO. *Psychiatric Opinion*, 1976, *13*, 27–31.

Patton, W. *Evaluation of the police response to domestic disturbance*. Unpublished manuscript, Oakland, California, Police Department, 1973.

Payne, E.C., Kravitz, A.R., Notman, M.T., & Anderson, J.V. Outcome following therapeutic abortion. *Archives of General Psychiatry*, 1976, *33*, 725–733.

Pearson, J. The Denver custody mediation project: A program description and literature review. *The Colorado Lawyer*, 1979, *8*, 1211–1230.

Pearson, J. *Methods of resolving child custody and visitation disputes: Evaluation of model divorce mediation services programs*. Denver, Co.: The Divorce Mediation Research Project, 1982, in preparation.

Perls F. *Gestalt therapy verbatim*. Lafayette, Calif.: Real People Press, 1969.

Perls, F., Hefferline, R.F., & Goodman, P. *Gestalt Therapy*. New York: Dell Publishing Co., 1951.

Peter, L.F., & Hull, R. *The Peter Principle*. New York: William Morrow & Co., 1969.

Peters, J.J. *The Philadelphia rape victim study*. The report presented at the First International Symposium of Victimology, Israel, September, 1973. Mimeograph copy from the center for rape concern, Philadelphia General Hospital, 1973.

Peters, J.J. *Social psychiatric study of victims reporting rape*. A study presented at the APA 128th Annual Meeting, Anaheim, Calif., May 7, 1975. Mimeographed copy from the Philadelphia Center for Rape Concern, Philadelphia General Hospital.

Phelps, S., & Austin, N. *The assertive woman*. San Luis Obispo, Calif.: Impact, 1975.

Phelps, L.G., Schwartz, J.A., & Liebman, D.A. Training an entire patrol division in domestic crisis intervention techniques. *The Police Chief*, 1971, *38*(July), 18.

Phillip, A.E., Cay, E., Vetter, N.J., & Stuckey, N. Short-term fluctuations in anxiety in patients with myocardial infarction. *Journal of Psychosomatic Research*, 1979, *23*, 277–280.

Phillips, B. *School stress and anxiety*. New York: Human Sciences Press, 1978.

Phillips, D.A. Crisis counseling. *The Police Chief*, 1975, *42*(3), 54–55.

Pisarcik, G., Zigmund, D., Summerfield, R., Mian, P., Johansen, C., & Devereaux, P. Psychiatric nurses in the emergency room. *American Journal of Nursing*, 1979, *79*, 1264–1266.

Poll, I.B., & DeNour, A.K. Locus of control and adjustment to chronic haemodialysis. *Psychological Medicine*, 1980, *10*, 153–157.

Powers, M.A. The benefits of anticipatory grief for the parents of dying children. *International Journal of Family Counseling*, 1977, *5*, 48–53.

Prazak, J.A. Learning job-seeking interview skills. In J.D. Krumboltz & C.E. Thorsen (Eds.), *Behavioral Counseling: Cases and Techniques*. New York: Holt, Rinehart & Winston, 1969.

Preiser, M.L. A crucial technique: The initial client interview in a personal injury case. *Trial*, December, 1979, 19–22.

Preston, J., Schoenfeld, L.S., & Adams, R.L. Evaluating the effectiveness of a telephone crisis center from the consumer's viewpoint. *Hospital and Community Psychiatry*, 1975, *26*, 719–720.

Pretzel, P.W. The role of the clergyman in suicide prevention. *Pastoral Psychology*. 1970a, *21*, 47–52.

Pretzel, P.W. The volunteer clinical worker at the suicide prevention center. *Bulletin of Suicidology*, 1970b, *6*, 27–34.

Price, S., & McCreary, C. Mental health consultation for a clinical law training program. *Journal of Community Psychology*, 1976, *4*, 168–173.

Pritchard, M.J. Measurement of illness behavior in patients on haemodialysis and awaiting cardiac surgery. *Journal of Psychosomatic Research*, 1979, *23*, 117–130.

Puryear, D.A. *Helping people in crisis*. San Francisco: Jossey-Bass Publishers, 1979.

Quarantelli, F.L., & Dynes, R.R. Response to social crisis and disaster. *Annual of Revised Sociology*, 1977, *3*, 23–49.

Quinsley, V.L., & Varney, G.W. Social skills game: A general method for the modeling and practice of adaptive behavior. *Behavior Therapy*, 1977, *8*, 279–281.

Raphael, B. Preventive intervention with the recently bereaved. *Archives of General Psychiatry*, 1977, *34*, 1450–1454.

Rapoport, L. The state of crisis: Some theoretical considerations. In H.J. Parad (Ed.), *Crisis intervention: Selected readings*. New York: Family Service Association of America, 1965.

Rapoport, R. Transition from engagement to marriage. *Acta Sociologica*, 1964, *8*, 36–55.

Rapoport, R., & Rapoport, R. *Growing through life*. New York: Harper & Row, 1980.

Rappaport, J. *Community psychology: Values, research and action*. New York: Holt, Rinehart, & Winston, 1977.

Rawls, E.S. *A handbook of yoga*. New York: Pyramid Book, 1974.

Reardon, R.W. Help for the troubled worker in a small company. *Personnel*, 1976, *58*, 50–54.

Reid, T.A. Training suburban police in the management of social interaction disturbances. *Crisis Intervention*, 1975, *6*(3), 2–12.

Reiff, R. Of cabbages and kings. The 1974 Division 27 annual for distinguished contributions to community mental health. *American Journal of Community Psychology*, 1975, *3*, 185–196.

Reiss, A., Jr. *The police and the public*. New Haven, Conn.: Yale University Press, 1971.

Resnik, H.L.P. A community anti-suicide organization: The friends of Dade County, Florida. In H.L.P. Resnik (Ed.), *Suicidal Behaviors Diagnosis and Management*, Boston: Little Brown & Co., 1968.

Riegel, K. Adult life crises: A dialectic interpretation of development. In N. Datan & L.H. Ginsberg (Eds.), *Life-span developmental psychology: Normative life crises*. New York: Academic Press, 1975.

Rimm, D.C. Thought stopping and covert assertion in the treatment of phobias. *Journal of Consulting and Clinical Psychology*, 1973, *41*, 466–467.

Rimm, D.C. & Masters, F.C. *Behavior therapy* (2nd ed.). New York: Academic Press, 1979, Chap. 4.

Robins, E., Gentry, K.A., Munoz, R.A., and Marten, S. A contrast of the three more common illnesses with the ten less common in a study and 18 months follow-up of 314 psychiatric emergency room patients: I, II and III. *Archives of General Psychiatry*, 1977, *34*, 259–291.

Robinson, G.E., Oldham, J., & Sniderman, M. The establishment of a rape crisis centre. *Canada's Mental Health Supplement*. 1975, *23*, 10–12.

Rogawski, A., and Edmundson, B. Factors affecting the outcome of psychiatric inter-agency referrals. *American Journal of Psychiatry*, 1971, *127*, 925–934.

Rogers, C. *On becoming a person*. Boston: Houghton Mifflin, 1961.

Rogers, C.R. *Client-centered therapy*. Boston: Houghton Mifflin, 1951.

Rollin, B. *First you cry*. Philadelphia: Lippincott, 1976.

Roosevelt, R., & Lofas F. *Living in step*. New York: Stein and Day, 1976.

Rose, R.M., Jenkins, D., & Hurst, M.W. Health change in air traffic controllers: A prospective study. *Psychosomatic Medicine*, 1978, *40*, 142-165.

Rosen, H. The impact of the psychiatric intensive care unit on patients and staff. *American Journal of Psychiatry*, 1975, *132*, 549-551.

Rosenbaum, A. & Calhoun, J.F. The use of the telephone hotline in crisis intervention: A review: *Journal of Community Psychology*, 1977, *5*, 325-339.

Rosenfeld, J.P. Social strain of probate. *Journal of Marital and Family Therapy*, 1980, *6*, 327-334.

Rosenthal, D.E. *Lawyer and Client: Who's in Charge?* New York: Russell Sage Foundation, 1974.

Roskies, E., & Lazarus, R. Coping theory and the teaching of coping skills. In Davidson, P. and Davidson, S. (Eds.), *Behavioral Medicine: Changing Health Lifestyles*, New York: Bruner/Mazel, 1980.

Rowland, K.F. Environmental events predicting death for the elderly. *Psychological Bulletin*, 1977, *84*, 349-372.

Rueveni, U. *Networking families in crisis: Intervention strategies with families and social networks*. New York: Human Sciences Press, 1979.

Ryan, W. *Distress in the cities*. Cleveland: Case Western Reserve University Press, 1969.

Sabalis, R.F., & Ayers, G.W. Emotional aspects of divorce and their effects on the legal process. *Family Coordinator*, 1977, *26*, 391-394.

Sager, L.B. The corporation and the alcoholic. *Across the Board*, 1979, *26*, 79-82.

Salter, A. *Conditioned reflex therapy*. New York: Creative Age, 1949.

Sanchez-Salazar, V., & Stark, A. The use of crisis intervention in the rehabilitation of laryngectomees. *Journal of Speech and Hearing Disorders*, 1972, *37*, 323-328.

Sank, L.I. Community disasters: Primary prevention and treatment in a health maintenance organization. *American Psychologist*, 1979, *34*, 334-338.

Sarason, S.B. Anxiety, intervention and the culture of the school. In C.D. Spielberger (Ed.), *Anxiety: Current trends in theory and research*. New York: Academic Press, 1972.

Satin, D.G. Help: Life stresses, and psychosocial problems in the hospital emergency unit. *Social Psychiatry*, 1972, *7*(3), 119-126.

Satir, V.M. *Conjoint family therapy: A guide to theory and technique*. (Rev. ed.). Palo Alto, Calif.: Science & Behavior Books, 1967.

Satir, V. *People making*. Palo Alto, Calif.: Science and Behavior Books, 1972.

Scarf, M. *Unfinished business: Pressure points in the lives of women*. New York: Doubleday, 1980.

Schaar, K. Crisis. *APA Monitor*, September/October 1980, 14–17.

Schild, S. Social work with genetic problems. *Health and Social Work*, 1977, *2*, 58–77.

Schinke, S.P., Smith, T.E., Myers, R.K., & Altman, D.C. Crisis intervention training with paraprofessionals. *Journal of Community Psychology*, 1979, *7*, 343–347.

Schnaper, N., & Cowley, R.A. Overviews: Psychiatric sequelae to multiple trauma. *American Journal of Psychiatry*, 1976, *133*, 883–890.

Schoenfeld, L.S., Preston, J., & Adams, R.L. Selection of volunteers for telephone crisis intervention center. *Psychological Reports*, 1976, *39*, 725–726.

Schoenfield, M.K., & Schoenfield, B.P. *Interviewing and counseling*. Philadelphia: The American Law Institute, 1981.

Schofield, W. *Psychotherapy: The purchase of friendship*. Englewood Cliffs, N.J.: Prentice-Hall, 1964.

Schuker, E. A treatment program for rape victims. *Alaska Medicine*, 1978, *20*, 48–55.

Schulberg, H.C., & Sheldon, A. The probability of crisis and strategies for preventive intervention. *Archives of General Psychiatry*, 1968, *18*, 553–558.

Schuller, D.S., Strommen, M.P., & Brekke, J.L. *Ministry in America*. New York: Harper & Row, 1980.

Schultz, J.H., & Luthe, W. *Autogenic training*. New York: Grune & Stratton, 1959.

Segal, J. Conquering crisis: Lessons from captivity. *Reader's Digest*, April, 1982, 139–142.

Seiler, J.A. *Systems analysis in organizational behavior*. Homewood, Ill.: Richard D. Irwin, Dorsey Press, 1967.

Selye, H. *The stress of life*. New York: McGraw Hill Book Co., 1976.

Selye, H. *Stress without distress*. New York: Signet, 1974.

Seyle, H. Stress and physical activity. *McGill Journal of Education*, 1976, *11*, 3–14.

Shaffer, T.L. *Legal intervention and counseling in a nutshell*. St. Paul: West Publishing Co., 1976.

Sheehy, G. *Passages*. New York: E.P. Dutton & Co., 1976.

Shelton, J.L., & Acherman, J.M. *Homework in counseling & psychotherapy*. Springfield, Ill.: Charles C. Thomas, 1974.

Shereshfsky, P.M., & Yarrow, L.J. (Eds.). *Psychological aspects of a first pregnancy and early post-natal adaptation*. New York: Raven Press, 1973.

Sherman, B., Gladesville hospital crisis services—a new concept in service delivery: *Australian Social Workers*, 1977, *30*, 41.

Sheskin, A., & Wallace, S.E. Differing bereavements: Suicide, natural and accidental death. *Omega: Journal of Death and Dying*, 1976, *7*, 229-242.

Shields, L. Crisis intervention: Implications for the nurse. *Journal of Psychiatric Nursing and Mental Health Services*, 1975, *13*, 37-42.

Shneidman, E.S., & Farberow, N.L. (Eds.). *Clues to suicide.* New York: McGraw-Hill Book Co., Inc., 1957.

Shulman, B.H. What is the life style. In B.H. Shulman, *Contributions to Individual Psychology.* Chicago: Alfred Adler Institute, 1973.

Silber, E., Hamburg, D.A., Coelho, G.V., Murphy, E.G., Rosenberg, M., & Perlin, L.I. Adaptive behavior in competent adolescence. *Archives of General Psychiatry*, 1961, *5*, 364-365.

Simon, H.A. A behavioral model of rational choice. *Quarterly Journal of Economics*, 1955, *69*, 99-118.

Simons, J.B. & Reidy, J. *The human art of counseling.* New York: Herder & Herder, 1971.

Simonton, O.C., Matthews-Simonton, S., & Creighton, J. *Getting well again.* Los Angeles: J.P. Tarcher, Inc., 1978.

Singer, J.L. *Imagery and daydream methods in psychotherapy and behavior modification.* New York: Academic Press, 1974.

Slaikeu, K.A. The clinical-community approach to community psychology. In B. Wolman (Ed.), *International Encyclopedia of Psychiatry, Psychology, Psychoanalysis & Neurology*, New York: Van Nostrand Reinhold, 1977.

Slaikeu, K.A. Crisis intervention by telephone. In L. Cohen, W. Claiborne & G. Specter (Eds.) *Crisis Intervention: Second Edition.* New York: Human Sciences Press, 1983.

Slaikeu, K.A. *Defusing the distraught client.* Austin, Tx.: The State Bar of Texas, 1978.

Slaikeu, K.A. Rehabilitation at post-release: Implications from crisis theory. In B. Bradshaw & D.J. Eck (Eds.), *Rehabilitation: What part of corrections?* Arlington, Tx.: The Institute of Urban Studies, University of Texas at Arlington, 1977, *5*, 59-82.

Slaikeu, K.A., Temporal variables in telephone crisis intervention: Their relationship to selected process and outcome variables. *Journal of Consulting and Clinic Psychology*, 1979, *47*, 193-195.

Slaikeu, K.A., & Duffy, M. Mental health consultation with campus ministers: A pilot program. *Professional Psychology*, 1979, 338-346.

Slaikeu, K.A., Lester, D., & Tulkin, S. Show versus no show: A comparison of telephone referral calls to a suicide prevention and crisis service. *Journal of Consulting and Clinical Psychology*, 1973, *40*, 481-486.

Slaikeu, K.A., Tulkin, S.R., & Speer, D.C. Process and outcome in the evaluation of telephone counseling referrals. *Journal of Consulting and Clinical Psychology*, 1975, *43*, 700–707.

Slaikeu, K.A., and Willis, M.A. Caller feedback on counselor performance in telephone crisis intervention: A follow-up study. *Crisis Intervention*, 1978, *4*, 42–49.

Smiley, O.R., & Smiley, C.W. The community health nurse and crisis intervention. *International Nursing Review*, 1974, *21*, 151–152.

Smith, L.L. Crisis intervention, theory and practice. *Community Mental Health Review*, 1977, *2*, 1; 5–13.

Soloff, P., & Bartel, A. Effects of denial on mood and performance in cardiovascular rehabilitation. *Journal of Chronic Disease*, 1979, *32*, 307–313.

Solomon, E.G., & Bumpus, A.K. The running meditation response: An adjunct to psychotherapy. *American Journal of Psychotherapy*, 1978, *32*, 583–592.

Soreff, S.M. Psychiatric consultation in the emergency department. *Psychiatric Annals*, 1978, *8*, 61–66.

Soreff, S.M., & Elkins, A.M. A community mental health center's consultation service in a general hospital. *Hospital and Community Psychiatry*, 1977, *28*, 749–752.

Sourkes, B.M. Facilitating family coping with childhood cancer. *Journal of Pediatric Psychology*, 1977, *2*, 65–67.

Specter, G.A., & Claiborne, W.L. (Eds.). *Crisis intervention*. New York: Human Sciences Press, 1973.

Speer, D.C. Project summary: Evaluative study of callers to a crisis hotline. *Final Report NIMH Grant*, MH–24902, 1976.

Speer, D.C. The role of the crisis intervention model in the rehabilitation of criminal offenders. *J.S.A.S. Catalog of Selected Documents in Psychology*, 1974, *4*, 133.

Spink, D. Crisis intervention for parents of the deaf child. *Health and Social Work*, 1976, *1*, 140–160.

Spitz, L. Evolution of a psychiatry emergency crisis intervention service in medical emergency room sitting room. *Comprehensive Psychiatry*, 1976, *17*, 99–113.

Sprott, J.A. Psychological aspects of estate planning. *Journal of Forensic Psychology*, 1973, *5*, 25–39.

Stahmann, R.F. Treatment forms for marital counseling. In R.F. Stahmann & W.J. Hiebert. *Counseling in Marital and Sexual Problems*, Baltimore, Md.: Williams & Williams, Co., 1977.

Stampfel, T.G. Impulsive therapy. Part I: The theory. In S.G. Armitage (Ed.), *Behavior Modification Techniques in the Treatment of Emotional Disorders*, Battle Creek, Mich.: U.S. Veteran Administration, 1966.

Stanko, B. Crisis intervention after the birth of a defective child. *Canadian Nurse*, 1973, *69*, 27–28.

Steinmetz, S.K., & Straus, M.A. (Eds.). *Violence in the family.* New York: Harper & Row, 1974.

Stern, M.J., & Pascale, L. Psychosocial adaptation post-myocardial infarction: The spouse's dilemma. *Journal of Psychosomatic Research*, 1979, *23*, 83–87.

Stevenson, J.S. *Issues and crises during middlescence.* New York: Appleton-Century-Crofts, 1977.

Stone, H.W. *Crisis counseling.* Philadelphia: Fortress Press, 1976.

Stratton, J.G. Effects of crisis intervention counseling on first or second time 601 or misdemeanor 602 juvenile offenders. Doctoral dissertation, University of Southern California, 1974. *Dissertation Abstracts International*, 1974, *35*, 525–B.

Straus, M.A. A general systems theory approach to a theory of violence between family members. *Social Science Information*, 1973, *12*, 105–125.

Straus, M.A. Sexual inequality, cultural norms, and wife beating. In E.C. Viano (Ed.), *Victims and society.* Washington, D.C.: Visage Press, 1976.

Strickler, M., & Bonnefil, M. Crisis intervention and social casework: Similarities and differences in problem solving. In S. Nass, *Crisis intervention.* Dubuque, Ia.: Kendall/Hunt, 1977.

Striegel-Moore, R., & Slaikeu, K. *Women in crisis: A reformulation of the rape trauma syndrome.* Unpublished manuscript, University of South Carolina, 1982.

Summers, W.K., Rund, D.A., & Levin, M. Psychiatric illness in a general urban emergency room: Daytime versus nighttime population. *Journal of Clinical Psychiatry*, 1979, *48*, 340–343.

Sund, A. Crisis intervention in situations with somatic trauma. *Acta Psychiatrica Scandinavica*, 1976, *265*, (Supplement), 27–28.

Susman, E.J., Hollenbeck, A.R., Nannis, E., & Strope, B.E. A developmental perspective on psychosocial aspects of childhood cancer. In J.L. Schulman & M.J. Kupst, (Eds.), *The Child With Cancer.* Springfield, Ill.: Thomas, 1980.

Susset, V., Vobecky, J., & Black, R. Disability outcome and self-assessment of disabled person: An analysis of 506 cases. *Archives of Physical Medicine and Rehabilitation*, 1979, *60*, 50–56.

Susskind, D.F. The idealized self-image (ISI): A new technique in confidence training. *Behavior Therapy*, 1970, *1*, 538–541.

Sutherland, S., & Scherl, D.J. Patterns of response among victims of rape. *American Journal of Orthopsychiatry*, 1970, *40*, 503–511.

Sutherland, S., & Scherl, D.J. Patterns of response among victims of rape. In R.H. Moos (Ed.), *Human adaptation: Coping with life crises*. Lexington, Mass.: D.C. Heath & Co., 1976.

Switzer, D.K. *The minister as crisis counselor*. Nashville: Abington Press, 1974.

Symonds, M. Victims of violence: Psychological effects and aftereffects. *American Journal of Psychoanalysis*, 1975, *35*, 19–26.

Taplin, J.R. Crisis theory: Critique and reformulation. *Community Mental Health Journal*, 1971, *7*, 13–23.

Tapp, J.T., & Spanier, D. Personal characteristics of volunteer phone counselors. *Journal of Consulting and Clinical Psychology*, 1973, *41*, 245–250.

Tavernier, G. Corporate aid for the alcoholic. *International Management*, 1979, *34*, 16–20.

Tay, A. *Making things better by making them worse*. New York: Hawthorne, 1978.

Tenor, D. *Super self. A woman's guide to self-management*, New York: Jovel HBJ, 1978.

Thomas, A., Chess, S., & Birch, H.G. *Temperament and Behavior Disorders in Children*. New York: New York University Press, 1969.

Thorn, G.W., Quinby, J.T., & Clinton, M. A comparison of the metabolic effects of isocaloric meals of varying compositions with special reference to the prevention of postprandial hypoglycemic symptoms. *Annals of Internal Medicine*, XVIII, 1943, 913.

Tietz, W., McSherry, L., & Britt, B. Family sequelae after a child's death due to cancer. *American Journal of Psychotherapy*, 1977, *31*, 417–425.

Titchener, J.L., & Levine, M. *Surgery as a human experience: The psychodynamics of surgical practice*. New York: Oxford University Press, 1960.

Titchener, J.L., Kapp, F.T., & Winget, C. The Buffalo Creek syndrome: Symptoms and character change after a major disaster. In H.J. Parad, H.L.P. Resnik, & L.G. Parad (Eds.), *Emergency and disaster management: A mental health sourcebook*. Bowie, Md.: The Charles Press Publishers, Inc., 1976.

Toffler, A. *Future shock*. New York: Bantam Books, 1971.

Tosi, D., & Moleski, R.L. Rational-emotive crisis intervention therapy. *Rationa. Living*, 1975, *10*, 32–37.

Trexler, L.D. A review of rational-emotive psychotherapy outcome studies. In J. Wolfe & E. Brand (Eds.), *Twenty Years of Rational Therapy*, New York: Institute for Rational Living, 1977.

Turk, D.C. Coping with pain: A review of cognitive control techniques. In M. Fenestein, L.B. Sacks, & I.D. Turkat (Eds.), *Psychological Approaches to Pain Control*, New York: Wiley-Interscience, in press.

Turk, D.C., & Genest, M. Regulation of pain: The application of cognitive and behavioral techniques for prevention and remediation. In P.C. Kendall and S.D. Hollon (Eds.), *Cognitive Behavioral Interventions*, New York: Academic Press, 1979.

Turk, D.C., Meichenbaum, D., & Berman, W.H. Application of biofeedback in the regulation of pain: A critical review. *Psychological Bulletin*, 1979, *86*, 1322–1338.

Twemlow, S.W., & Bowen, W.T. Psychedelic drug induced psychological crisis: Attitudes of the "crisis therapist." *Journal of Psychedelic Drugs*, 1979, *4*, 331–335.

Tyhurst, J.S. The role of transition states-including disasters-in mental illness. In *Symposium of Preventive and Social Psychiatry*. Sponsored by the Walter Reed Army Institute of Research, Walter Reed Army Medical Center, & the National Research Council. Washington, D.C.: Walter Reed Army Institute of Research, 1958.

Tyrer, P., Lee, I., & Alexander, J. Awareness of cardiac function in anxious, phobic, and hypochondriacal patients. *Psychological Medicine*, 1980, *10*, 171–174.

Unger, D.G., & Powell, D.R. Supporting families under stress: The role of social networks. *Family Relations*, 1980, *29*, 566–574.

Ungerleider, J. The psychiatric emergency: Analysis of 6 month's experience of a university hospital's consultation service. *Archives of General Psychiatry*, 1960, *3*, 593–601.

U.S. Congress: Community Mental Health Centers Acts of 1963. Public Law 88-164, Title II. Washington, D.C., U.S. Government Printing Office, 1963.

Uzoka, A.F. The myth of the nuclear family: Historical background and clinical implications. *American Psychologist*, 1979, *34*, 1095–1106.

Vachon, M.L. Grief and bereavement following the death of a spouse. *Canadian Psychiatric Association Journal*, 1976, *21*, 35–44.

Vachon, M.L.S. *The importance of social support in the longitudinal adaptation to bereavement in breast cancer*. Presented at the annual meeting of the American Psychological Association, New York, New York, September, 1979.

Vaillant, G.E. *Adaptation to life*. Boston: Little, Brown & Co., 1977.

Valle, J., & Axelberd, M. Brief report police intervention into family crisis: A training model. *Crisis Intervention*, 1977, *8*(3), 117–123.

Veronen, L.J., and Kilpatrick, D.G. *The response to rape: The impact of rape on self esteem*. Paper presented at the 26th Annual Convention of the Southwestern Psychological Association, Oklahoma City, April 11, 1980.

Veronen, L.J., Kilpatrick, D.G., & Resick, P.A. *Stress inoculation training for*

Association for Advancement of Behavior Therapy, Chicago, Ill., November 18, 1978.

Viney, L.L. The concept of crisis: A tool for clinical psychologists. *Bulletin of the British Psychological Society*, 1976, *29*, 387–395.

Viney, L.L. *Coping with crisis and the transition from school to university*. Paper read at the 25th World Mental Health Conference, Sidney, Australia, 1973.

Viney, L.L., & Bazeley, P. Affective responses of housewives to community relocation. *Journal of Community Psychology*, 1977, *5*, 37–45.

Viney, L.L., & Clarke, A.M. Children coping with crisis: An analogue study. *British Journal of Social and Clinical Psychology*, 1974, *13*, 305–313.

Viney, L.L., & Clarke, A.M. Children coping with crisis in Papua New Guinea and Australia: A cross-cultural application of an analogue. *Social Behavior and Personality*, 1976, *4*, 1–10.

Viney, L.L., & Westbrook, M.T. Cognitive anxiety: A method of content analysis for verbal samples. *Journal of Personality Assessment*, 1976, *40*, 140–145.

Vollman, R.R., Ganzert, A., Picher, L., & Williams, W.V. The reaction of family systems to sudden and unexpected death. *Omega*, 1971, *2*, 101–110.

Walfish, S. The effects of training and supervision on the performance of paraprofessional telephone counselors: An analogue study. Unpublished doctoral dissertation: University of South Florida, 1981.

Walfish, S., Tapp, J.T., Tulkin, S.R., Slaikeu, K.A., & Russell, M. The development of a contract negotiation scale for crisis counseling. *Crisis Intervention*, 1976, *7*, 136–148.

Walker, K.N., MacBride, A., & Vachon, M.L.S. Social support networks and the crisis of bereavement. *Social Science and Medicine*, 1977, *11*, 35–41.

Walker, L.E. Treatment alternatives for battered women. In J.R. Chapman & M. Gates (Eds.), *The victimization of women*. Beverly Hills: Sage Publications, 1978.

Wallace, M., & Schreiber, F.B. Crisis intervention training for police officers: A practical program for local police departments. *Journal of Psychiatric Nursing and Mental Health Services*, 1977, *15*(2), 25–29.

Wallerstein, J.S., & Kelly, J.B. *Surviving the breakup: How children and parents cope with divorce*. New York: Basic Books, Inc., 1980.

Walsh, J.A., & Witte, P.G. Police training in domestic crises: A suburban approach. *Community Mental Health Journal*, 1975, *11*(3), 301–306.

Wandersman, L.P., Wandersman, A., & Kahn, S. Social support in the transition to parenthood. *Journal of Community Psychology*, 1980, *8*(4), 332–342.

Warner, C.G. *Conflict intervention in social and domestic violence*. Bowie, Md.: Robert J. Brady, Co., 1981.

Watson, A.S. *The Lawyer in the interviewing and counseling process*. Indianapolis: The Bobbs-Merrill Company, Inc., 1976.

Watson, D.L., & Tharp, R.G. *Self-directed behavior: Self-modification for personal adjustment*. Monterey, Calif.: Brooks/Cole, 1972.

Watson, G.D. Utilization of emergency departments for psychiatric treatment. *Canadian Psychiatric Association Journal*, 1978, *23*, 143–148.

Watzlawick, P., Weakland, F., and Fisch, R. *Change: Principles of problem formation and problem resolution*. New York: W.W. Norton, 1974.

Weingarten, H., & Kulka, R. *Parental divorce in childhood and adult adjustment: A two generational view*. Presented at the annual meeting of the American Psychological Association, New York, New York, September, 1979.

Weisath, L. Physical threat and injury: Psychiatric crisis aspects. *Acta Psychiatrica Scandinavica*, 1976, *265* (Supplement), 27.

Weiskopf, S., & Binder, J.L. Grieving medical students: Educational and clinical considerations. *Comprehensive Psychiatry*, 1976, *17*, 623–630.

Weisman, A.D. Coping with untimely death. In R.H. Moos (Ed.), *Human Adaptation: Coping with life crises*. Lexington, Mass.: D.C. Heath & Co., 1976.

Weissberg, N.P. Emergency room medical clearance. An education problem: *American Journal of Psychiatry*, 1979, *136*, 787–790.

Weiss, R.L. Contracts, cognition, and change: A behavioral approach to marriage therapy. *Counseling Psychologist*, 1975, *5*, 15–26.

Weiss, R.S. *Marital Separation*. New York· Basic Books, Inc., 1975.

Wekstein, L. *Handbook of suiciodology Principles, problems, and practice*. New York: Brunner/Mazel, 1979.

Westbrook, M.T. Analyzing people's experience of events; A study of the child bearing years. Doctoral dissertation, McClary, 1975.

Wheeler, H. Silent victims of incest—peer group project. In A.W. Burgess & B.A. Baldwin (Eds.), *Crisis intervention: Theory and practice*, 1981, 258–274.

Whitaker, C. A family therapist looks at marital therapy. In A. Gurman & D. Rice (Eds.), *Couples in Conflicts: New Directions in Marital Therapy*, New York: Axronson, 1975.

White, G.F., & Haas, J.E. *Assessment of research on natural hazards*. Cambridge, Mass.: MIT Press, 1975.

Whitehead, T. A psychiatric presence in the accident and emergency department. *World Medicine*, 1978a, *13*, 93–95.

Whitehead, T. Psychiatry as an emergency service. *Nursing Mirror and Midwive's Journal*, 1978b, *147*, 17.

Whiteley, J., & Flowers, J. (Eds.). *Approach to assertion training*. Monterey, Ca.: Brooks/Cole, 1978.

Wilder, J., Plutchnik, R., & Conte, H. Compliance with psychiatric emergency room referrals. *Archives of General Psychiatry*, 1977, *34*, 930–933.

Wilhelm, R. *The Book of Changes* or *The I Ching*. Princeton, N.J.: Princeton University Press, 1967.

Wilkins, W. Desensitization: Social & cognitive factors underlying the effectiveness of Wolpe's procedure. *Psychological Bulletin*, 1971, *76*, 311–317.

Williams, C., & Rice, D.G. The intensive care unit: Social work intervention with families of critically ill patients. *Social Work in Health Care*, 1977, *2*, 391–398.

Williams, R.J. *Nutrition in a Nutshell*. New York: Doubleday, 1962.

Williams, T. (Ed.). *Post-traumatic stress disorders of the Vietnam veteran*. Cincinnati, Ohio: Disabled American Veterans, National Headquarters. 1980.

Williams, W.V., Lee, J., & Polak, P.R. Crisis intervention: Effects of crisis intervention on family survivors of sudden death situations. *Community Mental Health Journal*, 1976, *12*, 128–136.

Williams, W.V., & Polak, P.R. Follow-up research in primary prevention: A model of adjustment in acute grief. *Journal of Clinical Psychology*, 1979, *35*, 35–45.

Wilson, L. Thoughts on Tarasoff. *The Clinical Psychologist*, 1981, *34*, 37.

Winder, A.E. Family therapy: A necessary part of the cancer patient's care: A multi-disciplinary treatment concept. *Family Therapy*, 1978, *5*, 151–161.

Winters, R.A., & Modione, A. High school students as mental health workers. *The School Counselor*, 1975, *104*, 43–44.

Wise, D.J. Crisis intervention before cardiac surgery. *American Journal of Nursing*, 1975, *75*, 1316–1318.

Witkin, M.H. Psychosexual counseling of the mastectomy patient. *Journal of Sex & Marital Therapy*, 1978, *4*, 20–28.

Wolberg, L.R. *The technique of psychotherapy* (2nd. ed.). New York: Grune & Stratton, 1967.

Wolfolk, R., & Richardson, F. *Stress, sanity and survival*. New York: Simon & Schuster, 1978.

Wolpe, J. *The practice of behavior therapy* (1st ed.). Elmsford, N.Y.: Pergamon Press, 1969.

Wolpe, J. *Psychotherapy by reciprocal inhibition*. Stanford, Calif.: Stanford University Press, 1958.

Wooley, S.C., Blackwell, B., & Winget, C. A learning theory model of chronic illness behavior: Theory, treatment, and research. *Psychosomatic Medicine*, 1978, *40*, 379–401.

Woolfolk, R.L. A multimodal perspective on emotion. In A.A. Lazarus (Ed.), *Multimodal Behavior Therapy*. New York: Springer, 1976.

Yano, B., Alexander, L., & Kuwanoe, C. Crisis intervention: A guide for nurses. *Journal of Rehabilitation*, 1976, *42*, 23–26.

Yates, J.E. *Managing Stress*. New York, N.Y.: Amacon, 1979.

Yesudian, S. *Yoga week by week*. New York: Harper and Row, 1975.

Yowell, S., & Brose, C. Working with drug abuse in the emergency room. *American Journal of Nursing*, 1977, *77*, 82–85.

Zind, R.K. Deterrents to crisis intervention in the hospital unit. *Nursing clinics of North America*, 1974, *9*, 27–36.

Zonana, H., Henisz, J., & Levine, M. Psychiatric emergency services a decade later. *Psychiatry Medicine*, 1973, *3*, 273–290.

Zubin, J., & Spring, B. Vulnerability—a new view of schizophrenia. *Journal of Abnormal Psychology*, 1977, *86*, 103–126.

Zusman, J. Meeting mental health needs in a disaster: A public health review. In H.J. Parad, H.L.P. Resnik, & L.G. Parad (Eds.), *Emergency and disaster management: A mental health sourcebook*. Bowie, Maryland: The Charles Press Publishers, Inc., 1976.

Subject Index

A

A-B-C personality paradigm, 120
Abortion, 216–217, 223
Action, in psychological first aid
  "do's and don'ts" of, 103 *table*
  helper behavior, 87 *table*, 91–93, 99–100
  objectives of, 87 *table* 91–93
Active listening (technique), 295 *appendix*
Adolescence, 41 *table*
  identity crisis in, 4
  identity themes, 39
  pregnancy in, 216–217
Adult development framework, 46–49
  crisis intervention and, 46
  Erikson's developmental theory and, 46
Adulthood, 35, 36, 52
  middle 42–43 *table,* 44–45
  young, 39, 41–42 *table*
  see also Adult development framework
Affective modality, in BASIC personality profile,
  27 *table*, 118–119, 137
Age, suicidal risk and, 95 *table*
Age, old; *see* Old age
Alcohol, suicidal risk and, 95 *table*
Alcoholism, in work settings, 270, 271
Ambivalence, in suicidal feelings, 94, 99–100
Anger-control (technique), 295–296 *appendix*
Anger expression (technique), 296 *appendix*
Anger provocation (technique), 296–297 *appendix*
Anticipatory guidance (technique), 207, 221, 297 *appendix*
Anxiety management training; *see* Stress innoculation training
Assertiveness training, 297 *appendix*
Assessment
  assumptions underlying, 122–123
  BASIC personality profile and, 118–138
  checklist, 123–138
    context of crisis, 136
    Crisis Assessment Summary, 124–135 *table*
    crisis BASIC functioning, 137–138
    precipitating event, 123, 136
    pre-crisis BASIC functioning, 136–137
    presenting problem, 136

  in crisis intervention, 78–79
  guidelines for, 49–51
  instruments, 289–293 *appendix*, 291–295 *appendix*
  tasks in, 79
Attorneys, crisis intervention by, 183–190
  literature review, 185–187
  training for, 184, 189–190
Autogenic training, 297–298 *appendix*

B

BASIC personality profile
  assessment and, 118–138
  crisis and, 89, 137–138
  Crisis Assessment Summary and, 124–135 *table*
  Crisis Questionnaire and, 123
  crisis resolution and, 138–146
  definition of, 26, 27 *table*
  evaluation and, 147
  General systems theory and, 26, 31–32
  modalities of
    affective, 27 *table*, 118–119, 137
    behavioral, 27 *table*, 118, 137
    cognitive, 27 *table*, 120–122, 137–138
    interpersonal, 27 *table*, 119–120, 137
    somatic, 27 *table*, 119, 137
  multimodal crisis therapy and, 148
  pre-crisis, 89, 136–137
  psychological first aid and, 87 *table*
  research and, 277–280, 287
  variables in, 27 *table*
Behavior rehearsal (technique), 298 *appendix*
Behavioral modality, in BASIC personality profile,
  27 *table*, 118, 137
Bereavement, 57–58
  counseling, in work settings, 270–271
Bibliotherapy, 298 *appendix*
Biofeedback, 298, 299 *appendix*
Biological timing, 38
Book, plan of, 11
Breath control (technique), 299 *appendix*
Buffalo Creek flood, 63
  see also Disasters

Author Index

Author Index